GLADSTONE'S SCHOOL FOR WORLD CONQUERORS

CREATED BY

MARK ANDREW SMITH
& ARMAND VILLAVERT

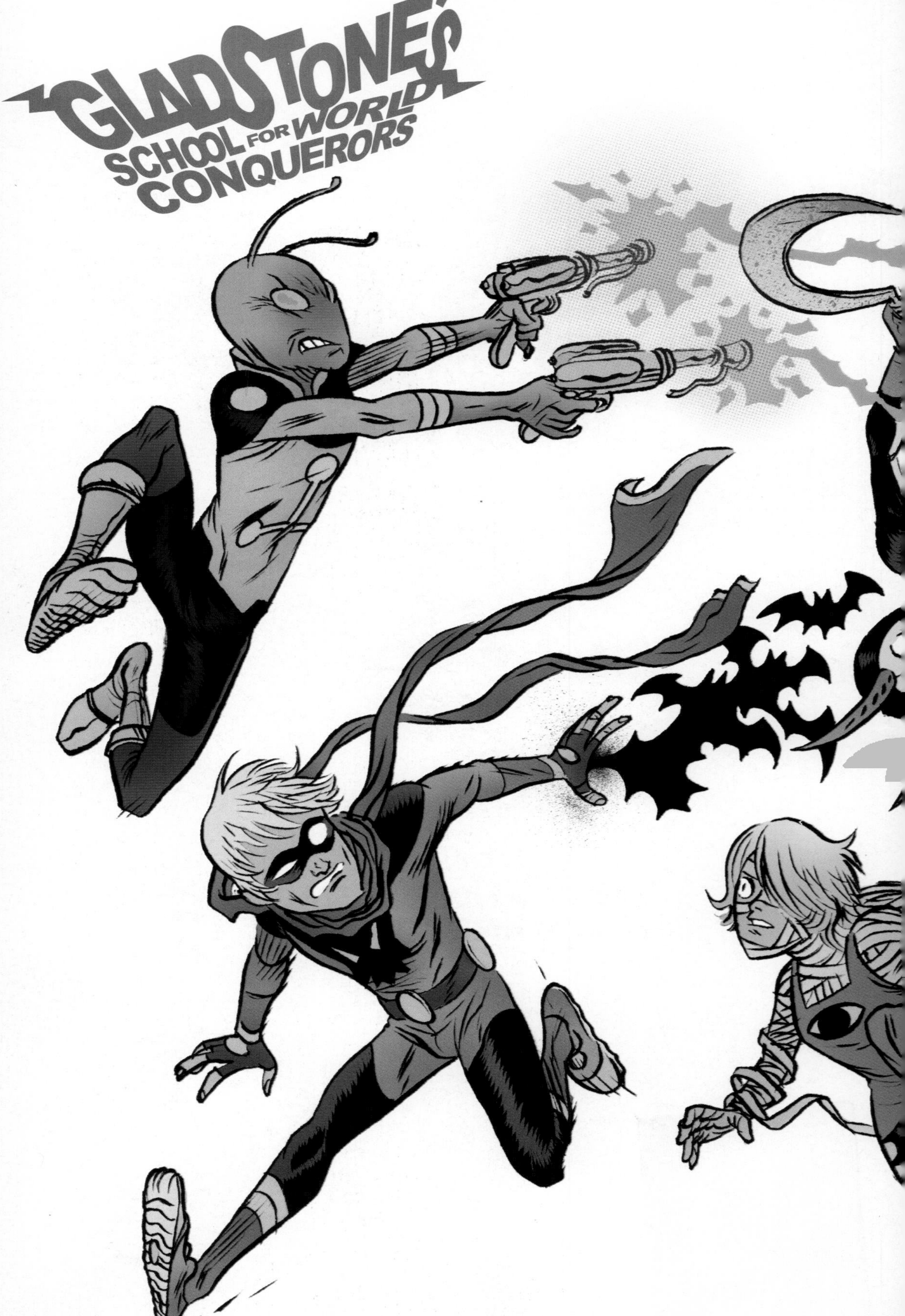
GLADSTONE'S
SCHOOL FOR WORLD CONQUERORS

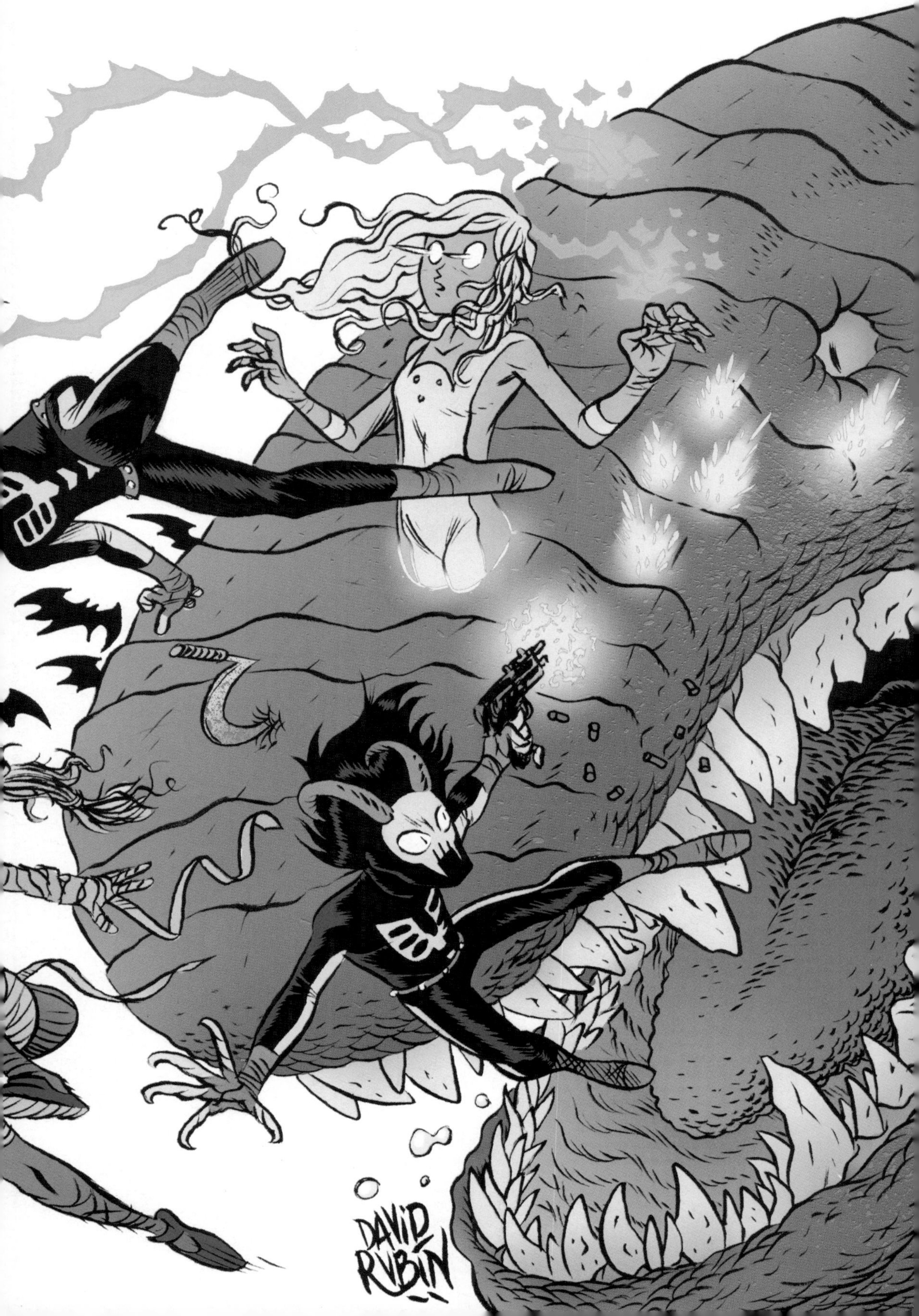
DAVID
RUBIN

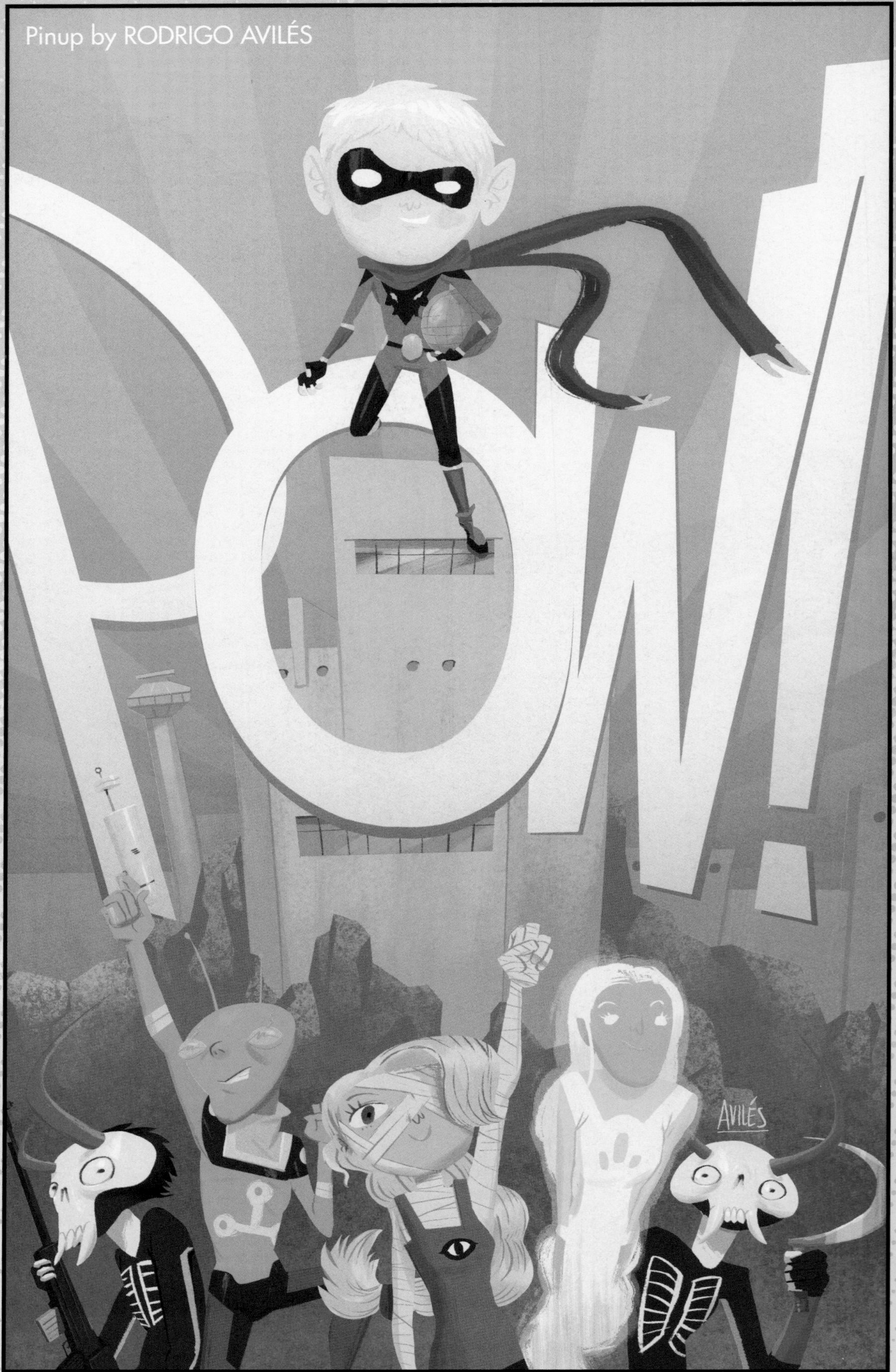
Pinup by RODRIGO AVILÉS
POW!
AVILÉS

WRITTEN BY:
MARK ANDREW SMITH

ILLUSTRATED BY:
ARMAND VILLAVERT

COLORED BY:
CARLOS CARRASCO
(CHAPTERS 1—2, 4)
ANDRE POULAIN
(CHAPTER 2)
POMMES
(CHAPTER 3)
RODRIGO AVILÉS
(CHAPTERS 5—6)

PINUPS BY:
DAVID RUBIN
(PAGES 2-3)
RODRIGO AVILÉS
(PAGE 4)
ARMAND VILLAVERT
(PAGES 159 & 192)
MATTHEW WELDON
(PAGE 191)

LETTERED BY:
FONOGRAFIKS
(CHAPTER 1)
THOMAS MAUER
(CHAPTERS 2—6)

*GLADSTONE'S SCHOOL FOR WORLD
CONQUERORS* LOGO BY:
DAN HIPP

EDITED BY:
D.J. KIRKBRIDE
(CHAPTER 1)
JUSTIN ROBINSON
(CHAPTERS 2, 4)
ERICK TAGGART
(CHAPTERS 3, 5—6)

PRODUCTION EDITS & DESIGN BY:
THOMAS MAUER

Image Comics, Inc.

Robert Kirkman - *Chief Operating Officer*
Erik Larsen - *Chief Financial Officer*
Todd McFarlane - *President*
Marc Silvestri - *Chief Executive Officer*
Jim Valentino - *Vice-President*

Eric Stephenson - *Publisher*
Todd Martinez - *Sales & Licensing Coordinator*
Sarah deLaine - *PR & Marketing Coordinator*
Branwyn Bigglestone - *Accounts Manager*
Emily Miller - *Administrative Assistant*
Jamie Parreno - *Marketing Assistant*
Kevin Yuen - *Digital Rights Coordinator*
Tyler Shainline - *Production Manager*
Drew Gill - *Art Director*
Jonathan Chan - Senior *Production Artist*
Monica Garcia - *Production Artist*
Vincent Kukua - *Production Artist*
Jana Cook - *Production Artist*

www.imagecomics.com

International Rights Representative:
Christine Meyer (christine@gfloystudio.com)

GLADSTONE'S SCHOOL FOR WORLD CONQUERORS, VOL. 1
ISBN: 978-1-60706-115-1
First Printing

Published by Image Comics, Inc. Office of publication:
2134 Allston Way, 2nd Floor, Berkeley, CA 94704. Copyright © 2011
Mark Andrew Smith and Armand Villavert. All rights reserved.
Originally published as GLADSTONE'S SCHOOL FOR WORLD CONQUERORS #1-6.
GLADSTONE'S SCHOOL FOR WORLD CONQUERORS™ (including all prominent
characters featured herein), its logo and all character likenesses are trademarks of
Mark Andrew Smith and Armand Villavert, unless otherwise noted.
El Campeon ™ & © Mark Andrew Smith & Dan Hipp.

Printed in the U.S.A.
For information regarding the CPSIA on this printed material call: 203-595-3636
and provide reference # EAST – 411208

CHAPTER 1

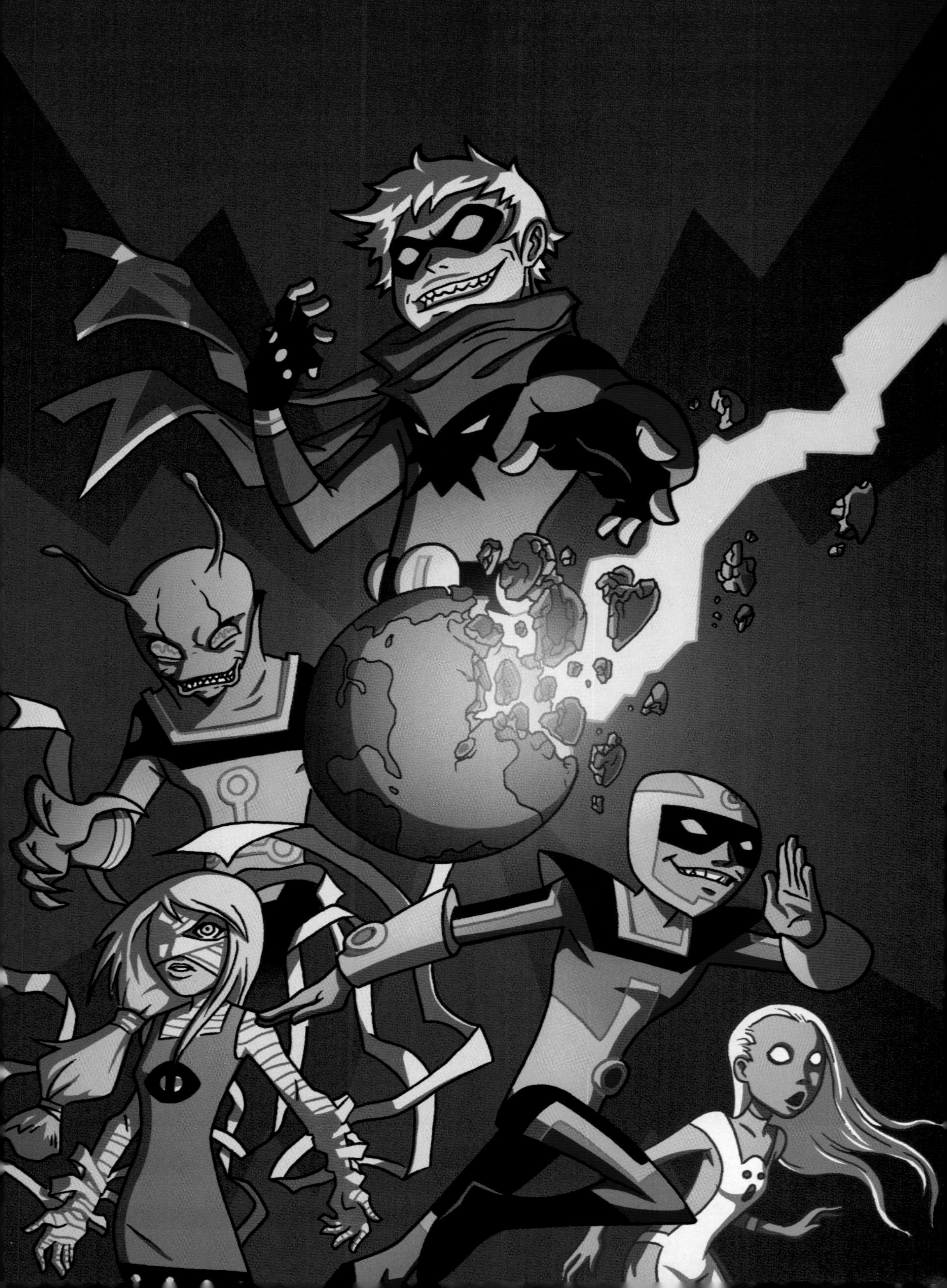

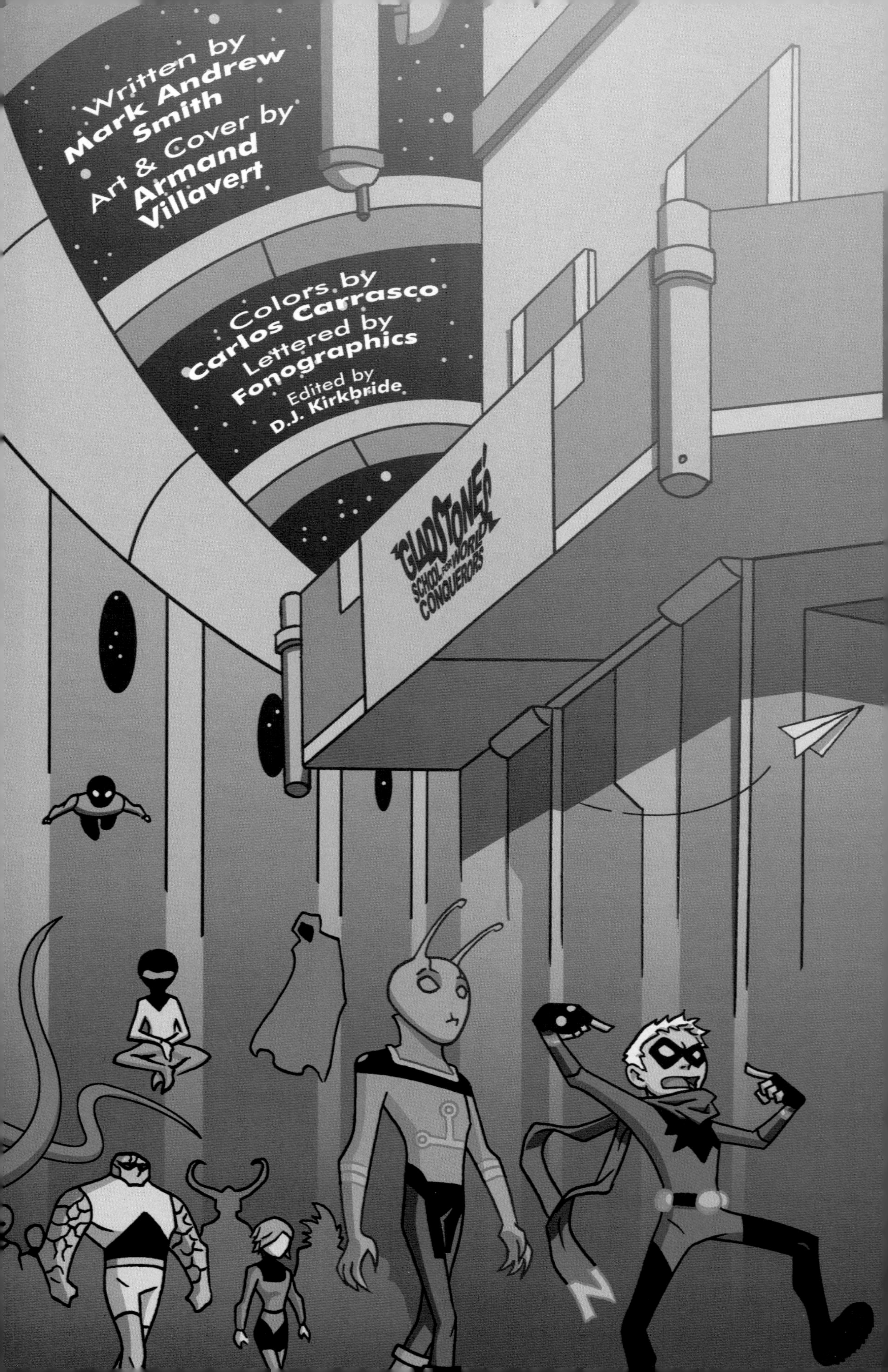

Written by
Mark Andrew Smith
Art & Cover by
Armand Villavert
Colors by
Carlos Carrasco
Lettered by
Fonographics
Edited by
D.J. Kirkbride
GLADSTONE'S SCHOOL FOR WORLD CONQUERORS

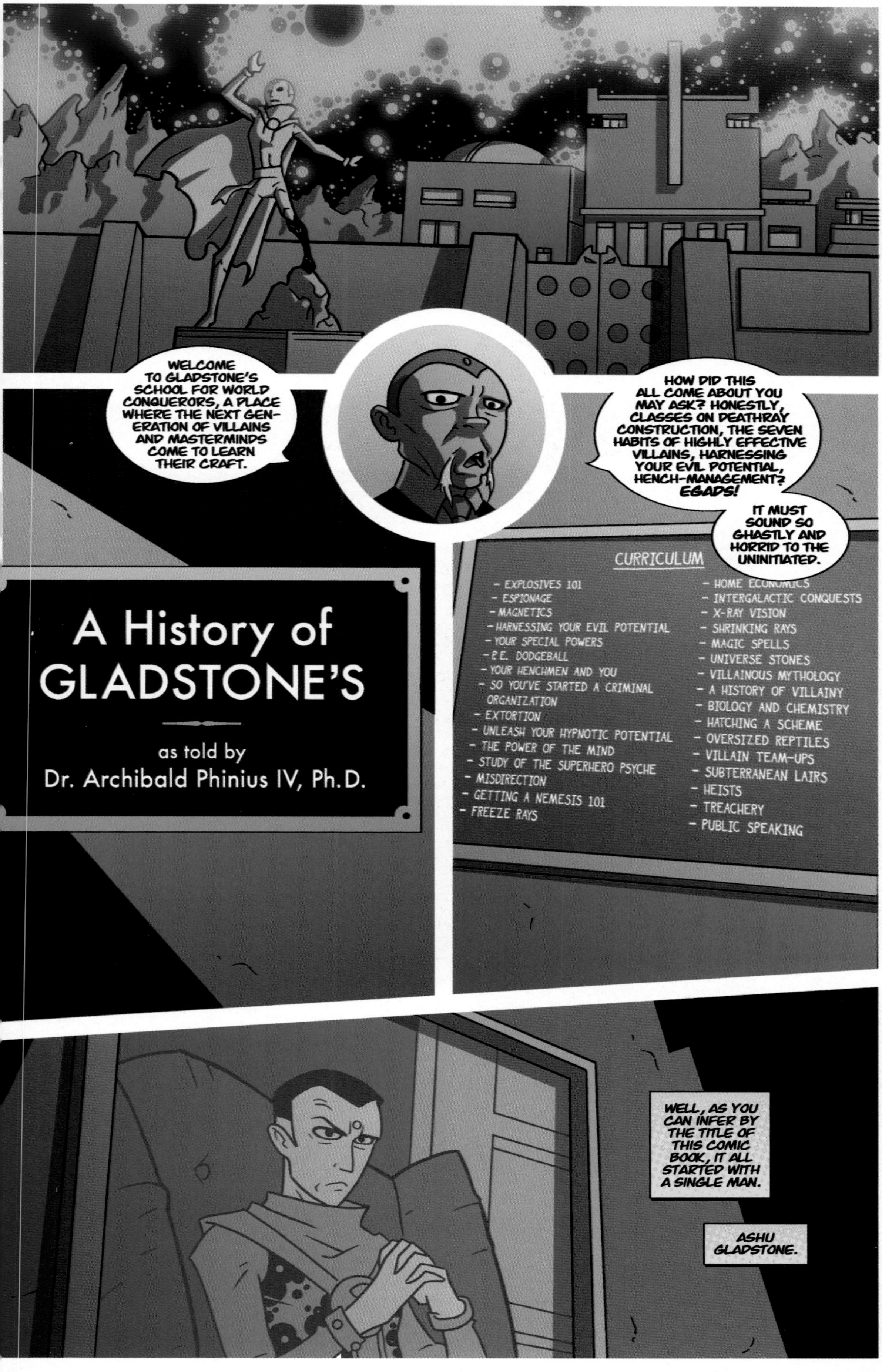
WELCOME TO GLADSTONE'S SCHOOL FOR WORLD CONQUERORS, A PLACE WHERE THE NEXT GENERATION OF VILLAINS AND MASTERMINDS COME TO LEARN THEIR CRAFT.
HOW DID THIS ALL COME ABOUT YOU MAY ASK? HONESTLY, CLASSES ON DEATHRAY CONSTRUCTION, THE SEVEN HABITS OF HIGHLY EFFECTIVE VILLAINS, HARNESSING YOUR EVIL POTENTIAL, HENCH-MANAGEMENT? EGADS!
IT MUST SOUND SO GHASTLY AND HORRID TO THE UNINITIATED.
A History of GLADSTONE'S
as told by
Dr. Archibald Phinius IV, Ph.D.
CURRICULUM
- EXPLOSIVES 101
- ESPIONAGE
- MAGNETICS
- HARNESSING YOUR EVIL POTENTIAL
- YOUR SPECIAL POWERS
- P.E. DODGEBALL
- YOUR HENCHMEN AND YOU
- SO YOU'VE STARTED A CRIMINAL ORGANIZATION
- EXTORTION
- UNLEASH YOUR HYPNOTIC POTENTIAL
- THE POWER OF THE MIND
- STUDY OF THE SUPERHERO PSYCHE
- MISDIRECTION
- GETTING A NEMESIS 101
- FREEZE RAYS
- HOME ECONOMICS
- INTERGALACTIC CONQUESTS
- X-RAY VISION
- SHRINKING RAYS
- MAGIC SPELLS
- UNIVERSE STONES
- VILLAINOUS MYTHOLOGY
- A HISTORY OF VILLAINY
- BIOLOGY AND CHEMISTRY
- HATCHING A SCHEME
- OVERSIZED REPTILES
- VILLAIN TEAM-UPS
- SUBTERRANEAN LAIRS
- HEISTS
- TREACHERY
- PUBLIC SPEAKING
WELL, AS YOU CAN INFER BY THE TITLE OF THIS COMIC BOOK, IT ALL STARTED WITH A SINGLE MAN.
ASHU GLADSTONE.

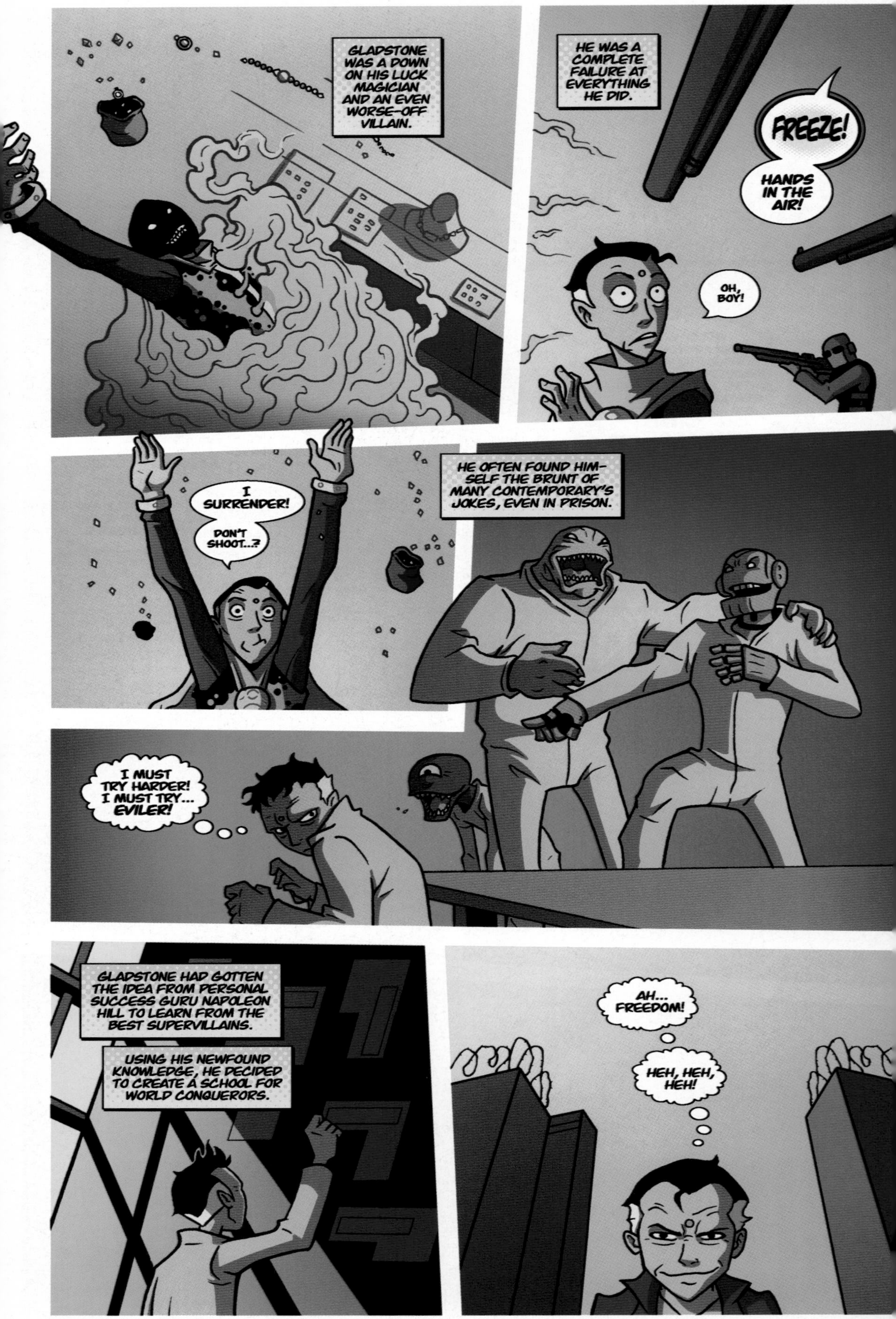
GLADSTONE WAS A DOWN ON HIS LUCK MAGICIAN AND AN EVEN WORSE-OFF VILLAIN.
HE WAS A COMPLETE FAILURE AT EVERYTHING HE DID.
FREEZE!
HANDS IN THE AIR!
OH, BOY!
I SURRENDER!
DON'T SHOOT...?
HE OFTEN FOUND HIM-SELF THE BRUNT OF MANY CONTEMPORARY'S JOKES, EVEN IN PRISON.
I MUST TRY HARDER! I MUST TRY... EVILER!
GLADSTONE HAD GOTTEN THE IDEA FROM PERSONAL SUCCESS GURU NAPOLEON HILL TO LEARN FROM THE BEST SUPERVILLAINS.
USING HIS NEWFOUND KNOWLEDGE, HE DECIDED TO CREATE A SCHOOL FOR WORLD CONQUERORS.
AH... FREEDOM!
HEH, HEH, HEH!

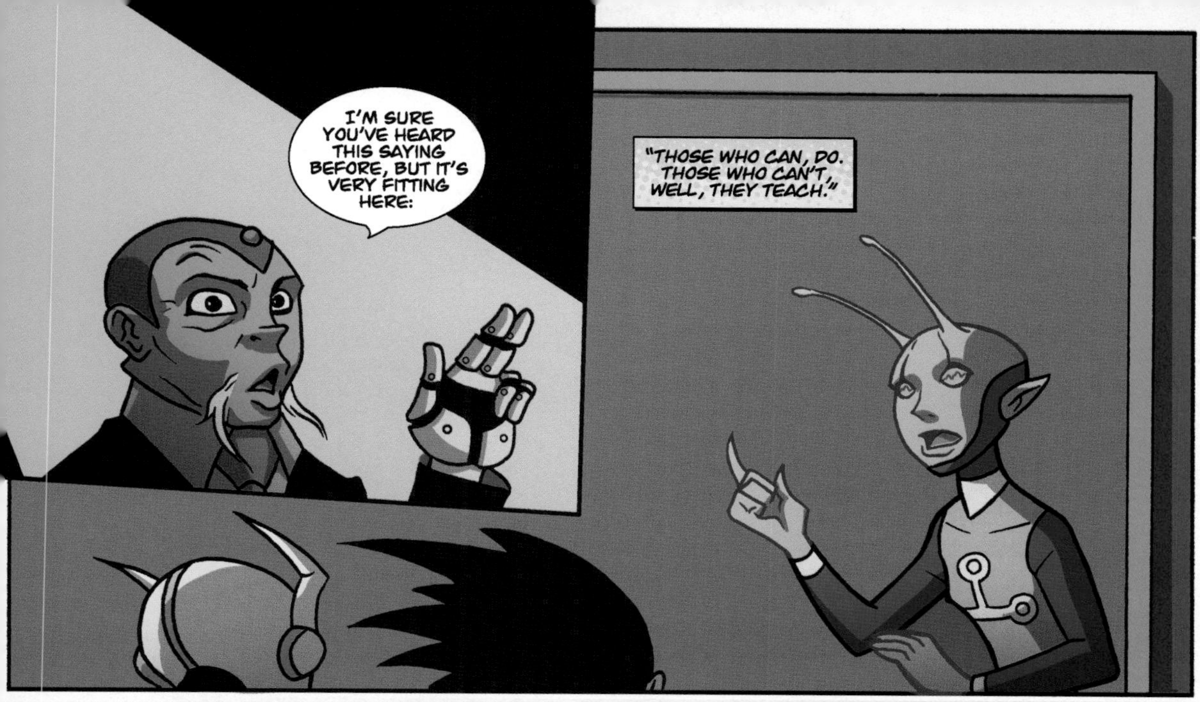
I'M SURE YOU'VE HEARD THIS SAYING BEFORE, BUT IT'S VERY FITTING HERE:
"THOSE WHO CAN, DO. THOSE WHO CAN'T, WELL, THEY TEACH."

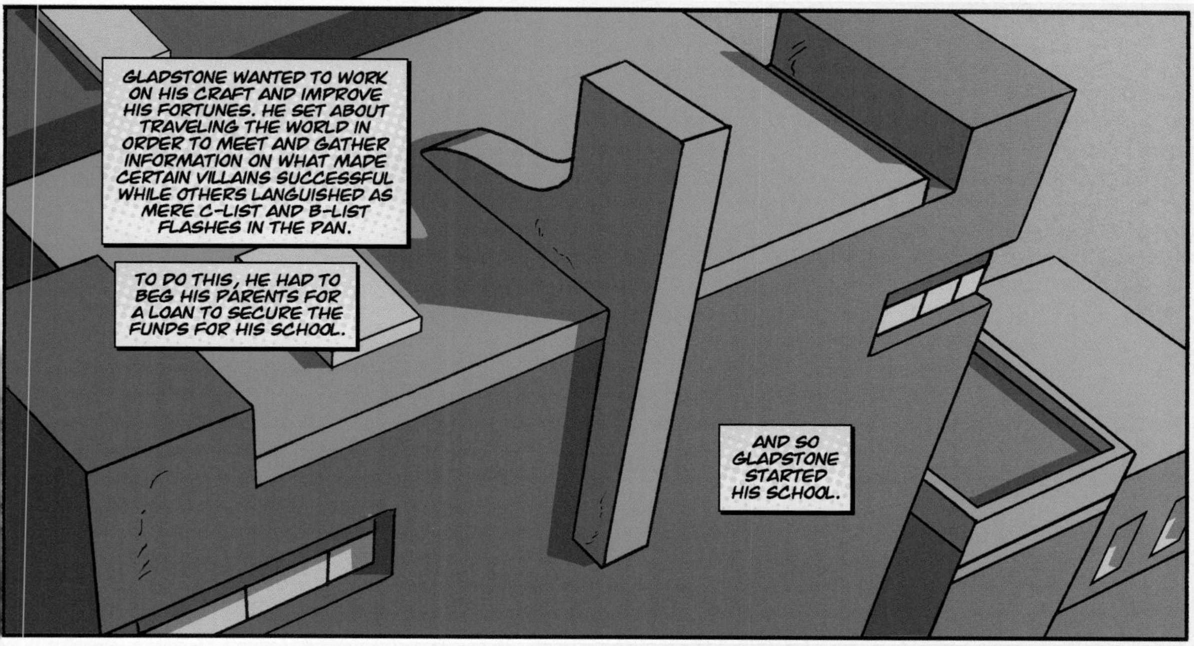
GLADSTONE WANTED TO WORK ON HIS CRAFT AND IMPROVE HIS FORTUNES. HE SET ABOUT TRAVELING THE WORLD IN ORDER TO MEET AND GATHER INFORMATION ON WHAT MADE CERTAIN VILLAINS SUCCESSFUL WHILE OTHERS LANGUISHED AS MERE C-LIST AND B-LIST FLASHES IN THE PAN.
TO DO THIS, HE HAD TO BEG HIS PARENTS FOR A LOAN TO SECURE THE FUNDS FOR HIS SCHOOL.
AND SO GLADSTONE STARTED HIS SCHOOL.

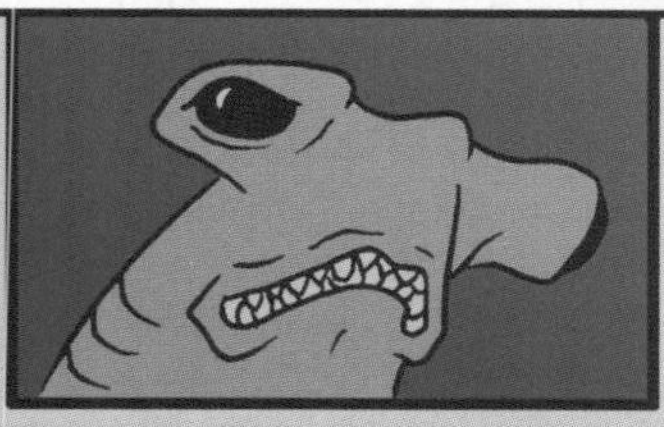

Aliquam erat volutpat. Ut wisi enim ad minim veniam, quis nostrud exerci tation ullamcorper suscipit lobortis nisl ut aliquip ex ea commodo consequat. Duis autem vel eum iriure dolor in hendrerit in vulputate velit esse molestie consequat, vel illum dolore eu feugiat nulla facilisis dolore magna aliquam erat volutpat. Ut wisi enim ad minim veniam, quis nostrud exerci tation ullamcorper suscipit lobortis nisl ut aliquip ex ea commodo consequat. Duis autem vel eum iriure dolor in hendrerit in vulputate velit esse molestie consequat dignissim qui blandit praesent luptatum.

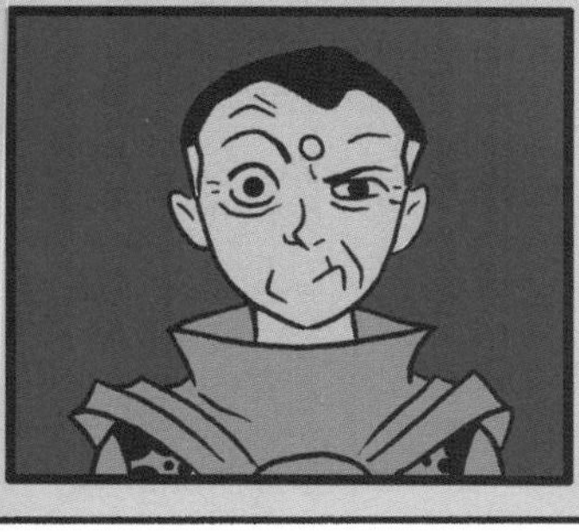

GLADSTONE, ASHU

Down-on-his-luck magician. Even worse-off villain.

INDEED, IT SEEMED GLADSTONE WAS DOOMED TO BE A MERE FOOTNOTE IN THE ANNALS OF VILLAINY. THAT IS, UNTIL ONE FATEFUL ENCOUNTER...

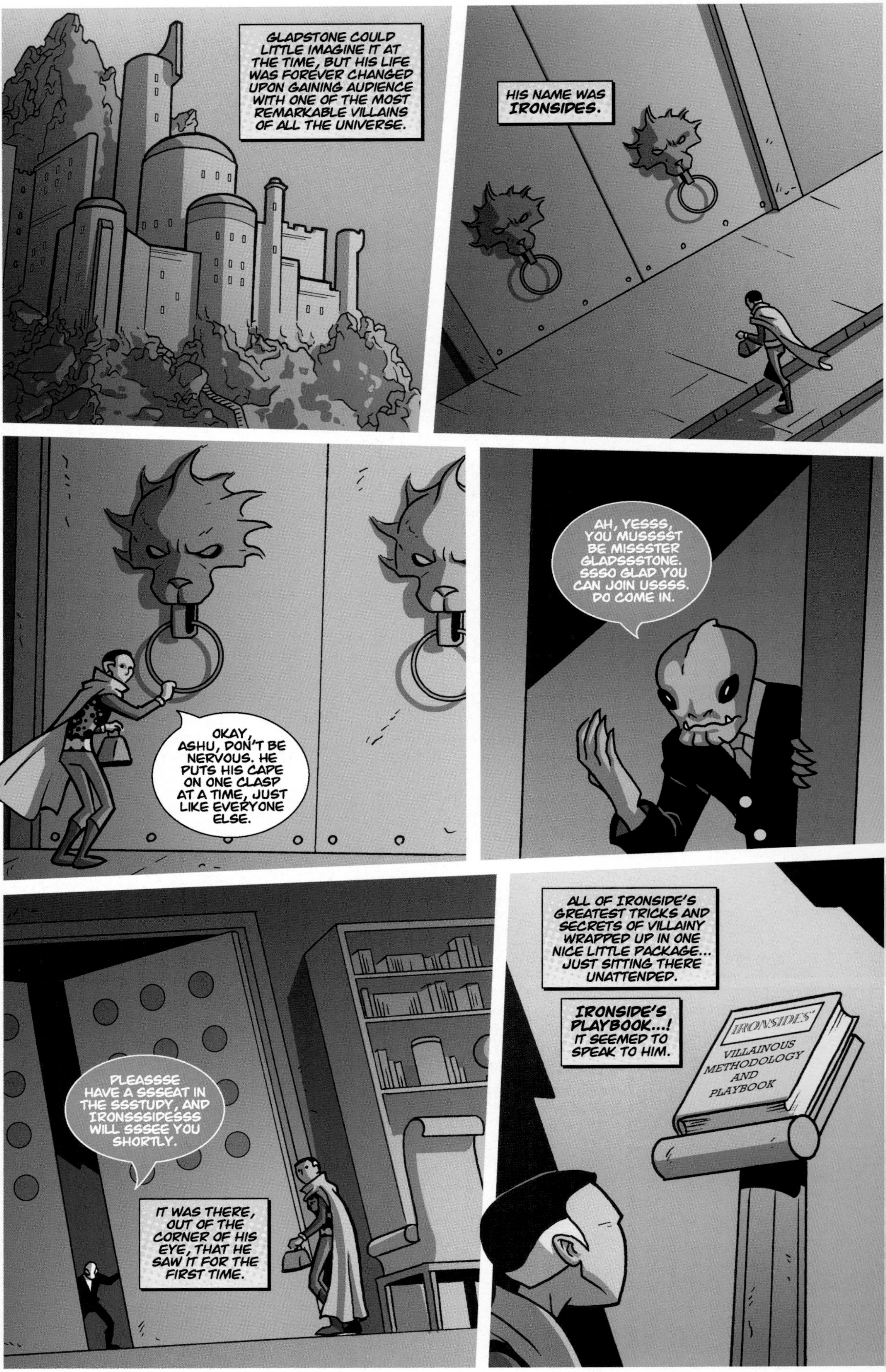
GLADSTONE COULD LITTLE IMAGINE IT AT THE TIME, BUT HIS LIFE WAS FOREVER CHANGED UPON GAINING AUDIENCE WITH ONE OF THE MOST REMARKABLE VILLAINS OF ALL THE UNIVERSE.
HIS NAME WAS IRONSIDES.
OKAY, ASHU, DON'T BE NERVOUS. HE PUTS HIS CAPE ON ONE CLASP AT A TIME, JUST LIKE EVERYONE ELSE.
AH, YESSS, YOU MUSSSST BE MISSSTER GLADSSSTONE. SSSO GLAD YOU CAN JOIN USSSS. DO COME IN.
PLEASSSE HAVE A SSSEAT IN THE SSSTUDY, AND IRONSSSIDESSS WILL SSSEE YOU SHORTLY.
IT WAS THERE, OUT OF THE CORNER OF HIS EYE, THAT HE SAW IT FOR THE FIRST TIME.
ALL OF IRONSIDE'S GREATEST TRICKS AND SECRETS OF VILLAINY WRAPPED UP IN ONE NICE LITTLE PACKAGE... JUST SITTING THERE UNATTENDED.
IRONSIDE'S PLAYBOOK...! IT SEEMED TO SPEAK TO HIM.
IRONSIDES'
VILLAINOUS METHODOLOGY AND PLAYBOOK

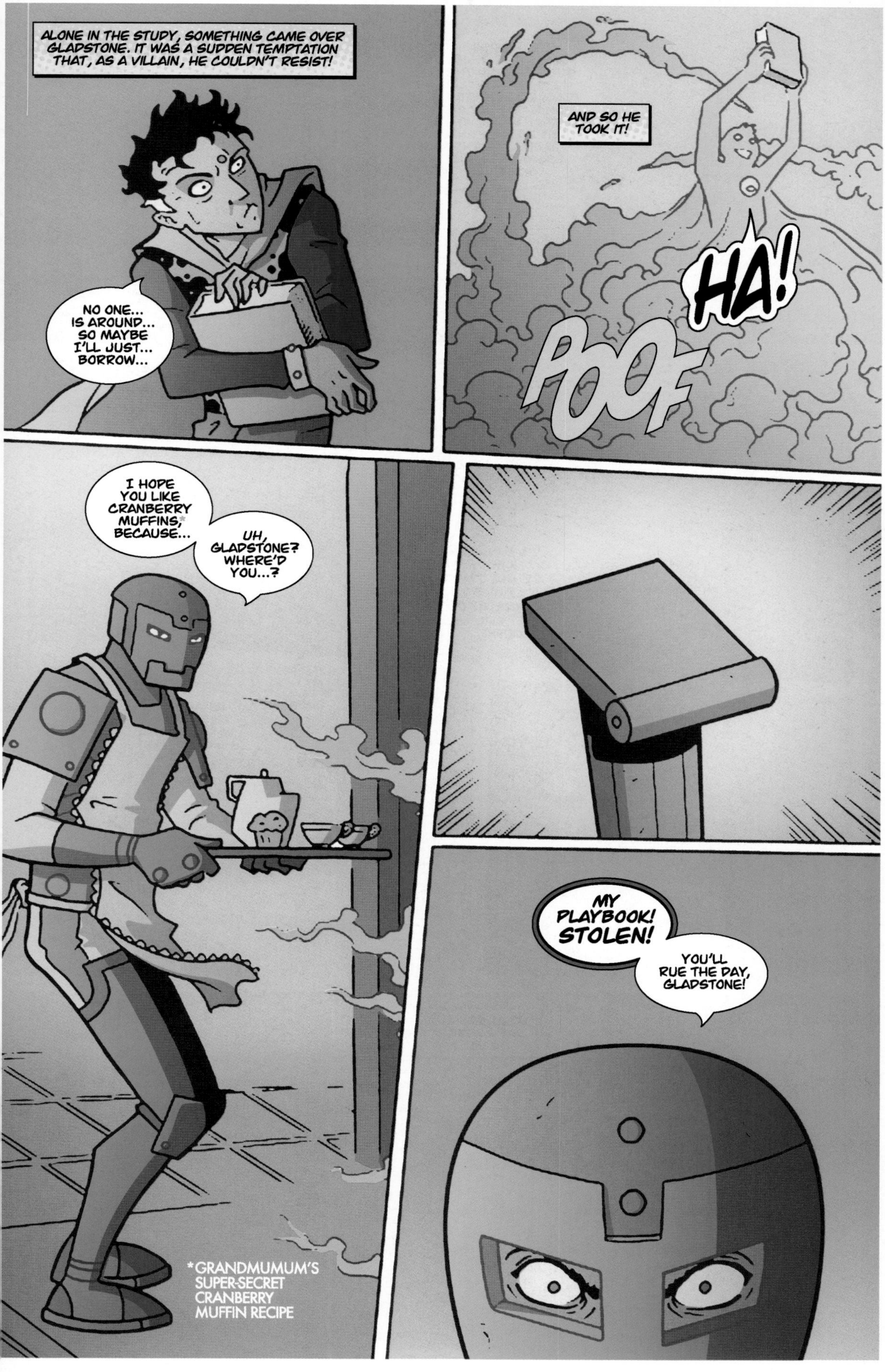
ALONE IN THE STUDY, SOMETHING CAME OVER GLADSTONE. IT WAS A SUDDEN TEMPTATION THAT, AS A VILLAIN, HE COULDN'T RESIST!
NO ONE... IS AROUND... SO MAYBE I'LL JUST... BORROW...
AND SO HE TOOK IT!
HA!
POOF
I HOPE YOU LIKE CRANBERRY MUFFINS,* BECAUSE...
UH, GLADSTONE? WHERE'D YOU...?
*GRANDMUMUM'S SUPER-SECRET CRANBERRY MUFFIN RECIPE
MY PLAYBOOK! STOLEN!
YOU'LL RUE THE DAY, GLADSTONE!

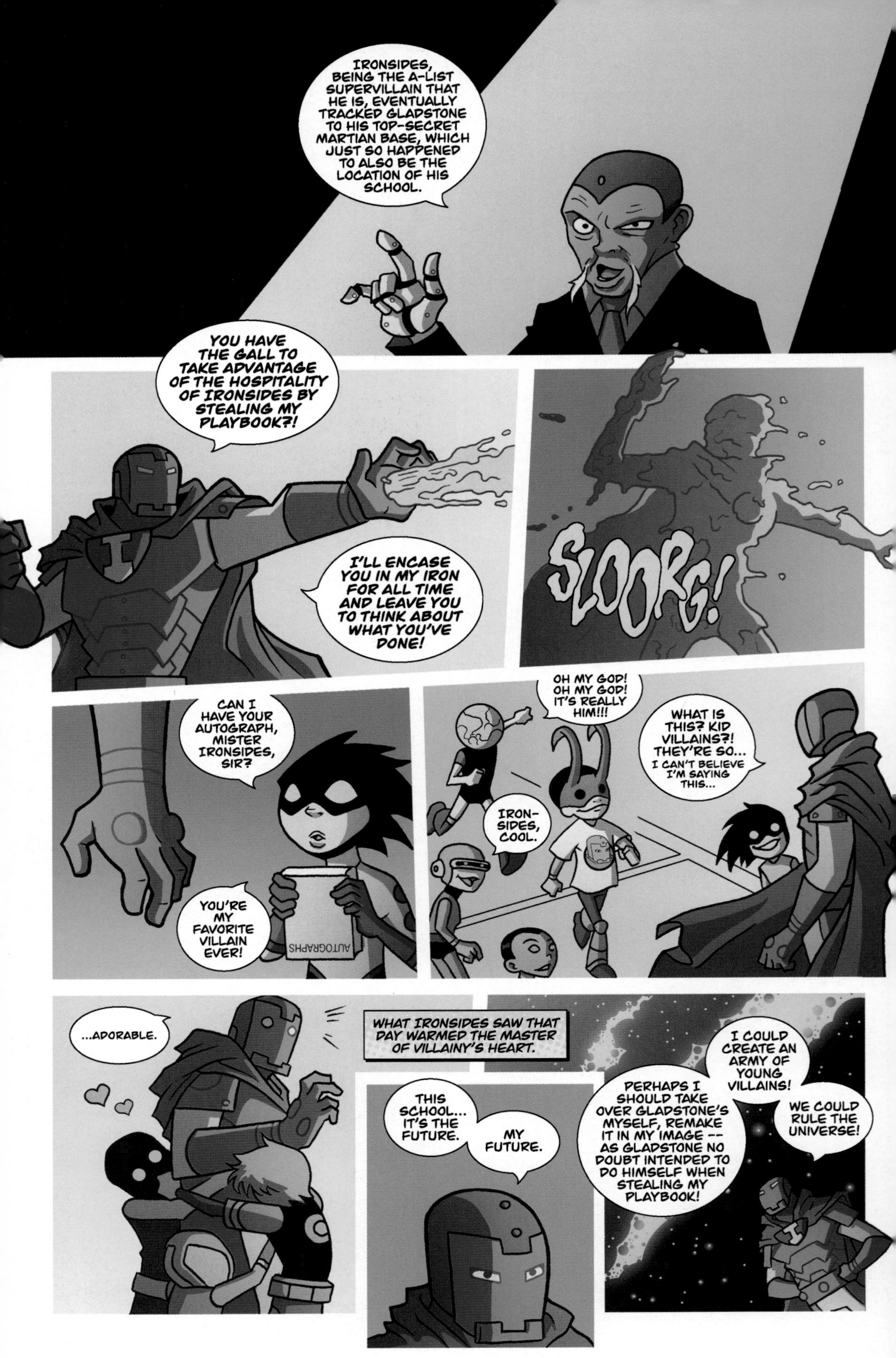
IRONSIDES, BEING THE A-LIST SUPERVILLAIN THAT HE IS, EVENTUALLY TRACKED GLADSTONE TO HIS TOP-SECRET MARTIAN BASE, WHICH JUST SO HAPPENED TO ALSO BE THE LOCATION OF HIS SCHOOL.
YOU HAVE THE GALL TO TAKE ADVANTAGE OF THE HOSPITALITY OF IRONSIDES BY STEALING MY PLAYBOOK?!
I'LL ENCASE YOU IN MY IRON FOR ALL TIME AND LEAVE YOU TO THINK ABOUT WHAT YOU'VE DONE!
SLOORG!
CAN I HAVE YOUR AUTOGRAPH, MISTER IRONSIDES, SIR?
YOU'RE MY FAVORITE VILLAIN EVER!
AUTOGRAPHS
OH MY GOD! OH MY GOD! IT'S REALLY HIM!!!
IRON-SIDES, COOL.
WHAT IS THIS? KID VILLAINS?! THEY'RE SO... I CAN'T BELIEVE I'M SAYING THIS...
...ADORABLE.
WHAT IRONSIDES SAW THAT DAY WARMED THE MASTER OF VILLAINY'S HEART.
THIS SCHOOL... IT'S THE FUTURE.
MY FUTURE.
PERHAPS I SHOULD TAKE OVER GLADSTONE'S MYSELF, REMAKE IT IN MY IMAGE -- AS GLADSTONE NO DOUBT INTENDED TO DO HIMSELF WHEN STEALING MY PLAYBOOK!
I COULD CREATE AN ARMY OF YOUNG VILLAINS!
WE COULD RULE THE UNIVERSE!

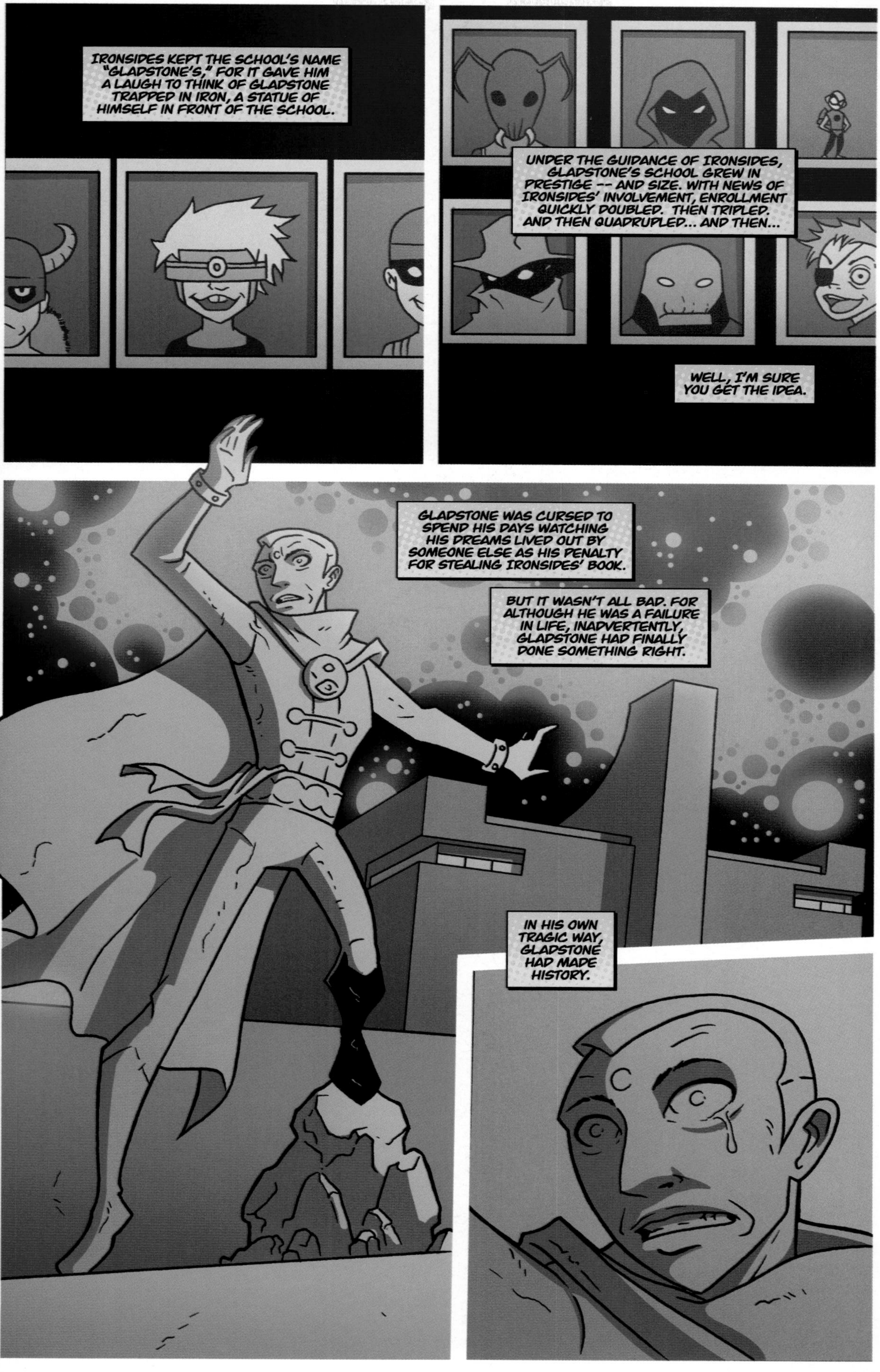
IRONSIDES KEPT THE SCHOOL'S NAME "GLADSTONE'S," FOR IT GAVE HIM A LAUGH TO THINK OF GLADSTONE TRAPPED IN IRON, A STATUE OF HIMSELF IN FRONT OF THE SCHOOL.
UNDER THE GUIDANCE OF IRONSIDES, GLADSTONE'S SCHOOL GREW IN PRESTIGE -- AND SIZE. WITH NEWS OF IRONSIDES' INVOLVEMENT, ENROLLMENT QUICKLY DOUBLED. THEN TRIPLED. AND THEN QUADRUPLED... AND THEN...
WELL, I'M SURE YOU GET THE IDEA.
GLADSTONE WAS CURSED TO SPEND HIS DAYS WATCHING HIS DREAMS LIVED OUT BY SOMEONE ELSE AS HIS PENALTY FOR STEALING IRONSIDES' BOOK.
BUT IT WASN'T ALL BAD. FOR ALTHOUGH HE WAS A FAILURE IN LIFE, INADVERTENTLY, GLADSTONE HAD FINALLY DONE SOMETHING RIGHT.
IN HIS OWN TRAGIC WAY, GLADSTONE HAD MADE HISTORY.

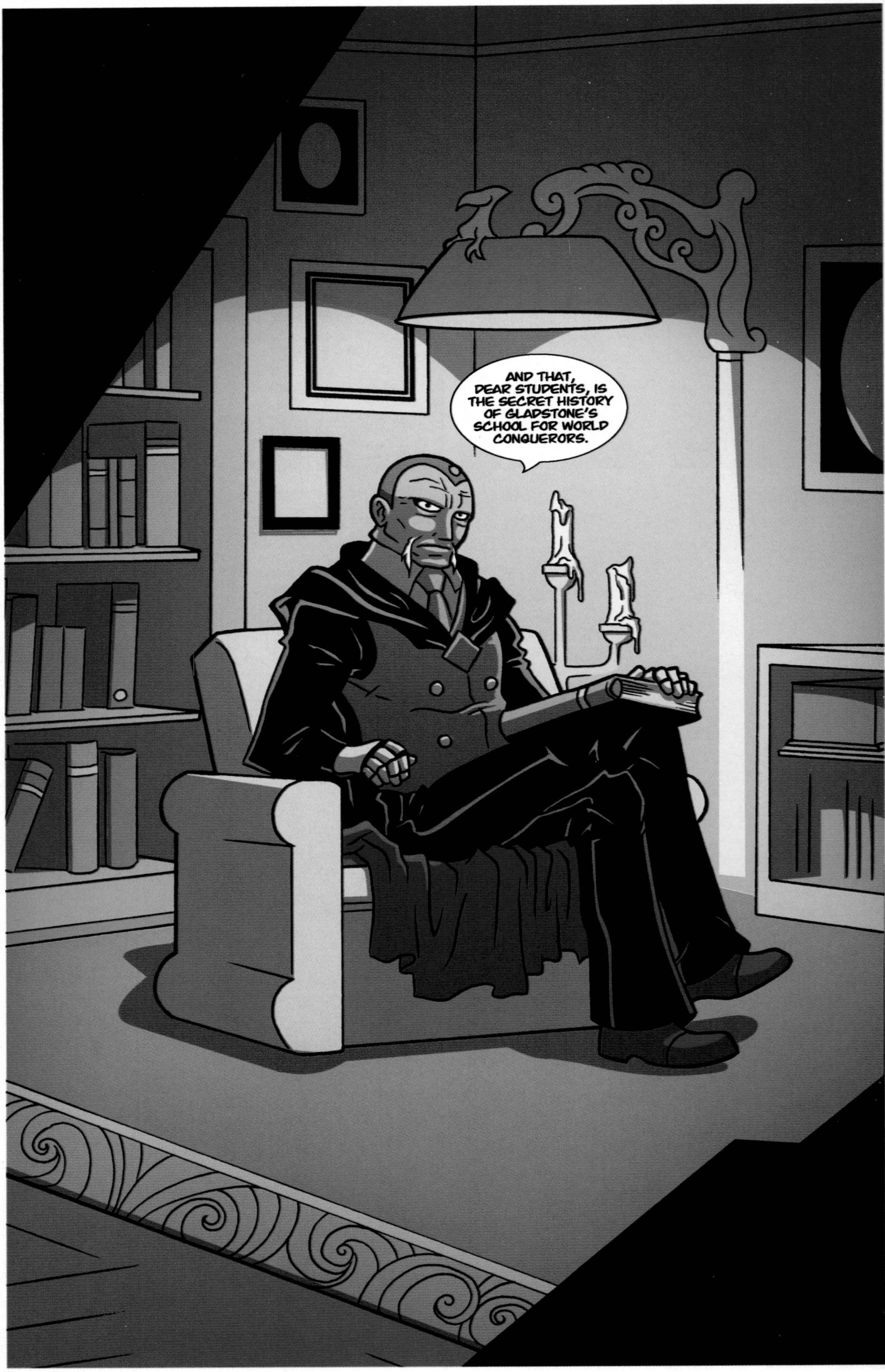
AND THAT, DEAR STUDENTS, IS THE SECRET HISTORY OF GLADSTONE'S SCHOOL FOR WORLD CONQUERORS.

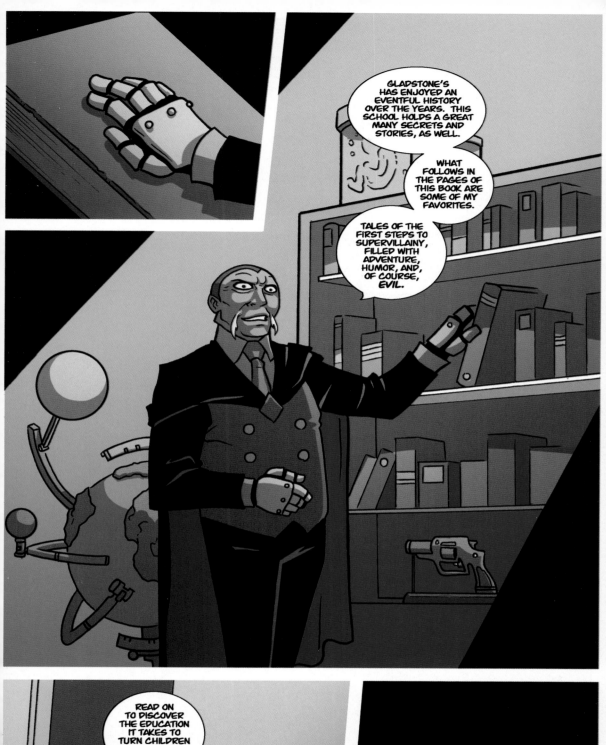

GLADSTONE'S HAS ENJOYED AN EVENTFUL HISTORY OVER THE YEARS. THIS SCHOOL HOLDS A GREAT MANY SECRETS AND STORIES, AS WELL.

WHAT FOLLOWS IN THE PAGES OF THIS BOOK ARE SOME OF MY FAVORITES.

TALES OF THE FIRST STEPS TO SUPERVILLAINY, FILLED WITH ADVENTURE, HUMOR, AND, OF COURSE, EVIL.

READ ON TO DISCOVER THE EDUCATION IT TAKES TO TURN CHILDREN INTO WORLD CONQUERORS...

...IF YOU DARE!

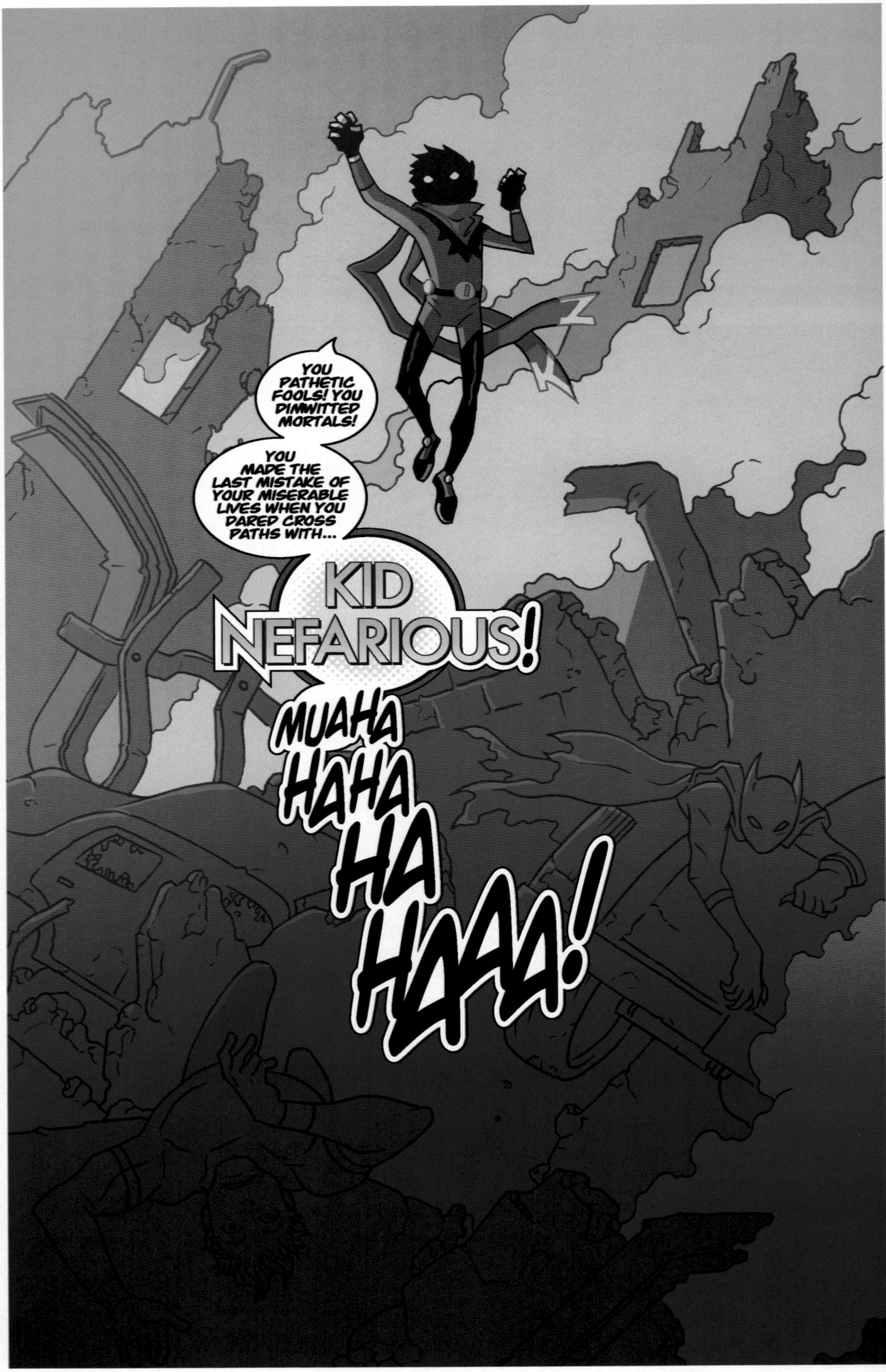
YOU PATHETIC FOOLS! YOU DIMWITTED MORTALS!
YOU MADE THE LAST MISTAKE OF YOUR MISERABLE LIVES WHEN YOU DARED CROSS PATHS WITH...
KID NEFARIOUS!
MUAHA HAHA HA HAAA!

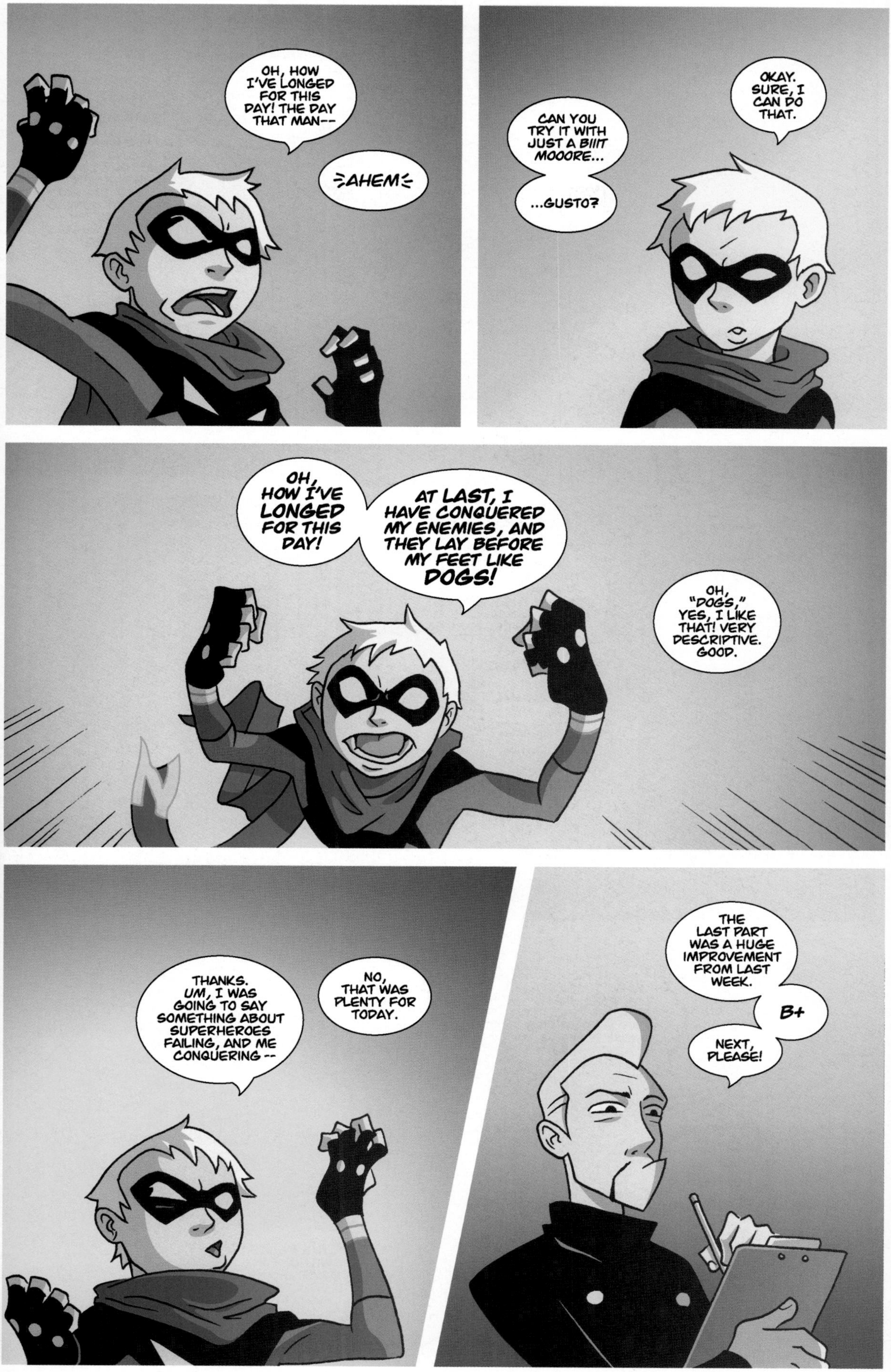
OH, HOW I'VE LONGED FOR THIS DAY! THE DAY THAT MAN--
AHEM
CAN YOU TRY IT WITH JUST A BIIIT MOOORE...
...GUSTO?
OKAY. SURE, I CAN DO THAT.
OH, HOW I'VE LONGED FOR THIS DAY!
AT LAST, I HAVE CONQUERED MY ENEMIES, AND THEY LAY BEFORE MY FEET LIKE DOGS!
OH, "DOGS," YES, I LIKE THAT! VERY DESCRIPTIVE. GOOD.
THANKS. UM, I WAS GOING TO SAY SOMETHING ABOUT SUPERHEROES FAILING, AND ME CONQUERING --
NO, THAT WAS PLENTY FOR TODAY.
THE LAST PART WAS A HUGE IMPROVEMENT FROM LAST WEEK.
B+
NEXT, PLEASE!

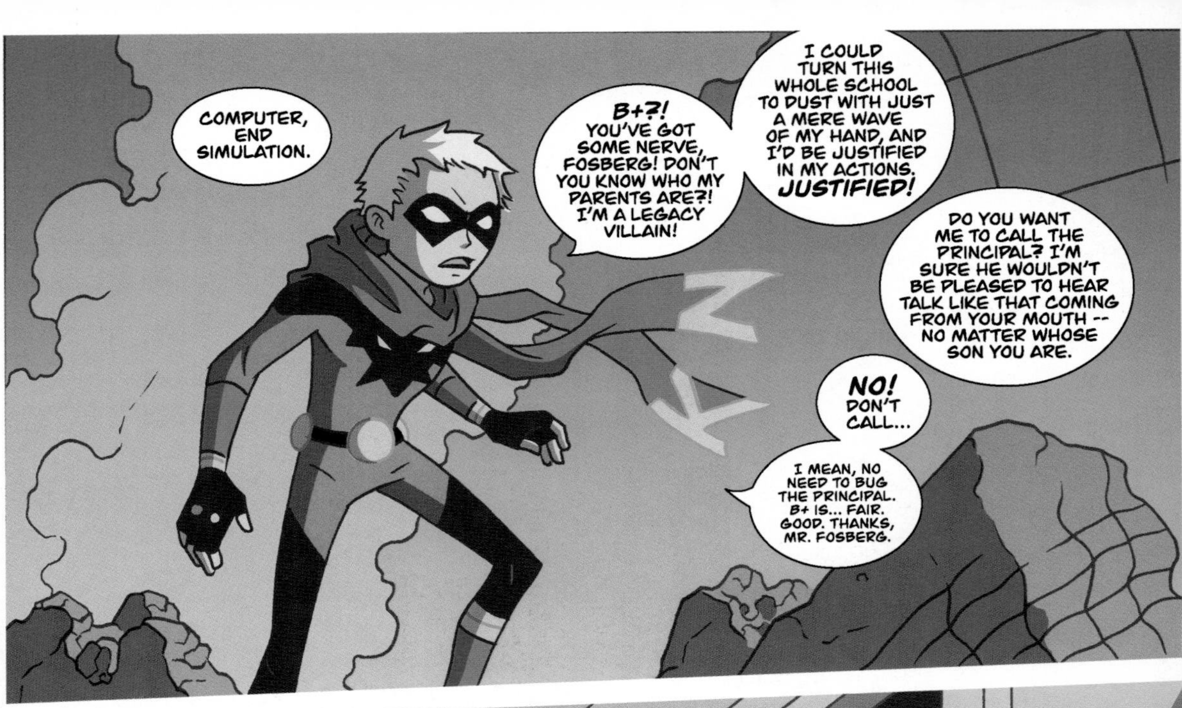
COMPUTER, END SIMULATION.
B+?! YOU'VE GOT SOME NERVE, FOSBERG! DON'T YOU KNOW WHO MY PARENTS ARE?! I'M A LEGACY VILLAIN!
I COULD TURN THIS WHOLE SCHOOL TO DUST WITH JUST A MERE WAVE OF MY HAND, AND I'D BE JUSTIFIED IN MY ACTIONS. JUSTIFIED!
DO YOU WANT ME TO CALL THE PRINCIPAL? I'M SURE HE WOULDN'T BE PLEASED TO HEAR TALK LIKE THAT COMING FROM YOUR MOUTH -- NO MATTER WHOSE SON YOU ARE.
NO! DON'T CALL...
I MEAN, NO NEED TO BUG THE PRINCIPAL. B+ IS... FAIR. GOOD. THANKS, MR. FOSBERG.

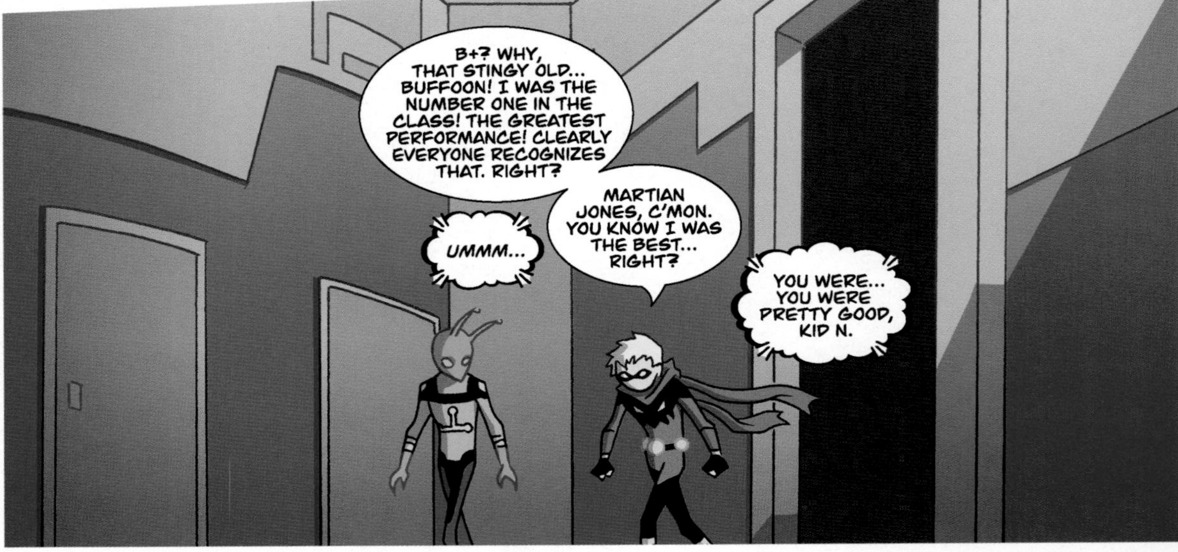
B+? WHY, THAT STINGY OLD... BUFFOON! I WAS THE NUMBER ONE IN THE CLASS! THE GREATEST PERFORMANCE! CLEARLY EVERYONE RECOGNIZES THAT. RIGHT?
UMMM...
MARTIAN JONES, C'MON. YOU KNOW I WAS THE BEST... RIGHT?
YOU WERE... YOU WERE PRETTY GOOD, KID N.

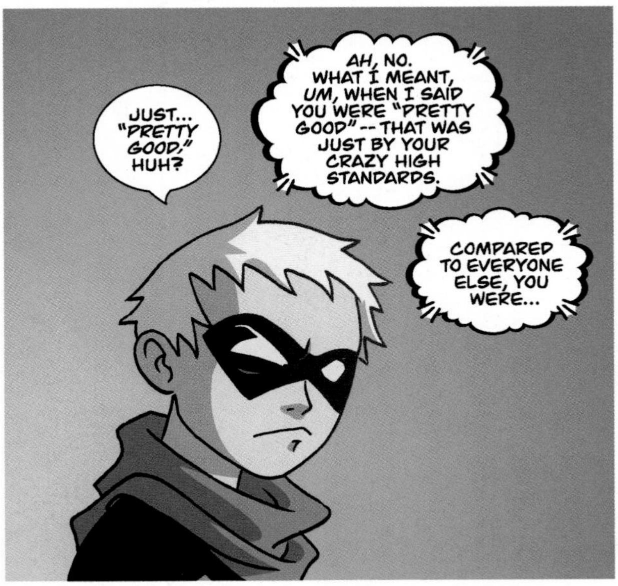
JUST... "PRETTY GOOD," HUH?
AH, NO. WHAT I MEANT, UM, WHEN I SAID YOU WERE "PRETTY GOOD" -- THAT WAS JUST BY YOUR CRAZY HIGH STANDARDS.
COMPARED TO EVERYONE ELSE, YOU WERE...

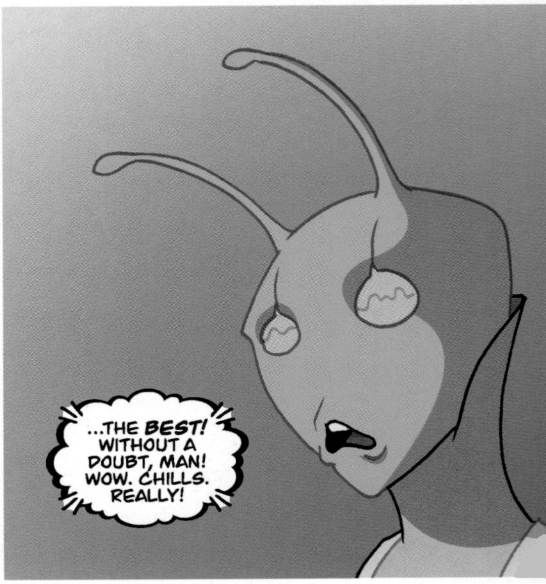
...THE BEST! WITHOUT A DOUBT, MAN! WOW. CHILLS. REALLY!

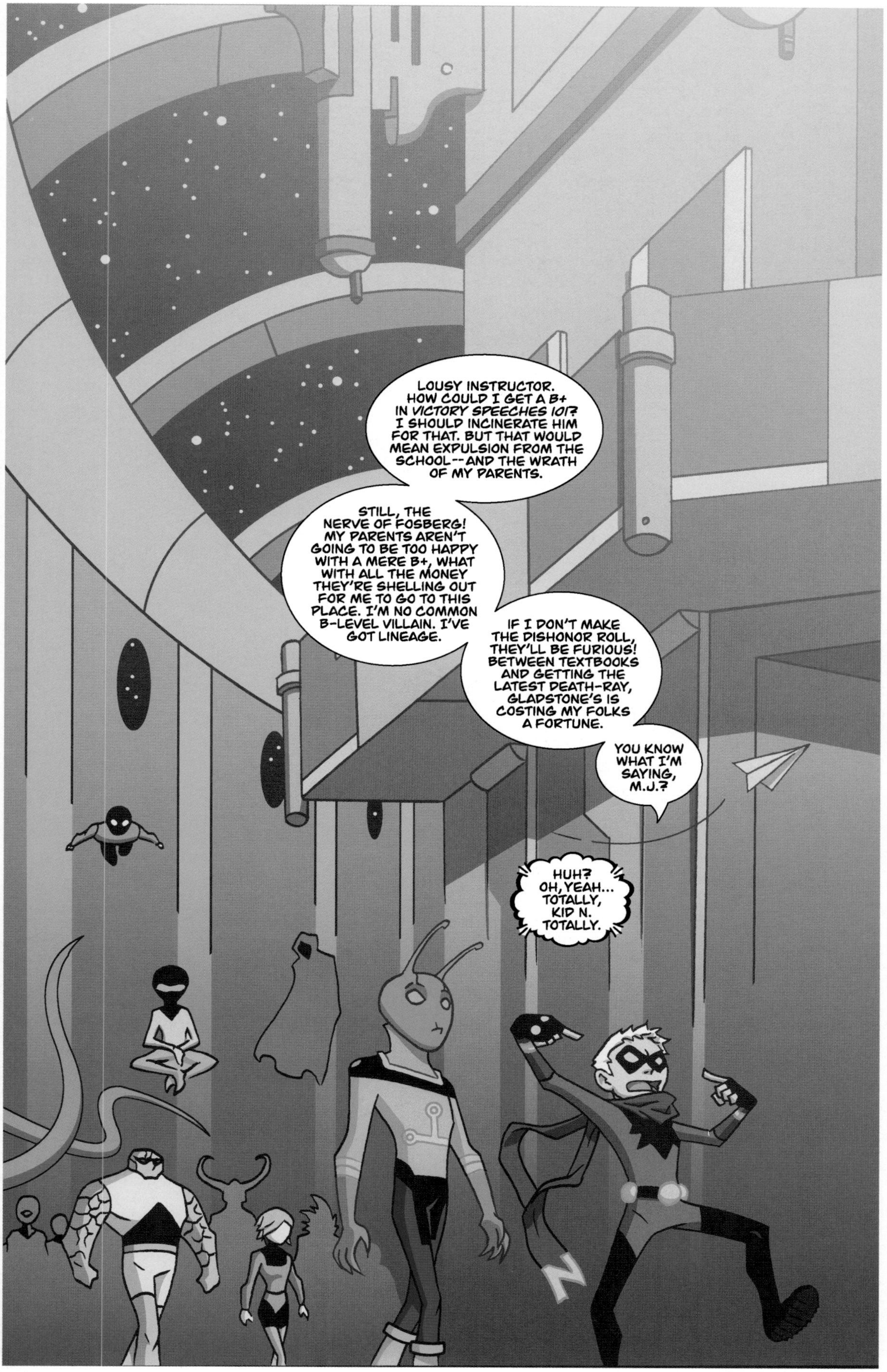
LOUSY INSTRUCTOR. HOW COULD I GET A B+ IN *VICTORY SPEECHES 101*? I SHOULD INCINERATE HIM FOR THAT. BUT THAT WOULD MEAN EXPULSION FROM THE SCHOOL--AND THE WRATH OF MY PARENTS.
STILL, THE NERVE OF FOSBERG! MY PARENTS AREN'T GOING TO BE TOO HAPPY WITH A MERE B+, WHAT WITH ALL THE MONEY THEY'RE SHELLING OUT FOR ME TO GO TO THIS PLACE. I'M NO COMMON B-LEVEL VILLAIN. I'VE GOT LINEAGE.
IF I DON'T MAKE THE DISHONOR ROLL, THEY'LL BE FURIOUS! BETWEEN TEXTBOOKS AND GETTING THE LATEST DEATH-RAY, GLADSTONE'S IS COSTING MY FOLKS A FORTUNE.
YOU KNOW WHAT I'M SAYING, M.J.?
HUH? OH, YEAH... TOTALLY, KID N. TOTALLY.

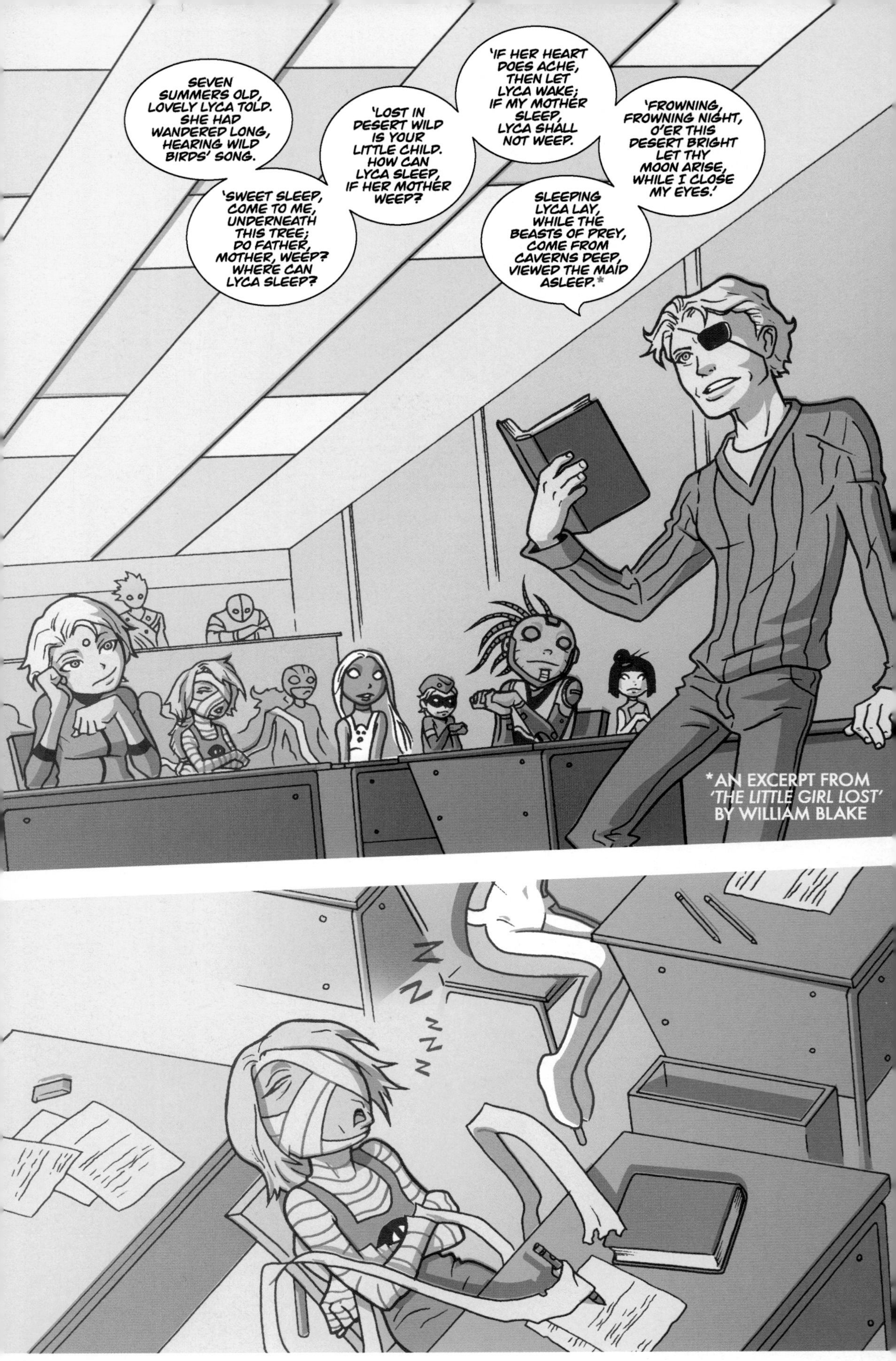
SEVEN SUMMERS OLD, LOVELY LYCA TOLD. SHE HAD WANDERED LONG, HEARING WILD BIRDS' SONG.
'SWEET SLEEP, COME TO ME, UNDERNEATH THIS TREE; DO FATHER, MOTHER, WEEP? WHERE CAN LYCA SLEEP?
'LOST IN DESERT WILD IS YOUR LITTLE CHILD. HOW CAN LYCA SLEEP, IF HER MOTHER WEEP?
'IF HER HEART DOES ACHE, THEN LET LYCA WAKE; IF MY MOTHER SLEEP, LYCA SHALL NOT WEEP.
'FROWNING, FROWNING NIGHT, O'ER THIS DESERT BRIGHT LET THY MOON ARISE, WHILE I CLOSE MY EYES.'
SLEEPING LYCA LAY, WHILE THE BEASTS OF PREY, COME FROM CAVERNS DEEP, VIEWED THE MAID ASLEEP.*
*AN EXCERPT FROM 'THE LITTLE GIRL LOST' BY WILLIAM BLAKE
Z Z Z Z Z

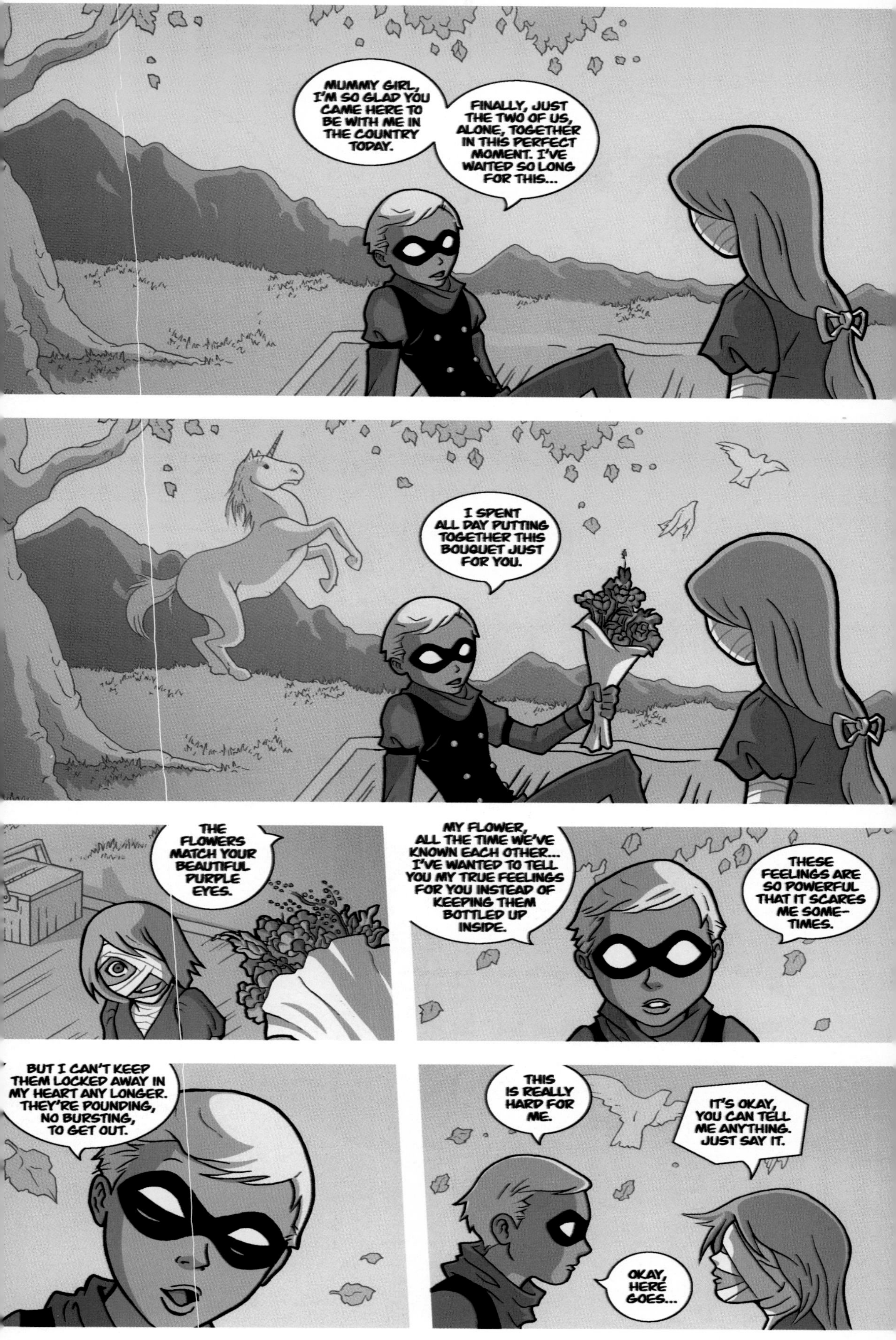
MUMMY GIRL, I'M SO GLAD YOU CAME HERE TO BE WITH ME IN THE COUNTRY TODAY.
FINALLY, JUST THE TWO OF US, ALONE, TOGETHER IN THIS PERFECT MOMENT. I'VE WAITED SO LONG FOR THIS...
I SPENT ALL DAY PUTTING TOGETHER THIS BOUQUET JUST FOR YOU.
THE FLOWERS MATCH YOUR BEAUTIFUL PURPLE EYES.
MY FLOWER, ALL THE TIME WE'VE KNOWN EACH OTHER... I'VE WANTED TO TELL YOU MY TRUE FEELINGS FOR YOU INSTEAD OF KEEPING THEM BOTTLED UP INSIDE.
THESE FEELINGS ARE SO POWERFUL THAT IT SCARES ME SOME-TIMES.
BUT I CAN'T KEEP THEM LOCKED AWAY IN MY HEART ANY LONGER. THEY'RE POUNDING, NO BURSTING, TO GET OUT.
THIS IS REALLY HARD FOR ME.
IT'S OKAY, YOU CAN TELL ME ANYTHING. JUST SAY IT.
OKAY, HERE GOES...

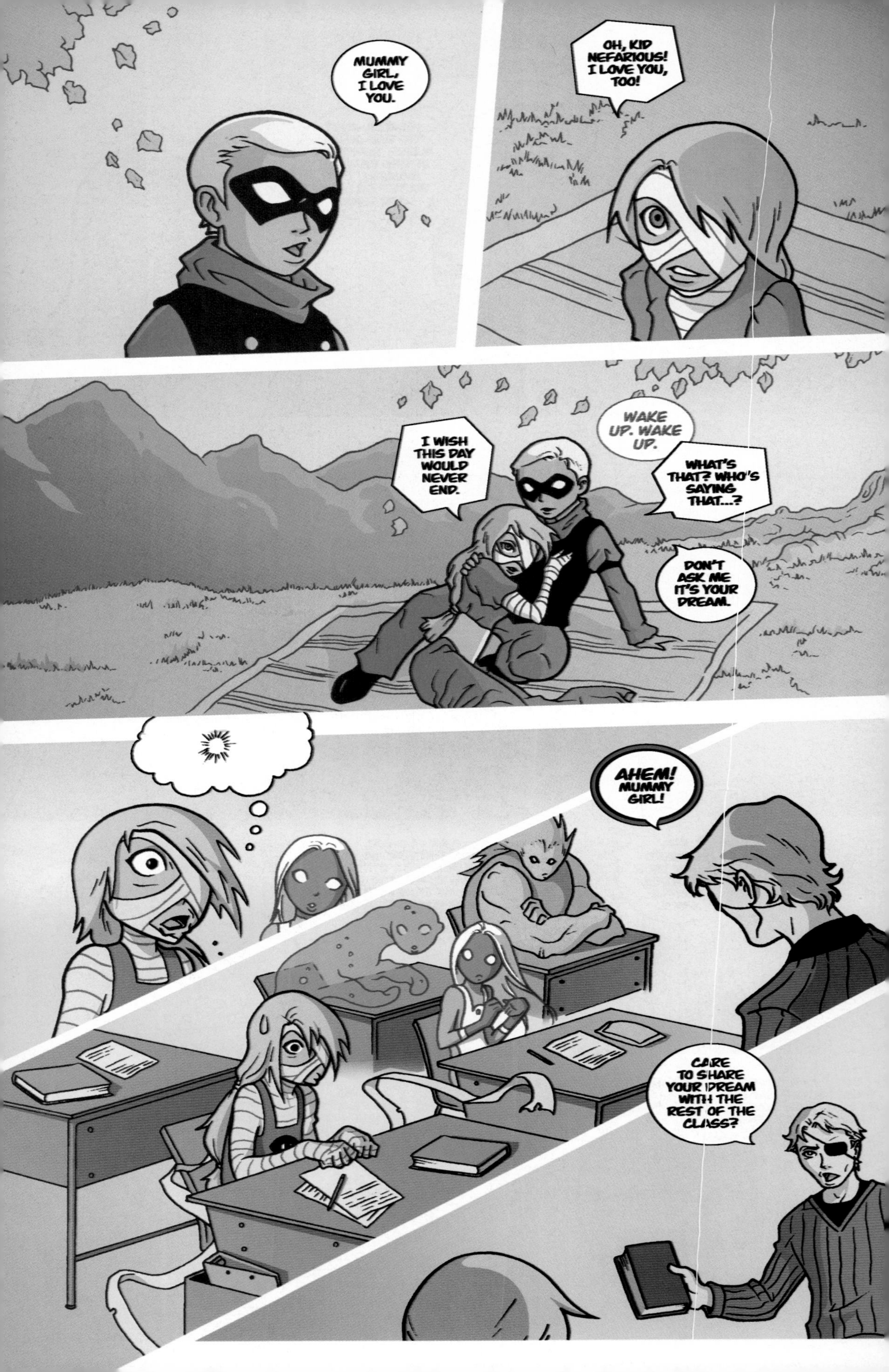
MUMMY GIRL, I LOVE YOU.
OH, KID NEFARIOUS! I LOVE YOU, TOO!
I WISH THIS DAY WOULD NEVER END.
WAKE UP. WAKE UP.
WHAT'S THAT? WHO'S SAYING THAT...?
DON'T ASK ME IT'S YOUR DREAM.
AHEM! MUMMY GIRL!
CARE TO SHARE YOUR DREAM WITH THE REST OF THE CLASS?

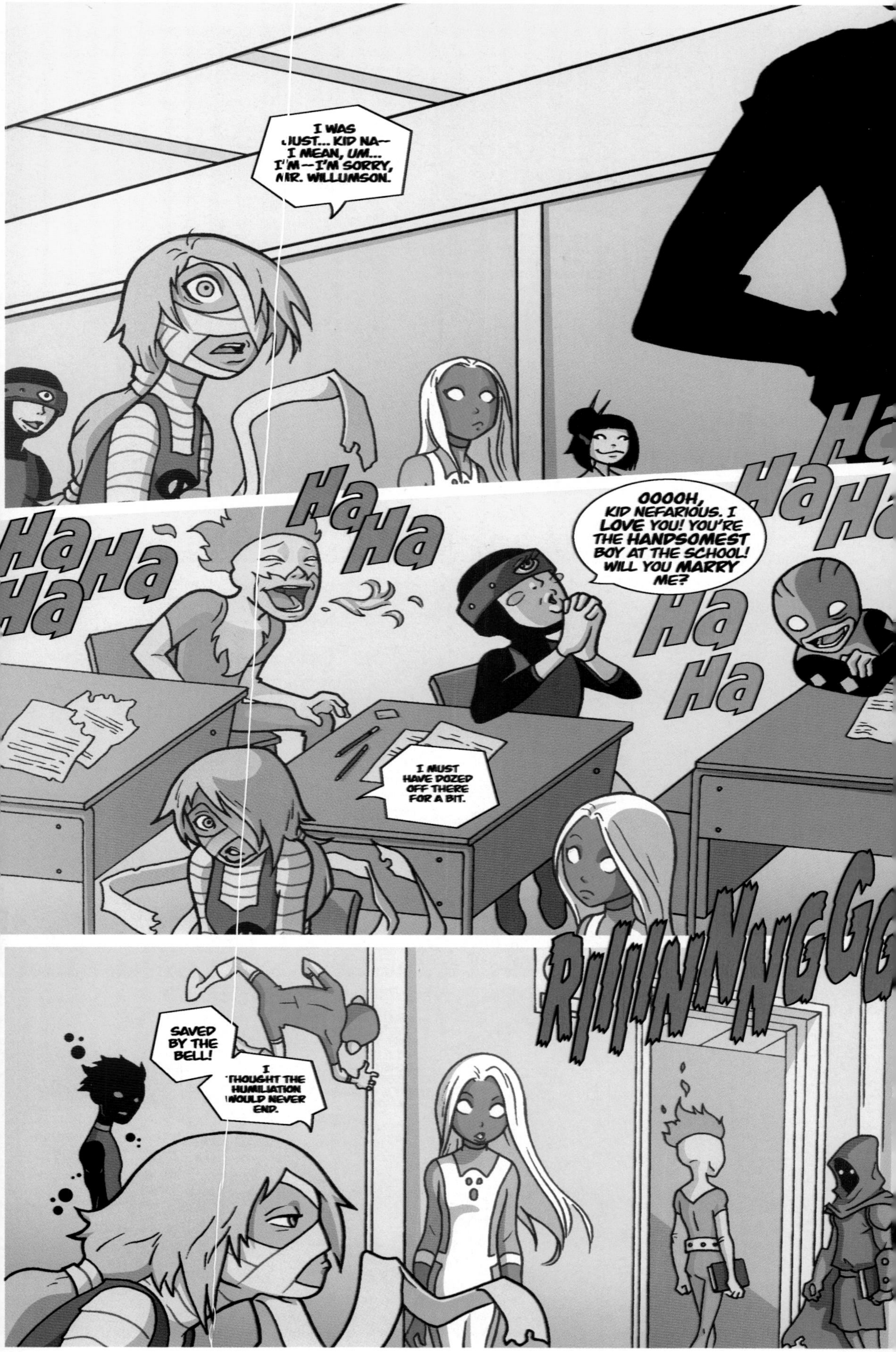
I WAS JUST... KID NA-- I MEAN, UM... I'M--I'M SORRY, MR. WILLUMSON.
HA HA HA HA
HA HA HA HA
HA HA
OOOOH, KID NEFARIOUS. I LOVE YOU! YOU'RE THE HANDSOMEST BOY AT THE SCHOOL! WILL YOU MARRY ME?
HA HA
I MUST HAVE DOZED OFF THERE FOR A BIT.
RIIIINNNGGG
SAVED BY THE BELL!
I THOUGHT THE HUMILIATION WOULD NEVER END.

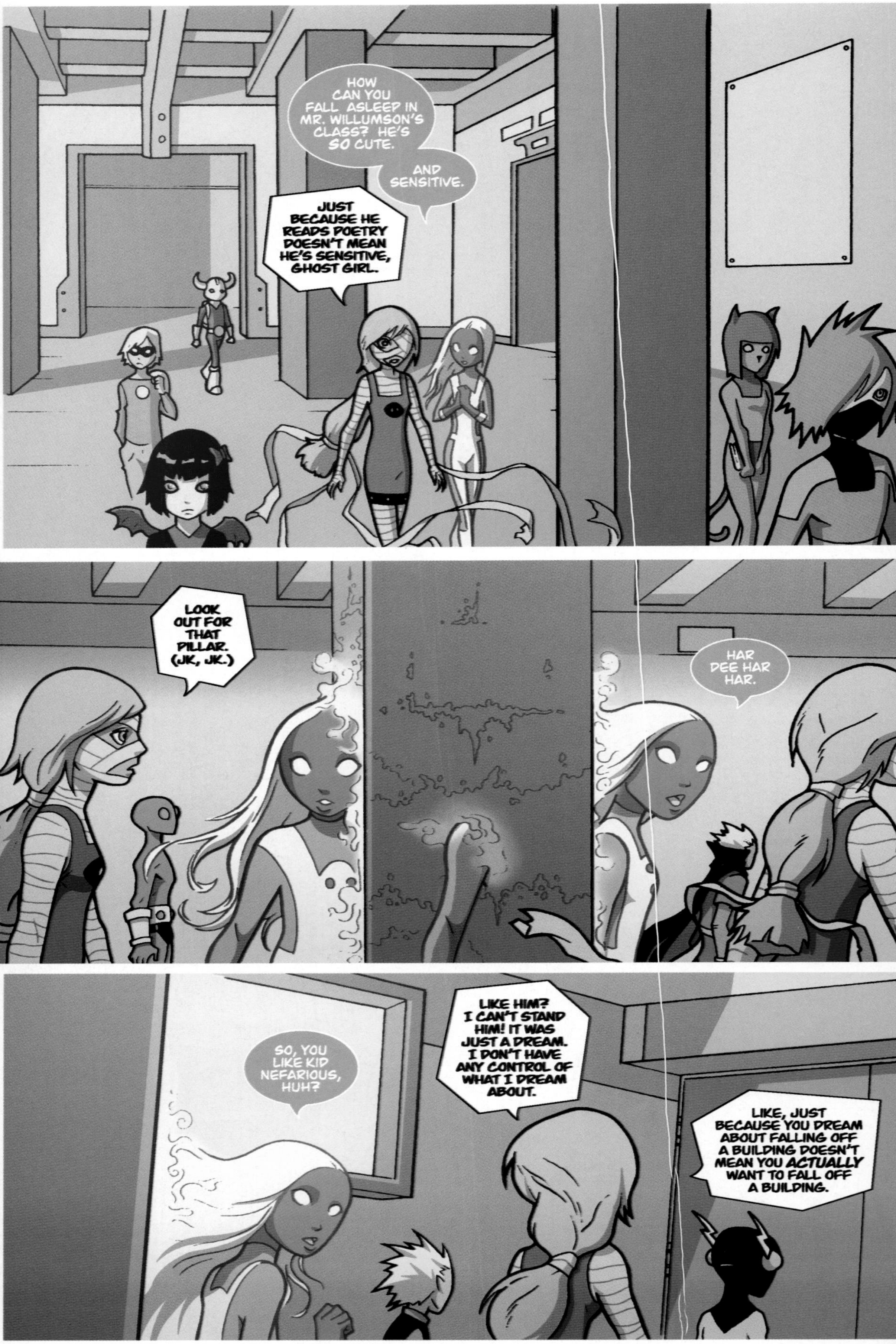
HOW CAN YOU FALL ASLEEP IN MR. WILLUMSON'S CLASS? HE'S SO CUTE.
AND SENSITIVE.
JUST BECAUSE HE READS POETRY DOESN'T MEAN HE'S SENSITIVE, GHOST GIRL.
LOOK OUT FOR THAT PILLAR. (JK, JK.)
HAR DEE HAR HAR.
SO, YOU LIKE KID NEFARIOUS, HUH?
LIKE HIM? I CAN'T STAND HIM! IT WAS JUST A DREAM. I DON'T HAVE ANY CONTROL OF WHAT I DREAM ABOUT.
LIKE, JUST BECAUSE YOU DREAM ABOUT FALLING OFF A BUILDING DOESN'T MEAN YOU ACTUALLY WANT TO FALL OFF A BUILDING.

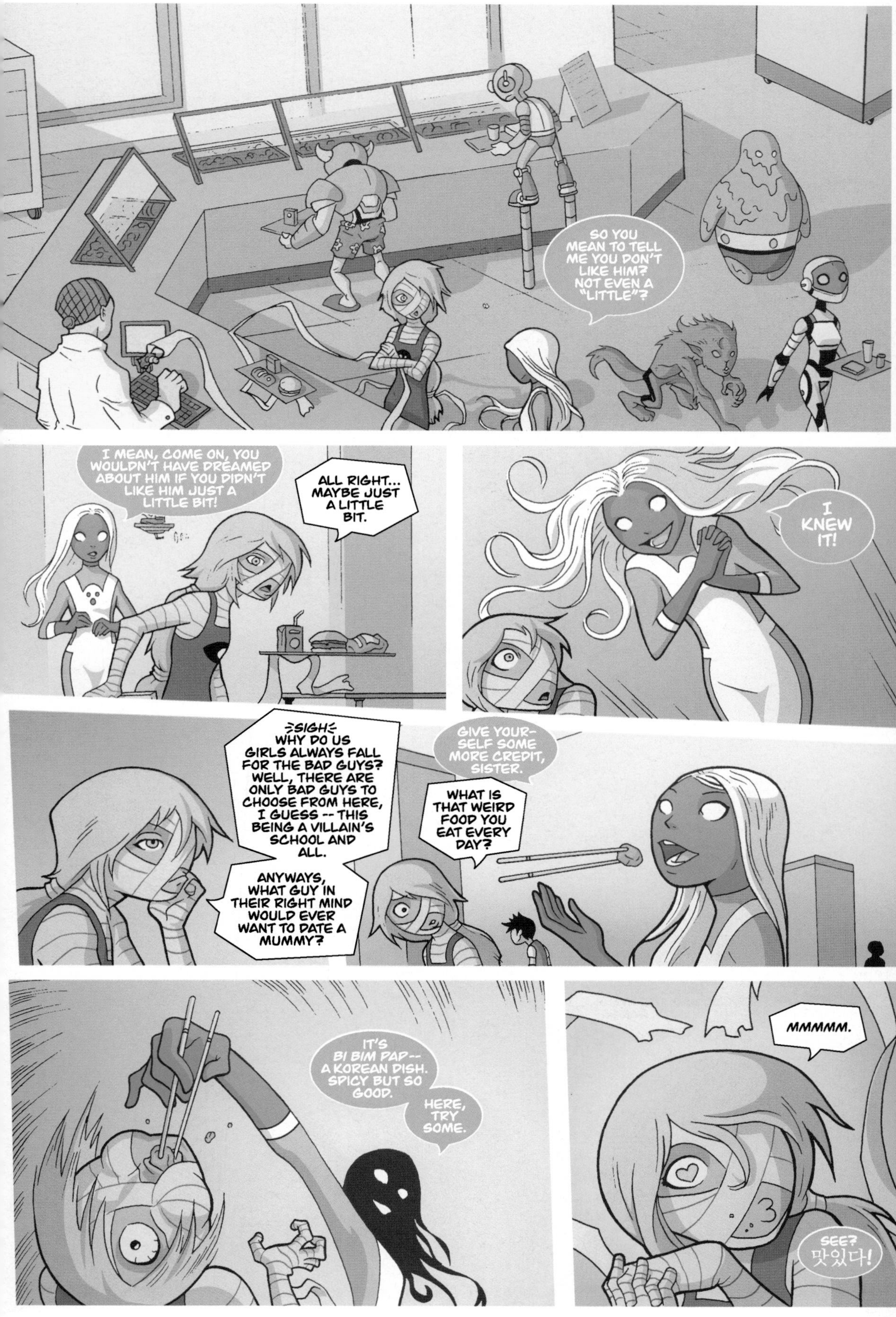
SO YOU MEAN TO TELL ME YOU DON'T LIKE HIM? NOT EVEN A "LITTLE"?
I MEAN, COME ON, YOU WOULDN'T HAVE DREAMED ABOUT HIM IF YOU DIDN'T LIKE HIM JUST A LITTLE BIT!
ALL RIGHT... MAYBE JUST A LITTLE BIT.
I KNEW IT!
SIGH
WHY DO US GIRLS ALWAYS FALL FOR THE BAD GUYS? WELL, THERE ARE ONLY BAD GUYS TO CHOOSE FROM HERE, I GUESS -- THIS BEING A VILLAIN'S SCHOOL AND ALL.
ANYWAYS, WHAT GUY IN THEIR RIGHT MIND WOULD EVER WANT TO DATE A MUMMY?
GIVE YOURSELF SOME MORE CREDIT, SISTER.
WHAT IS THAT WEIRD FOOD YOU EAT EVERY DAY?
IT'S BI BIM PAP-- A KOREAN DISH. SPICY BUT SO GOOD.
HERE, TRY SOME.
MMMMM.
SEE? 맛있다!

RECESS

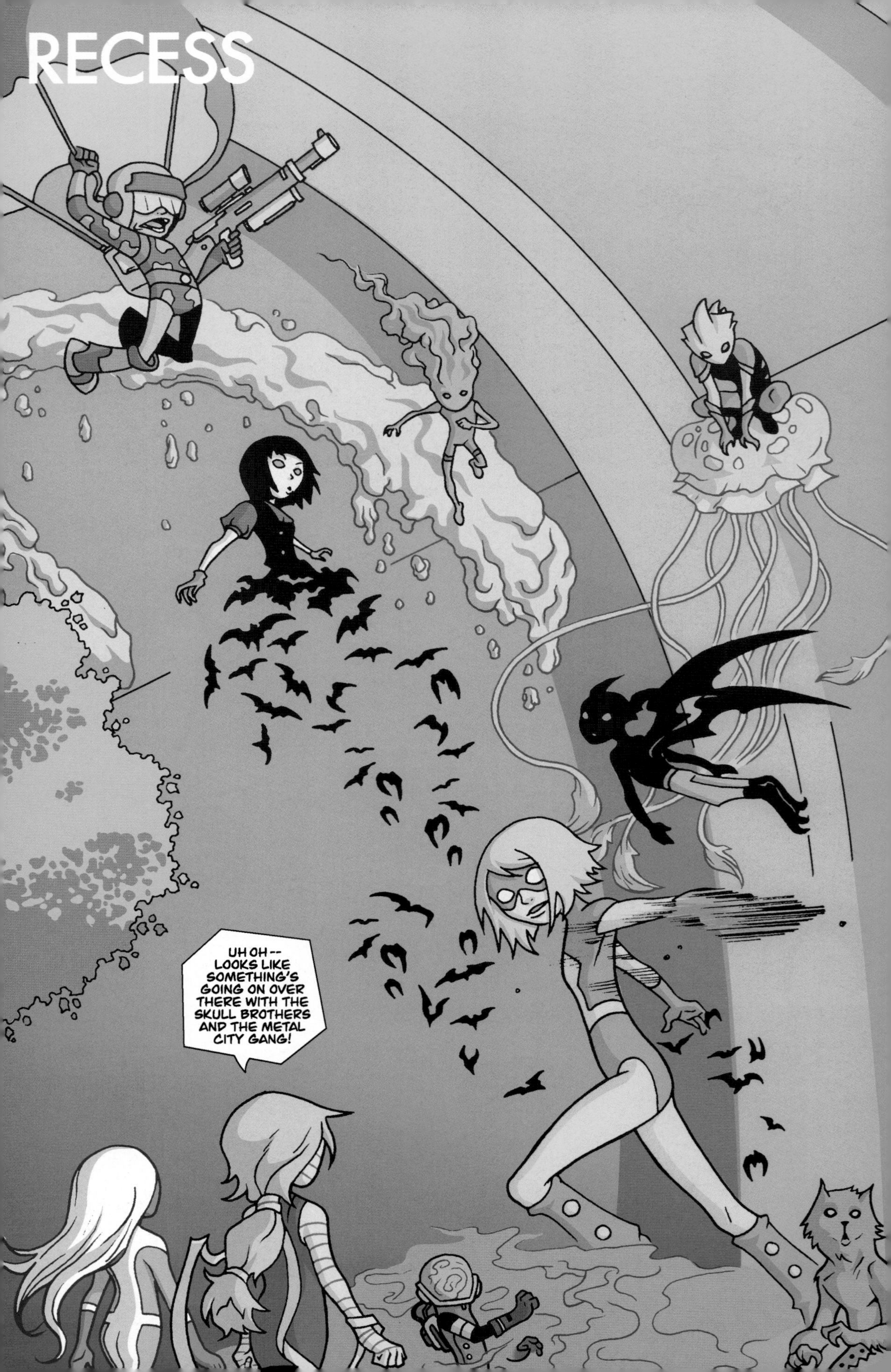
UH OH -- LOOKS LIKE SOMETHING'S GOING ON OVER THERE WITH THE SKULL BROTHERS AND THE METAL CITY GANG!

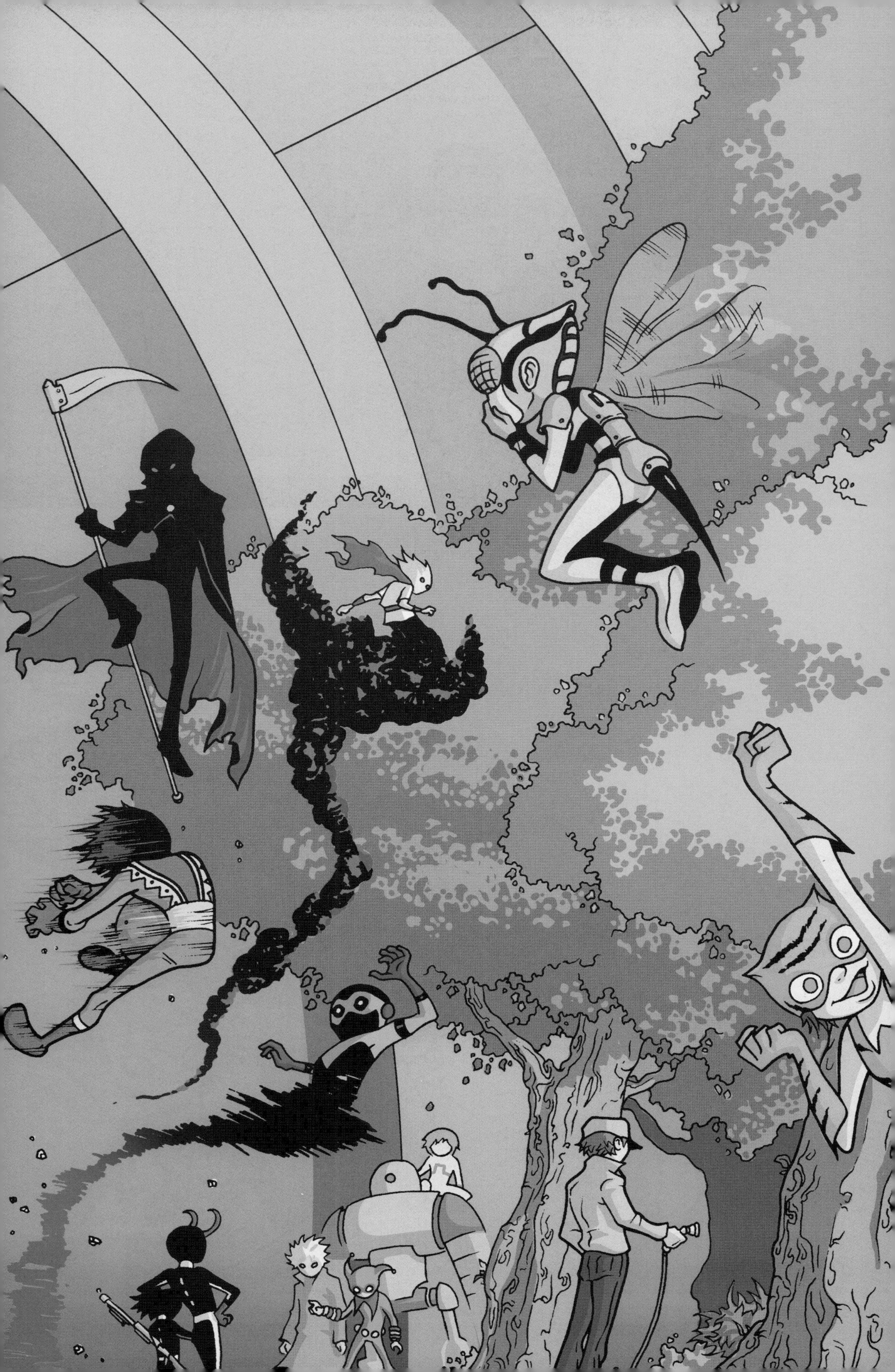

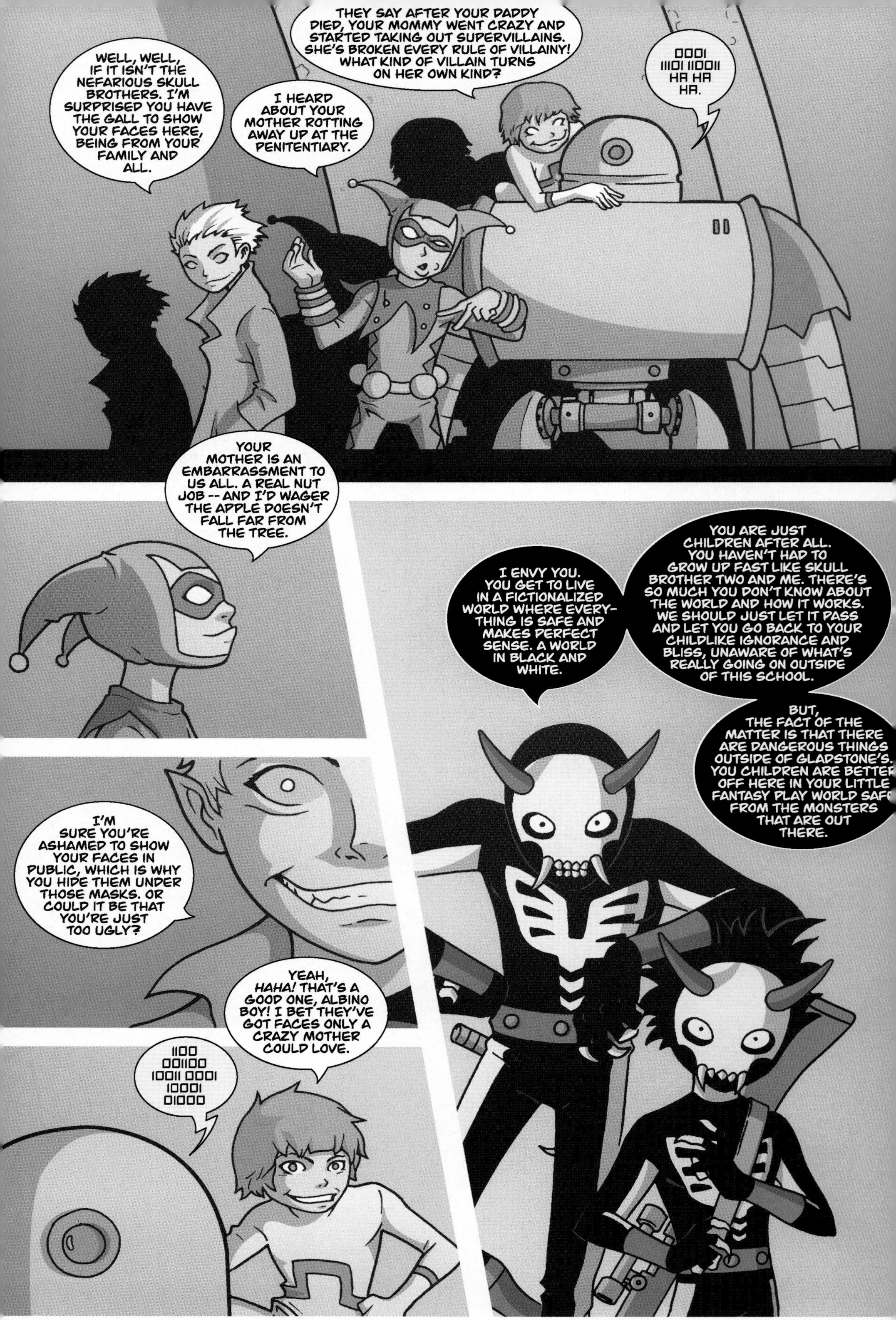
WELL, WELL, IF IT ISN'T THE NEFARIOUS SKULL BROTHERS. I'M SURPRISED YOU HAVE THE GALL TO SHOW YOUR FACES HERE, BEING FROM YOUR FAMILY AND ALL.
I HEARD ABOUT YOUR MOTHER ROTTING AWAY UP AT THE PENITENTIARY.
THEY SAY AFTER YOUR DADDY DIED, YOUR MOMMY WENT CRAZY AND STARTED TAKING OUT SUPERVILLAINS. SHE'S BROKEN EVERY RULE OF VILLAINY! WHAT KIND OF VILLAIN TURNS ON HER OWN KIND?
0001 11101 110011 HA HA HA.
YOUR MOTHER IS AN EMBARRASSMENT TO US ALL. A REAL NUT JOB -- AND I'D WAGER THE APPLE DOESN'T FALL FAR FROM THE TREE.
I'M SURE YOU'RE ASHAMED TO SHOW YOUR FACES IN PUBLIC, WHICH IS WHY YOU HIDE THEM UNDER THOSE MASKS. OR COULD IT BE THAT YOU'RE JUST TOO UGLY?
YEAH, HAHA! THAT'S A GOOD ONE, ALBINO BOY! I BET THEY'VE GOT FACES ONLY A CRAZY MOTHER COULD LOVE.
1100 001100 10011 0001 10001 01000
I ENVY YOU. YOU GET TO LIVE IN A FICTIONALIZED WORLD WHERE EVERY-THING IS SAFE AND MAKES PERFECT SENSE. A WORLD IN BLACK AND WHITE.
YOU ARE JUST CHILDREN AFTER ALL. YOU HAVEN'T HAD TO GROW UP FAST LIKE SKULL BROTHER TWO AND ME. THERE'S SO MUCH YOU DON'T KNOW ABOUT THE WORLD AND HOW IT WORKS. WE SHOULD JUST LET IT PASS AND LET YOU GO BACK TO YOUR CHILDLIKE IGNORANCE AND BLISS, UNAWARE OF WHAT'S REALLY GOING ON OUTSIDE OF THIS SCHOOL.
BUT, THE FACT OF THE MATTER IS THAT THERE ARE DANGEROUS THINGS OUTSIDE OF GLADSTONE'S. YOU CHILDREN ARE BETTER OFF HERE IN YOUR LITTLE FANTASY PLAY WORLD SAFE FROM THE MONSTERS THAT ARE OUT THERE.

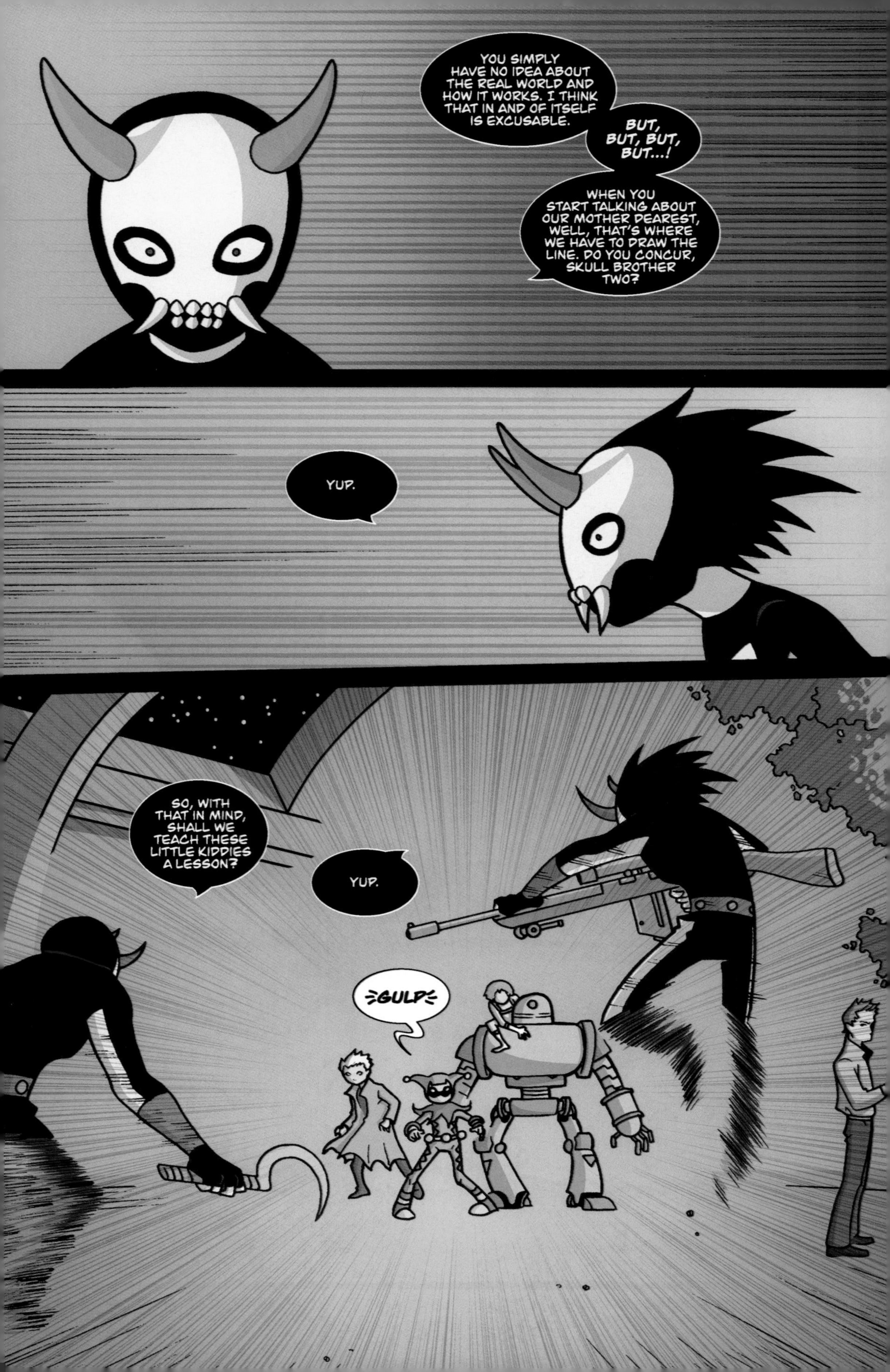

YOU SIMPLY HAVE NO IDEA ABOUT THE REAL WORLD AND HOW IT WORKS. I THINK THAT IN AND OF ITSELF IS EXCUSABLE.
BUT, BUT, BUT, BUT...!
WHEN YOU START TALKING ABOUT OUR MOTHER DEAREST, WELL, THAT'S WHERE WE HAVE TO DRAW THE LINE. DO YOU CONCUR, SKULL BROTHER TWO?
YUP.
SO, WITH THAT IN MIND, SHALL WE TEACH THESE LITTLE KIDDIES A LESSON?
YUP.
GULP

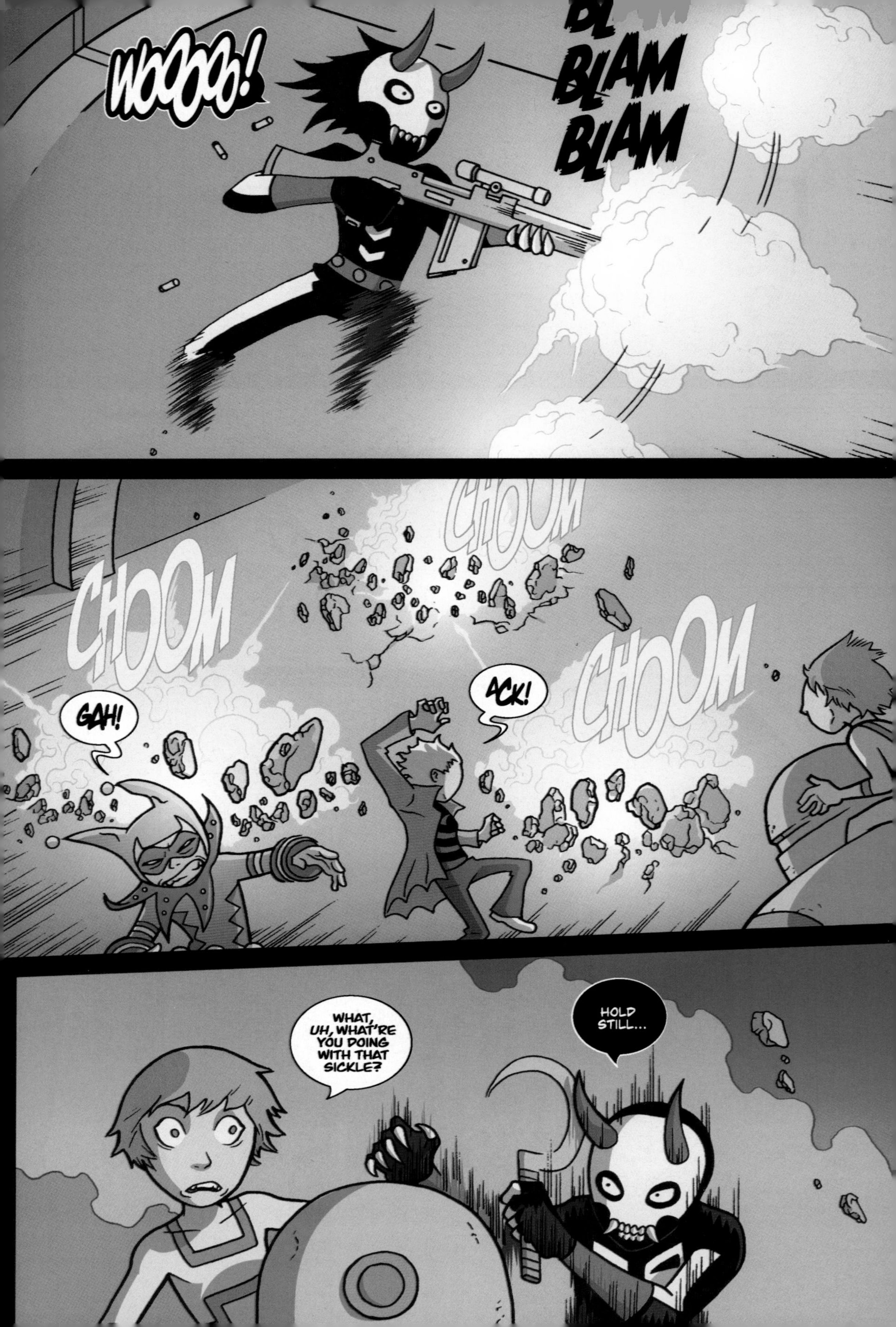
WOOOOO!
BL BLAM BLAM
CHOOM
CHOOM
GAH!
ACK!
CHOOM
WHAT, UH, WHAT'RE YOU DOING WITH THAT SICKLE?
HOLD STILL...

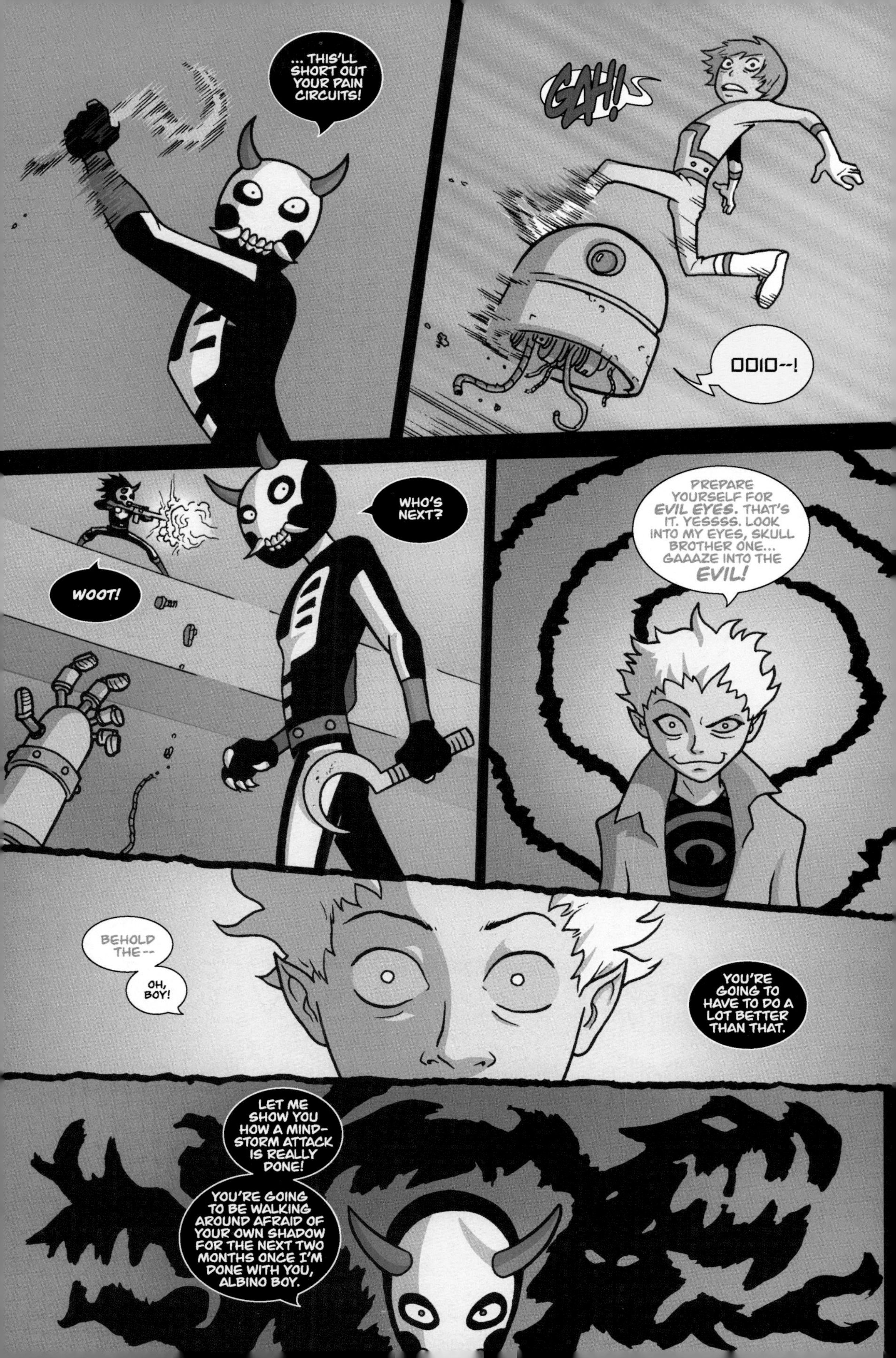
... THIS'LL SHORT OUT YOUR PAIN CIRCUITS!
GAH!
OOIO--!
WHO'S NEXT?
WOOT!
PREPARE YOURSELF FOR EVIL EYES. THAT'S IT. YESSSS. LOOK INTO MY EYES, SKULL BROTHER ONE... GAAAZE INTO THE EVIL!
BEHOLD THE--
OH, BOY!
YOU'RE GOING TO HAVE TO DO A LOT BETTER THAN THAT.
LET ME SHOW YOU HOW A MIND-STORM ATTACK IS REALLY DONE!
YOU'RE GOING TO BE WALKING AROUND AFRAID OF YOUR OWN SHADOW FOR THE NEXT TWO MONTHS ONCE I'M DONE WITH YOU, ALBINO BOY.

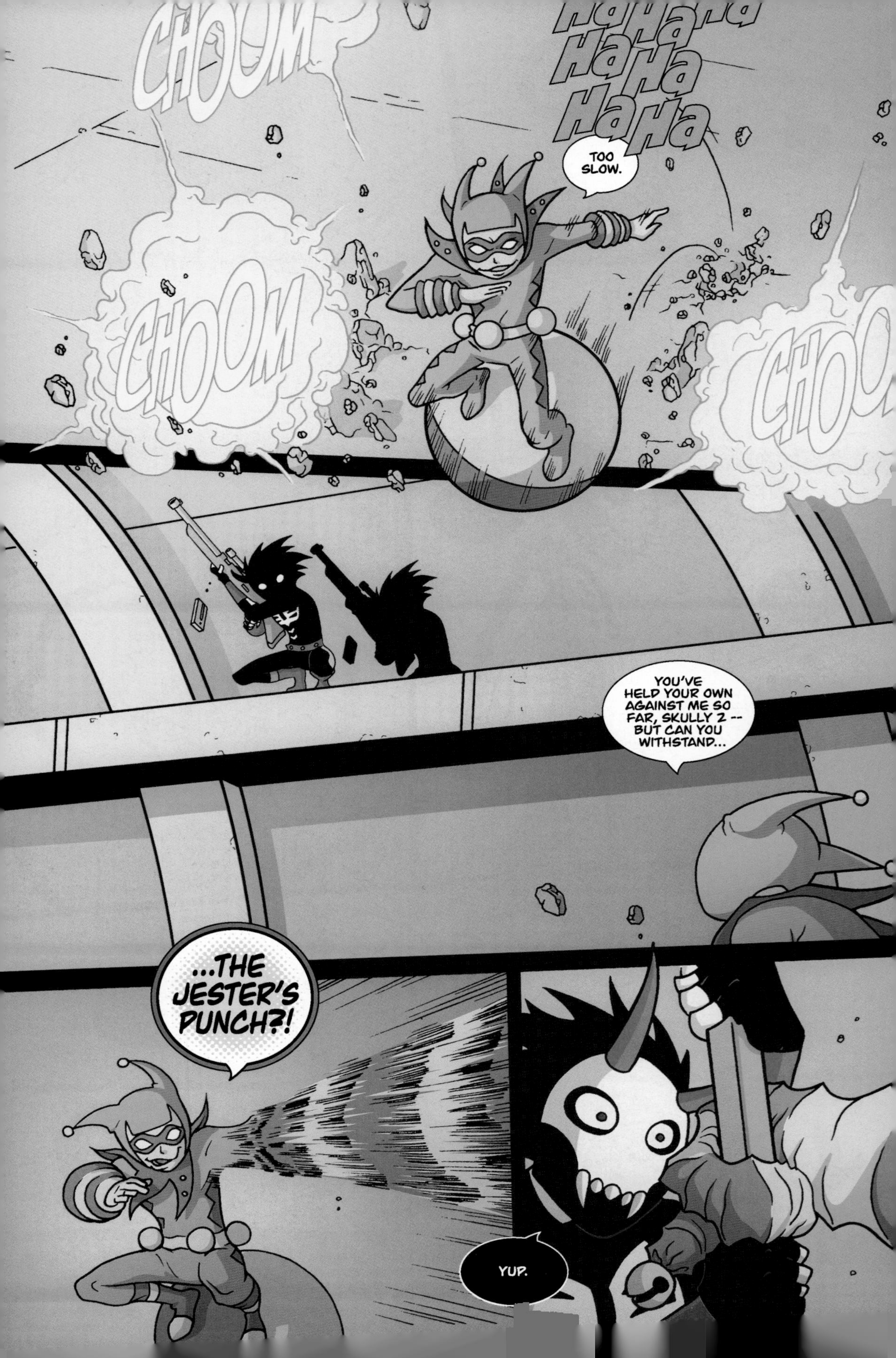
CHOOM
HaHaHa
HaHa
HaHa
TOO SLOW.
CHOOM
CHOO
YOU'VE HELD YOUR OWN AGAINST ME SO FAR, SKULLY 2 -- BUT CAN YOU WITHSTAND...
...THE JESTER'S PUNCH?!
YUP.

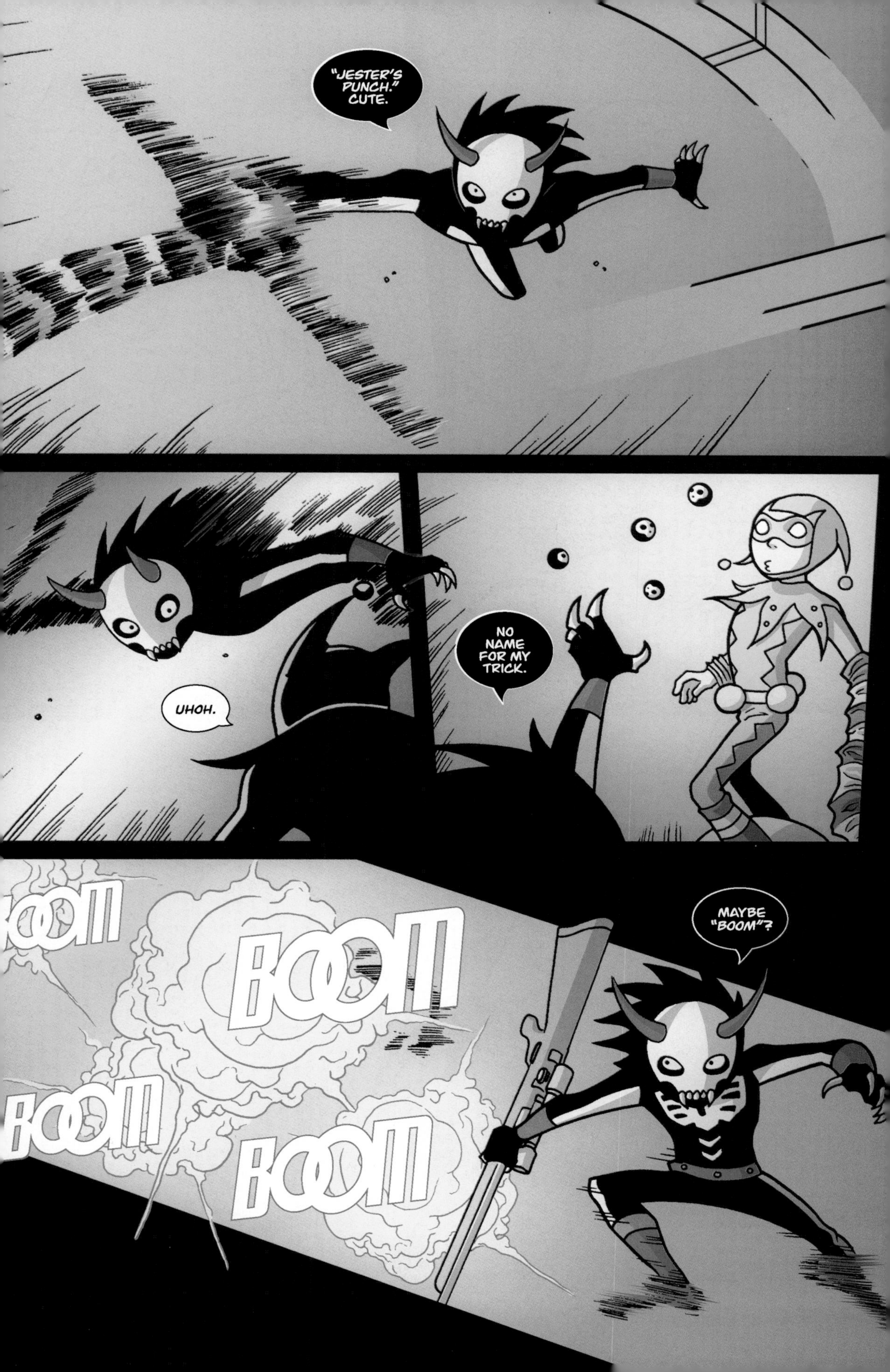
"JESTER'S PUNCH." CUTE.
UHOH.
NO NAME FOR MY TRICK.
MAYBE "BOOM"?
BOOM
BOOM
BOOM
BOOM

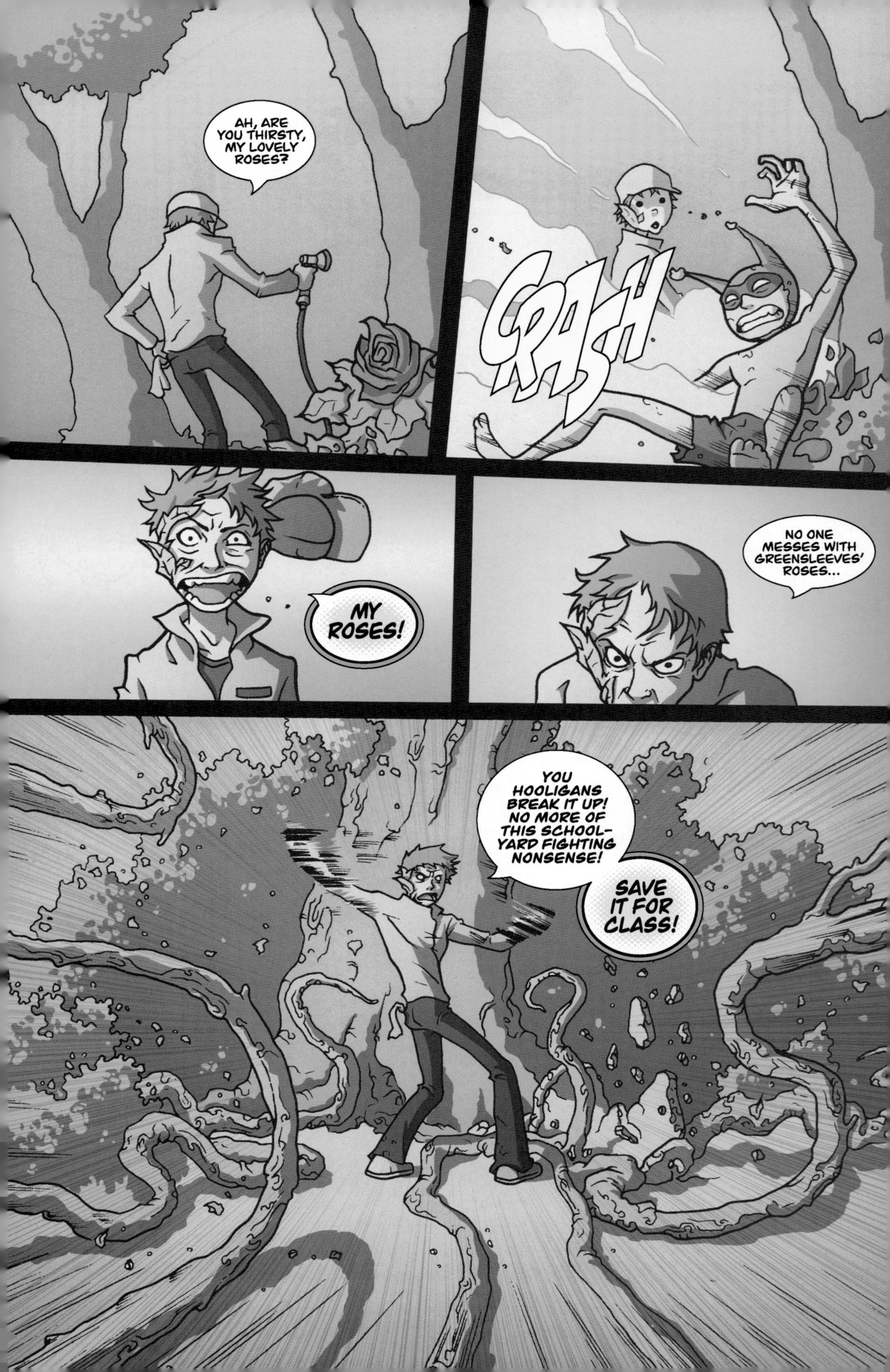
AH, ARE YOU THIRSTY, MY LOVELY ROSES?
CRASH
MY ROSES!
NO ONE MESSES WITH GREENSLEEVES' ROSES...
YOU HOOLIGANS BREAK IT UP! NO MORE OF THIS SCHOOL-YARD FIGHTING NONSENSE!
SAVE IT FOR CLASS!

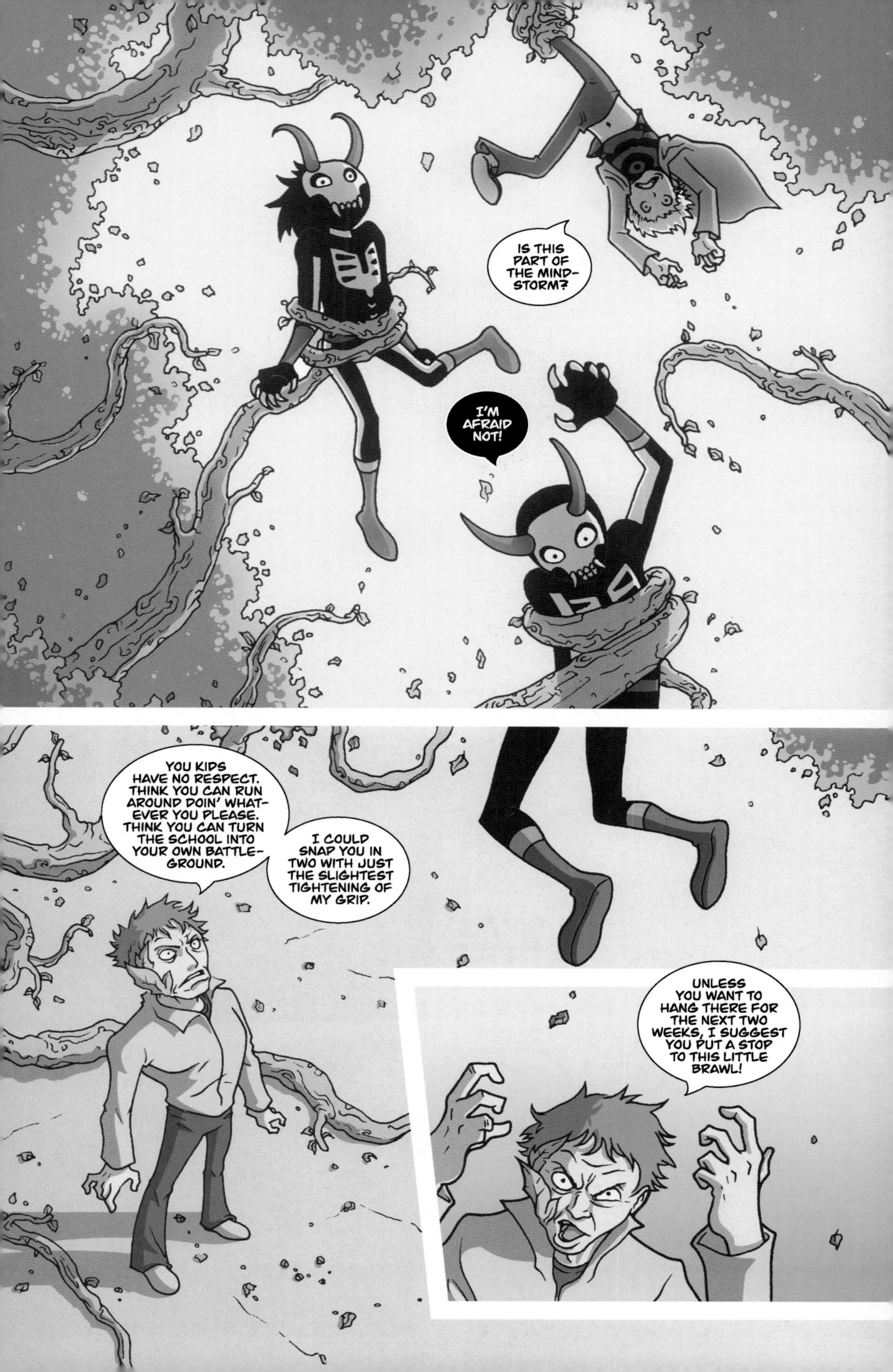
IS THIS PART OF THE MIND-STORM?
I'M AFRAID NOT!
YOU KIDS HAVE NO RESPECT. THINK YOU CAN RUN AROUND DOIN' WHAT-EVER YOU PLEASE. THINK YOU CAN TURN THE SCHOOL INTO YOUR OWN BATTLE-GROUND.
I COULD SNAP YOU IN TWO WITH JUST THE SLIGHTEST TIGHTENING OF MY GRIP.
UNLESS YOU WANT TO HANG THERE FOR THE NEXT TWO WEEKS, I SUGGEST YOU PUT A STOP TO THIS LITTLE BRAWL!

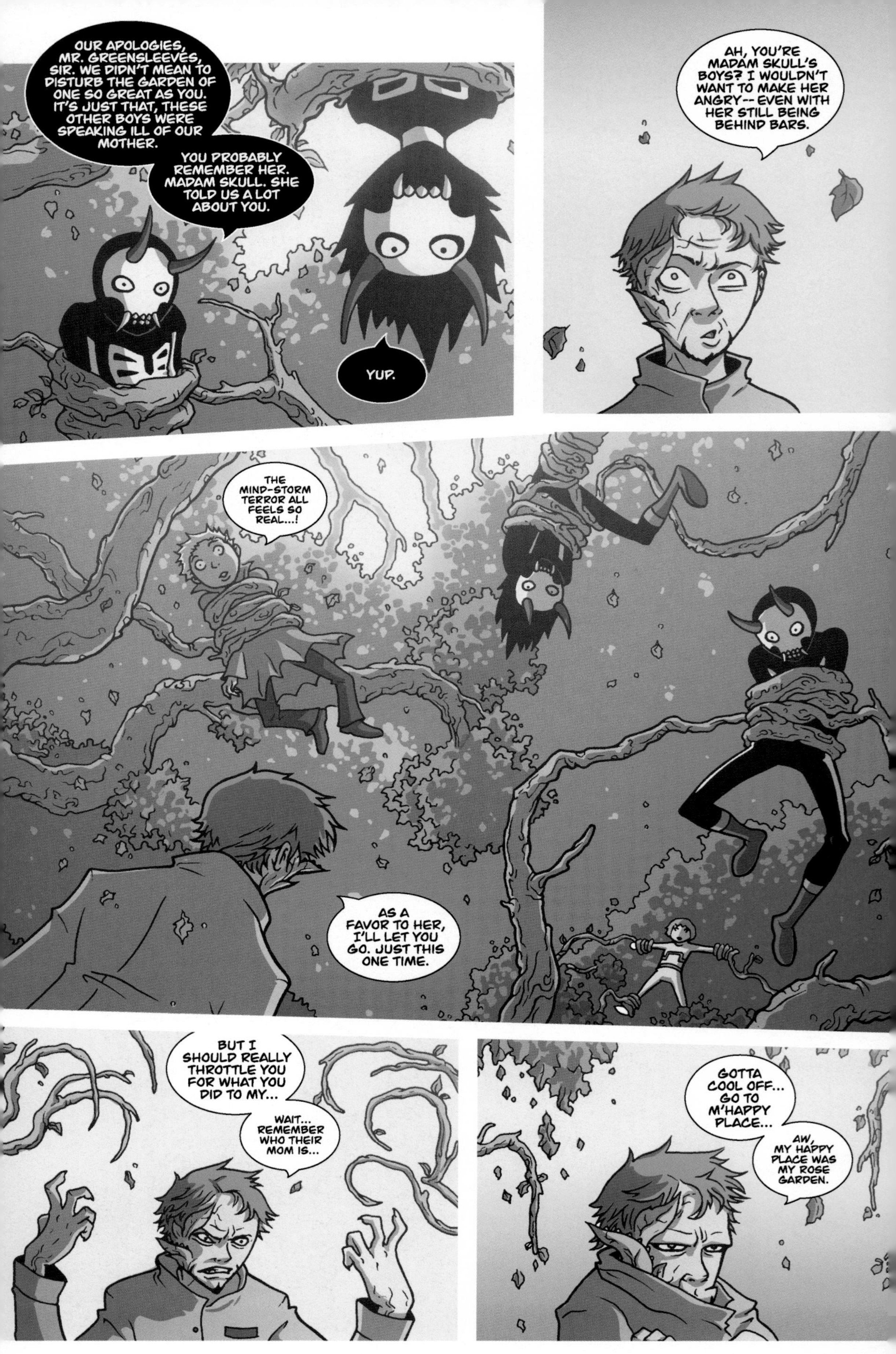
OUR APOLOGIES, MR. GREENSLEEVES, SIR. WE DIDN'T MEAN TO DISTURB THE GARDEN OF ONE SO GREAT AS YOU. IT'S JUST THAT, THESE OTHER BOYS WERE SPEAKING ILL OF OUR MOTHER.
YOU PROBABLY REMEMBER HER. MADAM SKULL. SHE TOLD US A LOT ABOUT YOU.
YUP.
AH, YOU'RE MADAM SKULL'S BOYS? I WOULDN'T WANT TO MAKE HER ANGRY-- EVEN WITH HER STILL BEING BEHIND BARS.
THE MIND-STORM TERROR ALL FEELS SO REAL...!
AS A FAVOR TO HER, I'LL LET YOU GO. JUST THIS ONE TIME.
BUT I SHOULD REALLY THROTTLE YOU FOR WHAT YOU DID TO MY...
WAIT... REMEMBER WHO THEIR MOM IS...
GOTTA COOL OFF... GO TO M'HAPPY PLACE...
AW, MY HAPPY PLACE WAS MY ROSE GARDEN.

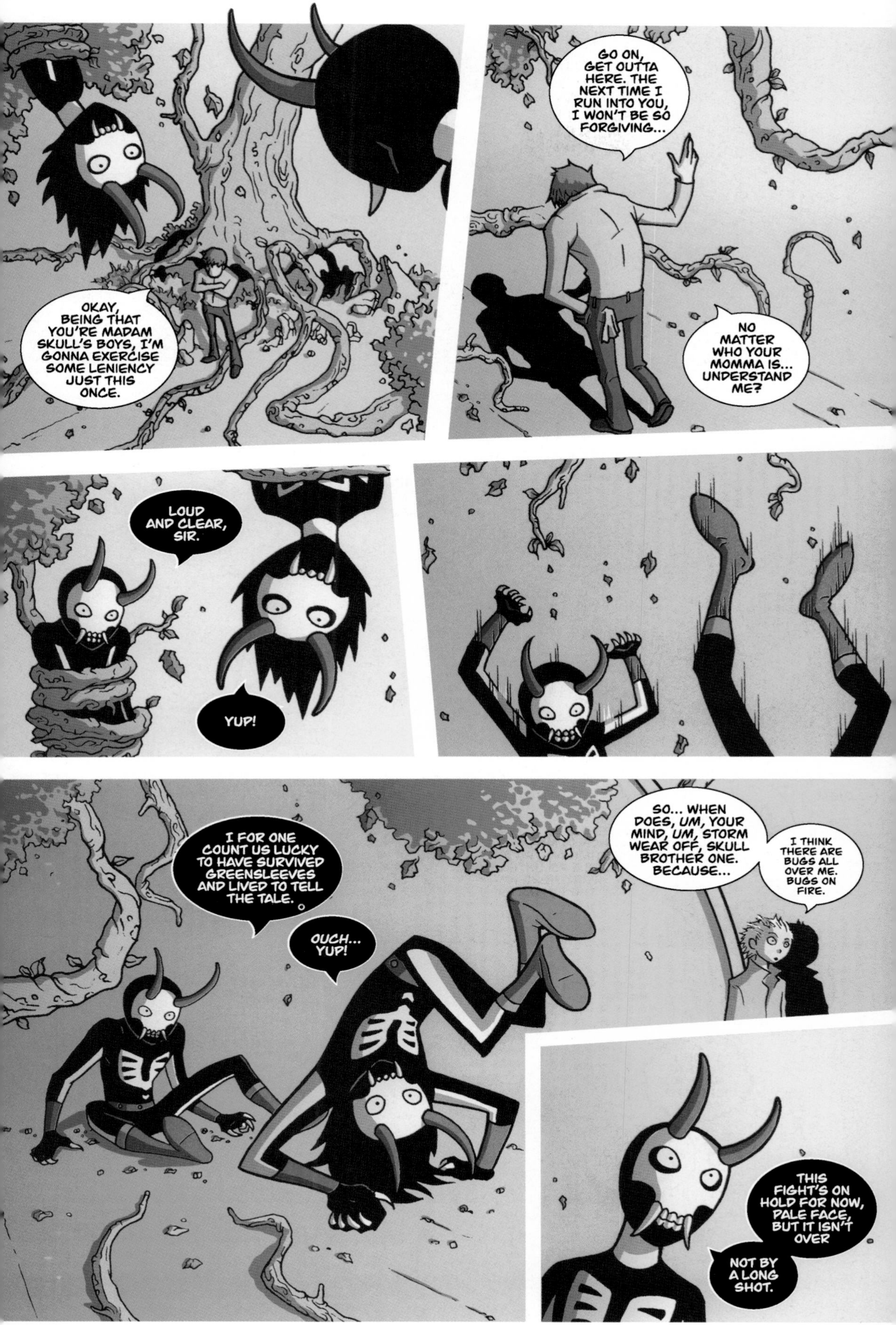
OKAY, BEING THAT YOU'RE MADAM SKULL'S BOYS, I'M GONNA EXERCISE SOME LENIENCY JUST THIS ONCE.
GO ON, GET OUTTA HERE. THE NEXT TIME I RUN INTO YOU, I WON'T BE SO FORGIVING...
NO MATTER WHO YOUR MOMMA IS... UNDERSTAND ME?
LOUD AND CLEAR, SIR.
YUP!
I FOR ONE COUNT US LUCKY TO HAVE SURVIVED GREENSLEEVES AND LIVED TO TELL THE TALE.
OUCH... YUP!
SO... WHEN DOES, *UM*, YOUR MIND, *UM*, STORM WEAR OFF, SKULL BROTHER ONE. BECAUSE...
I THINK THERE ARE BUGS ALL OVER ME. BUGS ON FIRE.
THIS FIGHT'S ON HOLD FOR NOW, PALE FACE, BUT IT ISN'T OVER
NOT BY A LONG SHOT.

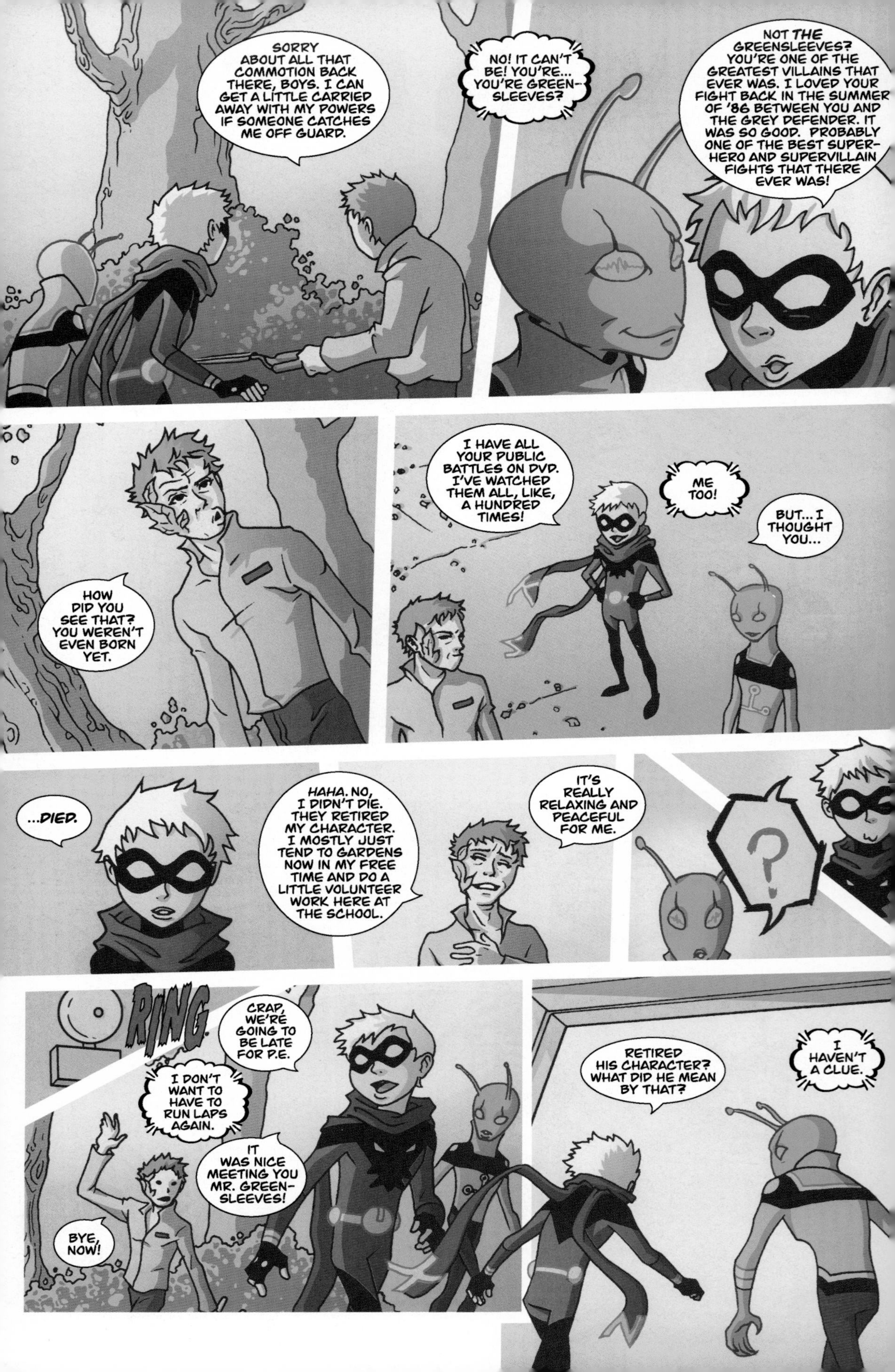
SORRY ABOUT ALL THAT COMMOTION BACK THERE, BOYS. I CAN GET A LITTLE CARRIED AWAY WITH MY POWERS IF SOMEONE CATCHES ME OFF GUARD.
NO! IT CAN'T BE! YOU'RE... YOU'RE GREEN-SLEEVES?
NOT THE GREENSLEEVES? YOU'RE ONE OF THE GREATEST VILLAINS THAT EVER WAS. I LOVED YOUR FIGHT BACK IN THE SUMMER OF '86 BETWEEN YOU AND THE GREY DEFENDER. IT WAS SO GOOD. PROBABLY ONE OF THE BEST SUPER-HERO AND SUPERVILLAIN FIGHTS THAT THERE EVER WAS!
HOW DID YOU SEE THAT? YOU WEREN'T EVEN BORN YET.
I HAVE ALL YOUR PUBLIC BATTLES ON DVD. I'VE WATCHED THEM ALL, LIKE, A HUNDRED TIMES!
ME TOO!
BUT... I THOUGHT YOU...
...DIED.
HAHA. NO, I DIDN'T DIE. THEY RETIRED MY CHARACTER. I MOSTLY JUST TEND TO GARDENS NOW IN MY FREE TIME AND DO A LITTLE VOLUNTEER WORK HERE AT THE SCHOOL.
IT'S REALLY RELAXING AND PEACEFUL FOR ME.
?
RING
CRAP, WE'RE GOING TO BE LATE FOR P.E.
I DON'T WANT TO HAVE TO RUN LAPS AGAIN.
IT WAS NICE MEETING YOU MR. GREEN-SLEEVES!
BYE, NOW!
RETIRED HIS CHARACTER? WHAT DID HE MEAN BY THAT?
I HAVEN'T A CLUE.

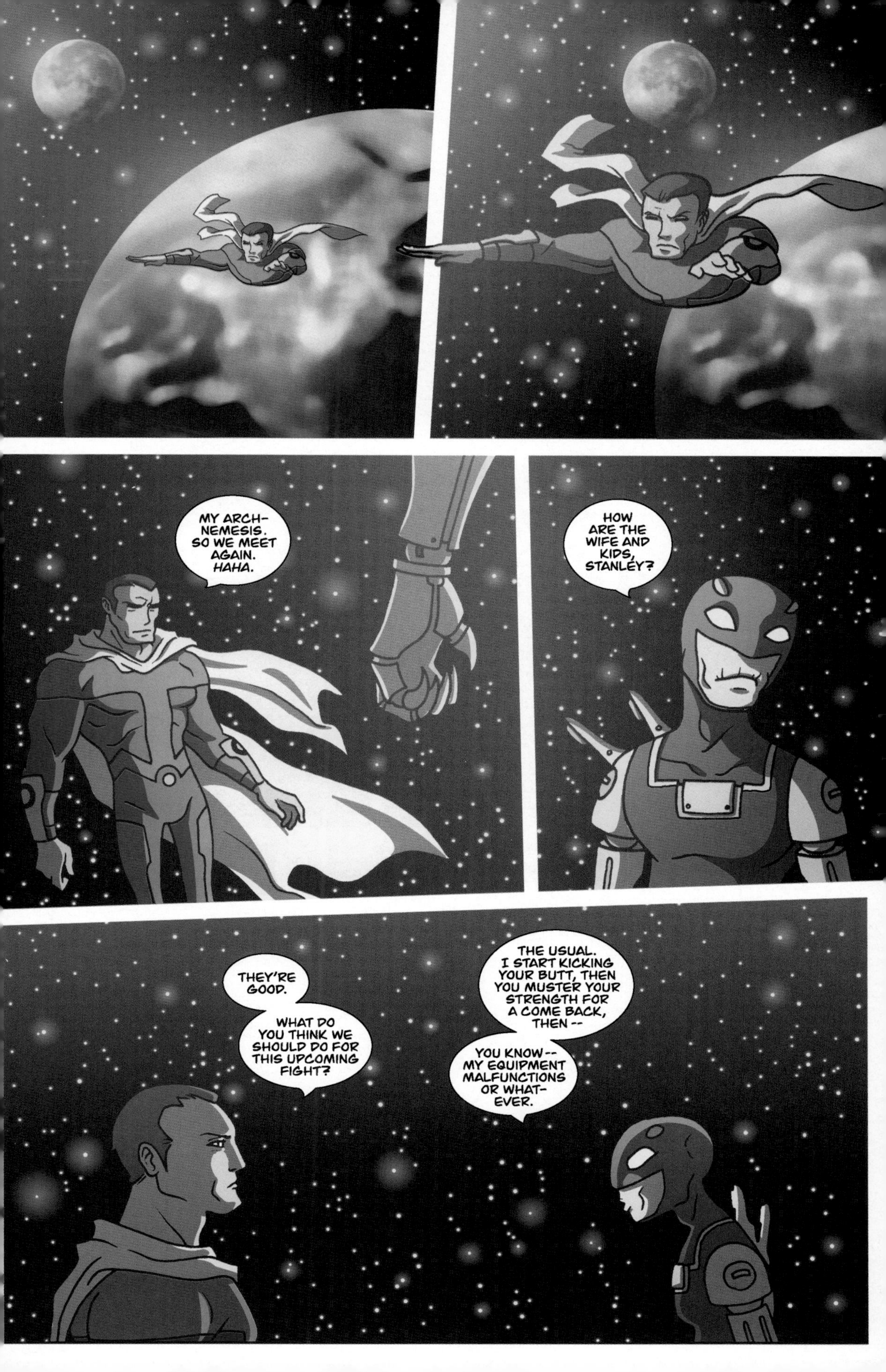
MY ARCH-NEMESIS. SO WE MEET AGAIN. HAHA.
HOW ARE THE WIFE AND KIDS, STANLEY?
THEY'RE GOOD.
WHAT DO YOU THINK WE SHOULD DO FOR THIS UPCOMING FIGHT?
THE USUAL. I START KICKING YOUR BUTT, THEN YOU MUSTER YOUR STRENGTH FOR A COME BACK, THEN --
YOU KNOW -- MY EQUIPMENT MALFUNCTIONS OR WHAT-EVER.

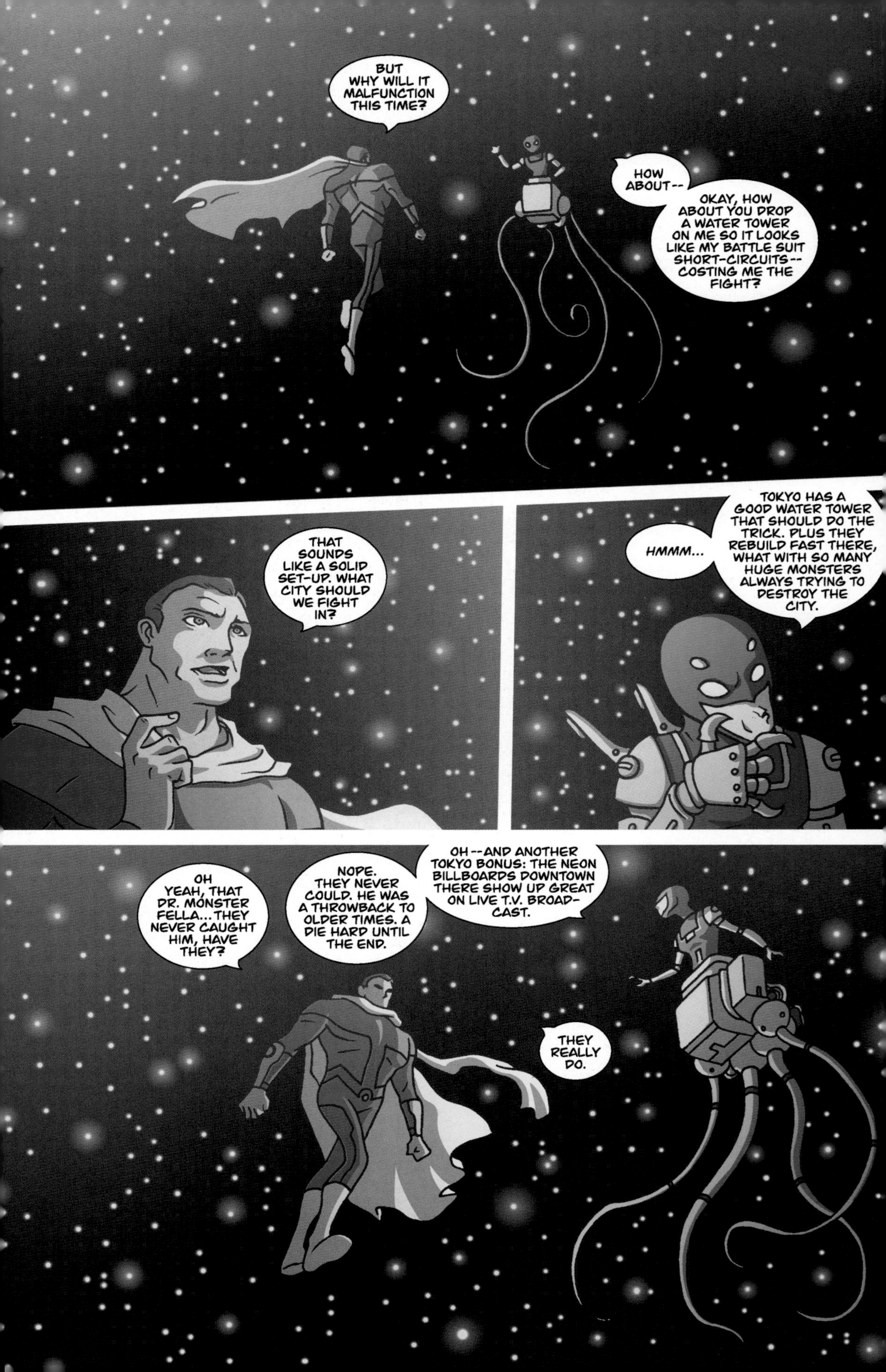
BUT WHY WILL IT MALFUNCTION THIS TIME?
HOW ABOUT--
OKAY, HOW ABOUT YOU DROP A WATER TOWER ON ME SO IT LOOKS LIKE MY BATTLE SUIT SHORT-CIRCUITS-- COSTING ME THE FIGHT?
THAT SOUNDS LIKE A SOLID SET-UP. WHAT CITY SHOULD WE FIGHT IN?
HMMM...
TOKYO HAS A GOOD WATER TOWER THAT SHOULD DO THE TRICK. PLUS THEY REBUILD FAST THERE, WHAT WITH SO MANY HUGE MONSTERS ALWAYS TRYING TO DESTROY THE CITY.
OH YEAH, THAT DR. MONSTER FELLA... THEY NEVER CAUGHT HIM, HAVE THEY?
NOPE. THEY NEVER COULD. HE WAS A THROWBACK TO OLDER TIMES. A DIE HARD UNTIL THE END.
OH --AND ANOTHER TOKYO BONUS: THE NEON BILLBOARDS DOWNTOWN THERE SHOW UP GREAT ON LIVE T.V. BROAD-CAST.
THEY REALLY DO.

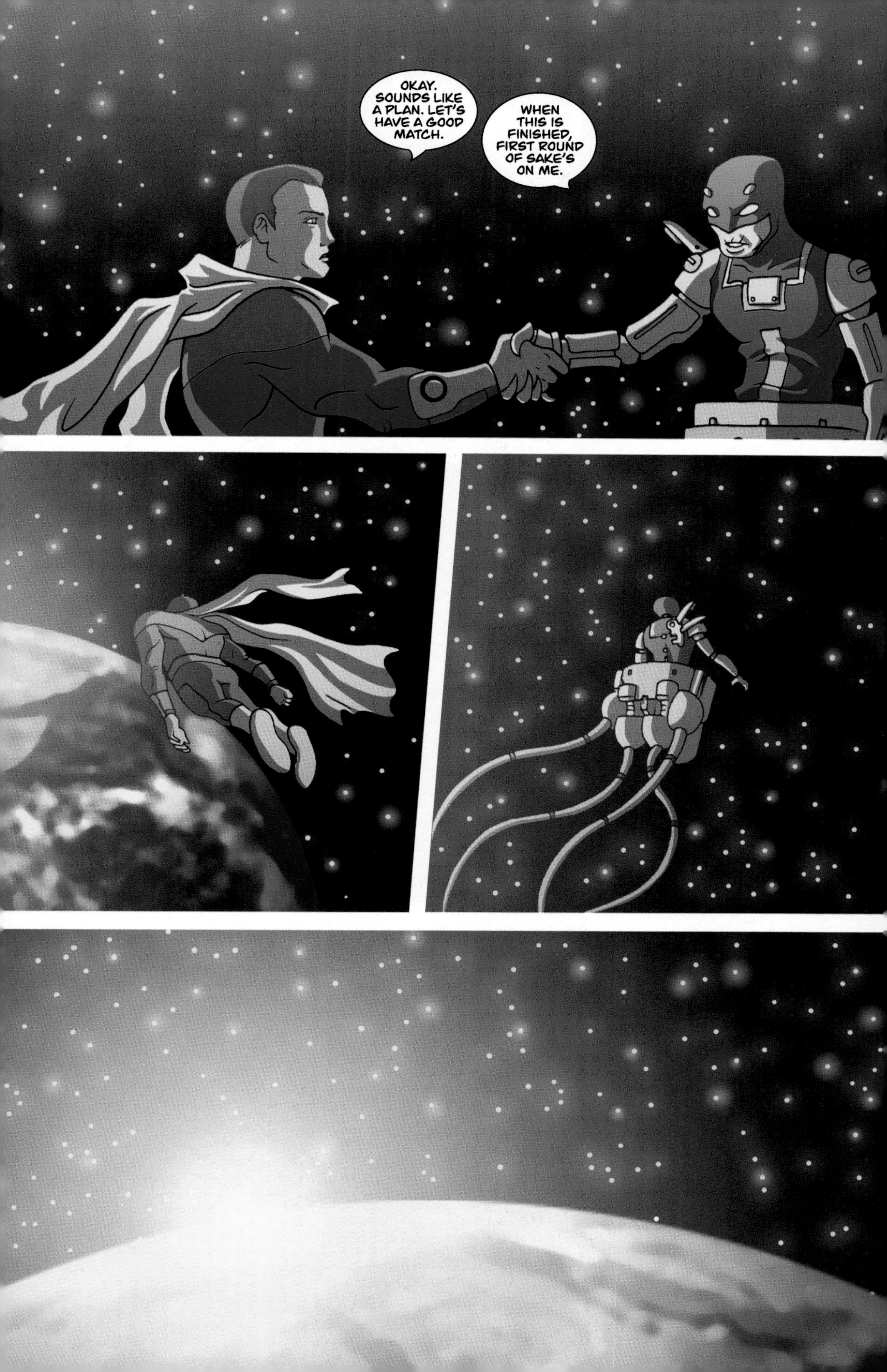
OKAY. SOUNDS LIKE A PLAN. LET'S HAVE A GOOD MATCH.
WHEN THIS IS FINISHED, FIRST ROUND OF SAKE'S ON ME.

CHAPTER 2

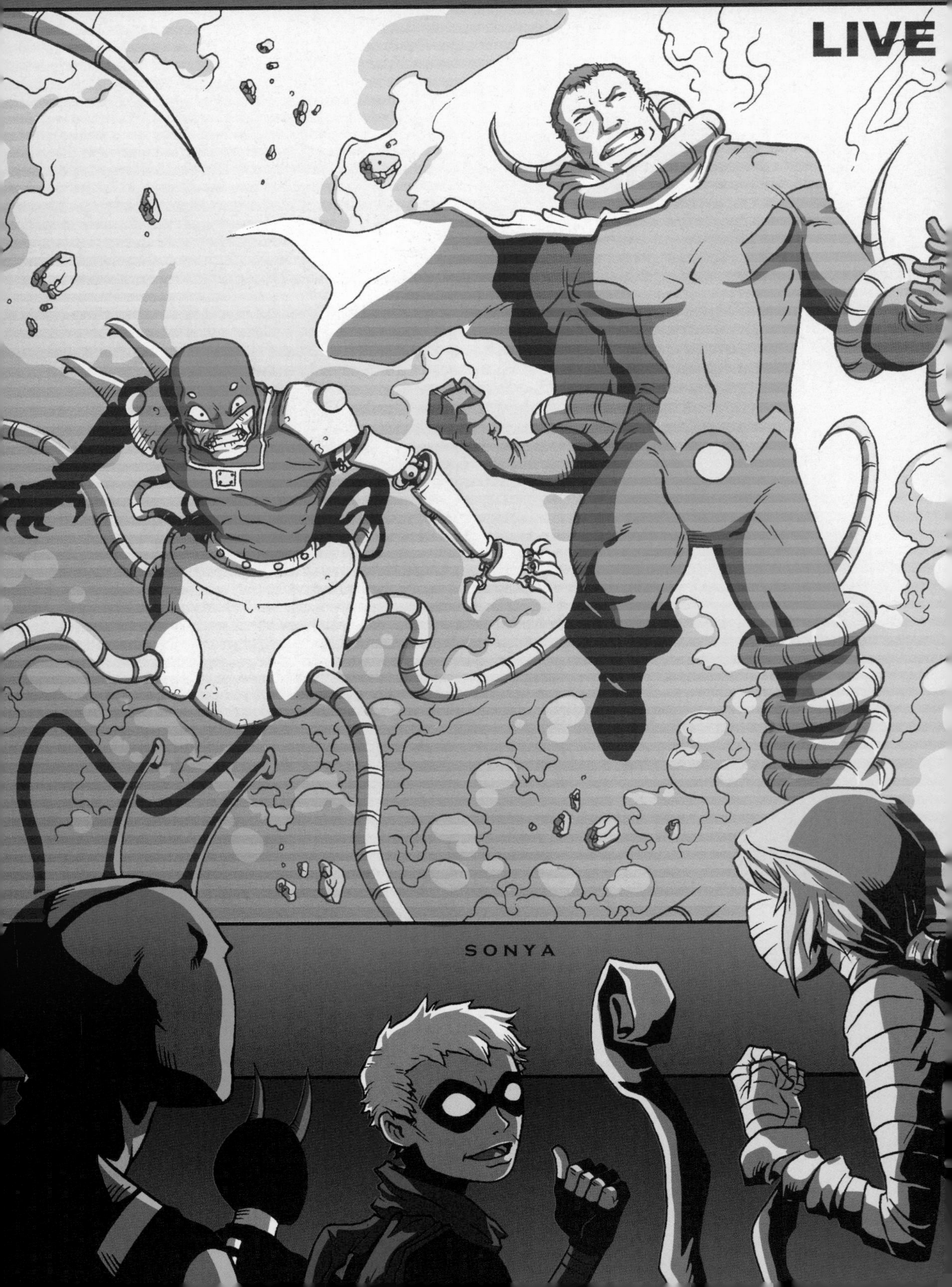
LIVE
SONYA

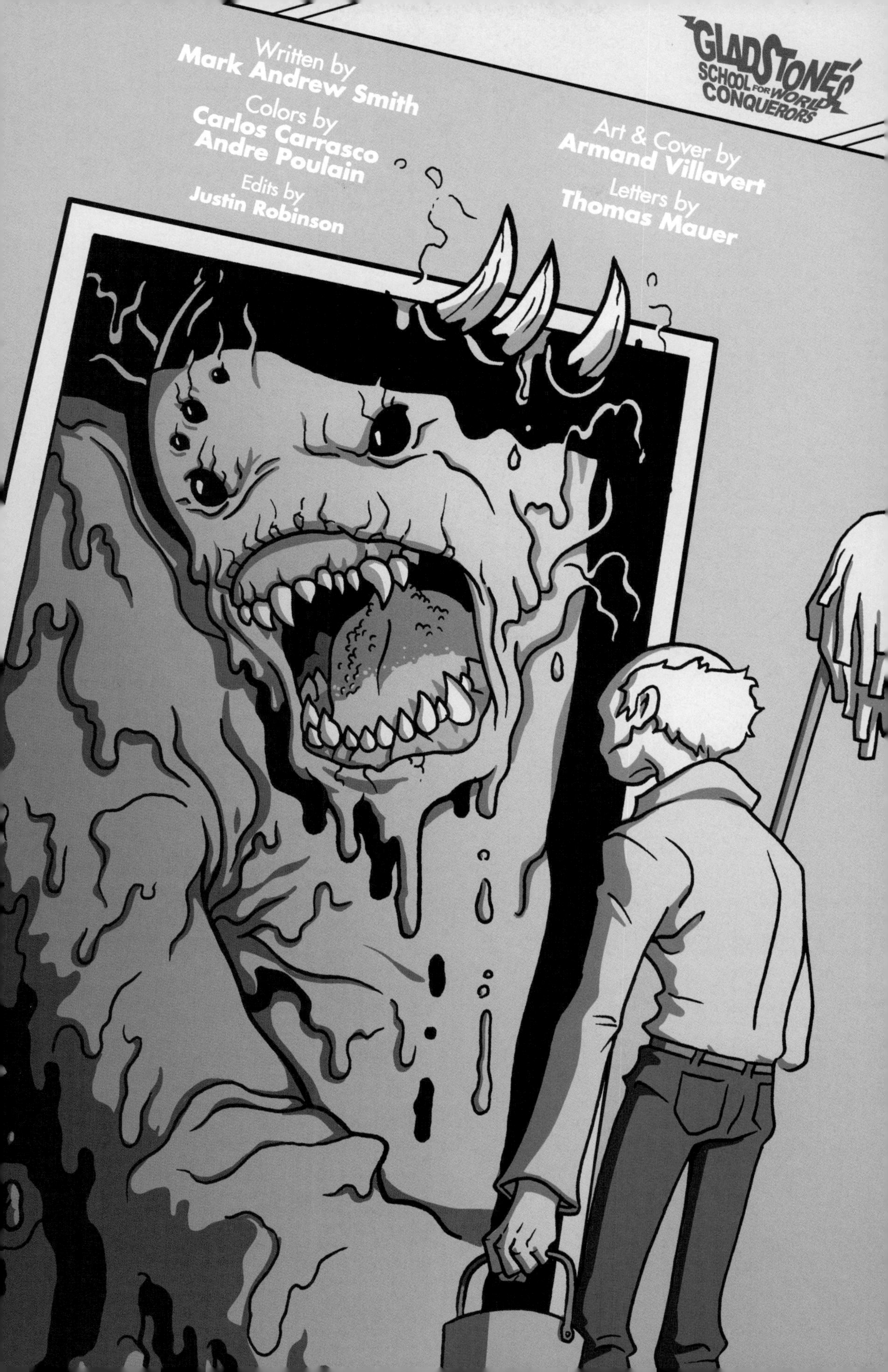
Gladstone's School for World Conquerors
Written by
Mark Andrew Smith
Colors by
Carlos Carrasco
Andre Poulain
Edits by
Justin Robinson
Art & Cover by
Armand Villavert
Letters by
Thomas Mauer

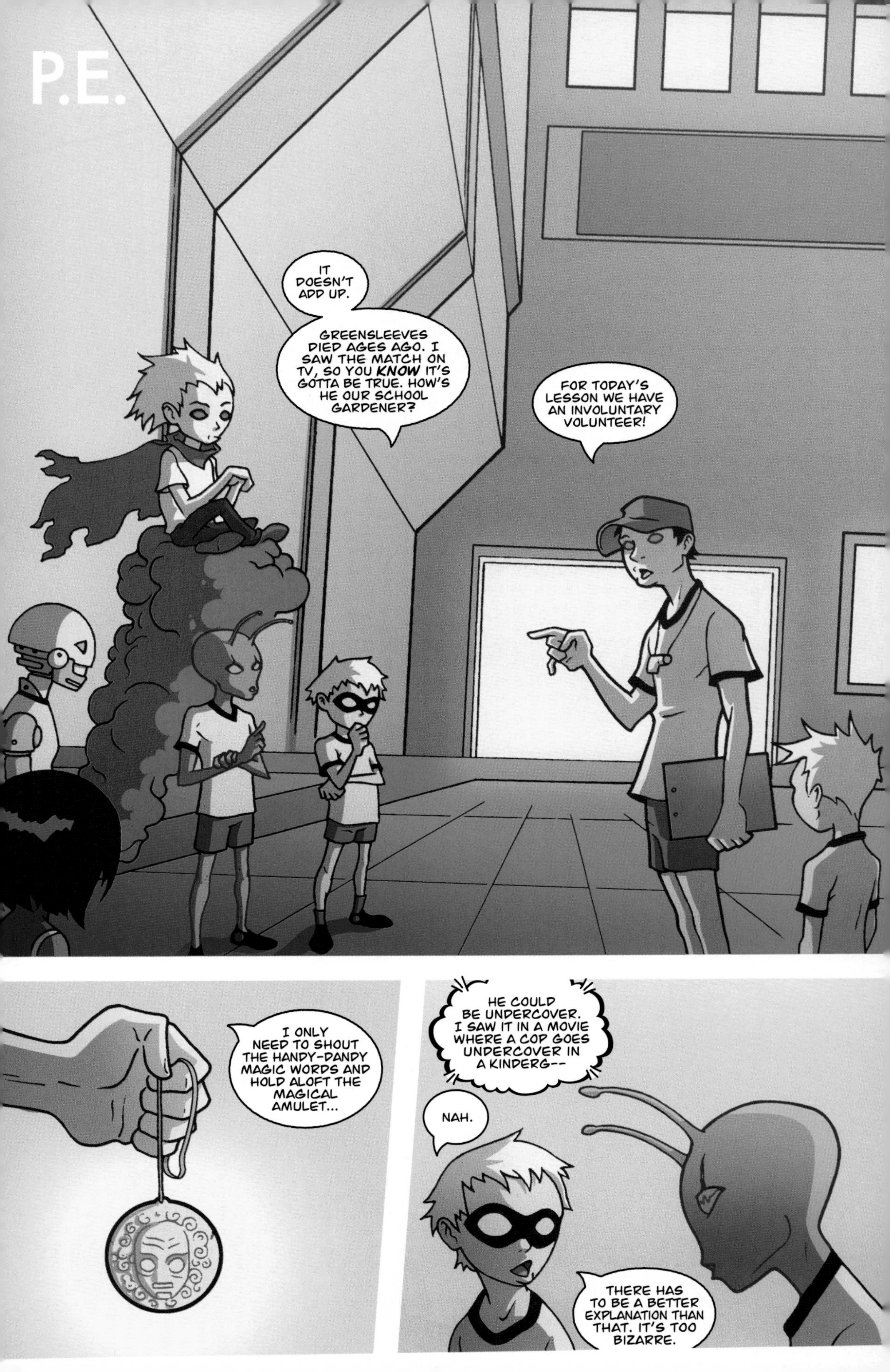
P.E.
IT DOESN'T ADD UP.
GREENSLEEVES DIED AGES AGO. I SAW THE MATCH ON TV, SO YOU KNOW IT'S GOTTA BE TRUE. HOW'S HE OUR SCHOOL GARDENER?
FOR TODAY'S LESSON WE HAVE AN INVOLUNTARY VOLUNTEER!
I ONLY NEED TO SHOUT THE HANDY-DANDY MAGIC WORDS AND HOLD ALOFT THE MAGICAL AMULET...
HE COULD BE UNDERCOVER. I SAW IT IN A MOVIE WHERE A COP GOES UNDERCOVER IN A KINDERG--
NAH.
THERE HAS TO BE A BETTER EXPLANATION THAN THAT. IT'S TOO BIZARRE.

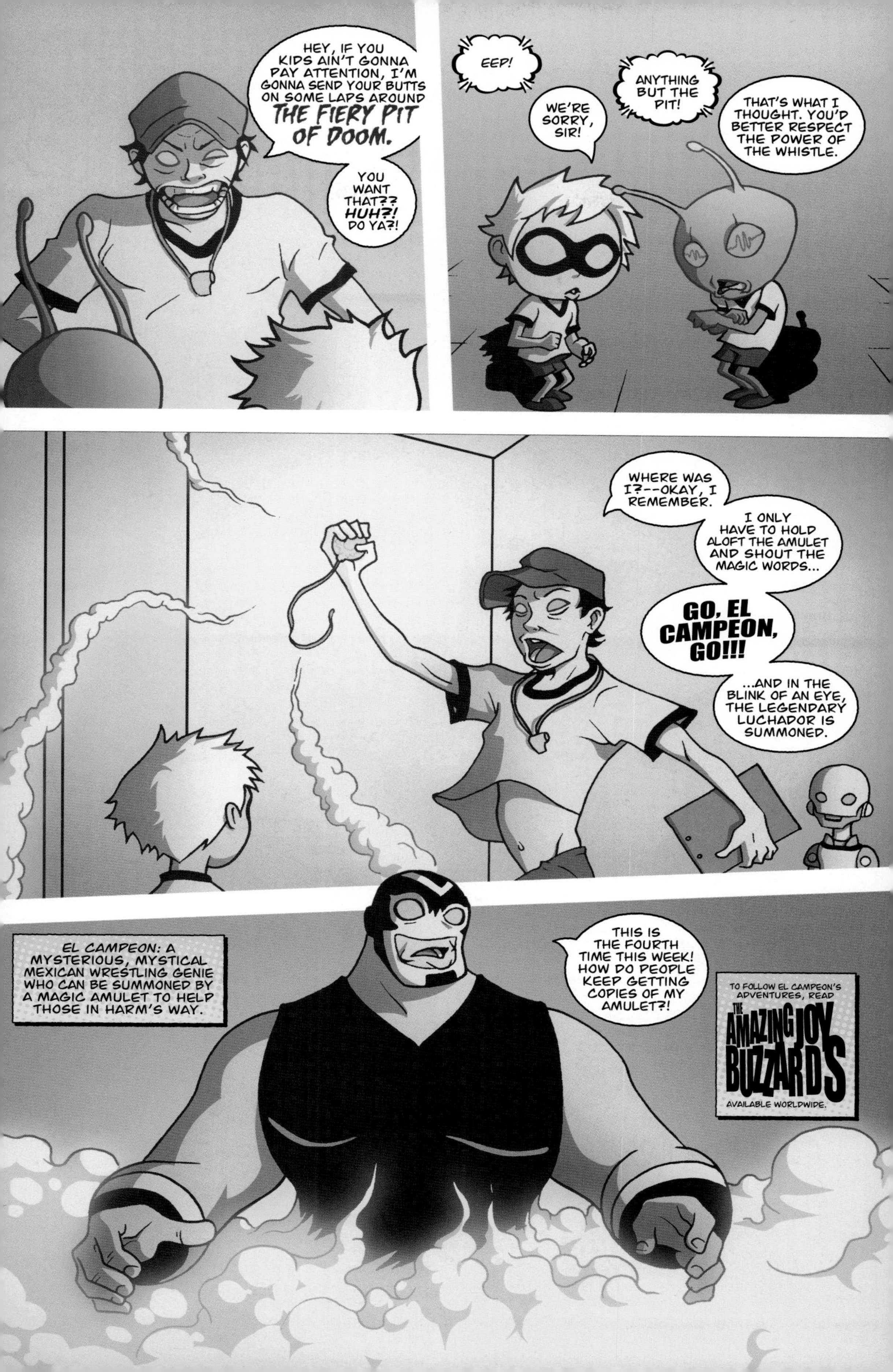
HEY, IF YOU KIDS AIN'T GONNA PAY ATTENTION, I'M GONNA SEND YOUR BUTTS ON SOME LAPS AROUND THE FIERY PIT OF DOOM.
YOU WANT THAT?? HUH?! DO YA?!
EEP!
WE'RE SORRY, SIR!
ANYTHING BUT THE PIT!
THAT'S WHAT I THOUGHT. YOU'D BETTER RESPECT THE POWER OF THE WHISTLE.
WHERE WAS I?--OKAY, I REMEMBER.
I ONLY HAVE TO HOLD ALOFT THE AMULET AND SHOUT THE MAGIC WORDS...
GO, EL CAMPEON, GO!!!
...AND IN THE BLINK OF AN EYE, THE LEGENDARY LUCHADOR IS SUMMONED.
EL CAMPEON: A MYSTERIOUS, MYSTICAL MEXICAN WRESTLING GENIE WHO CAN BE SUMMONED BY A MAGIC AMULET TO HELP THOSE IN HARM'S WAY.
THIS IS THE FOURTH TIME THIS WEEK! HOW DO PEOPLE KEEP GETTING COPIES OF MY AMULET?!
TO FOLLOW EL CAMPEON'S ADVENTURES, READ
THE AMAZING JOY BUZZARDS
AVAILABLE WORLDWIDE.

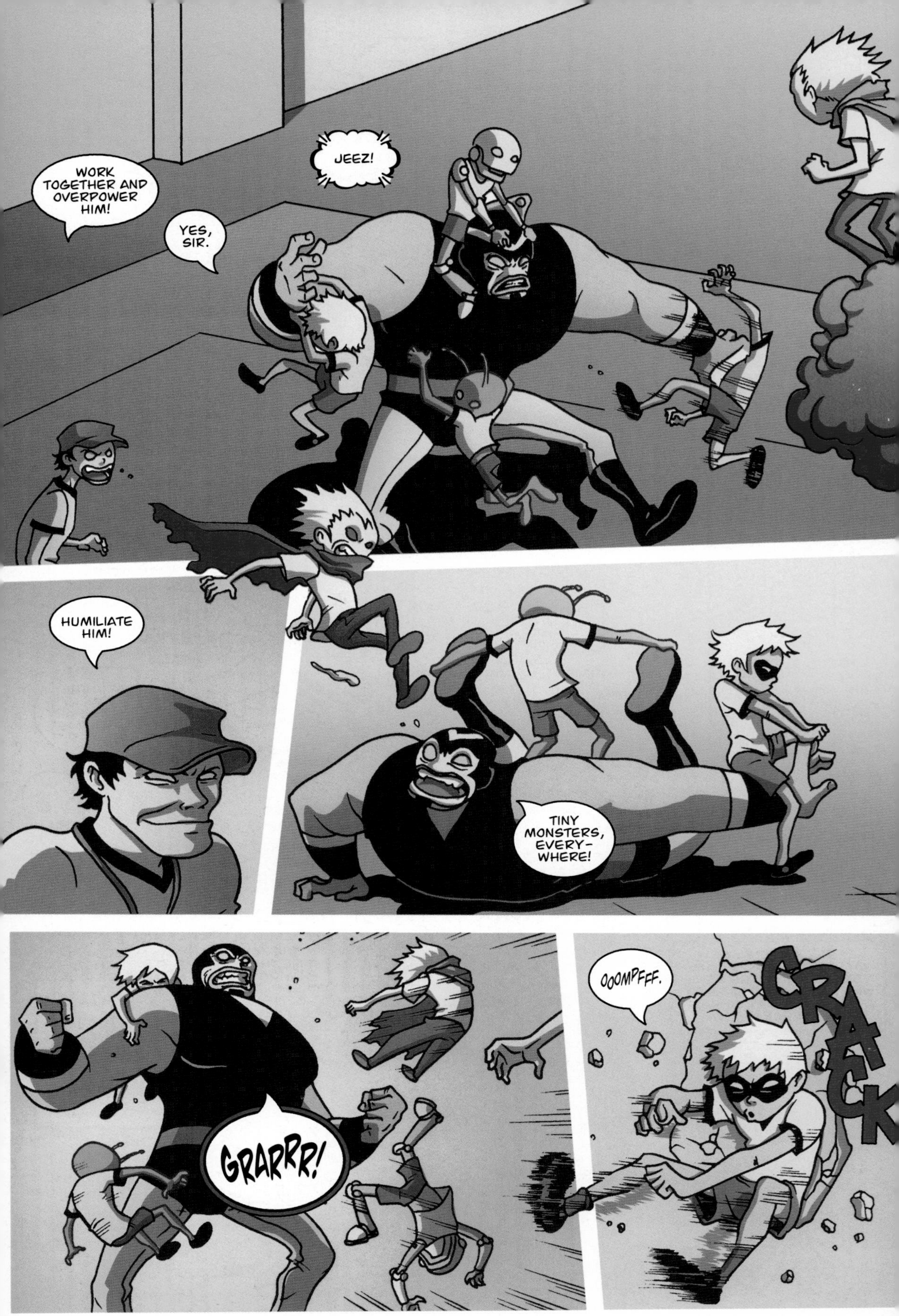
WORK TOGETHER AND OVERPOWER HIM!
YES, SIR.
JEEZ!
HUMILIATE HIM!
TINY MONSTERS, EVERY-WHERE!
GRARRR!
OOOMPFFF.
CRACK

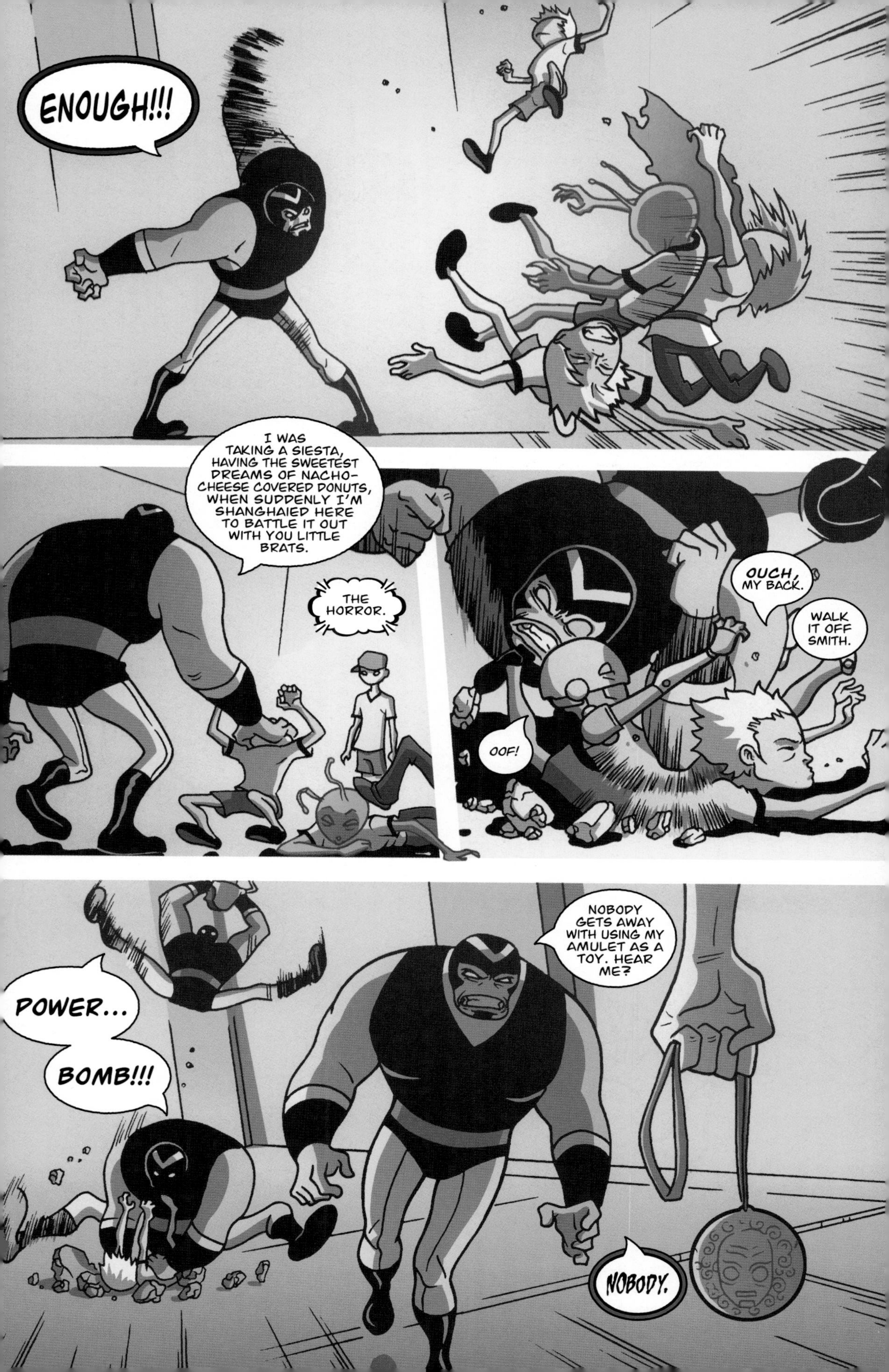
ENOUGH!!!
I WAS TAKING A SIESTA, HAVING THE SWEETEST DREAMS OF NACHO-CHEESE COVERED DONUTS, WHEN SUDDENLY I'M SHANGHAIED HERE TO BATTLE IT OUT WITH YOU LITTLE BRATS.
THE HORROR.
OUCH, MY BACK.
WALK IT OFF SMITH.
OOF!
POWER...
BOMB!!!
NOBODY GETS AWAY WITH USING MY AMULET AS A TOY. HEAR ME?
NOBODY.

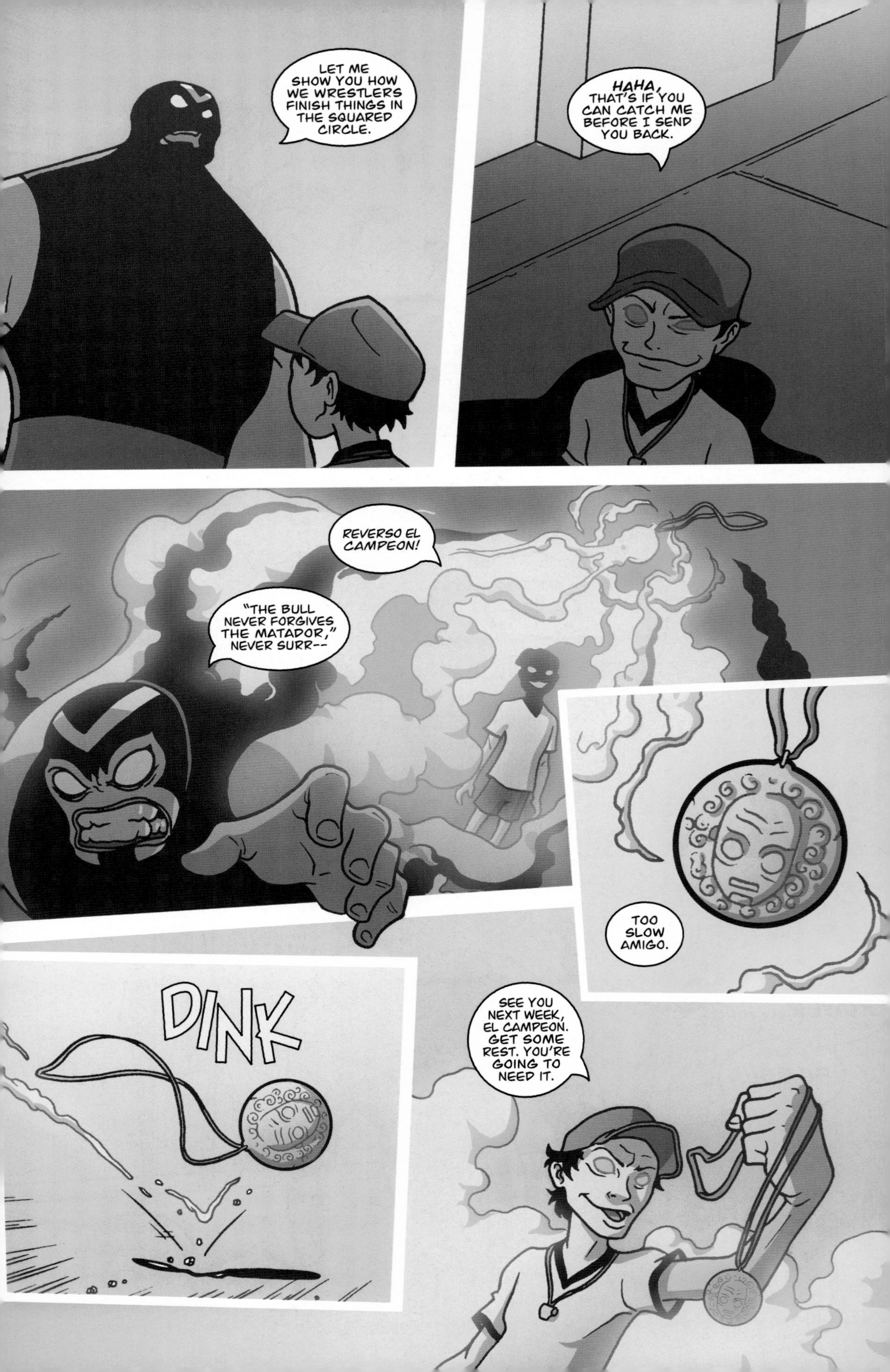
LET ME SHOW YOU HOW WE WRESTLERS FINISH THINGS IN THE SQUARED CIRCLE.
HAHA, THAT'S IF YOU CAN CATCH ME BEFORE I SEND YOU BACK.
REVERSO EL CAMPEON!
"THE BULL NEVER FORGIVES THE MATADOR," NEVER SURR--
TOO SLOW AMIGO.
DINK
SEE YOU NEXT WEEK, EL CAMPEON. GET SOME REST. YOU'RE GOING TO NEED IT.

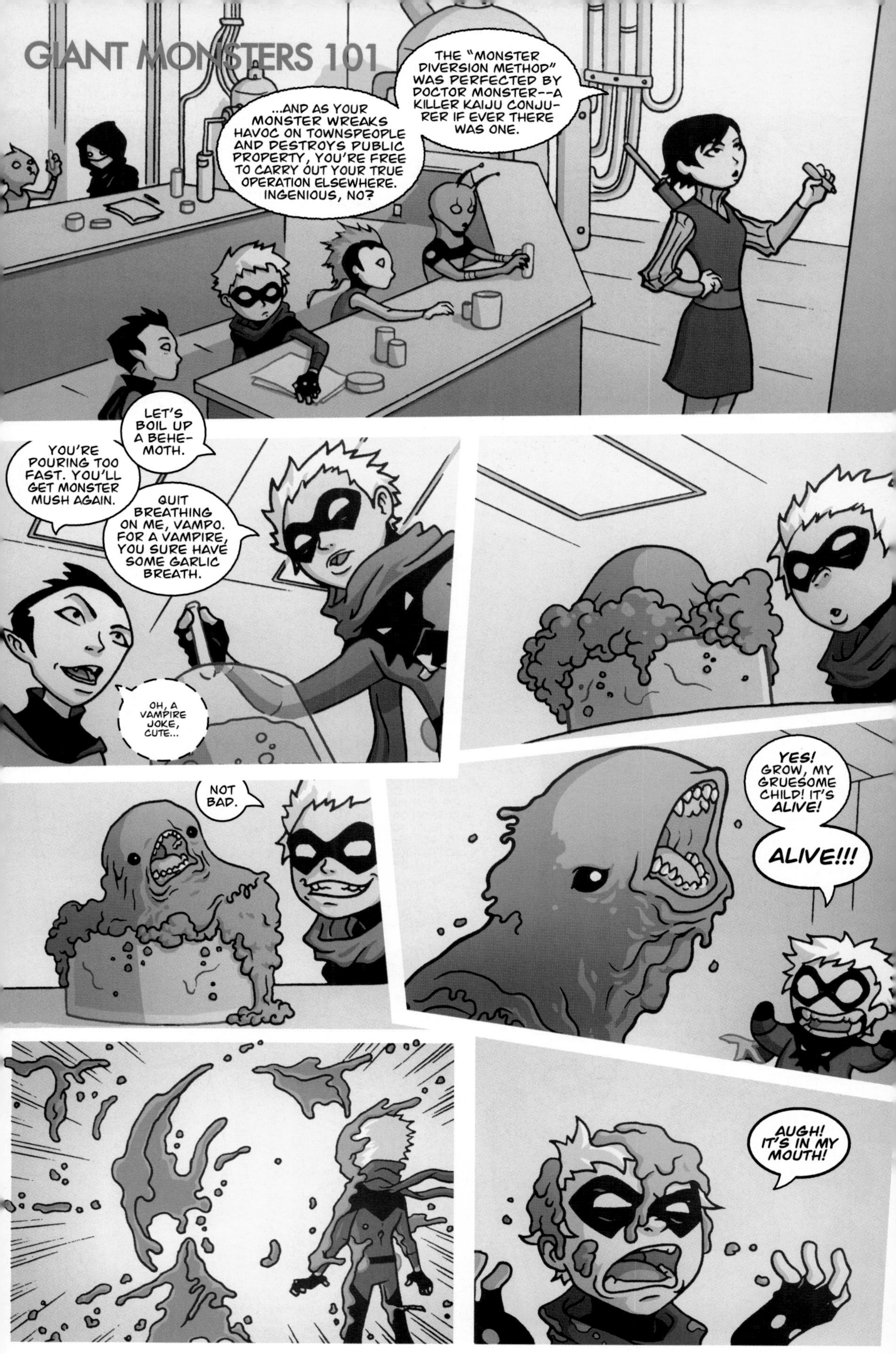
GIANT MONSTERS 101
...AND AS YOUR MONSTER WREAKS HAVOC ON TOWNSPEOPLE AND DESTROYS PUBLIC PROPERTY, YOU'RE FREE TO CARRY OUT YOUR TRUE OPERATION ELSEWHERE. INGENIOUS, NO?
THE "MONSTER DIVERSION METHOD" WAS PERFECTED BY DOCTOR MONSTER--A KILLER KAIJU CONJURER IF EVER THERE WAS ONE.
YOU'RE POURING TOO FAST. YOU'LL GET MONSTER MUSH AGAIN.
LET'S BOIL UP A BEHEMOTH.
QUIT BREATHING ON ME, VAMPO. FOR A VAMPIRE, YOU SURE HAVE SOME GARLIC BREATH.
OH, A VAMPIRE JOKE, CUTE...
NOT BAD.
YES! GROW, MY GRUESOME CHILD! IT'S ALIVE!
ALIVE!!!
AUGH! IT'S IN MY MOUTH!

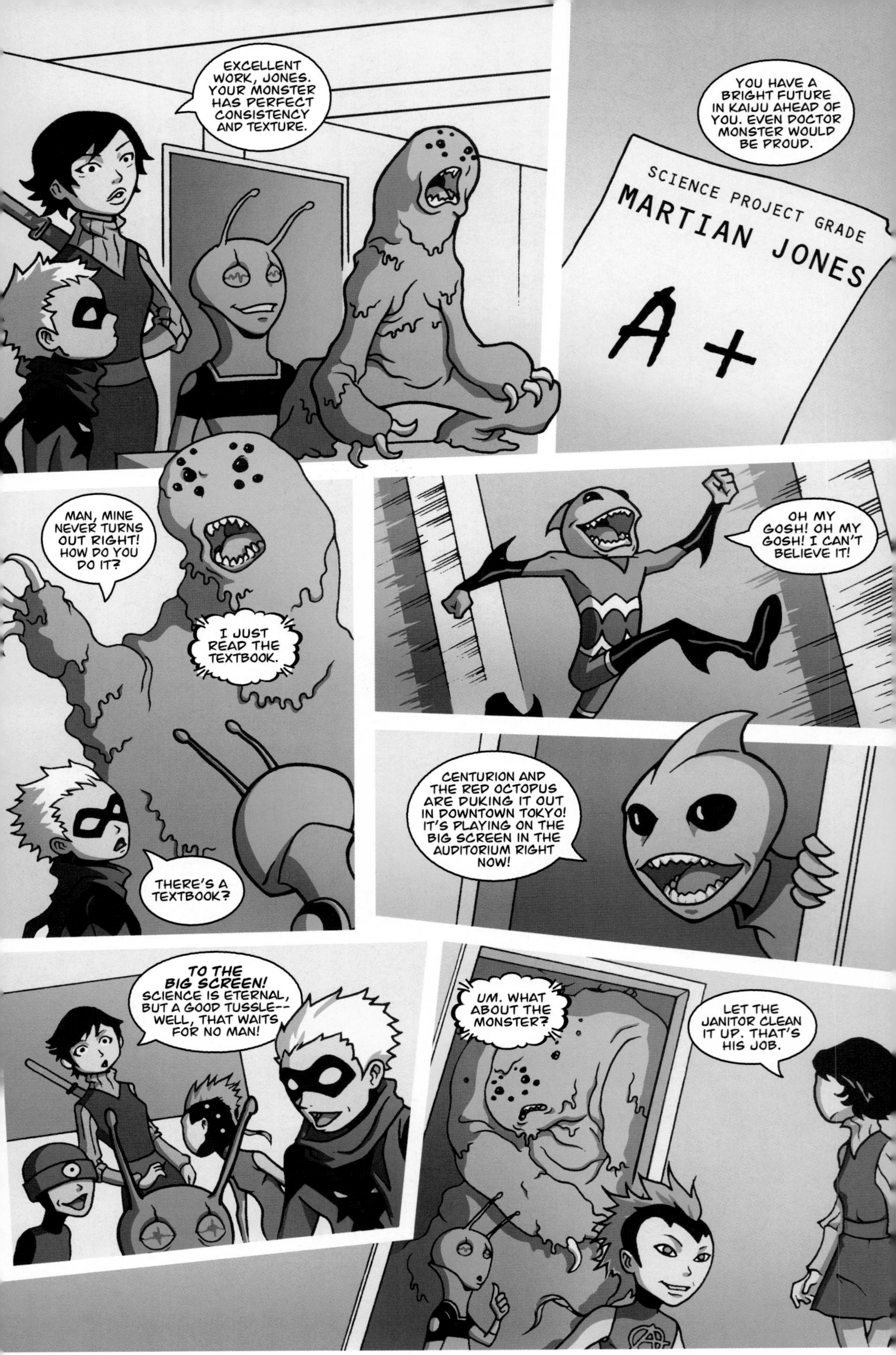
EXCELLENT WORK, JONES. YOUR MONSTER HAS PERFECT CONSISTENCY AND TEXTURE.
YOU HAVE A BRIGHT FUTURE IN KAIJU AHEAD OF YOU. EVEN DOCTOR MONSTER WOULD BE PROUD.
SCIENCE PROJECT GRADE
MARTIAN JONES
A+
MAN, MINE NEVER TURNS OUT RIGHT! HOW DO YOU DO IT?
I JUST READ THE TEXTBOOK.
THERE'S A TEXTBOOK?
OH MY GOSH! OH MY GOSH! I CAN'T BELIEVE IT!
CENTURION AND THE RED OCTOPUS ARE DUKING IT OUT IN DOWNTOWN TOKYO! IT'S PLAYING ON THE BIG SCREEN IN THE AUDITORIUM RIGHT NOW!
TO THE BIG SCREEN! SCIENCE IS ETERNAL, BUT A GOOD TUSSLE--WELL, THAT WAITS FOR NO MAN!
UM. WHAT ABOUT THE MONSTER?
LET THE JANITOR CLEAN IT UP. THAT'S HIS JOB.

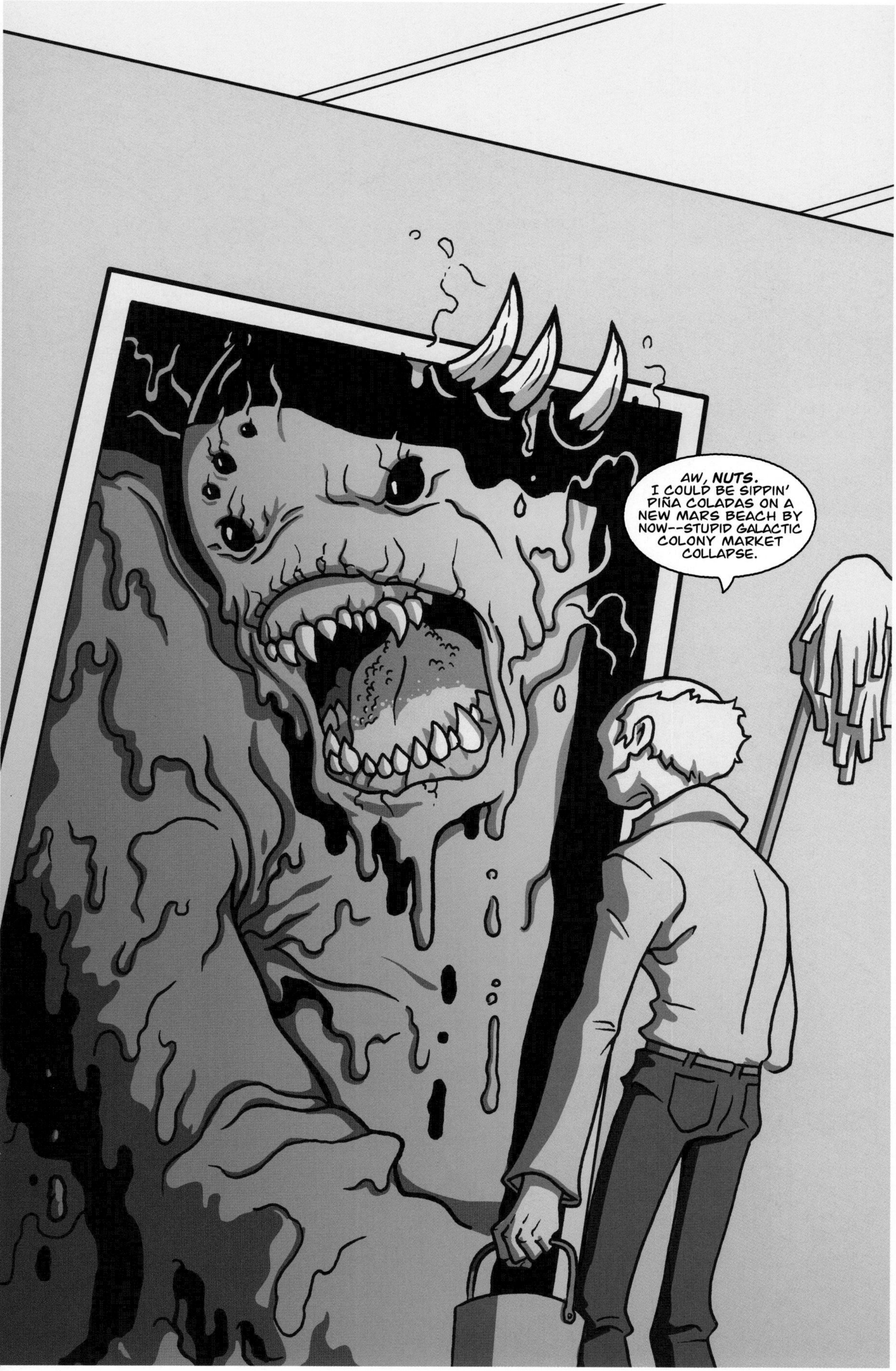
AW, NUTS. I COULD BE SIPPIN' PIÑA COLADAS ON A NEW MARS BEACH BY NOW--STUPID GALACTIC COLONY MARKET COLLAPSE.

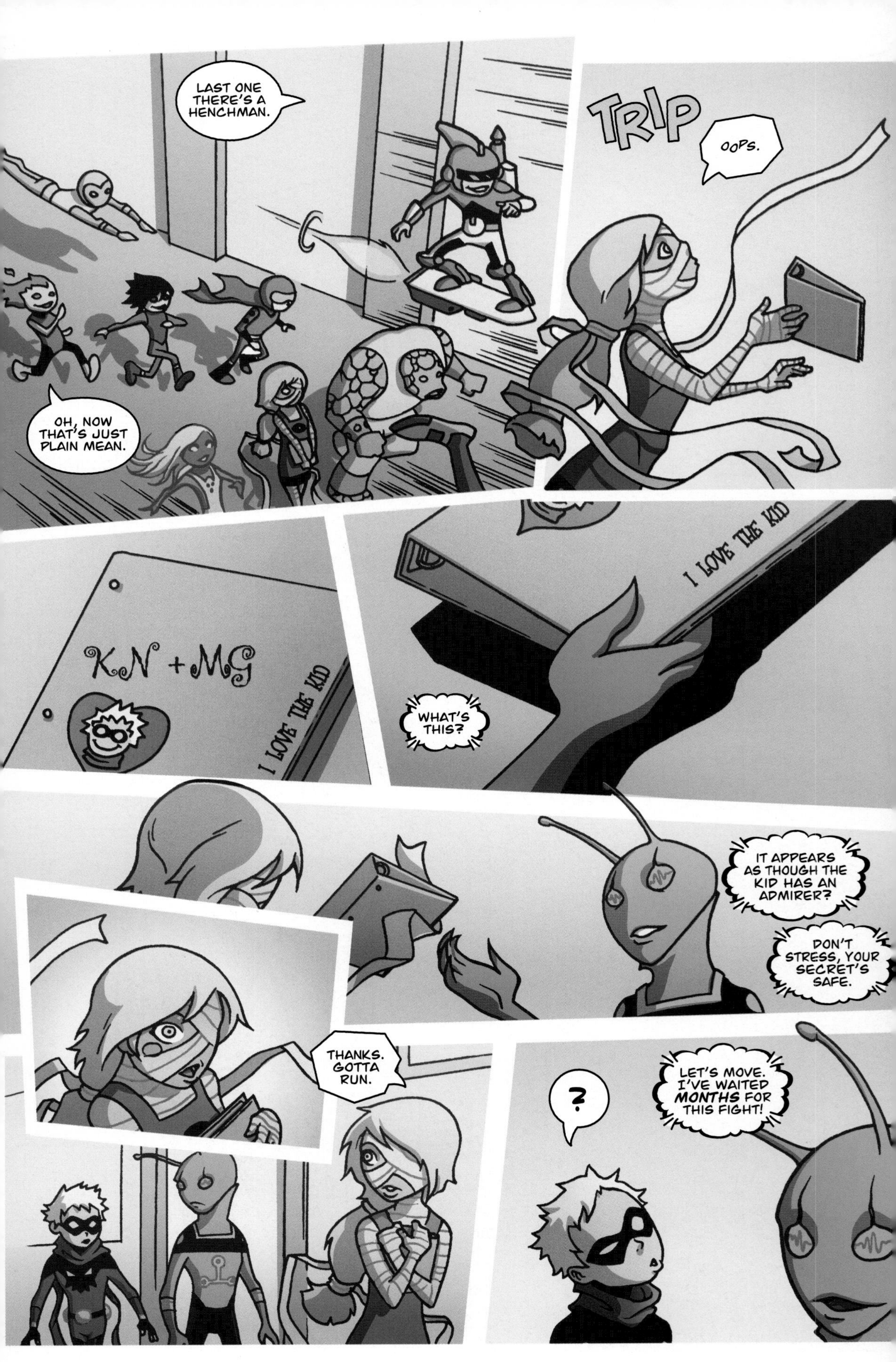
LAST ONE THERE'S A HENCHMAN.
OH, NOW THAT'S JUST PLAIN MEAN.
TRIP
OOPS.
KN + MG
I LOVE THE KID
I LOVE THE KID
WHAT'S THIS?
IT APPEARS AS THOUGH THE KID HAS AN ADMIRER?
DON'T STRESS, YOUR SECRET'S SAFE.
THANKS. GOTTA RUN.
?
LET'S MOVE. I'VE WAITED MONTHS FOR THIS FIGHT!

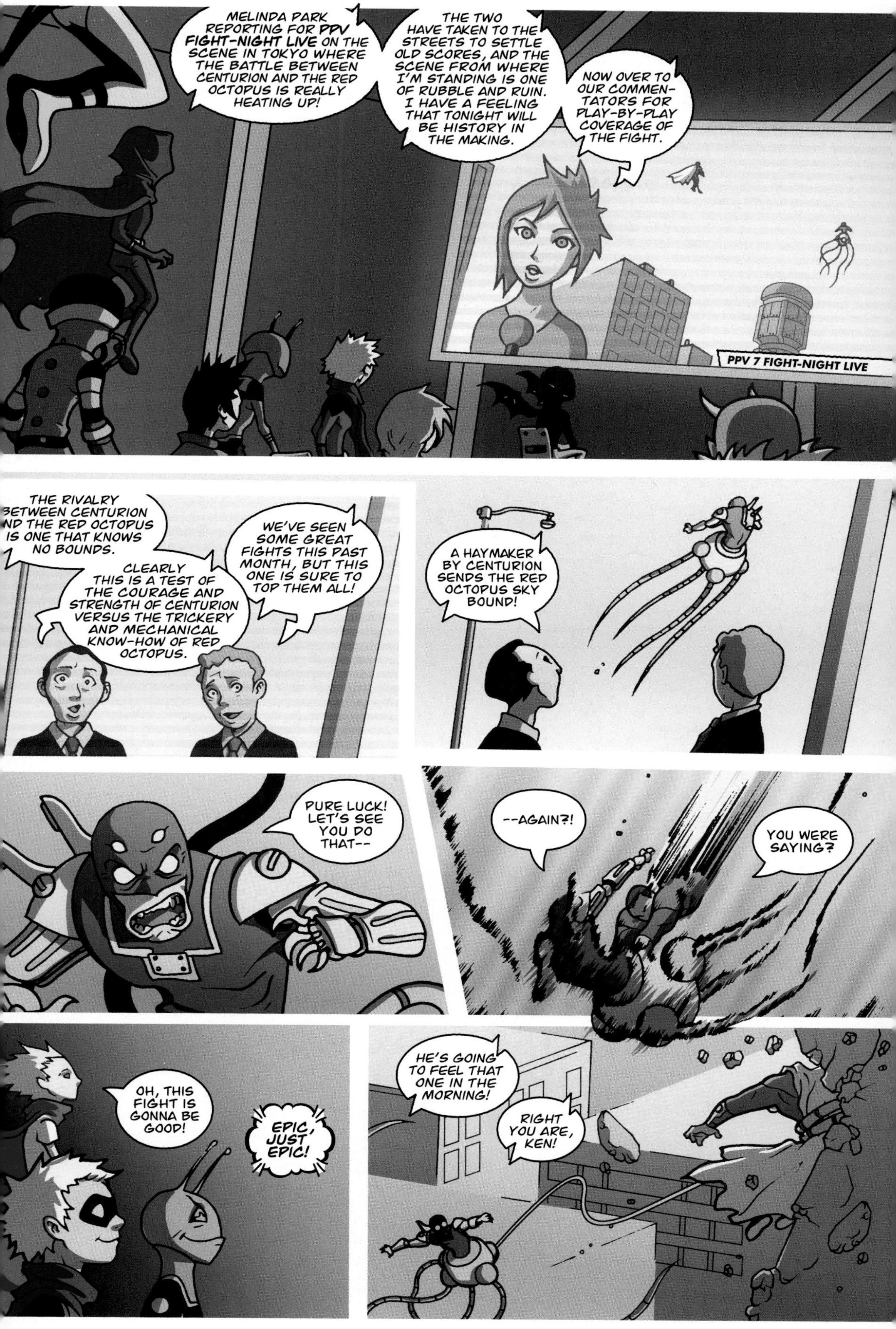
MELINDA PARK REPORTING FOR PPV FIGHT-NIGHT LIVE ON THE SCENE IN TOKYO WHERE THE BATTLE BETWEEN CENTURION AND THE RED OCTOPUS IS REALLY HEATING UP!
THE TWO HAVE TAKEN TO THE STREETS TO SETTLE OLD SCORES, AND THE SCENE FROM WHERE I'M STANDING IS ONE OF RUBBLE AND RUIN. I HAVE A FEELING THAT TONIGHT WILL BE HISTORY IN THE MAKING.
NOW OVER TO OUR COMMENTATORS FOR PLAY-BY-PLAY COVERAGE OF THE FIGHT.
PPV 7 FIGHT-NIGHT LIVE
THE RIVALRY ETWEEN CENTURION ND THE RED OCTOPUS IS ONE THAT KNOWS NO BOUNDS.
CLEARLY THIS IS A TEST OF THE COURAGE AND STRENGTH OF CENTURION VERSUS THE TRICKERY AND MECHANICAL KNOW-HOW OF RED OCTOPUS.
WE'VE SEEN SOME GREAT FIGHTS THIS PAST MONTH, BUT THIS ONE IS SURE TO TOP THEM ALL!
A HAYMAKER BY CENTURION SENDS THE RED OCTOPUS SKY BOUND!
PURE LUCK! LET'S SEE YOU DO THAT--
--AGAIN?!
YOU WERE SAYING?
OH, THIS FIGHT IS GONNA BE GOOD!
EPIC, JUST EPIC!
HE'S GOING TO FEEL THAT ONE IN THE MORNING!
RIGHT YOU ARE, KEN!

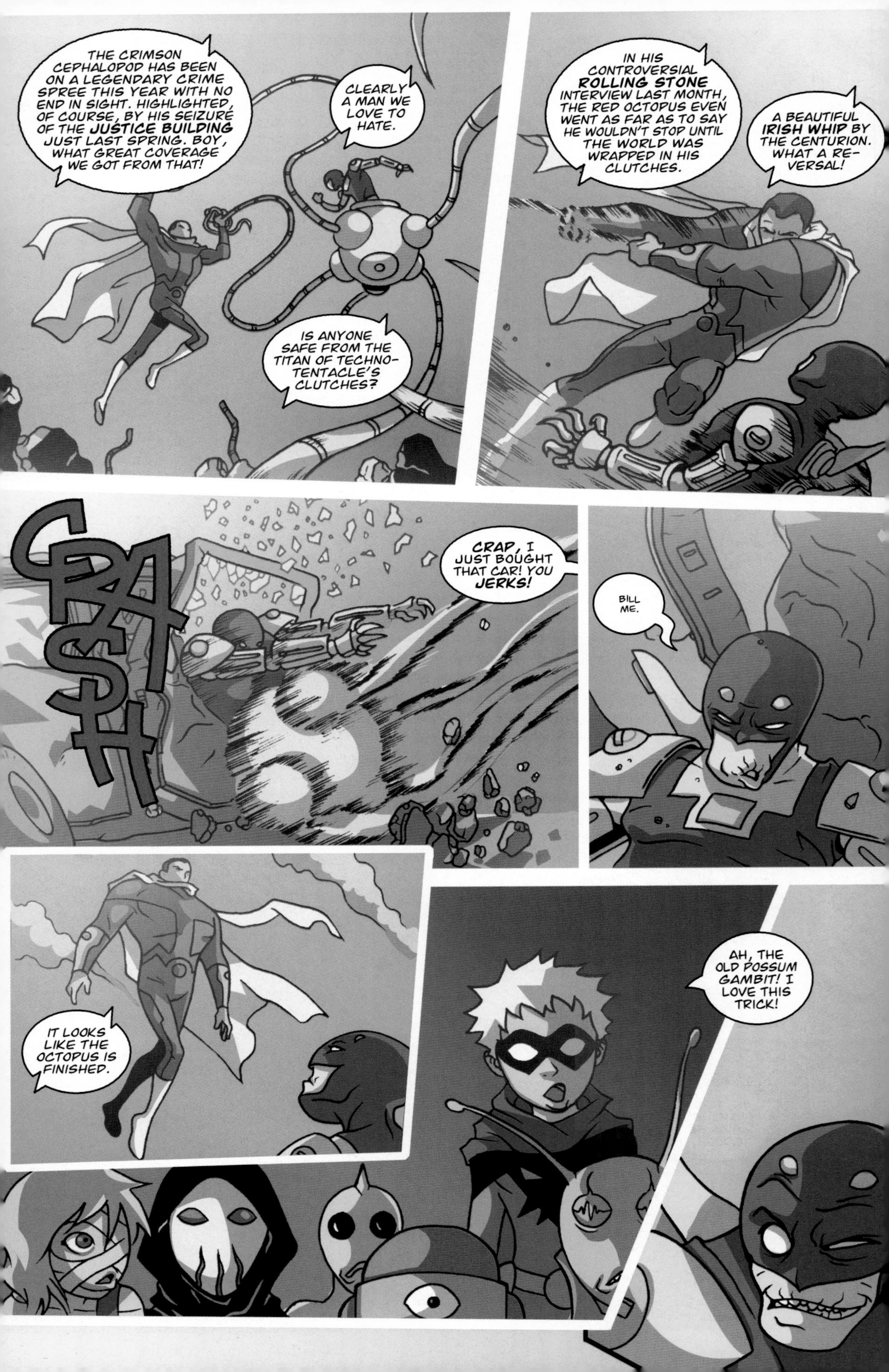
THE CRIMSON CEPHALOPOD HAS BEEN ON A LEGENDARY CRIME SPREE THIS YEAR WITH NO END IN SIGHT. HIGHLIGHTED, OF COURSE, BY HIS SEIZURE OF THE **JUSTICE BUILDING** JUST LAST SPRING. BOY, WHAT GREAT COVERAGE WE GOT FROM THAT!
CLEARLY A MAN WE LOVE TO HATE.
IS ANYONE SAFE FROM THE TITAN OF TECHNO-TENTACLE'S CLUTCHES?
IN HIS CONTROVERSIAL **ROLLING STONE** INTERVIEW LAST MONTH, THE RED OCTOPUS EVEN WENT AS FAR AS TO SAY HE WOULDN'T STOP UNTIL THE WORLD WAS WRAPPED IN HIS CLUTCHES.
A BEAUTIFUL **IRISH WHIP** BY THE CENTURION. WHAT A RE-VERSAL!
CRASH
CRAP, I JUST BOUGHT THAT CAR! YOU **JERKS!**
BILL ME.
IT LOOKS LIKE THE OCTOPUS IS FINISHED.
AH, THE OLD POSSUM GAMBIT! I LOVE THIS TRICK!

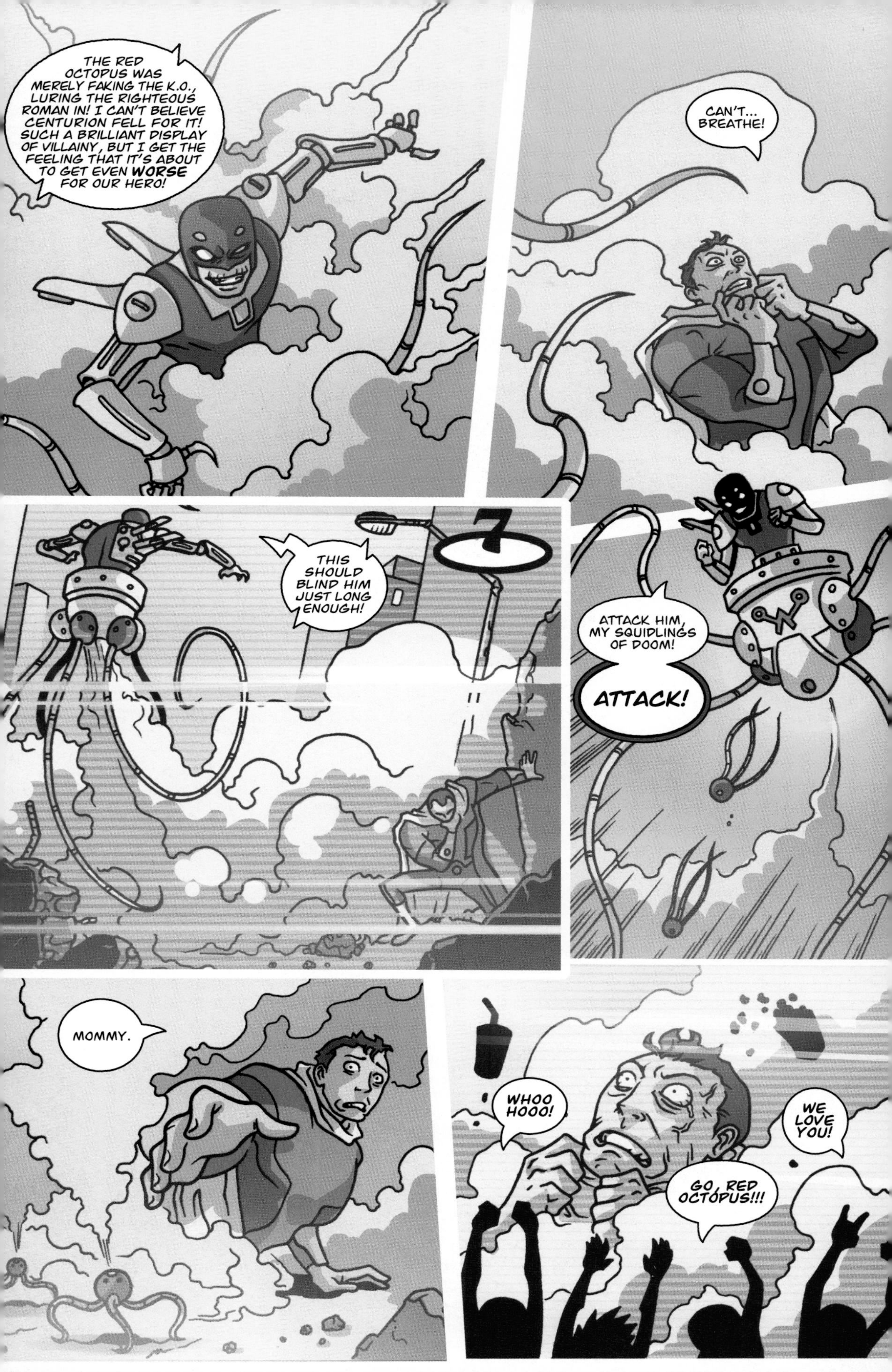
THE RED OCTOPUS WAS MERELY FAKING THE K.O., LURING THE RIGHTEOUS ROMAN IN! I CAN'T BELIEVE CENTURION FELL FOR IT! SUCH A BRILLIANT DISPLAY OF VILLAINY, BUT I GET THE FEELING THAT IT'S ABOUT TO GET EVEN **WORSE** FOR OUR HERO!
CAN'T... BREATHE!
THIS SHOULD BLIND HIM JUST LONG ENOUGH!
7
ATTACK HIM, MY SQUIDLINGS OF DOOM!
ATTACK!
MOMMY.
WHOO HOOO!
WE LOVE YOU!
GO, RED OCTOPUS!!!

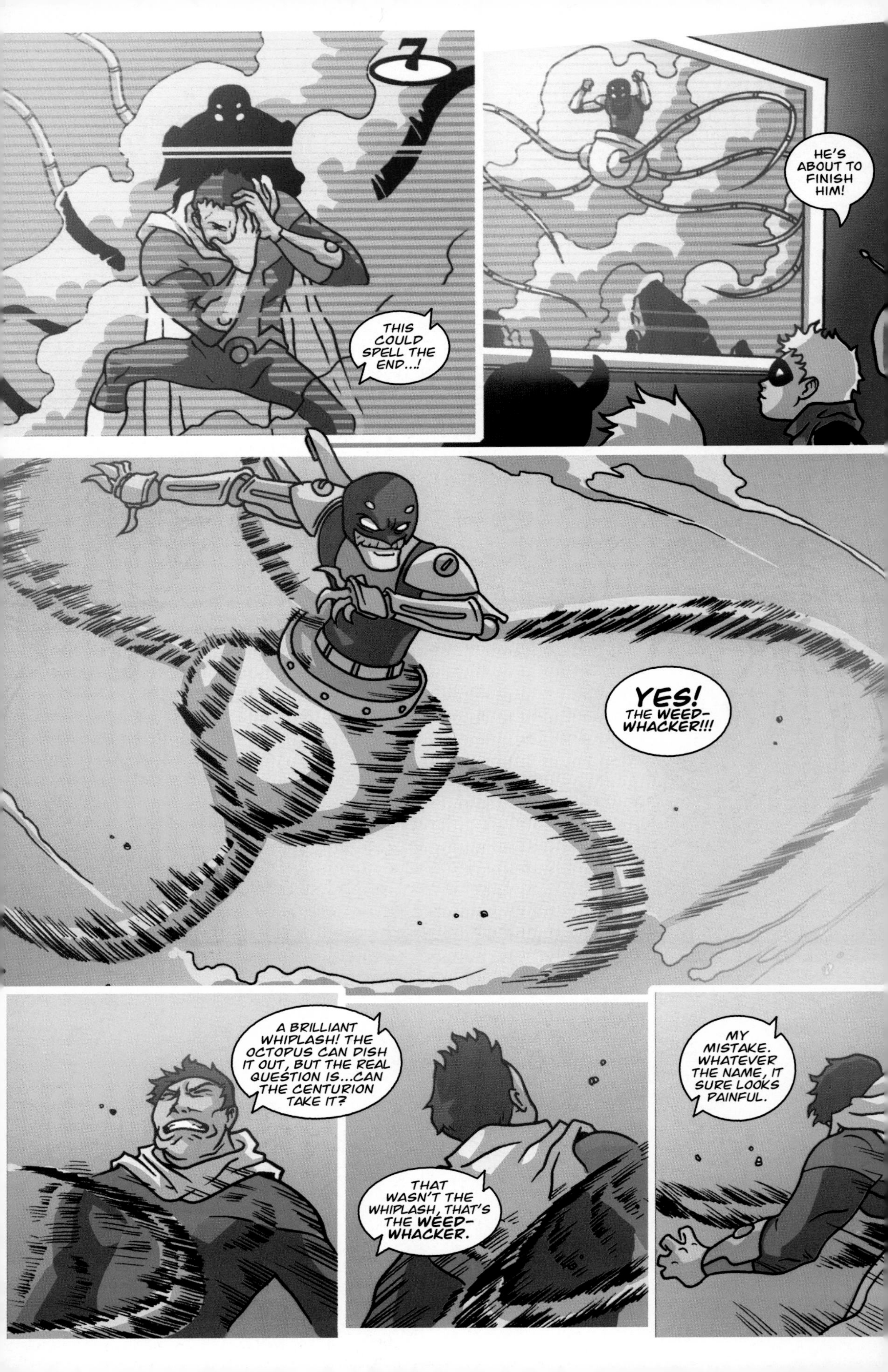
7
THIS COULD SPELL THE END...!
HE'S ABOUT TO FINISH HIM!
YES! THE WEED-WHACKER!!!
A BRILLIANT WHIPLASH! THE OCTOPUS CAN DISH IT OUT, BUT THE REAL QUESTION IS...CAN THE CENTURION TAKE IT?
THAT WASN'T THE WHIPLASH, THAT'S THE WEED-WHACKER.
MY MISTAKE. WHATEVER THE NAME, IT SURE LOOKS PAINFUL.

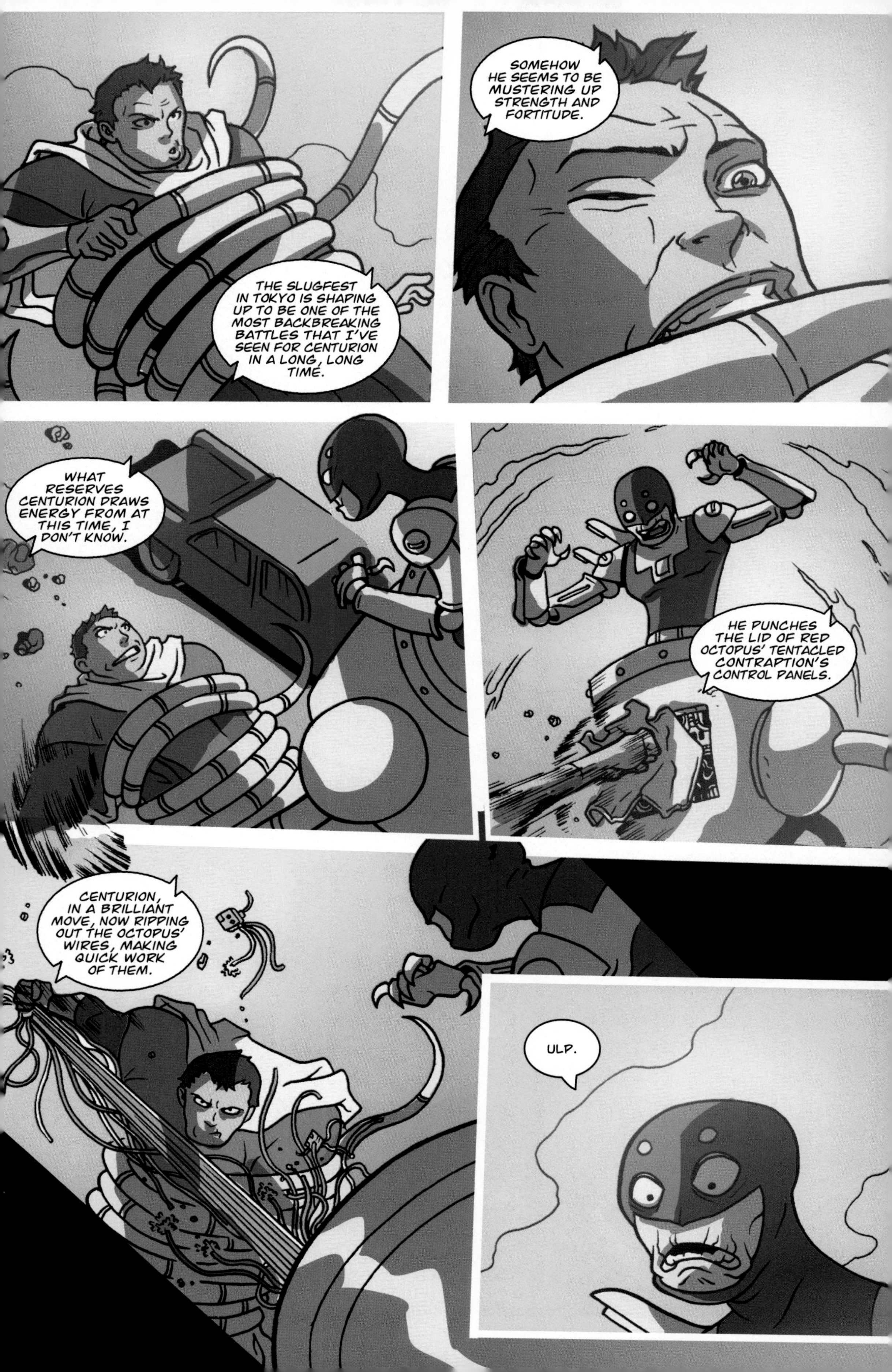
THE SLUGFEST IN TOKYO IS SHAPING UP TO BE ONE OF THE MOST BACKBREAKING BATTLES THAT I'VE SEEN FOR CENTURION IN A LONG, LONG TIME.
SOMEHOW HE SEEMS TO BE MUSTERING UP STRENGTH AND FORTITUDE.
WHAT RESERVES CENTURION DRAWS ENERGY FROM AT THIS TIME, I DON'T KNOW.
HE PUNCHES THE LID OF RED OCTOPUS' TENTACLED CONTRAPTION'S CONTROL PANELS.
CENTURION, IN A BRILLIANT MOVE, NOW RIPPING OUT THE OCTOPUS' WIRES, MAKING QUICK WORK OF THEM.
ULP.

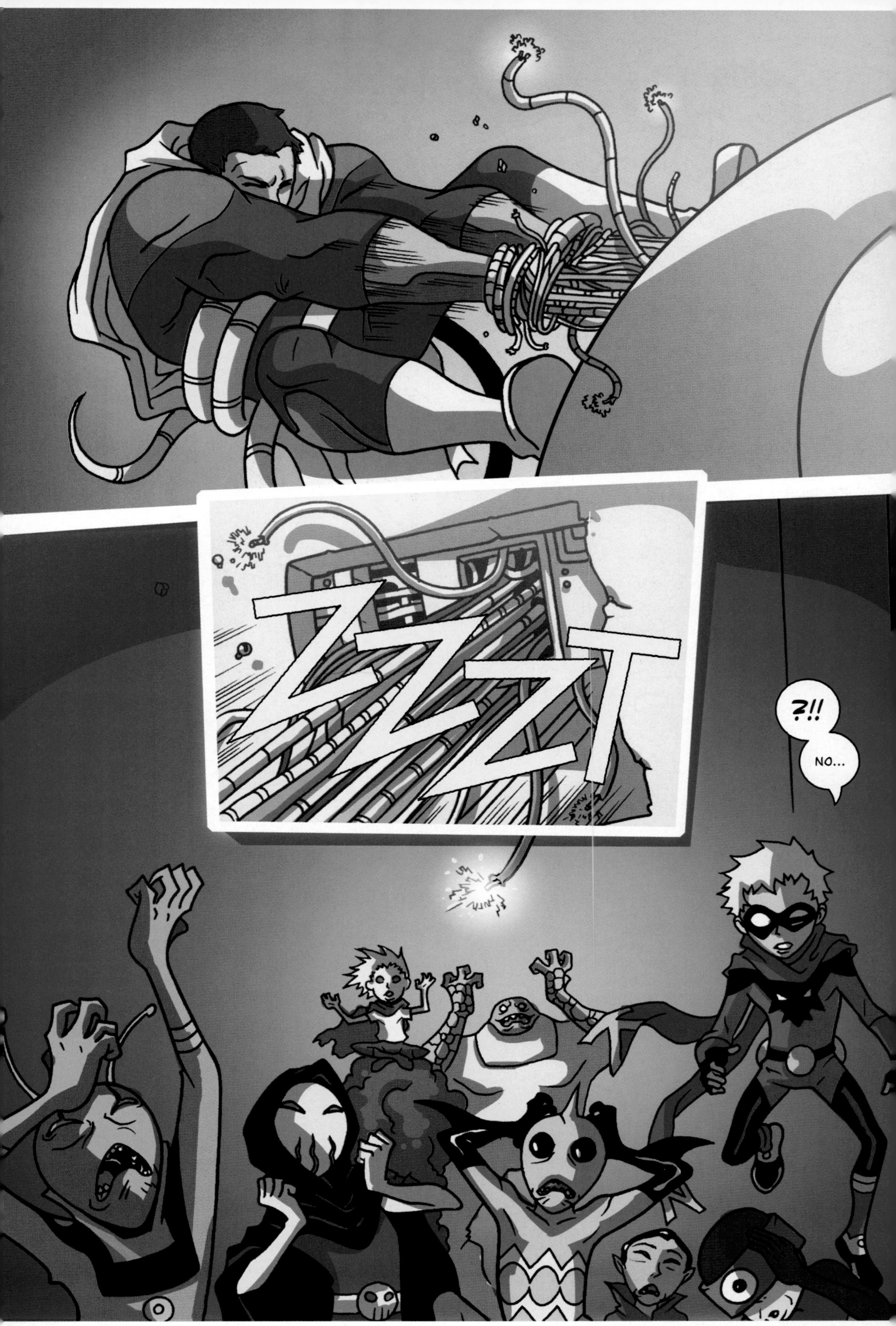
ZZZT
?!!
NO...

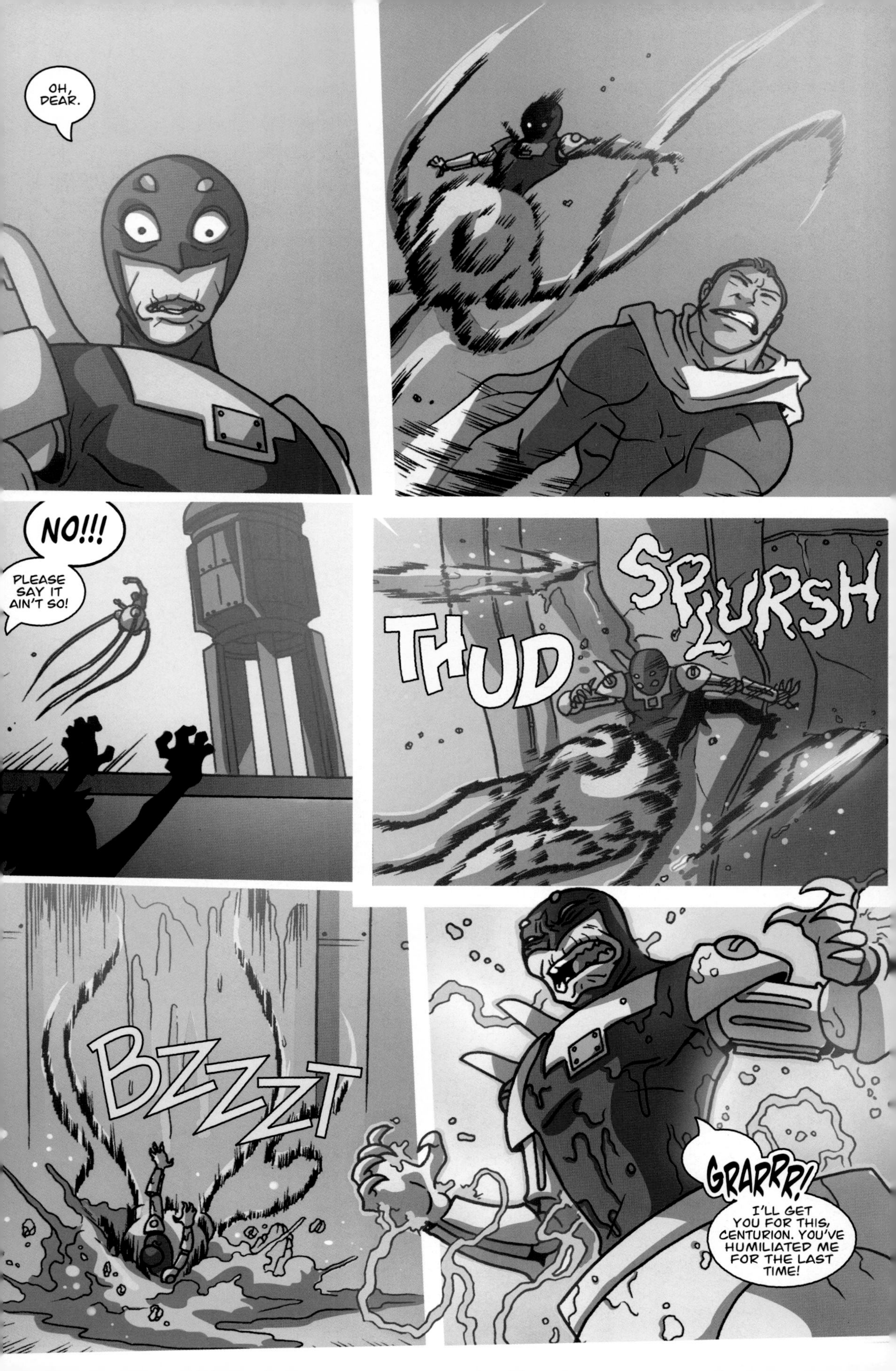
OH, DEAR.
NO!!!
PLEASE SAY IT AIN'T SO!
THUD
SPLURSH
BZZZZT
GRARRR!
I'LL GET YOU FOR THIS, CENTURION. YOU'VE HUMILIATED ME FOR THE LAST TIME!

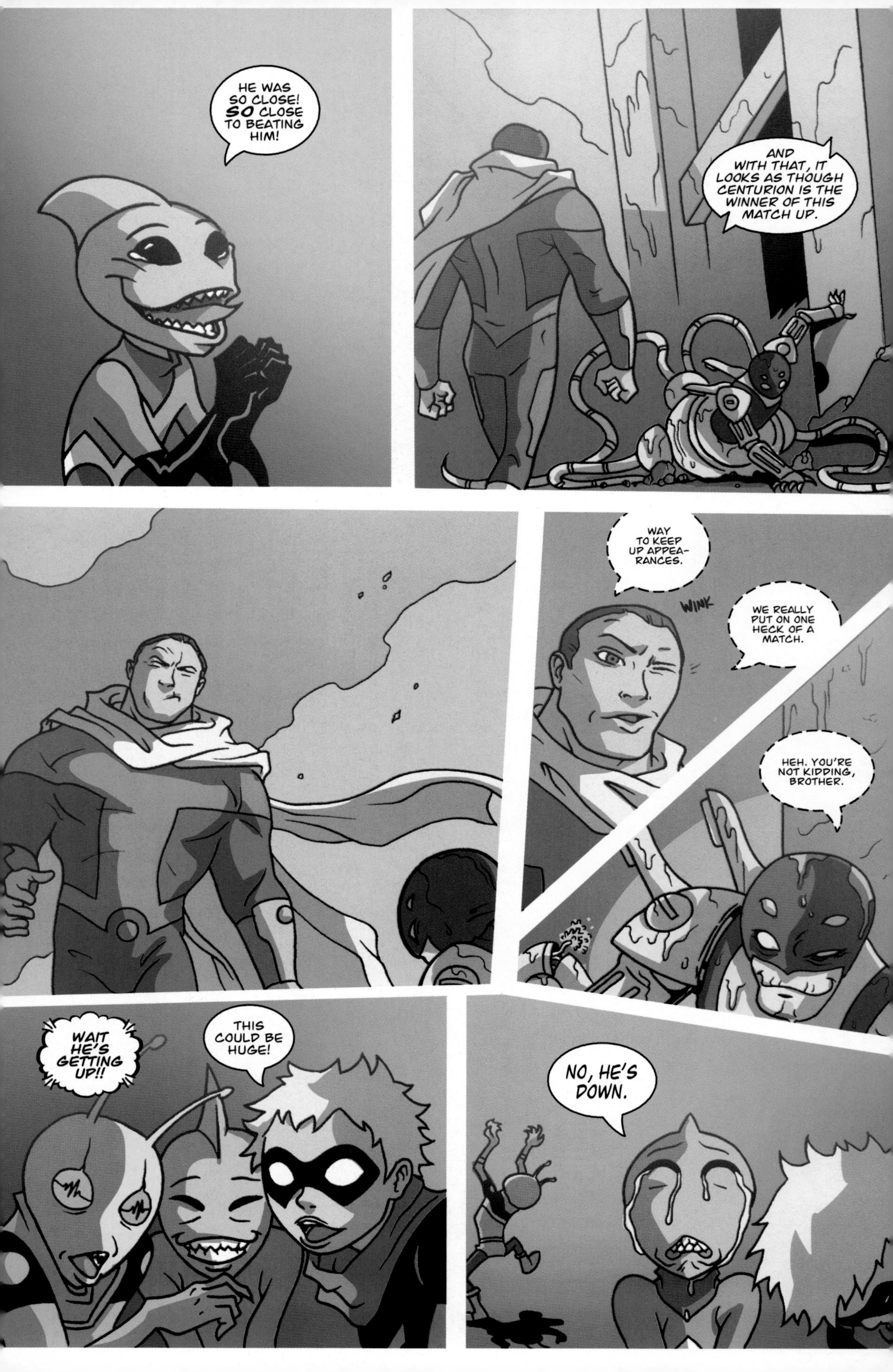
HE WAS SO CLOSE! SO CLOSE TO BEATING HIM!
AND WITH THAT, IT LOOKS AS THOUGH CENTURION IS THE WINNER OF THIS MATCH UP.
WAY TO KEEP UP APPEA-RANCES.
WINK
WE REALLY PUT ON ONE HECK OF A MATCH.
HEH. YOU'RE NOT KIDDING, BROTHER.
WAIT HE'S GETTING UP!!
THIS COULD BE HUGE!
NO, HE'S DOWN.

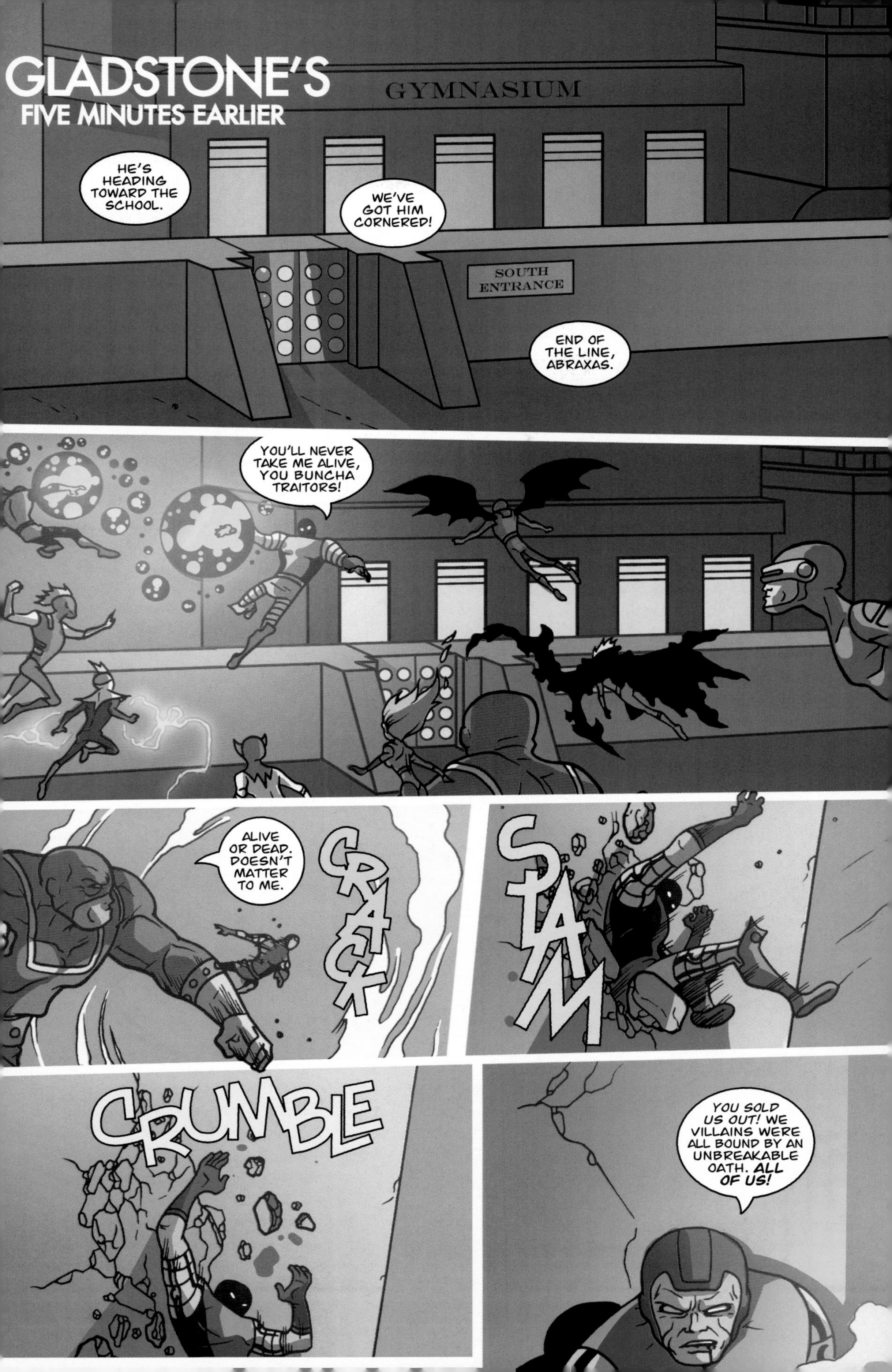
GLADSTONE'S
FIVE MINUTES EARLIER
GYMNASIUM
HE'S HEADING TOWARD THE SCHOOL.
WE'VE GOT HIM CORNERED!
SOUTH ENTRANCE
END OF THE LINE, ABRAXAS.
YOU'LL NEVER TAKE ME ALIVE, YOU BUNCHA TRAITORS!
ALIVE OR DEAD. DOESN'T MATTER TO ME.
CRACK
SLAM
CRUMBLE
YOU SOLD US OUT! WE VILLAINS WERE ALL BOUND BY AN UNBREAKABLE OATH. **ALL OF US!**

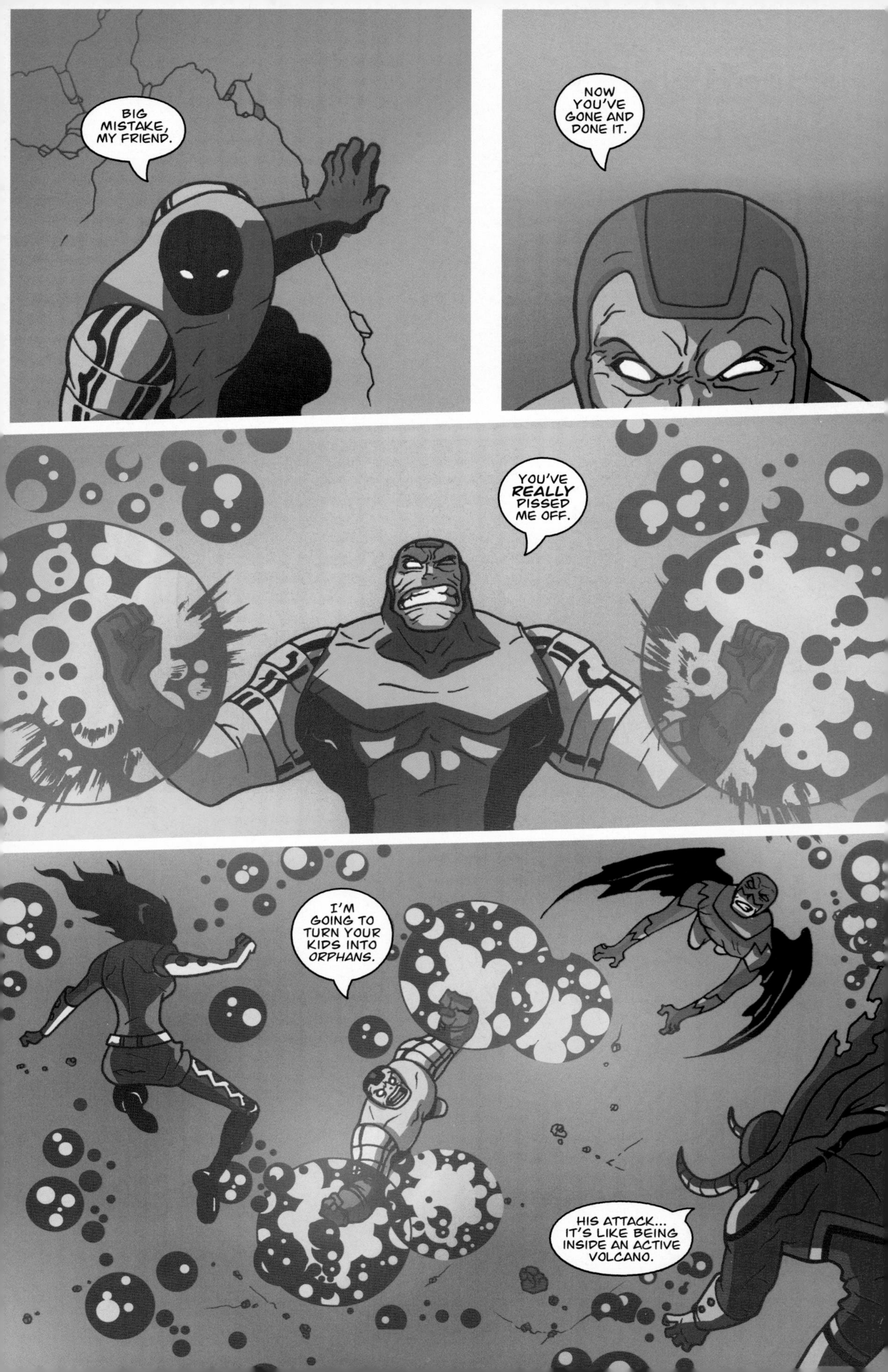
BIG MISTAKE, MY FRIEND.
NOW YOU'VE GONE AND DONE IT.
YOU'VE **REALLY** PISSED ME OFF.
I'M GOING TO TURN YOUR KIDS INTO ORPHANS.
HIS ATTACK... IT'S LIKE BEING INSIDE AN ACTIVE VOLCANO.

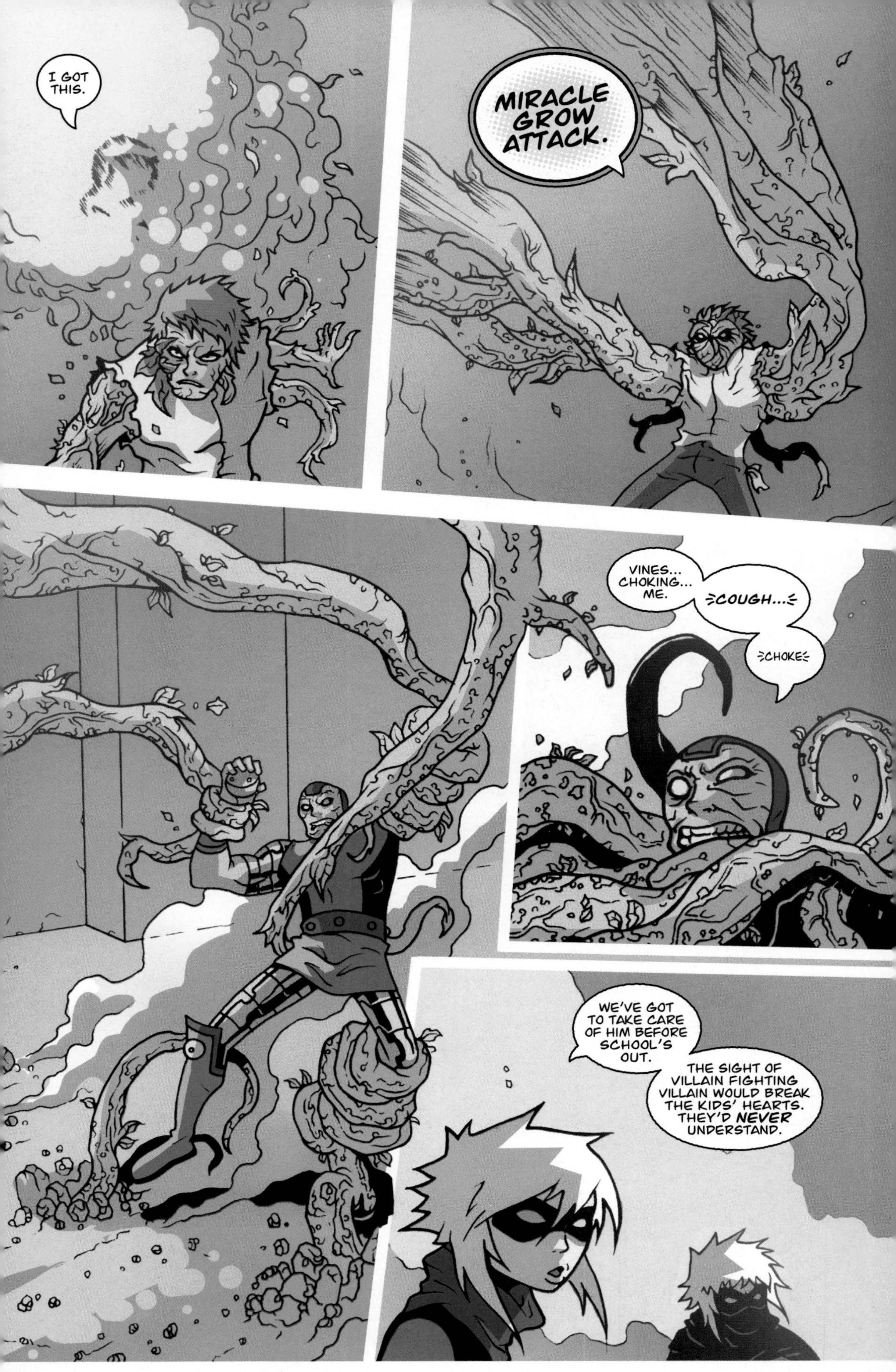
I GOT THIS.
MIRACLE GROW ATTACK.
VINES... CHOKING... ME.
COUGH...
CHOKE
WE'VE GOT TO TAKE CARE OF HIM BEFORE SCHOOL'S OUT.
THE SIGHT OF VILLAIN FIGHTING VILLAIN WOULD BREAK THE KIDS' HEARTS. THEY'D NEVER UNDERSTAND.

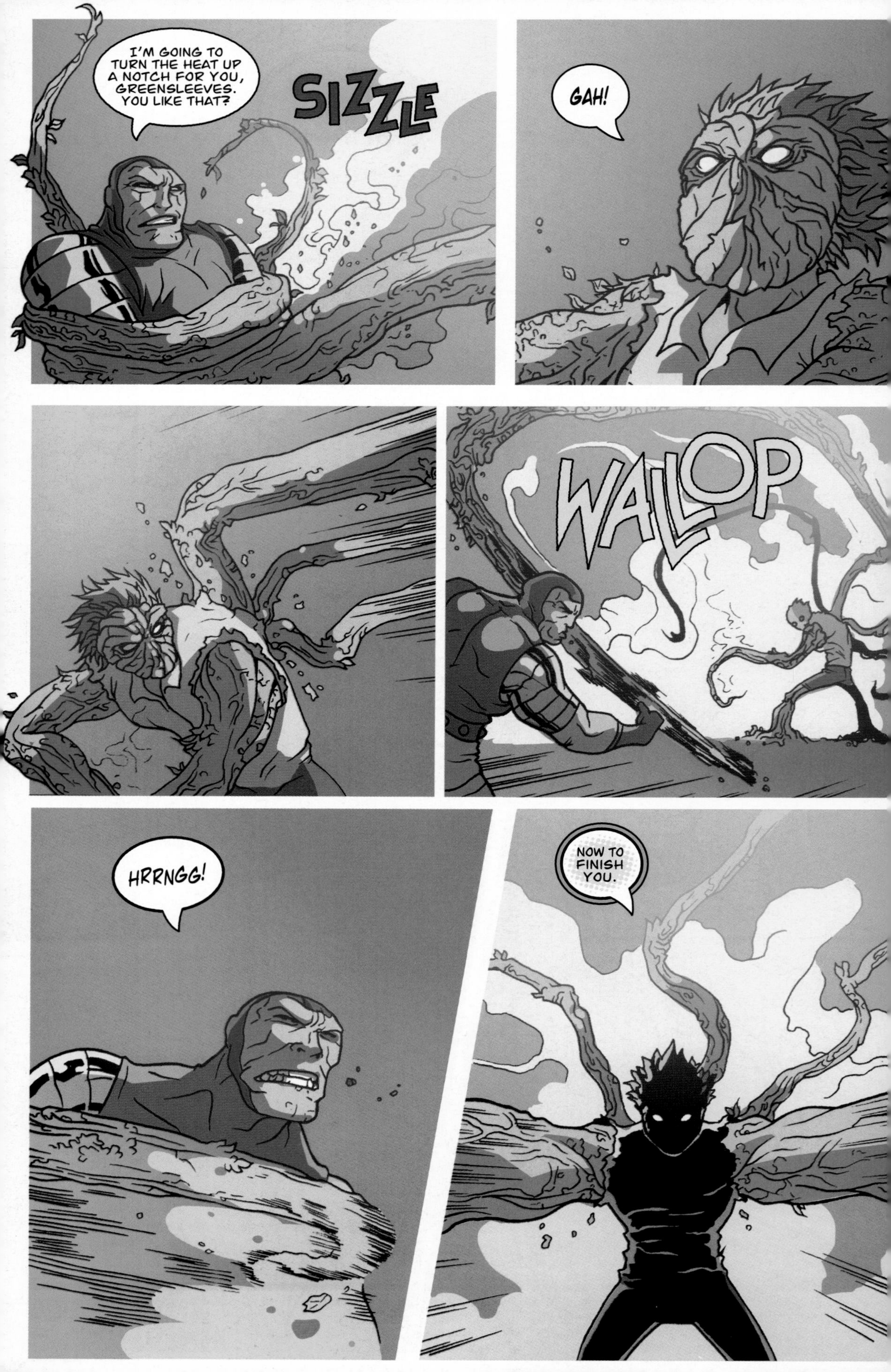
I'M GOING TO TURN THE HEAT UP A NOTCH FOR YOU, GREENSLEEVES. YOU LIKE THAT?
SIZZLE
GAH!
WALLOP
HRRNGG!
NOW TO FINISH YOU.

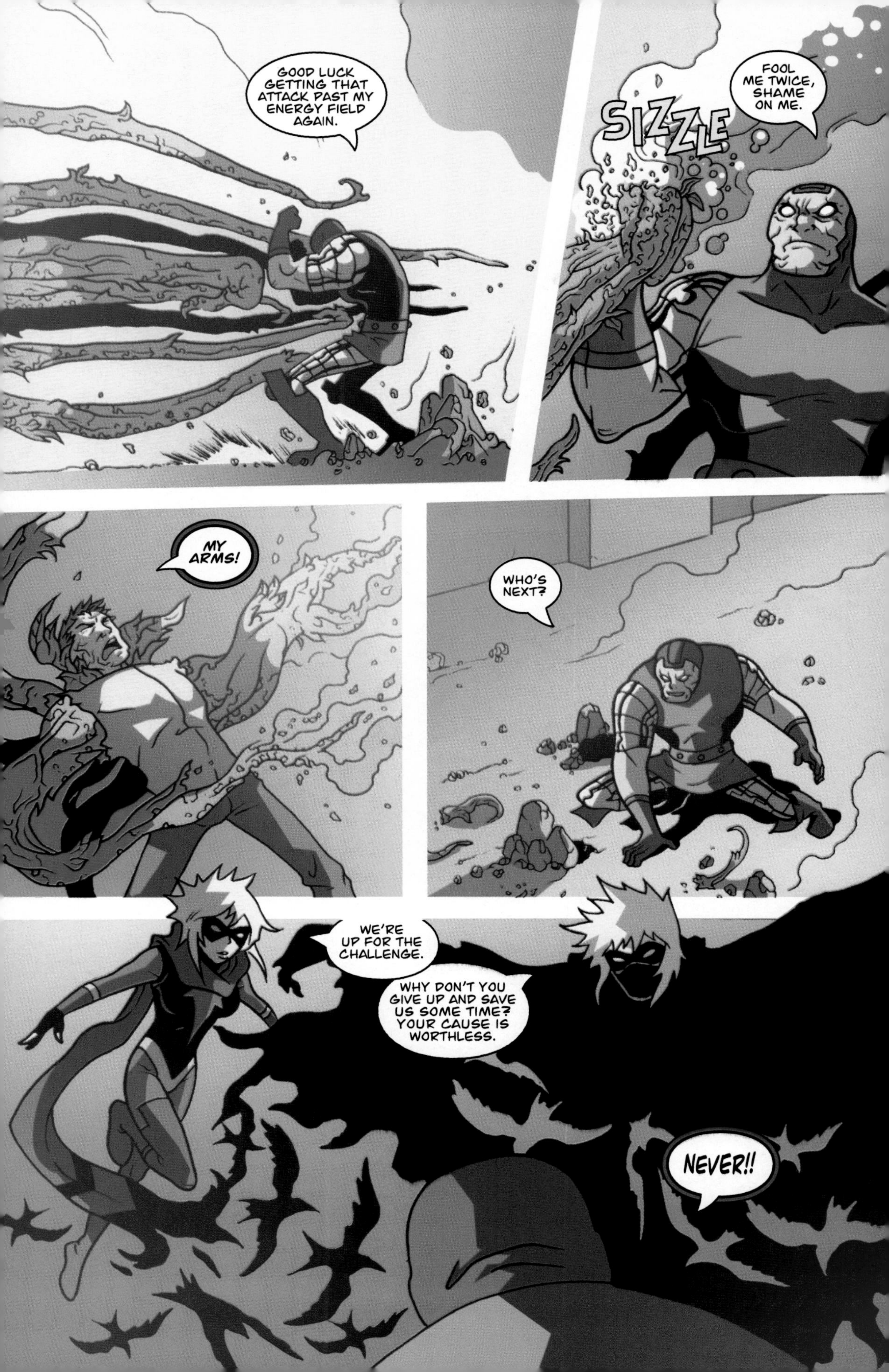
GOOD LUCK GETTING THAT ATTACK PAST MY ENERGY FIELD AGAIN.
SIZZLE
FOOL ME TWICE, SHAME ON ME.
MY ARMS!
WHO'S NEXT?
WE'RE UP FOR THE CHALLENGE.
WHY DON'T YOU GIVE UP AND SAVE US SOME TIME? YOUR CAUSE IS WORTHLESS.
NEVER!!

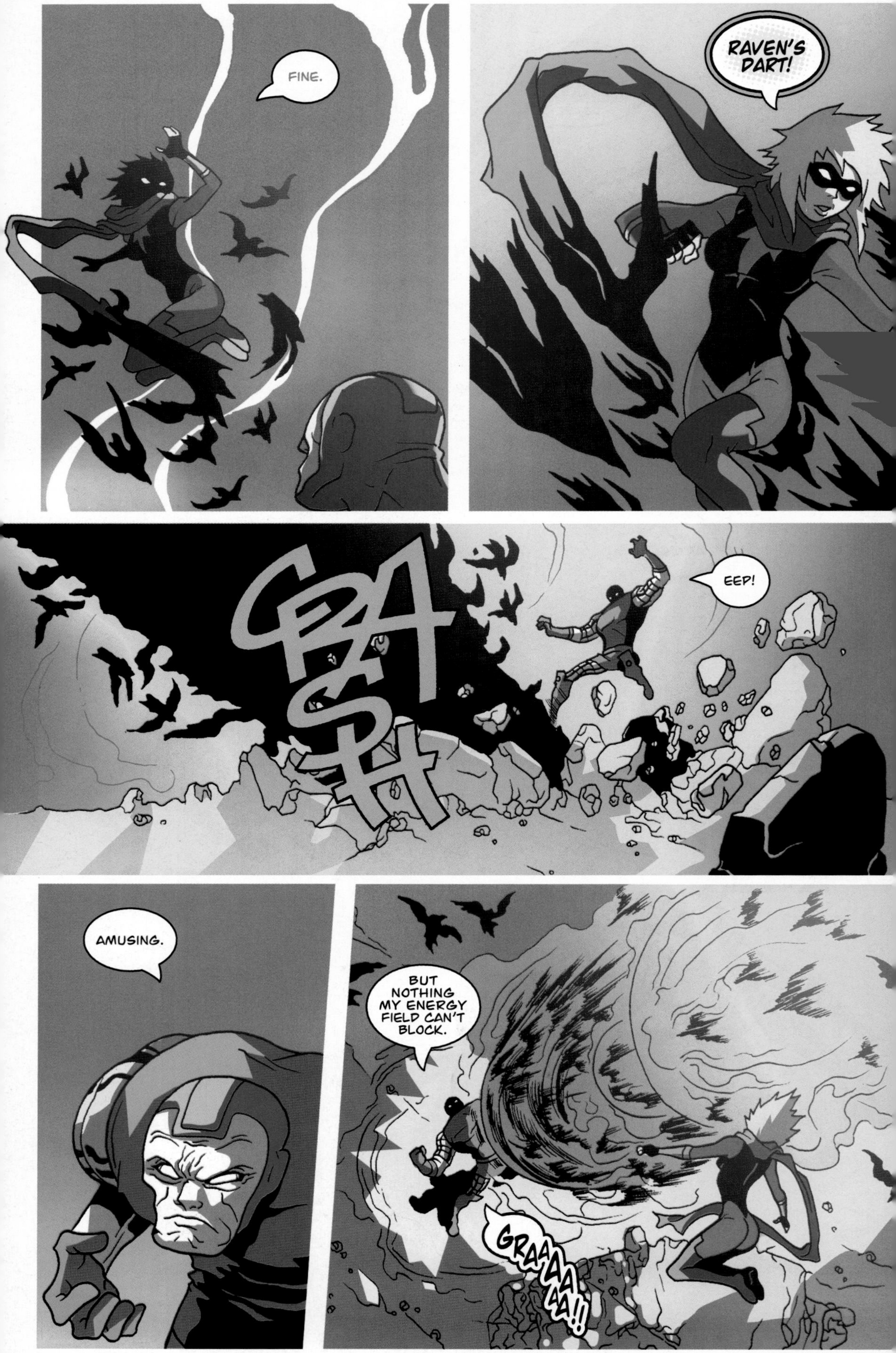
FINE.
RAVEN'S DART!
CRASH
EEP!
AMUSING.
BUT NOTHING MY ENERGY FIELD CAN'T BLOCK.
GRAAAAAAAA!!

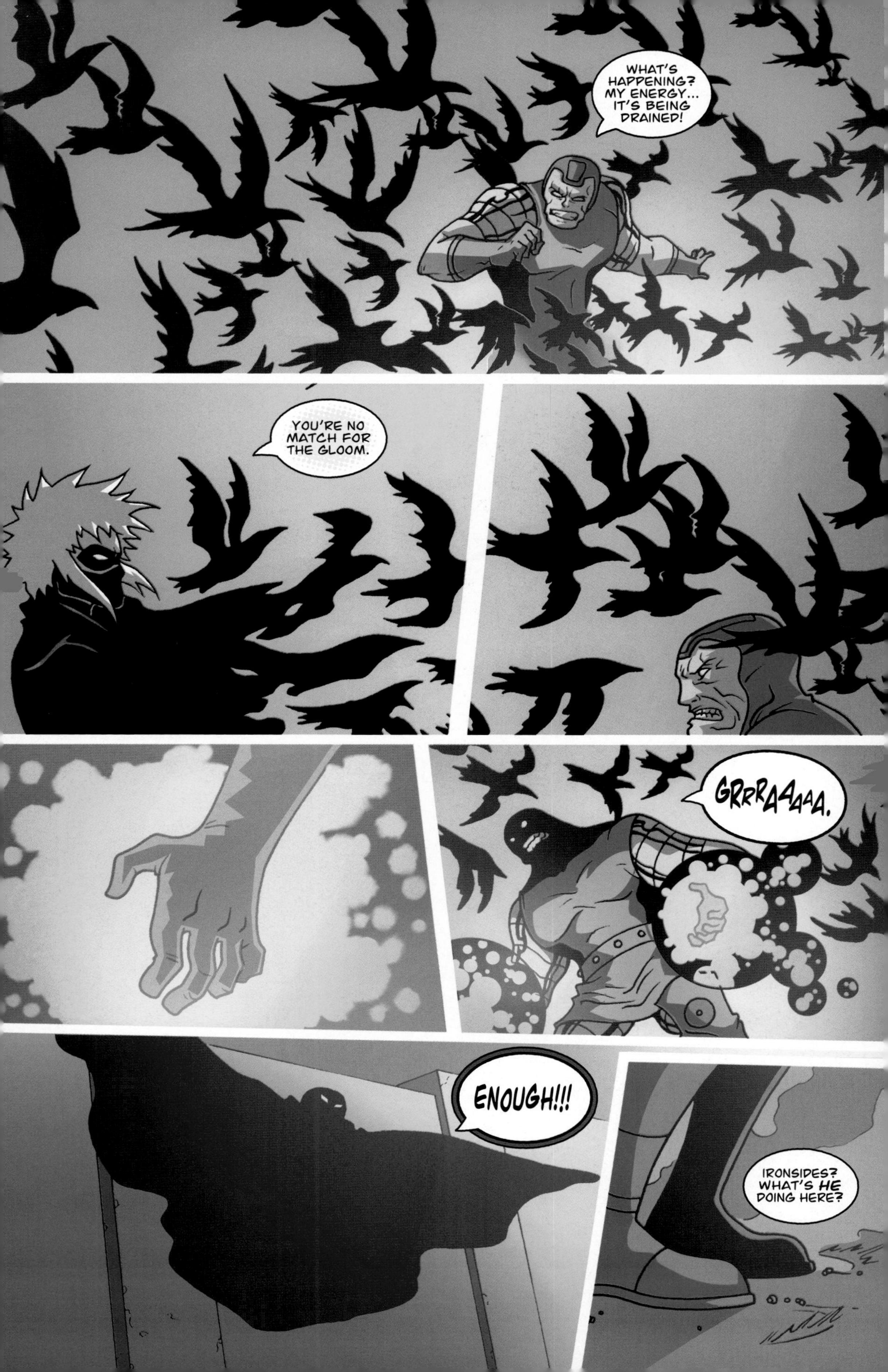
WHAT'S HAPPENING? MY ENERGY... IT'S BEING DRAINED!
YOU'RE NO MATCH FOR THE GLOOM.
GRRRAAAAA.
ENOUGH!!!
IRONSIDES? WHAT'S HE DOING HERE?

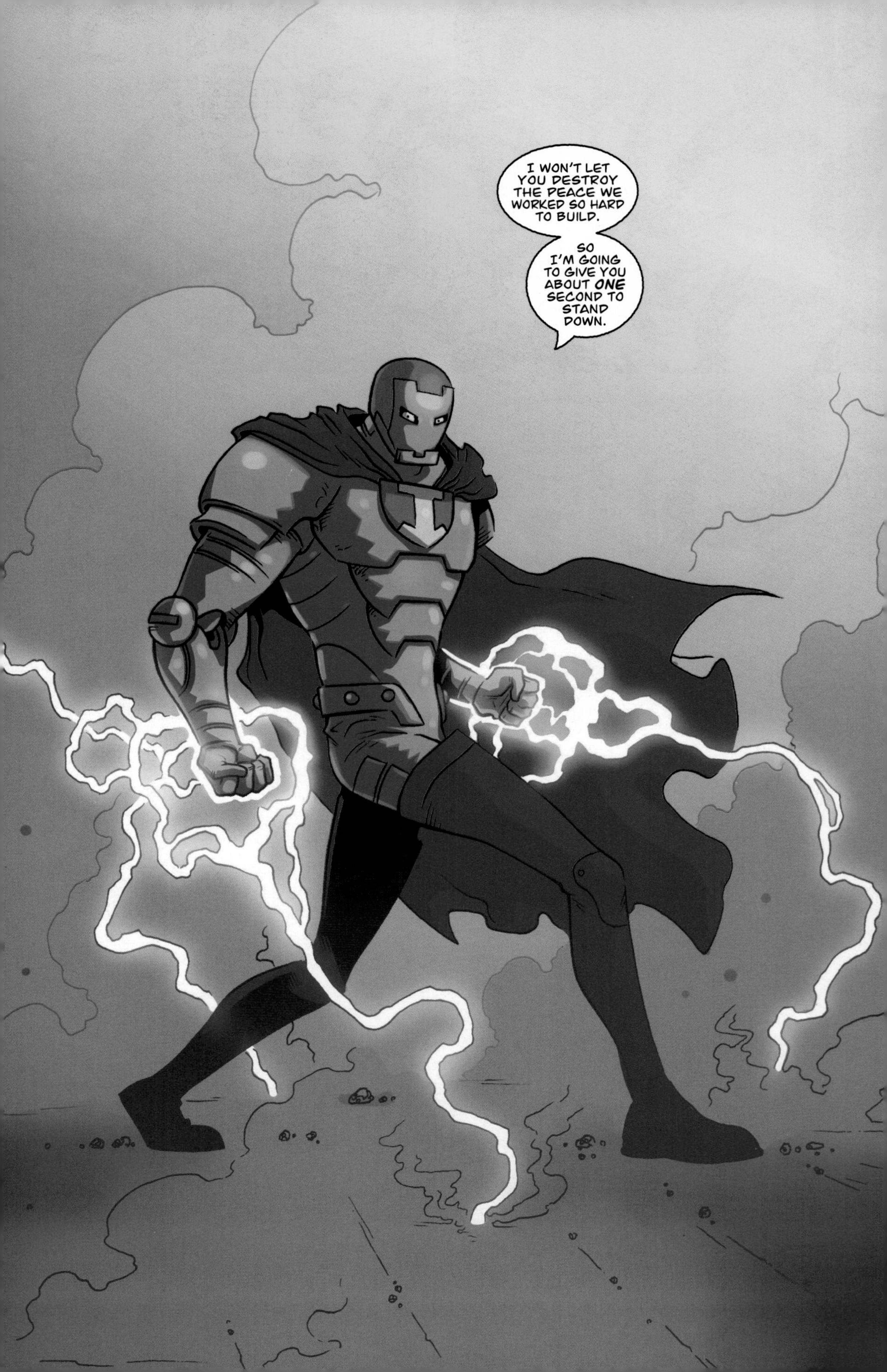
I WON'T LET YOU DESTROY THE PEACE WE WORKED SO HARD TO BUILD.
SO I'M GOING TO GIVE YOU ABOUT **ONE** SECOND TO STAND DOWN.

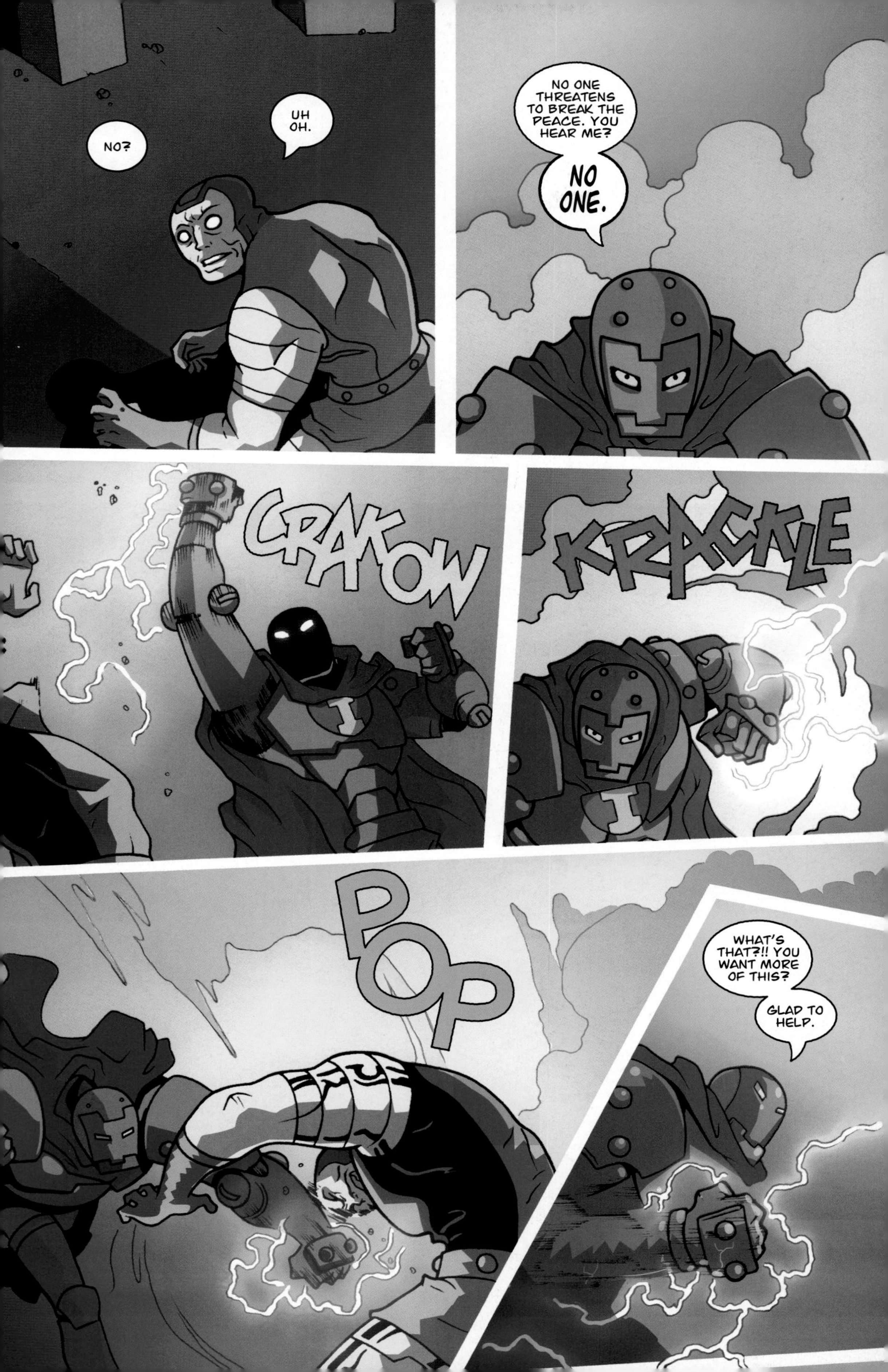
NO?
UH OH.
NO ONE THREATENS TO BREAK THE PEACE. YOU HEAR ME?
NO ONE.
CRAKOW
KRACKLE
POP
WHAT'S THAT?!! YOU WANT MORE OF THIS?
GLAD TO HELP.

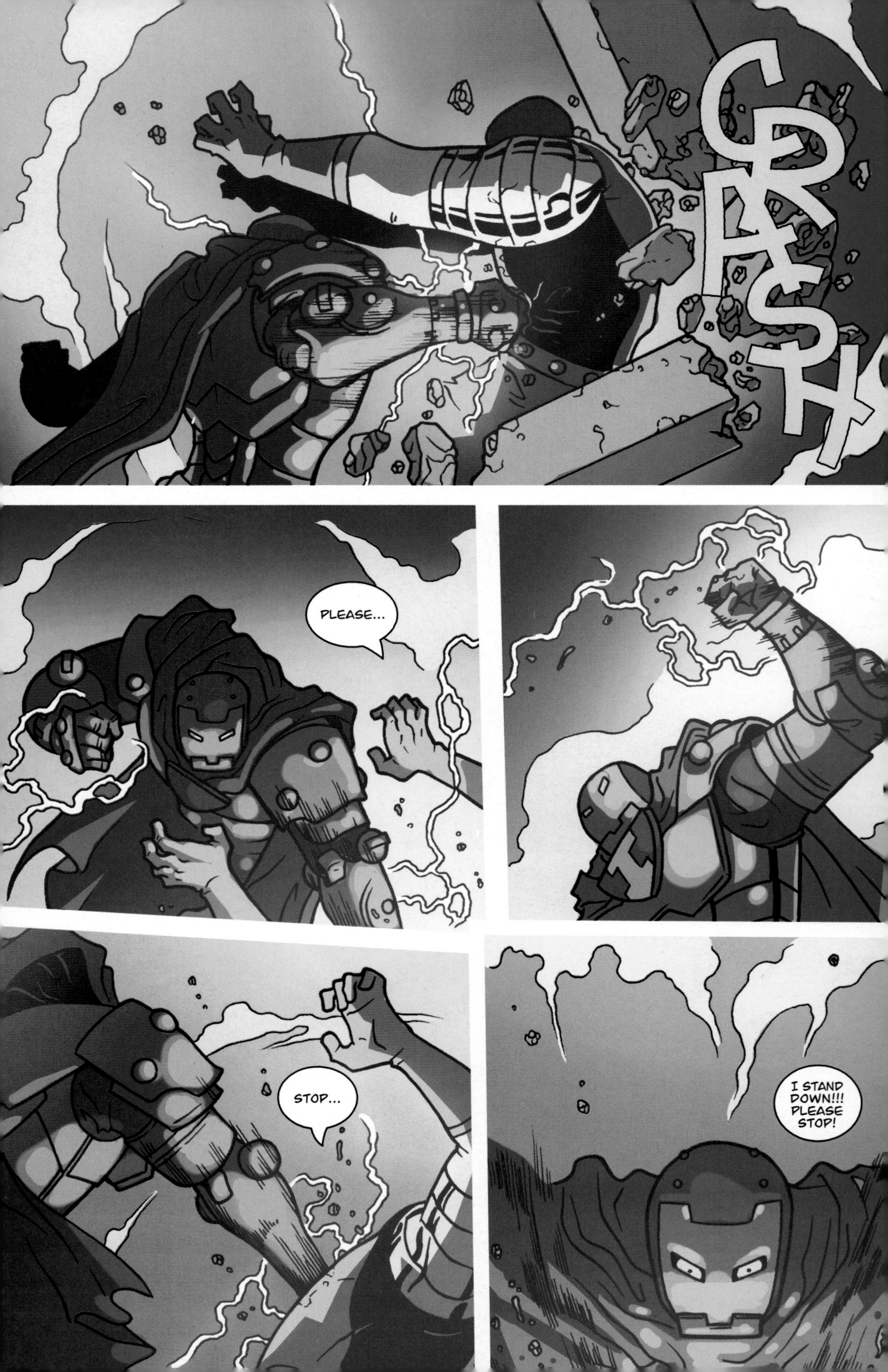
CRASH!
PLEASE...
STOP...
I STAND DOWN!!! PLEASE STOP!

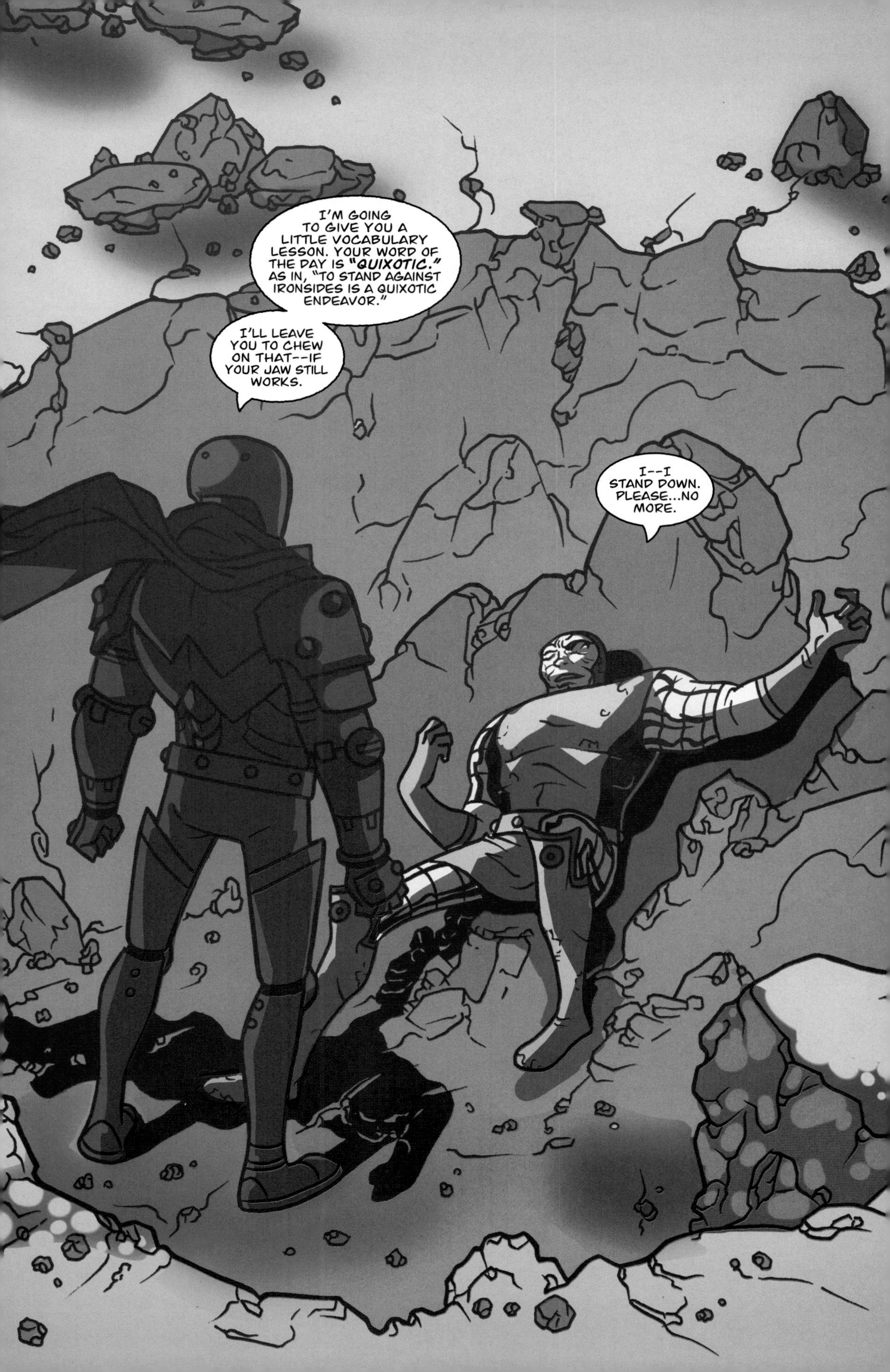
I'M GOING TO GIVE YOU A LITTLE VOCABULARY LESSON. YOUR WORD OF THE DAY IS "QUIXOTIC." AS IN, "TO STAND AGAINST IRONSIDES IS A QUIXOTIC ENDEAVOR."
I'LL LEAVE YOU TO CHEW ON THAT--IF YOUR JAW STILL WORKS.
I--I STAND DOWN. PLEASE...NO MORE.

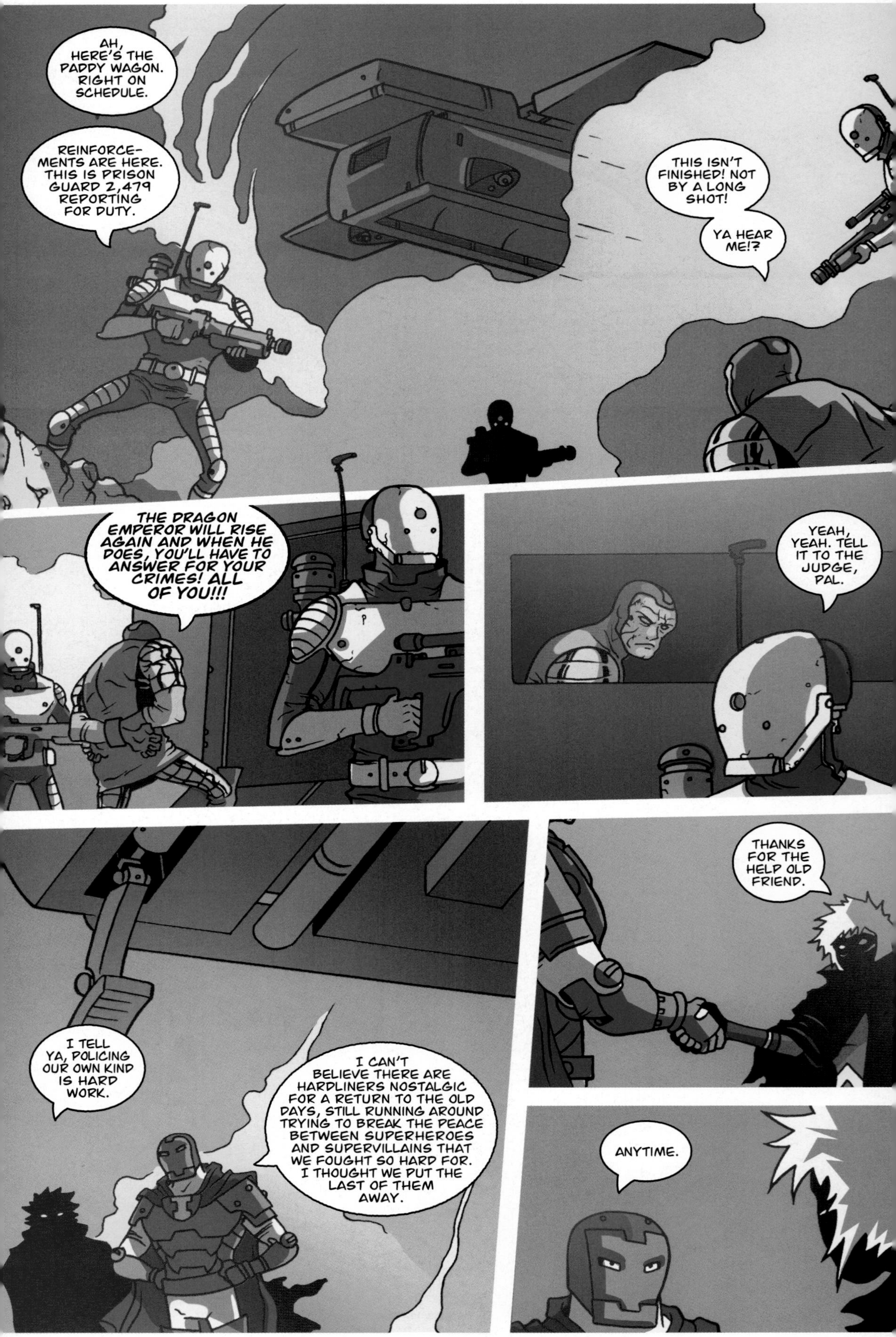
AH, HERE'S THE PADDY WAGON. RIGHT ON SCHEDULE.
REINFORCE-MENTS ARE HERE. THIS IS PRISON GUARD 2,479 REPORTING FOR DUTY.
THIS ISN'T FINISHED! NOT BY A LONG SHOT!
YA HEAR ME!?
THE DRAGON EMPEROR WILL RISE AGAIN AND WHEN HE DOES, YOU'LL HAVE TO ANSWER FOR YOUR CRIMES! ALL OF YOU!!!
YEAH, YEAH. TELL IT TO THE JUDGE, PAL.
I TELL YA, POLICING OUR OWN KIND IS HARD WORK.
I CAN'T BELIEVE THERE ARE HARDLINERS NOSTALGIC FOR A RETURN TO THE OLD DAYS, STILL RUNNING AROUND TRYING TO BREAK THE PEACE BETWEEN SUPERHEROES AND SUPERVILLAINS THAT WE FOUGHT SO HARD FOR. I THOUGHT WE PUT THE LAST OF THEM AWAY.
THANKS FOR THE HELP OLD FRIEND.
ANYTIME.

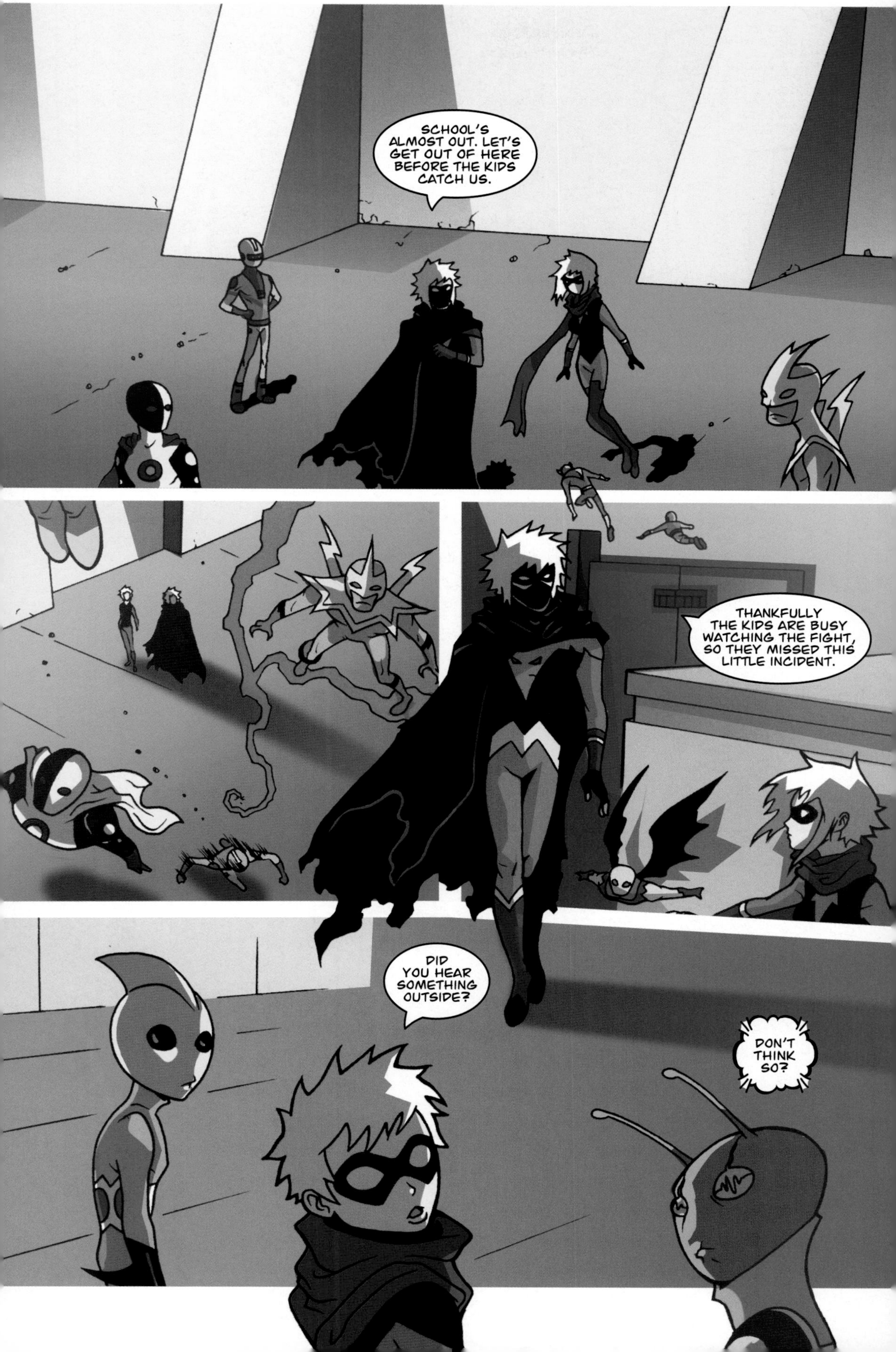
SCHOOL'S ALMOST OUT. LET'S GET OUT OF HERE BEFORE THE KIDS CATCH US.
THANKFULLY THE KIDS ARE BUSY WATCHING THE FIGHT, SO THEY MISSED THIS LITTLE INCIDENT.
DID YOU HEAR SOMETHING OUTSIDE?
DON'T THINK SO?

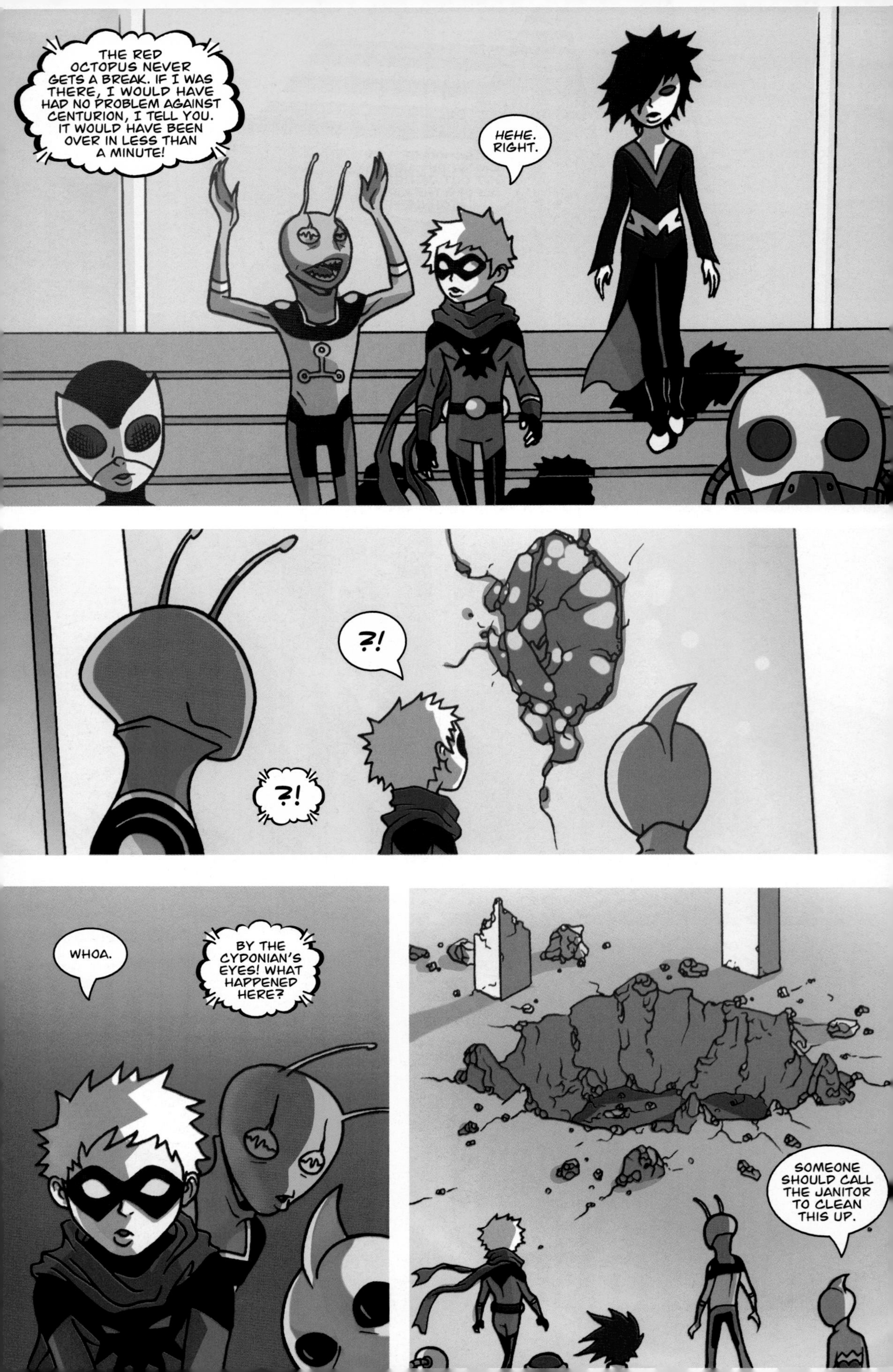
THE RED OCTOPUS NEVER GETS A BREAK. IF I WAS THERE, I WOULD HAVE HAD NO PROBLEM AGAINST CENTURION, I TELL YOU. IT WOULD HAVE BEEN OVER IN LESS THAN A MINUTE!
HEHE. RIGHT.
?!
?!
WHOA.
BY THE CYDONIAN'S EYES! WHAT HAPPENED HERE?
SOMEONE SHOULD CALL THE JANITOR TO CLEAN THIS UP.

CHAPTER 3

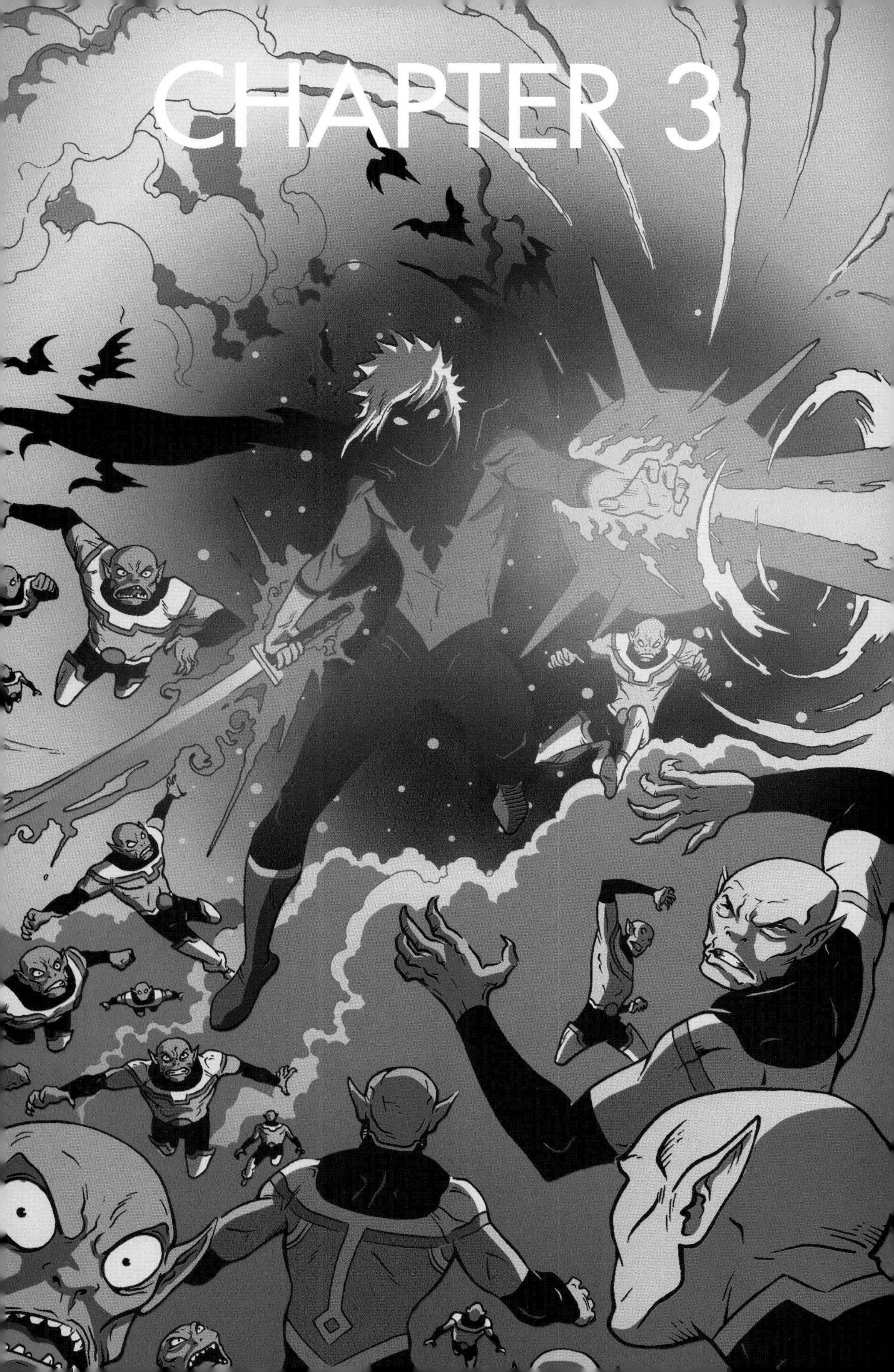

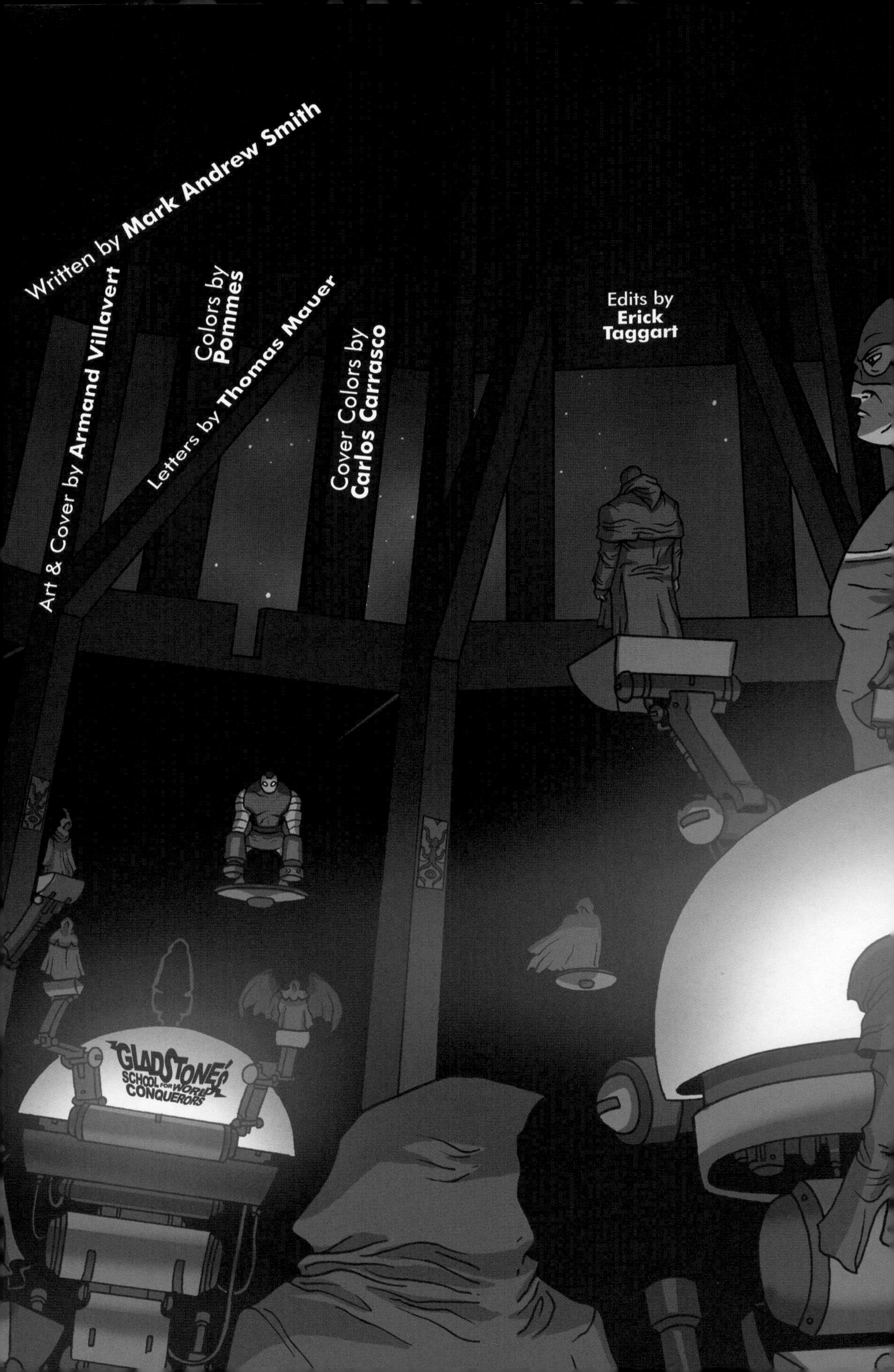

Written by Mark Andrew Smith
Art & Cover by Armand Villavert
Colors by Pommes
Letters by Thomas Mauer
Cover Colors by Carlos Carrasco
Edits by Erick Taggart
GLADSTONE'S SCHOOL FOR WORLD CONQUERORS

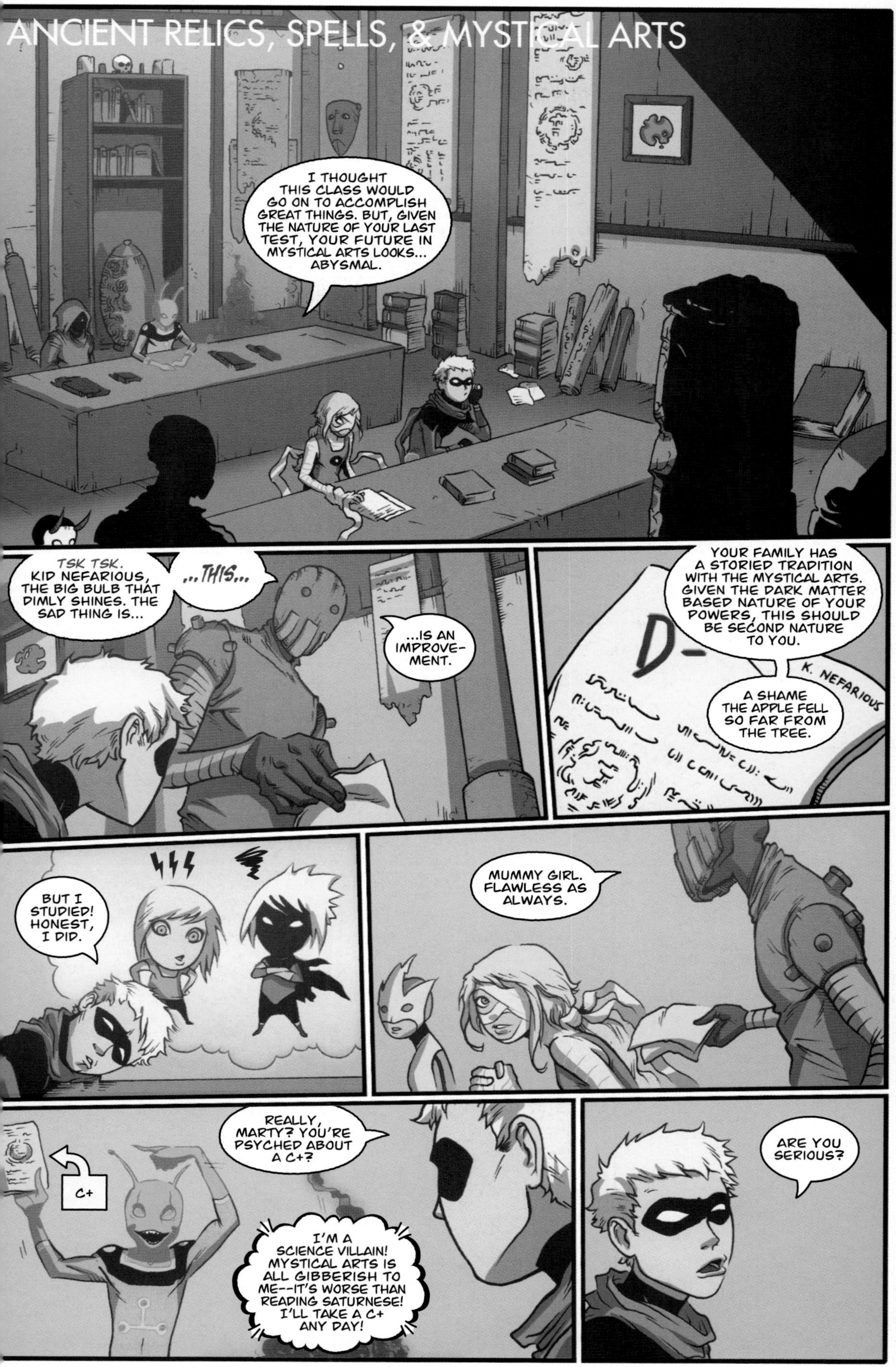
ANCIENT RELICS, SPELLS, & MYSTICAL ARTS
I THOUGHT THIS CLASS WOULD GO ON TO ACCOMPLISH GREAT THINGS. BUT, GIVEN THE NATURE OF YOUR LAST TEST, YOUR FUTURE IN MYSTICAL ARTS LOOKS... ABYSMAL.
TSK TSK. KID NEFARIOUS, THE BIG BULB THAT DIMLY SHINES. THE SAD THING IS...
...THIS...
...IS AN IMPROVEMENT.
YOUR FAMILY HAS A STORIED TRADITION WITH THE MYSTICAL ARTS. GIVEN THE DARK MATTER BASED NATURE OF YOUR POWERS, THIS SHOULD BE SECOND NATURE TO YOU.
D-
K. NEFARIOUS
A SHAME THE APPLE FELL SO FAR FROM THE TREE.
BUT I STUDIED! HONEST, I DID.
MUMMY GIRL. FLAWLESS AS ALWAYS.
C+
REALLY, MARTY? YOU'RE PSYCHED ABOUT A C+?
I'M A SCIENCE VILLAIN! MYSTICAL ARTS IS ALL GIBBERISH TO ME--IT'S WORSE THAN READING SATURNESE! I'LL TAKE A C+ ANY DAY!
ARE YOU SERIOUS?

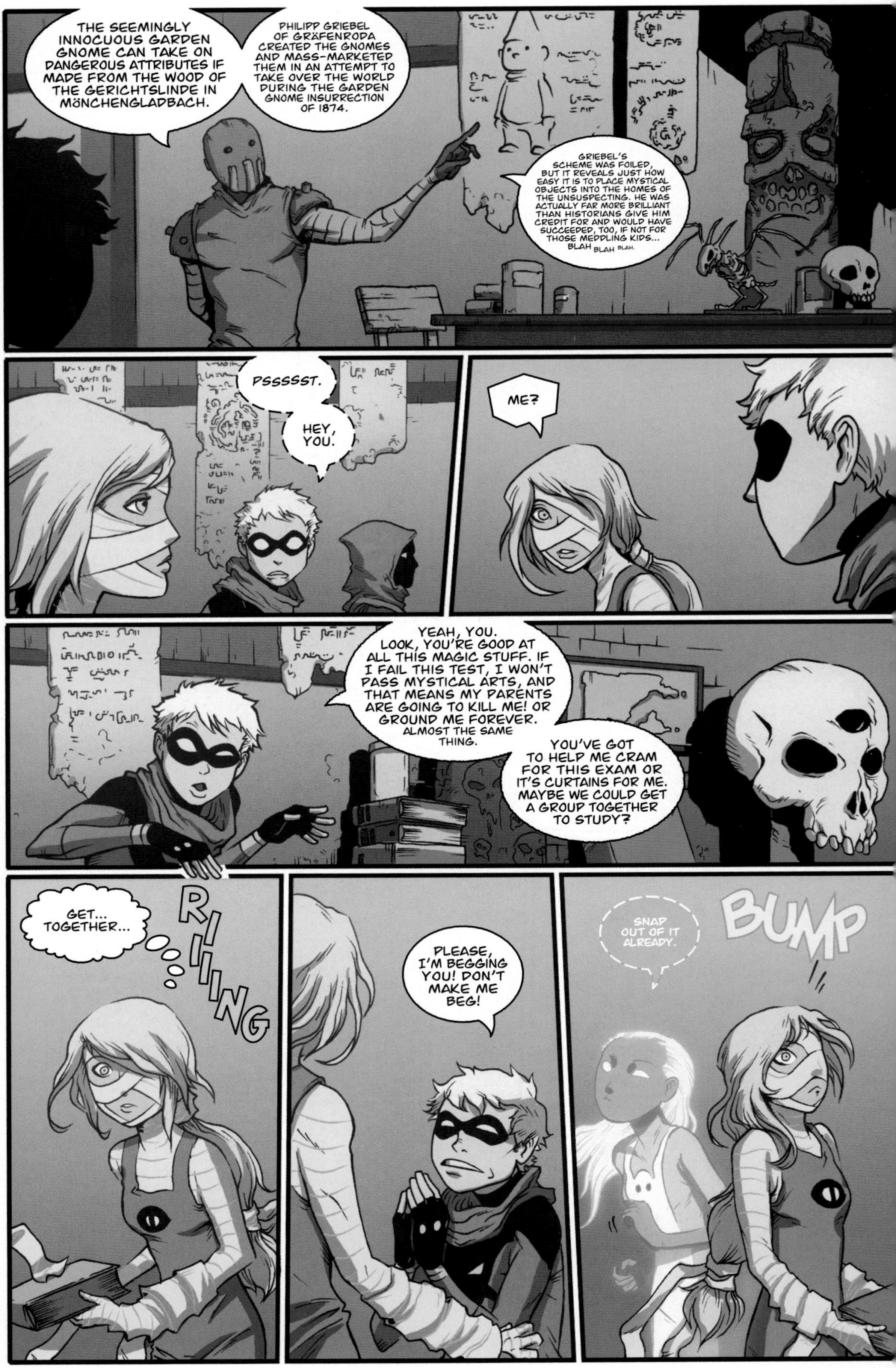
THE SEEMINGLY INNOCUOUS GARDEN GNOME CAN TAKE ON DANGEROUS ATTRIBUTES IF MADE FROM THE WOOD OF THE GERICHTSLINDE IN MÖNCHENGLADBACH.
PHILIPP GRIEBEL OF GRÄFENRODA CREATED THE GNOMES AND MASS-MARKETED THEM IN AN ATTEMPT TO TAKE OVER THE WORLD DURING THE GARDEN GNOME INSURRECTION OF 1874.
GRIEBEL'S SCHEME WAS FOILED, BUT IT REVEALS JUST HOW EASY IT IS TO PLACE MYSTICAL OBJECTS INTO THE HOMES OF THE UNSUSPECTING. HE WAS ACTUALLY FAR MORE BRILLIANT THAN HISTORIANS GIVE HIM CREDIT FOR AND WOULD HAVE SUCCEEDED, TOO, IF NOT FOR THOSE MEDDLING KIDS... BLAH BLAH BLAH.
PSSSSST.
HEY, YOU.
ME?
YEAH, YOU. LOOK, YOU'RE GOOD AT ALL THIS MAGIC STUFF. IF I FAIL THIS TEST, I WON'T PASS MYSTICAL ARTS, AND THAT MEANS MY PARENTS ARE GOING TO KILL ME! OR GROUND ME FOREVER. ALMOST THE SAME THING.
YOU'VE GOT TO HELP ME CRAM FOR THIS EXAM OR IT'S CURTAINS FOR ME. MAYBE WE COULD GET A GROUP TOGETHER TO STUDY?
GET... TOGETHER...
RIIIING
PLEASE, I'M BEGGING YOU! DON'T MAKE ME BEG!
SNAP OUT OF IT ALREADY.
BUMP

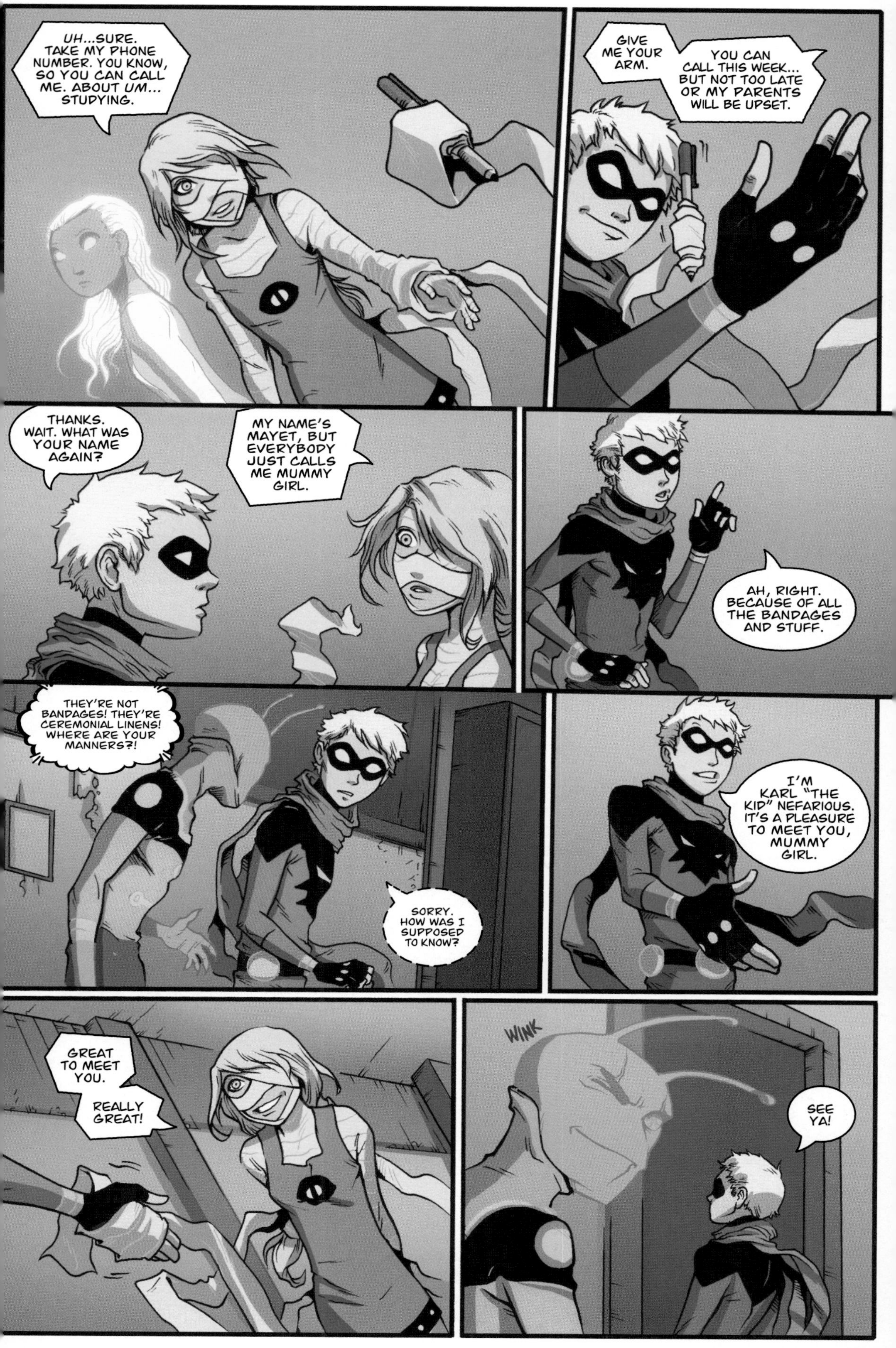
UH...SURE. TAKE MY PHONE NUMBER. YOU KNOW, SO YOU CAN CALL ME. ABOUT UM... STUDYING.
GIVE ME YOUR ARM.
YOU CAN CALL THIS WEEK... BUT NOT TOO LATE OR MY PARENTS WILL BE UPSET.
THANKS. WAIT. WHAT WAS YOUR NAME AGAIN?
MY NAME'S MAYET, BUT EVERYBODY JUST CALLS ME MUMMY GIRL.
AH, RIGHT. BECAUSE OF ALL THE BANDAGES AND STUFF.
THEY'RE NOT BANDAGES! THEY'RE CEREMONIAL LINENS! WHERE ARE YOUR MANNERS?!
SORRY. HOW WAS I SUPPOSED TO KNOW?
I'M KARL "THE KID" NEFARIOUS. IT'S A PLEASURE TO MEET YOU, MUMMY GIRL.
GREAT TO MEET YOU.
REALLY GREAT!
WINK
SEE YA!

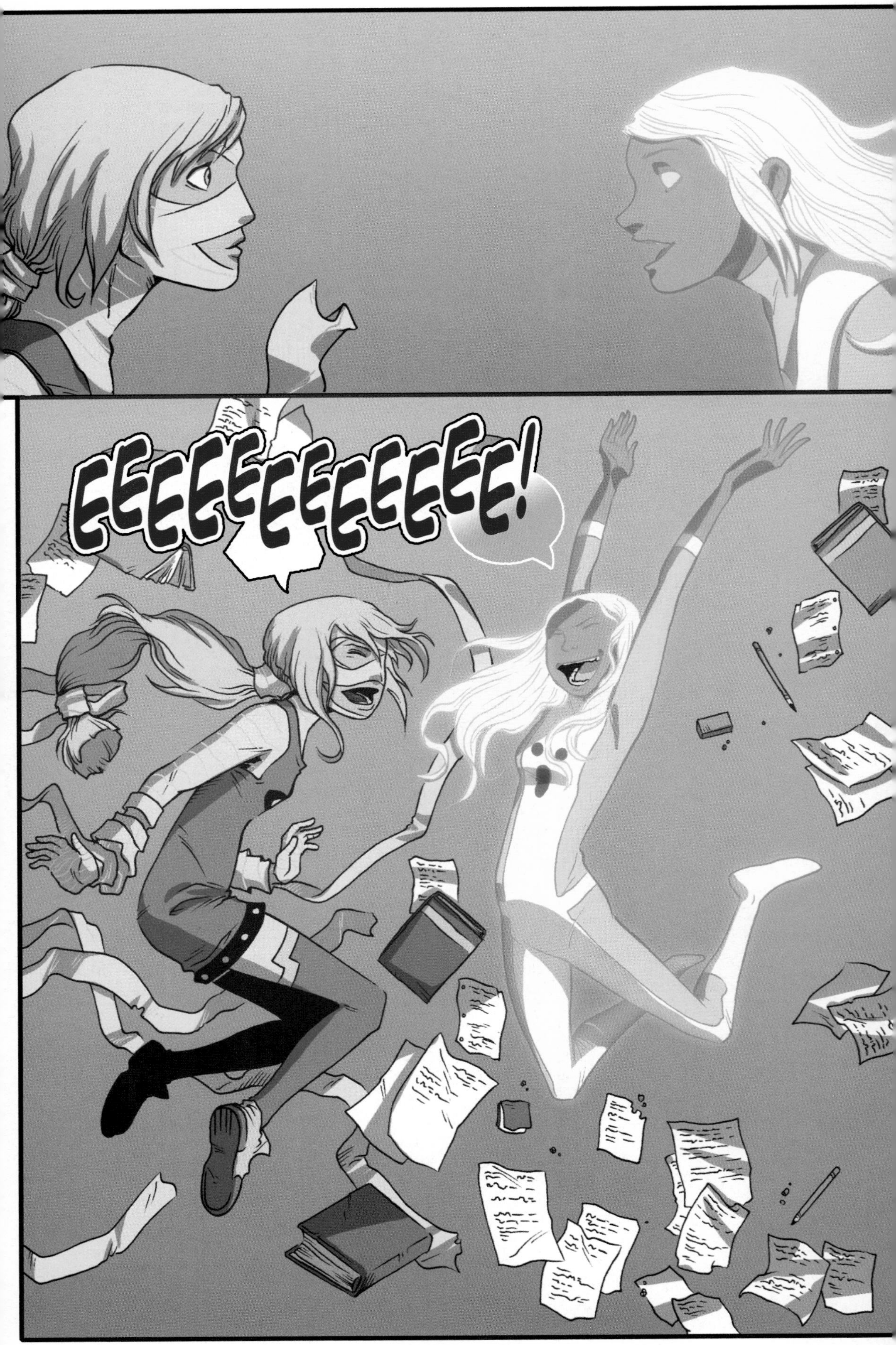
EEEEEEEEEEEE!

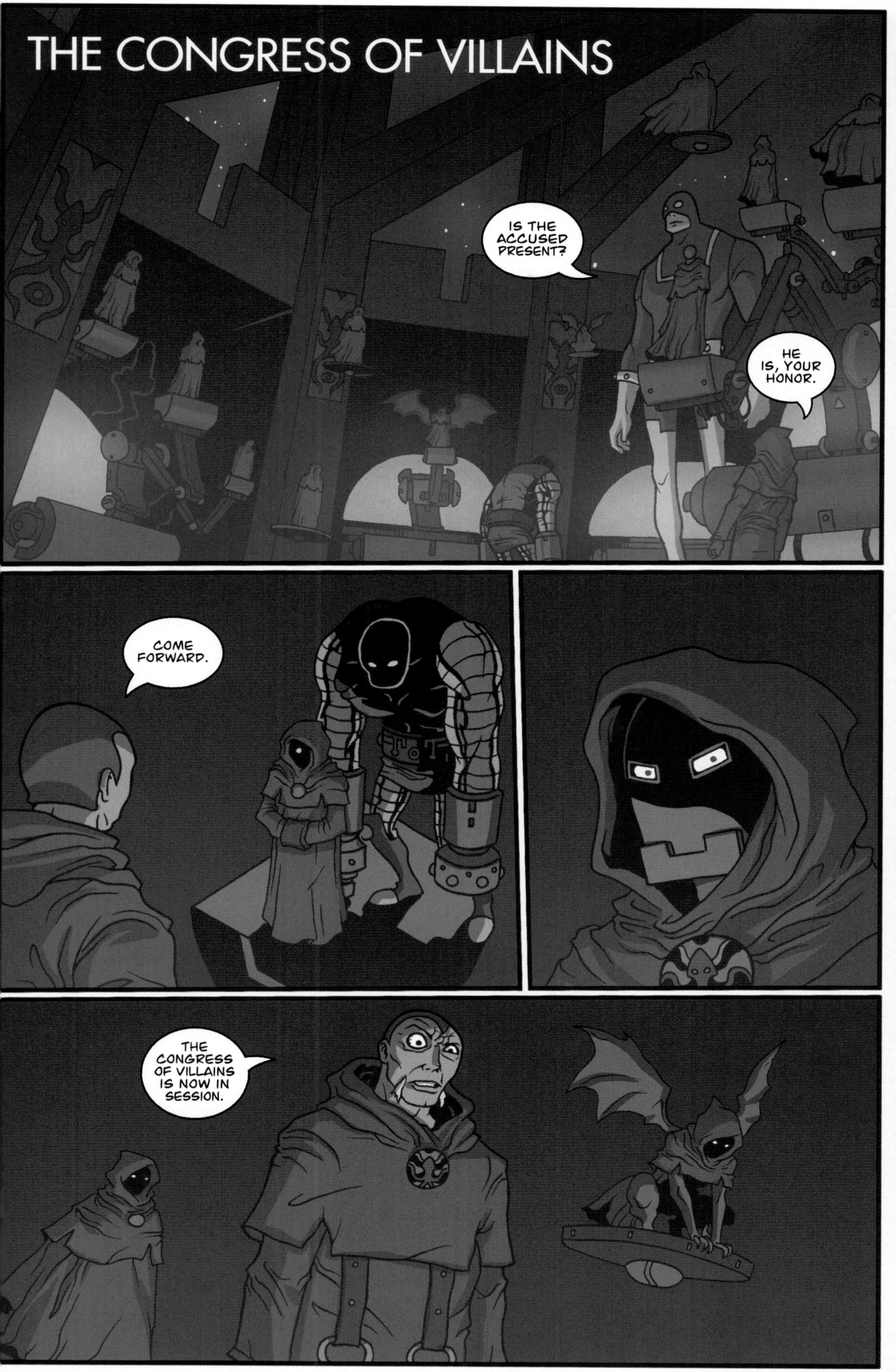
THE CONGRESS OF VILLAINS
IS THE ACCUSED PRESENT?
HE IS, YOUR HONOR.
COME FORWARD.
THE CONGRESS OF VILLAINS IS NOW IN SESSION.

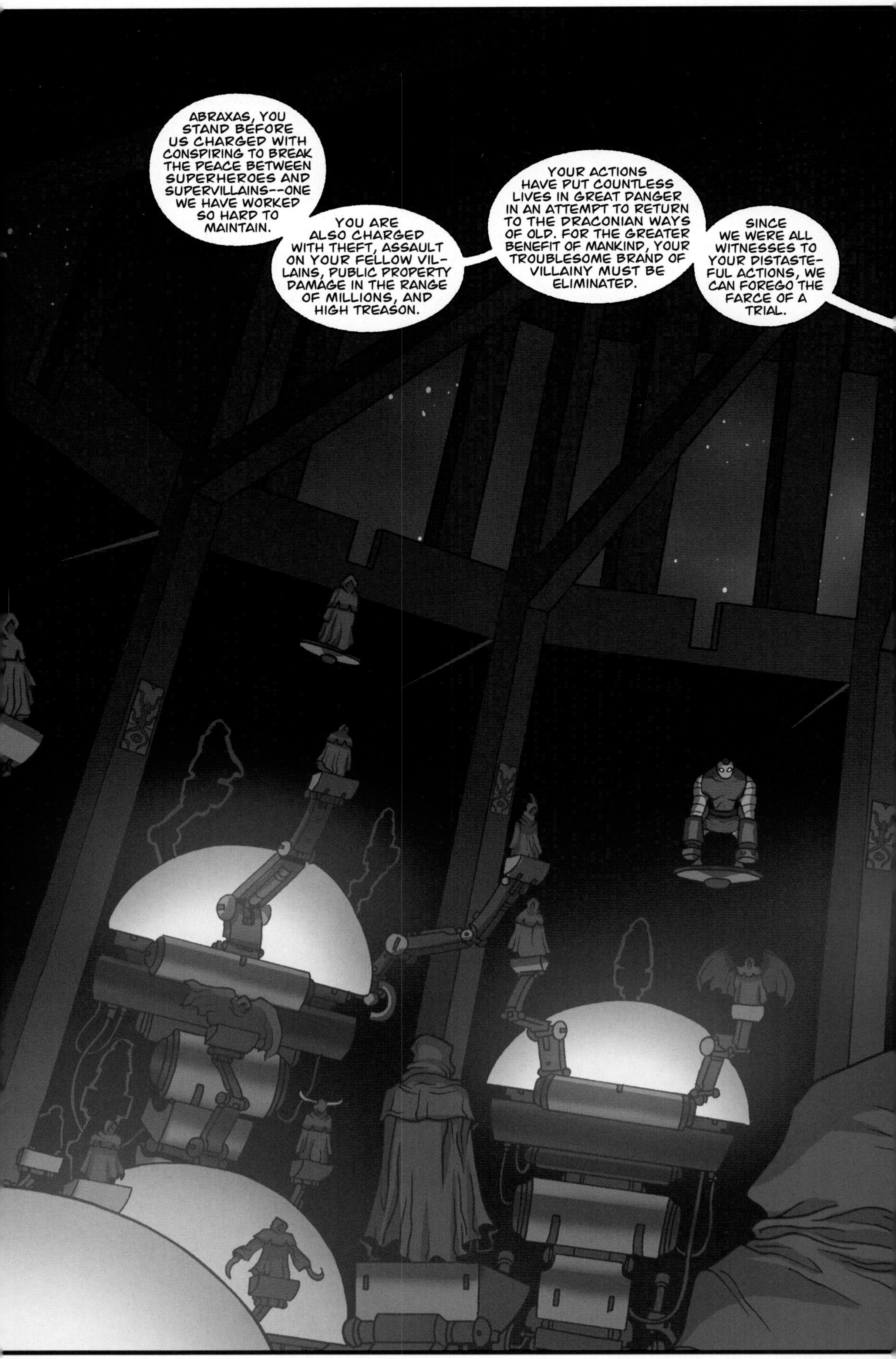
ABRAXAS, YOU STAND BEFORE US CHARGED WITH CONSPIRING TO BREAK THE PEACE BETWEEN SUPERHEROES AND SUPERVILLAINS--ONE WE HAVE WORKED SO HARD TO MAINTAIN.
YOU ARE ALSO CHARGED WITH THEFT, ASSAULT ON YOUR FELLOW VIL-LAINS, PUBLIC PROPERTY DAMAGE IN THE RANGE OF MILLIONS, AND HIGH TREASON.
YOUR ACTIONS HAVE PUT COUNTLESS LIVES IN GREAT DANGER IN AN ATTEMPT TO RETURN TO THE DRACONIAN WAYS OF OLD. FOR THE GREATER BENEFIT OF MANKIND, YOUR TROUBLESOME BRAND OF VILLAINY MUST BE ELIMINATED.
SINCE WE WERE ALL WITNESSES TO YOUR DISTASTE-FUL ACTIONS, WE CAN FOREGO THE FARCE OF A TRIAL.

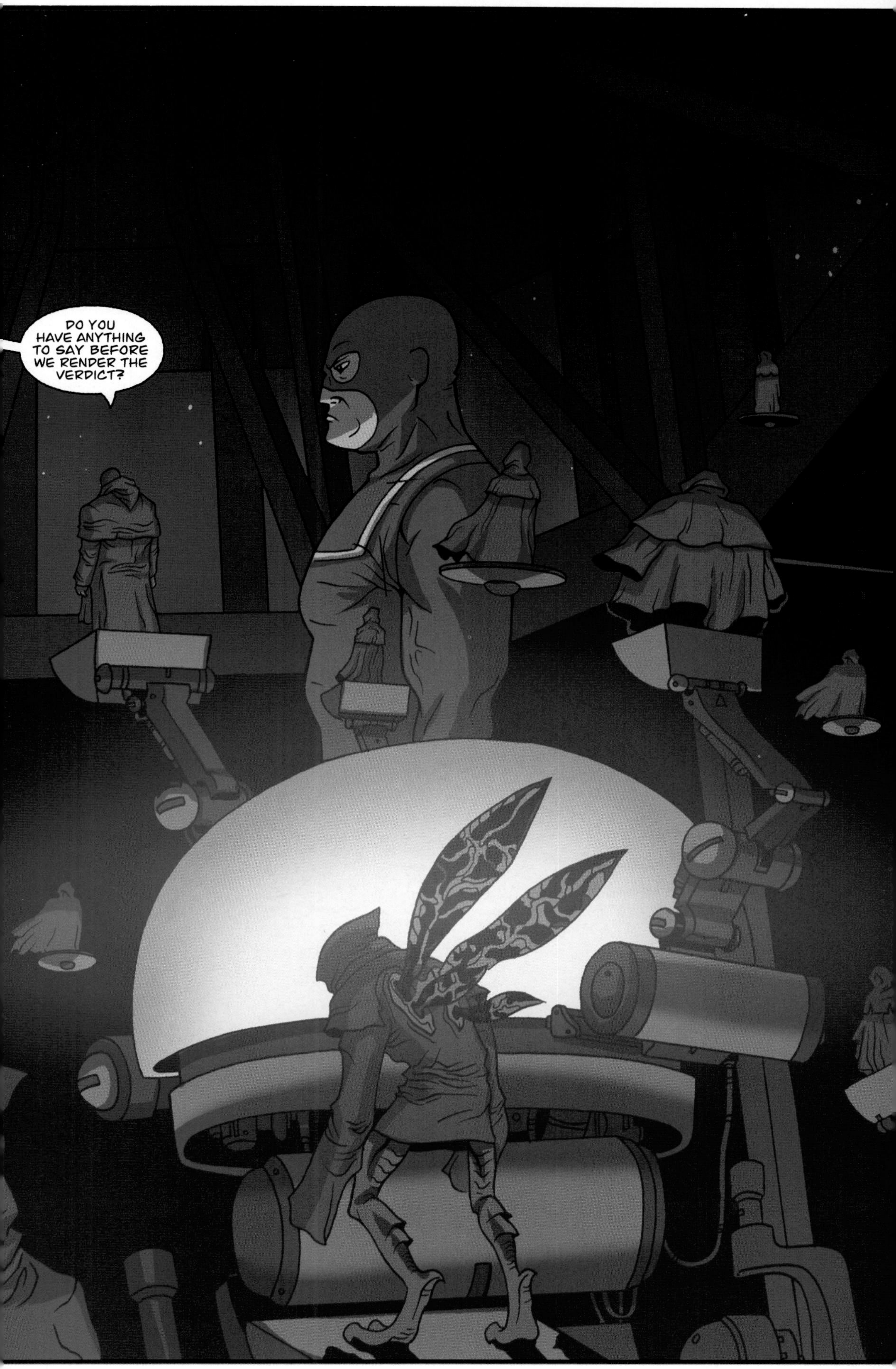
DO YOU HAVE ANYTHING TO SAY BEFORE WE RENDER THE VERDICT?

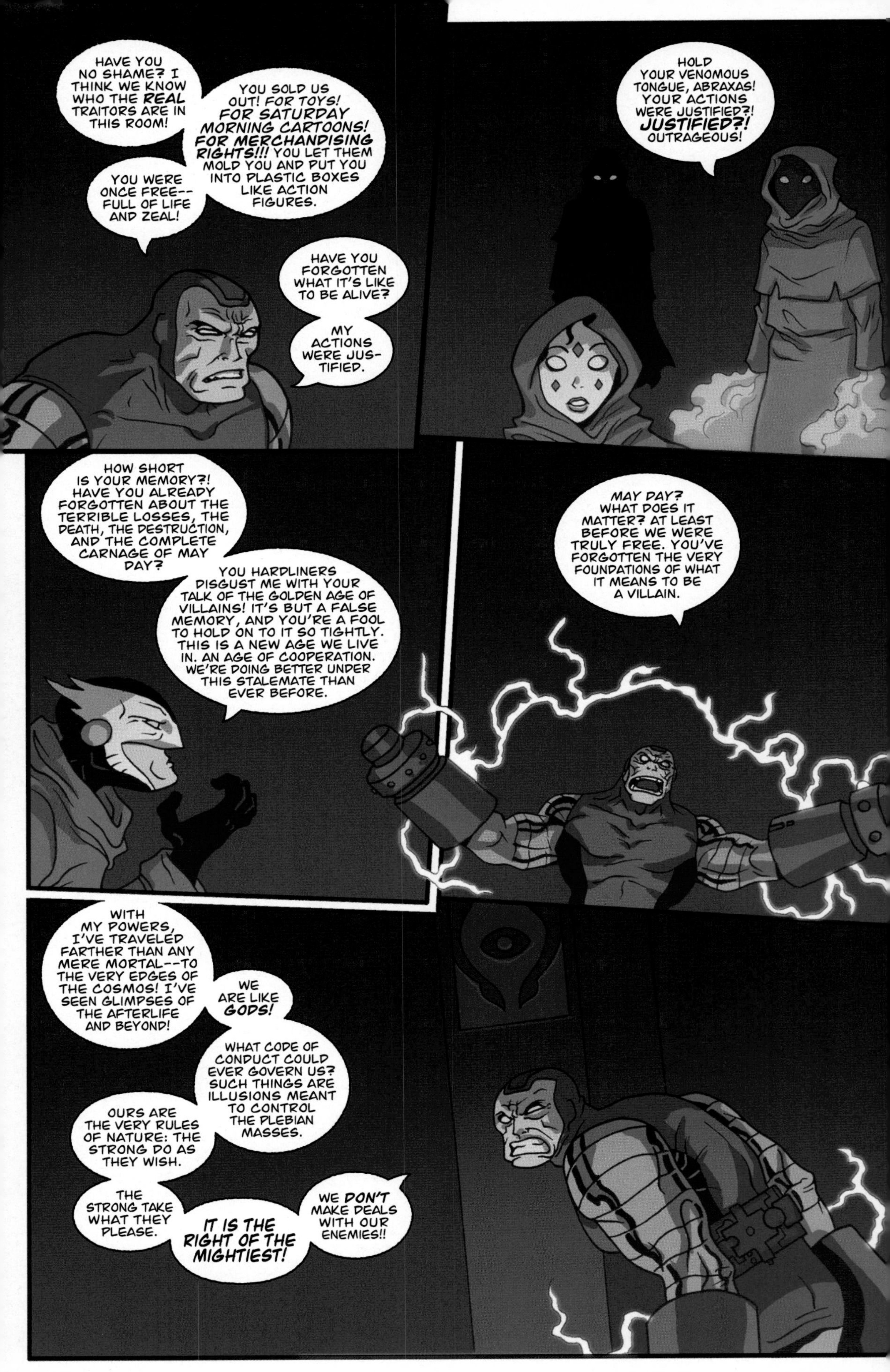

HAVE YOU NO SHAME? I THINK WE KNOW WHO THE REAL TRAITORS ARE IN THIS ROOM!
YOU SOLD US OUT! FOR TOYS! FOR SATURDAY MORNING CARTOONS! FOR MERCHANDISING RIGHTS!!! YOU LET THEM MOLD YOU AND PUT YOU INTO PLASTIC BOXES LIKE ACTION FIGURES.
YOU WERE ONCE FREE--FULL OF LIFE AND ZEAL!
HAVE YOU FORGOTTEN WHAT IT'S LIKE TO BE ALIVE?
MY ACTIONS WERE JUSTIFIED.
HOLD YOUR VENOMOUS TONGUE, ABRAXAS! YOUR ACTIONS WERE JUSTIFIED?! JUSTIFIED?! OUTRAGEOUS!
HOW SHORT IS YOUR MEMORY?! HAVE YOU ALREADY FORGOTTEN ABOUT THE TERRIBLE LOSSES, THE DEATH, THE DESTRUCTION, AND THE COMPLETE CARNAGE OF MAY DAY?
YOU HARDLINERS DISGUST ME WITH YOUR TALK OF THE GOLDEN AGE OF VILLAINS! IT'S BUT A FALSE MEMORY, AND YOU'RE A FOOL TO HOLD ON TO IT SO TIGHTLY. THIS IS A NEW AGE WE LIVE IN. AN AGE OF COOPERATION. WE'RE DOING BETTER UNDER THIS STALEMATE THAN EVER BEFORE.
MAY DAY? WHAT DOES IT MATTER? AT LEAST BEFORE WE WERE TRULY FREE. YOU'VE FORGOTTEN THE VERY FOUNDATIONS OF WHAT IT MEANS TO BE A VILLAIN.
WITH MY POWERS, I'VE TRAVELED FARTHER THAN ANY MERE MORTAL--TO THE VERY EDGES OF THE COSMOS! I'VE SEEN GLIMPSES OF THE AFTERLIFE AND BEYOND!
WE ARE LIKE GODS!
WHAT CODE OF CONDUCT COULD EVER GOVERN US? SUCH THINGS ARE ILLUSIONS MEANT TO CONTROL THE PLEBIAN MASSES.
OURS ARE THE VERY RULES OF NATURE: THE STRONG DO AS THEY WISH.
THE STRONG TAKE WHAT THEY PLEASE.
IT IS THE RIGHT OF THE MIGHTIEST!
WE DON'T MAKE DEALS WITH OUR ENEMIES!!

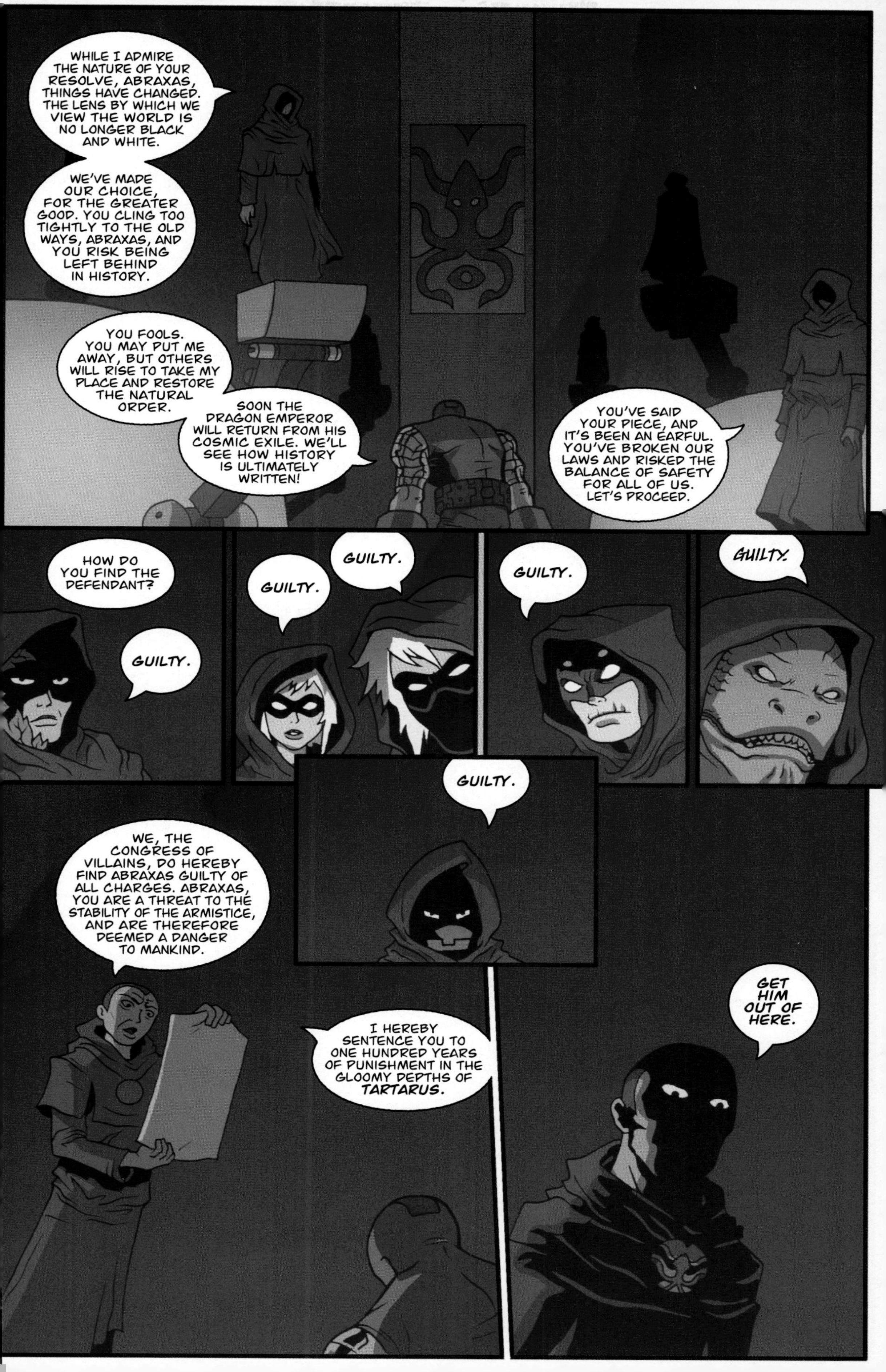
WHILE I ADMIRE THE NATURE OF YOUR RESOLVE, ABRAXAS, THINGS HAVE CHANGED. THE LENS BY WHICH WE VIEW THE WORLD IS NO LONGER BLACK AND WHITE.
WE'VE MADE OUR CHOICE, FOR THE GREATER GOOD. YOU CLING TOO TIGHTLY TO THE OLD WAYS, ABRAXAS, AND YOU RISK BEING LEFT BEHIND IN HISTORY.
YOU FOOLS. YOU MAY PUT ME AWAY, BUT OTHERS WILL RISE TO TAKE MY PLACE AND RESTORE THE NATURAL ORDER.
SOON THE DRAGON EMPEROR WILL RETURN FROM HIS COSMIC EXILE. WE'LL SEE HOW HISTORY IS ULTIMATELY WRITTEN!
YOU'VE SAID YOUR PIECE, AND IT'S BEEN AN EARFUL. YOU'VE BROKEN OUR LAWS AND RISKED THE BALANCE OF SAFETY FOR ALL OF US. LET'S PROCEED.
HOW DO YOU FIND THE DEFENDANT?
GUILTY.
GUILTY.
GUILTY.
GUILTY.
GUILTY.
GUILTY.
WE, THE CONGRESS OF VILLAINS, DO HEREBY FIND ABRAXAS GUILTY OF ALL CHARGES. ABRAXAS, YOU ARE A THREAT TO THE STABILITY OF THE ARMISTICE, AND ARE THEREFORE DEEMED A DANGER TO MANKIND.
I HEREBY SENTENCE YOU TO ONE HUNDRED YEARS OF PUNISHMENT IN THE GLOOMY DEPTHS OF TARTARUS.
GET HIM OUT OF HERE.

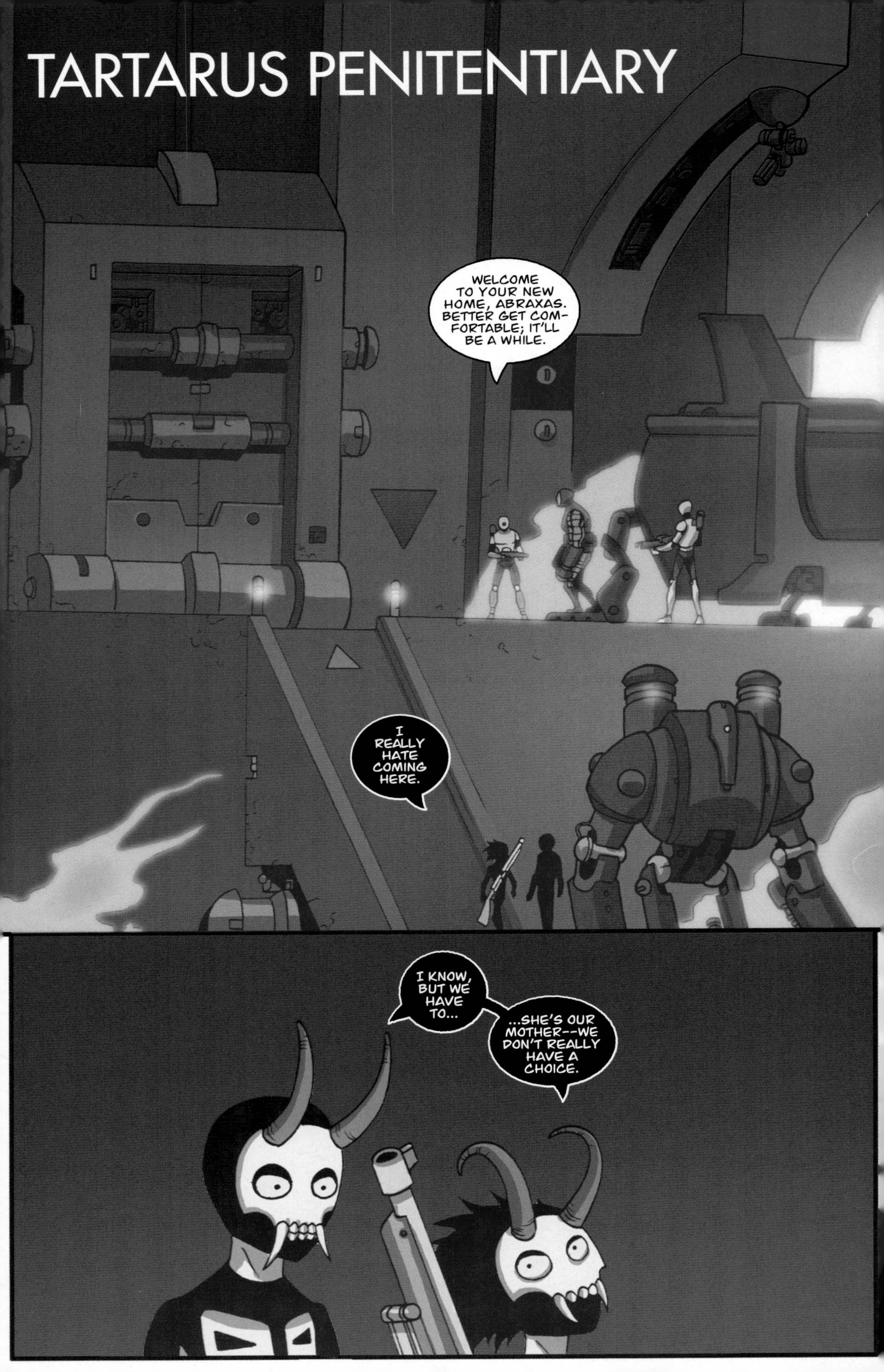
TARTARUS PENITENTIARY
WELCOME TO YOUR NEW HOME, ABRAXAS. BETTER GET COM-FORTABLE; IT'LL BE A WHILE.
I REALLY HATE COMING HERE.
I KNOW, BUT WE HAVE TO...
...SHE'S OUR MOTHER--WE DON'T REALLY HAVE A CHOICE.

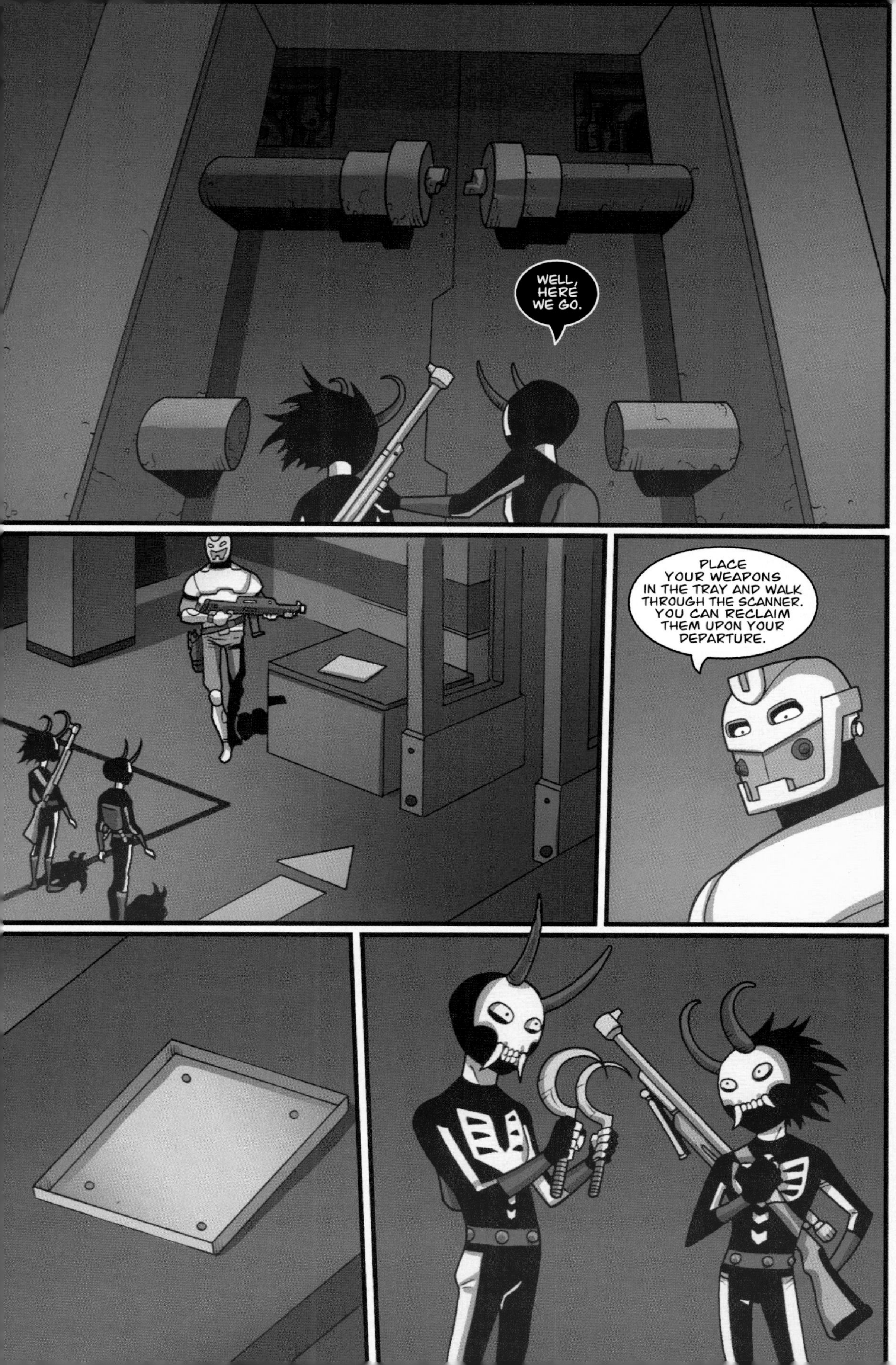
WELL, HERE WE GO.
PLACE YOUR WEAPONS IN THE TRAY AND WALK THROUGH THE SCANNER. YOU CAN RECLAIM THEM UPON YOUR DEPARTURE.

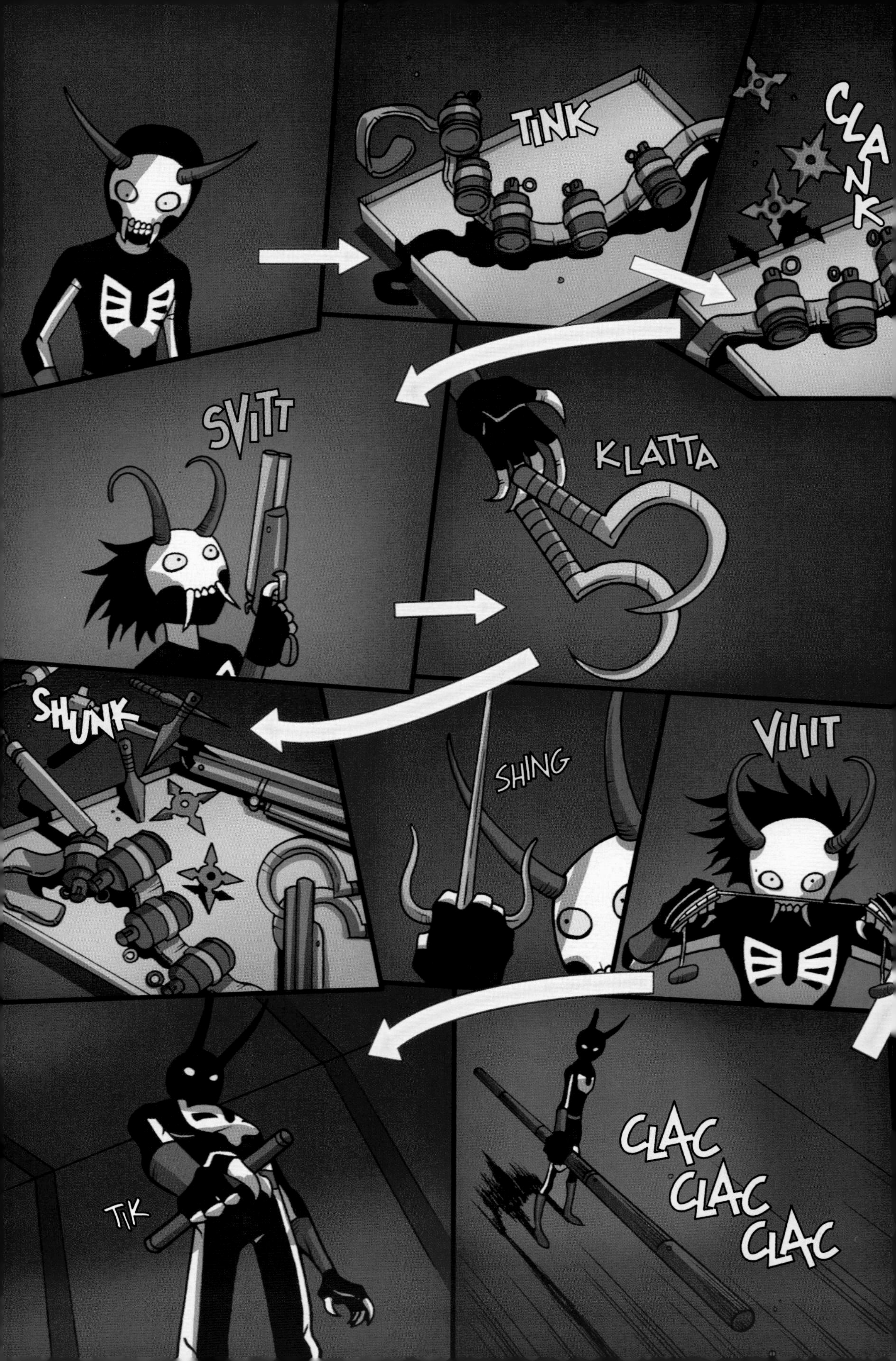
TINK
CLANK
SVITT
KLATTA
SHUNK
SHING
VIIIIT
TIK
CLAC
CLAC
CLAC

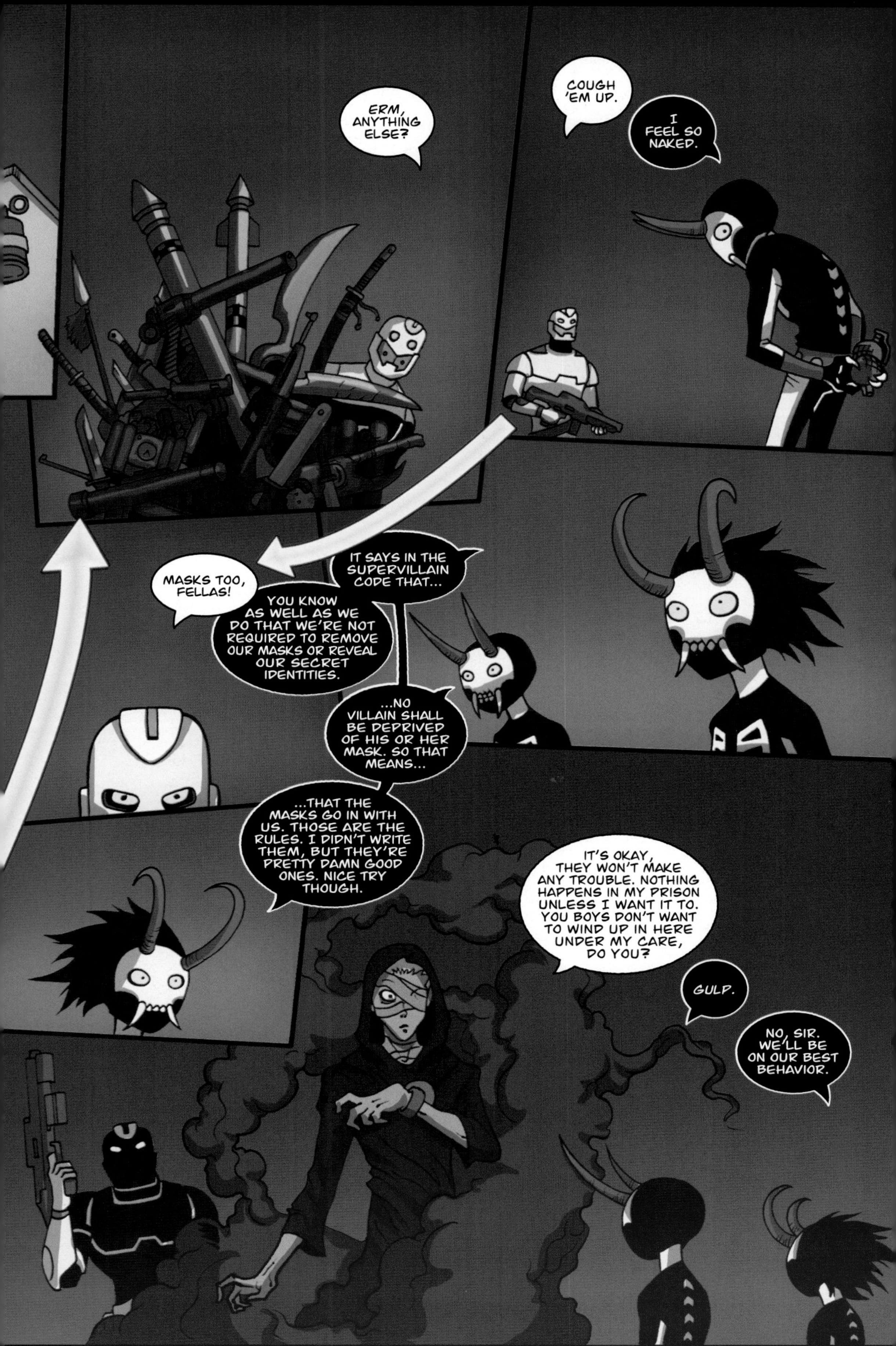
ERM, ANYTHING ELSE?
COUGH 'EM UP.
I FEEL SO NAKED.
MASKS TOO, FELLAS!
IT SAYS IN THE SUPERVILLAIN CODE THAT...
YOU KNOW AS WELL AS WE DO THAT WE'RE NOT REQUIRED TO REMOVE OUR MASKS OR REVEAL OUR SECRET IDENTITIES.
...NO VILLAIN SHALL BE DEPRIVED OF HIS OR HER MASK. SO THAT MEANS...
...THAT THE MASKS GO IN WITH US. THOSE ARE THE RULES. I DIDN'T WRITE THEM, BUT THEY'RE PRETTY DAMN GOOD ONES. NICE TRY THOUGH.
IT'S OKAY, THEY WON'T MAKE ANY TROUBLE. NOTHING HAPPENS IN MY PRISON UNLESS I WANT IT TO. YOU BOYS DON'T WANT TO WIND UP IN HERE UNDER MY CARE, DO YOU?
GULP.
NO, SIR. WE'LL BE ON OUR BEST BEHAVIOR.

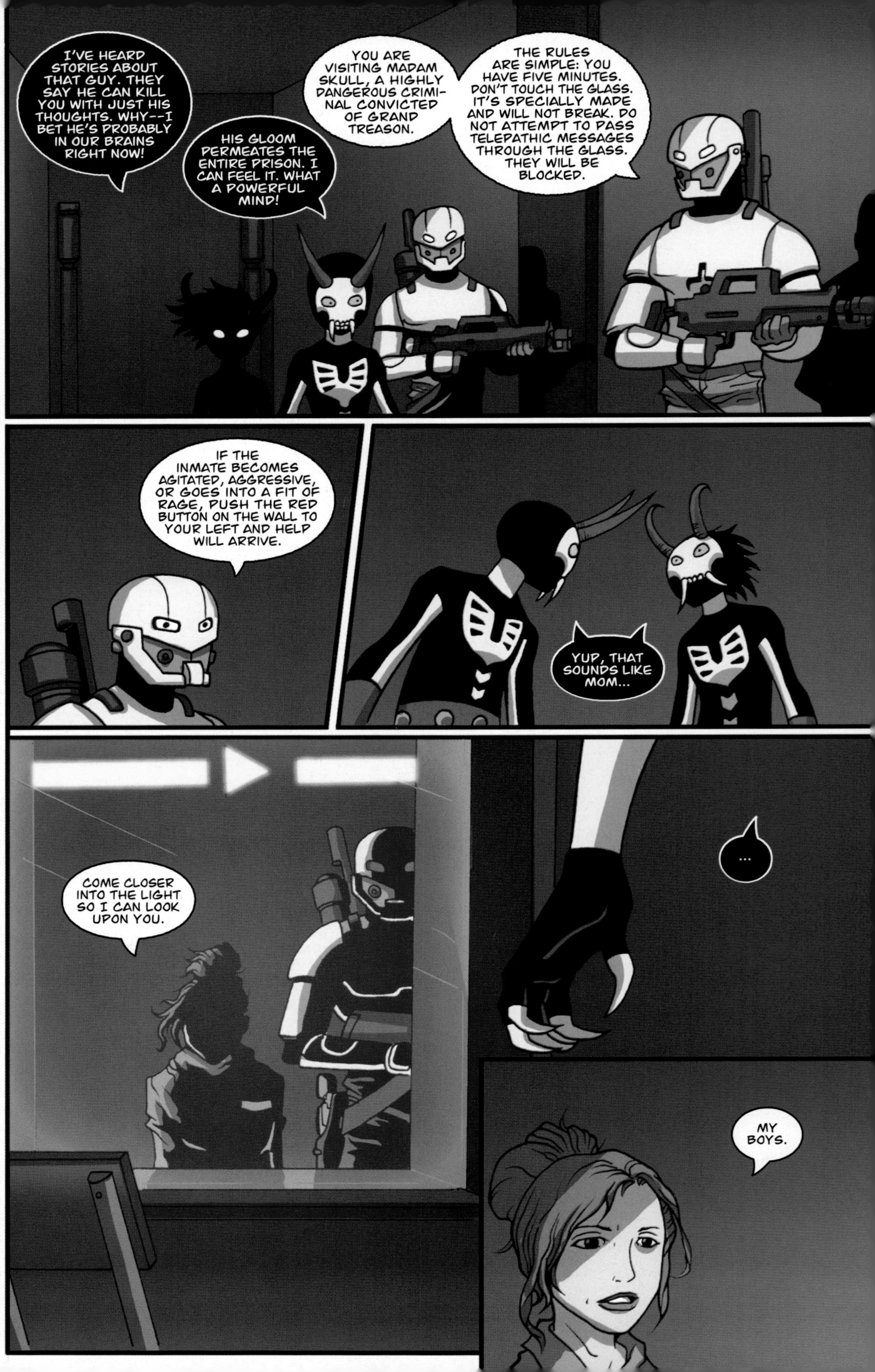
I'VE HEARD STORIES ABOUT THAT GUY. THEY SAY HE CAN KILL YOU WITH JUST HIS THOUGHTS. WHY--I BET HE'S PROBABLY IN OUR BRAINS RIGHT NOW!
HIS GLOOM PERMEATES THE ENTIRE PRISON. I CAN FEEL IT. WHAT A POWERFUL MIND!
YOU ARE VISITING MADAM SKULL, A HIGHLY DANGEROUS CRIMINAL CONVICTED OF GRAND TREASON.
THE RULES ARE SIMPLE: YOU HAVE FIVE MINUTES. DON'T TOUCH THE GLASS. IT'S SPECIALLY MADE AND WILL NOT BREAK. DO NOT ATTEMPT TO PASS TELEPATHIC MESSAGES THROUGH THE GLASS. THEY WILL BE BLOCKED.
IF THE INMATE BECOMES AGITATED, AGGRESSIVE, OR GOES INTO A FIT OF RAGE, PUSH THE RED BUTTON ON THE WALL TO YOUR LEFT AND HELP WILL ARRIVE.
YUP, THAT SOUNDS LIKE MOM...
COME CLOSER INTO THE LIGHT SO I CAN LOOK UPON YOU.
...
MY BOYS.

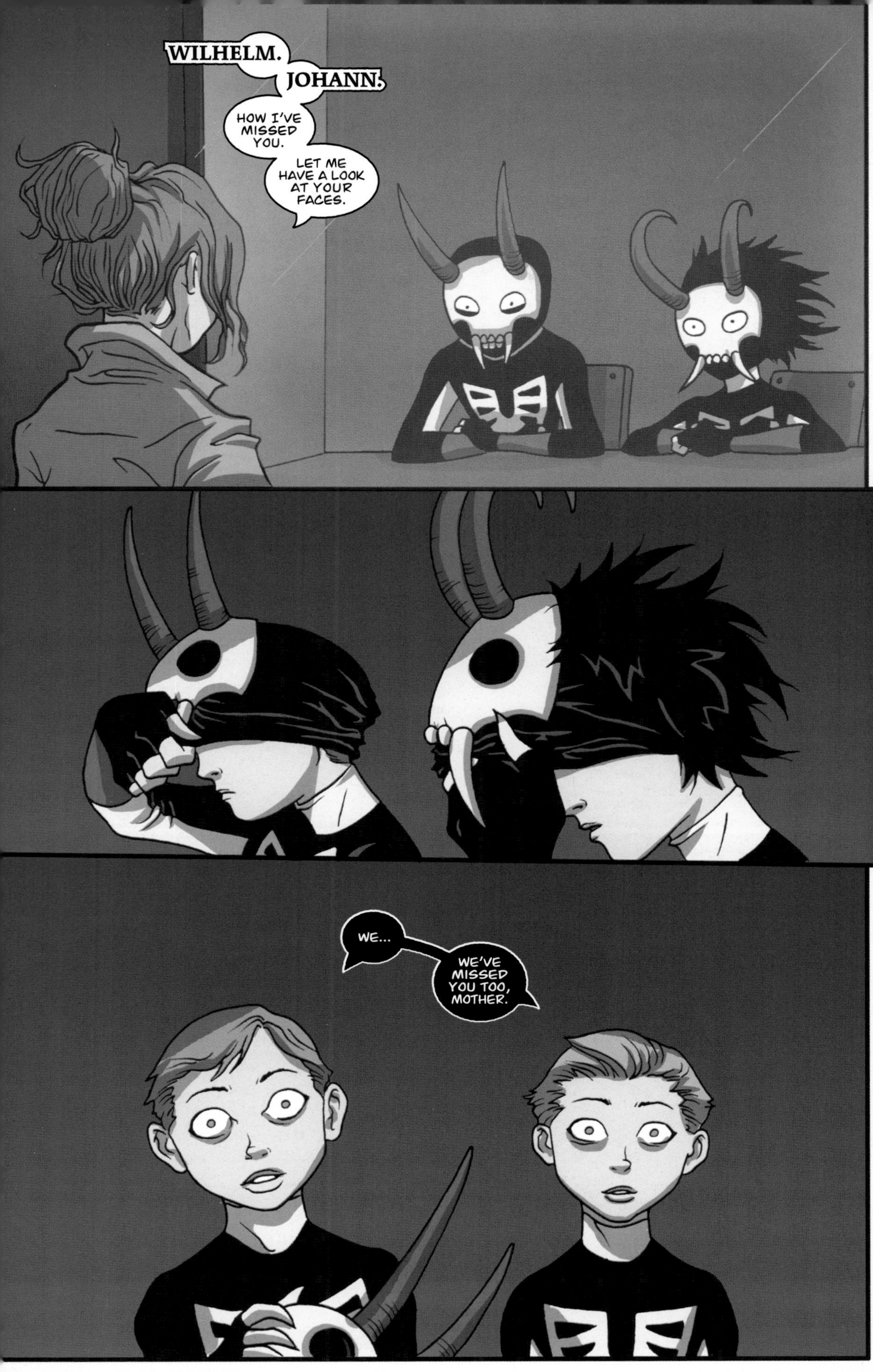
WILHELM.
JOHANN.
HOW I'VE MISSED YOU.
LET ME HAVE A LOOK AT YOUR FACES.
WE...
WE'VE MISSED YOU TOO, MOTHER.

YOU'RE BOTH SO HANDSOME, JUST LIKE YOUR FATHER. LOOKING AT YOUR FACES MAKES ME SAD--BECAUSE WHEN I LOOK AT YOU, I THINK OF HIM, AND I'M REMINDED OF WHAT HAS BECOME OF OUR FAMILY.

TO PROTECT THEIR YOUNG, THE CONGRESS OF VILLAINS DECIDED THAT NO CHILD SHOULD KNOW OF THE ARMISTICE ARRANGEMENT UNTIL THEY TURNED SEVENTEEN.

GIVEN OUR FAMILY'S LONG AND COMPLICATED HISTORY, THAT'S JUST NOT POSSIBLE FOR US.

I WISH YOU COULD BE LIKE NORMAL CHILDREN YOUR AGE. YOU'VE HAD TO GROW UP SO FAST.

I KNOW THIS KNOWLEDGE AND OUR FAMILY SECRET IS SUCH A HUGE BURDEN FOR YOU TO BEAR.

THEY TOLD US YOU COULD LEAVE ANY TIME. THEY SAID YOU JUST HAVE TO AGREE TO CHANGE YOUR WAYS. YOU ONLY HAVE TO SIGN THE ARMISTICE AND THEY'LL LET YOU OUT OF THIS PLACE.

YOU SHOULD JUST LIE, LIKE SO MANY OTHERS HAVE. THEN YOU CAN COME HOME WITH US!

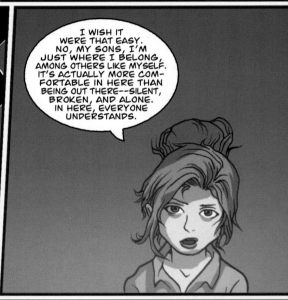

I WISH IT WERE THAT EASY. NO, MY SONS, I'M JUST WHERE I BELONG, AMONG OTHERS LIKE MYSELF. IT'S ACTUALLY MORE COMFORTABLE IN HERE THAN BEING OUT THERE--SILENT, BROKEN, AND ALONE. IN HERE, EVERYONE UNDERSTANDS.

AFTER THEY TOOK YOUR FATHER FROM US--HOW COULD I EVER FORGIVE THEM FOR THAT? THEY MADE A DEAL WITH THOSE...DOGS....THOSE... *SUPERHEROES* AND ACTED LIKE OUR LOSSES NEVER HAPPENED. LIKE YOUR FATHER'S DEATH...NO, HIS *MURDER*...NEVER HAPPENED.

I WILL *NEVER* SIGN THAT AGREEMENT. THOSE TURNCOATS AND SCAVENGERS MURDERED YOUR FATHER AND RIPPED OUR FAMILY APART! WOLFGANG SKULL'S BLOOD AND SO MUCH MORE IS ON THE HANDS OF THOSE HEROES...AND ON THOSE SO-CALLED VILLAINS.

I WILL NOT SOIL YOUR FATHER'S MEMORY OR GIVE THESE DOGS THE SATISFACTION. THE EVENTS OF MAY DAY WERE A GRAVE INJUSTICE, AND ONE DAY THEY'LL ALL BURN FOR IT.

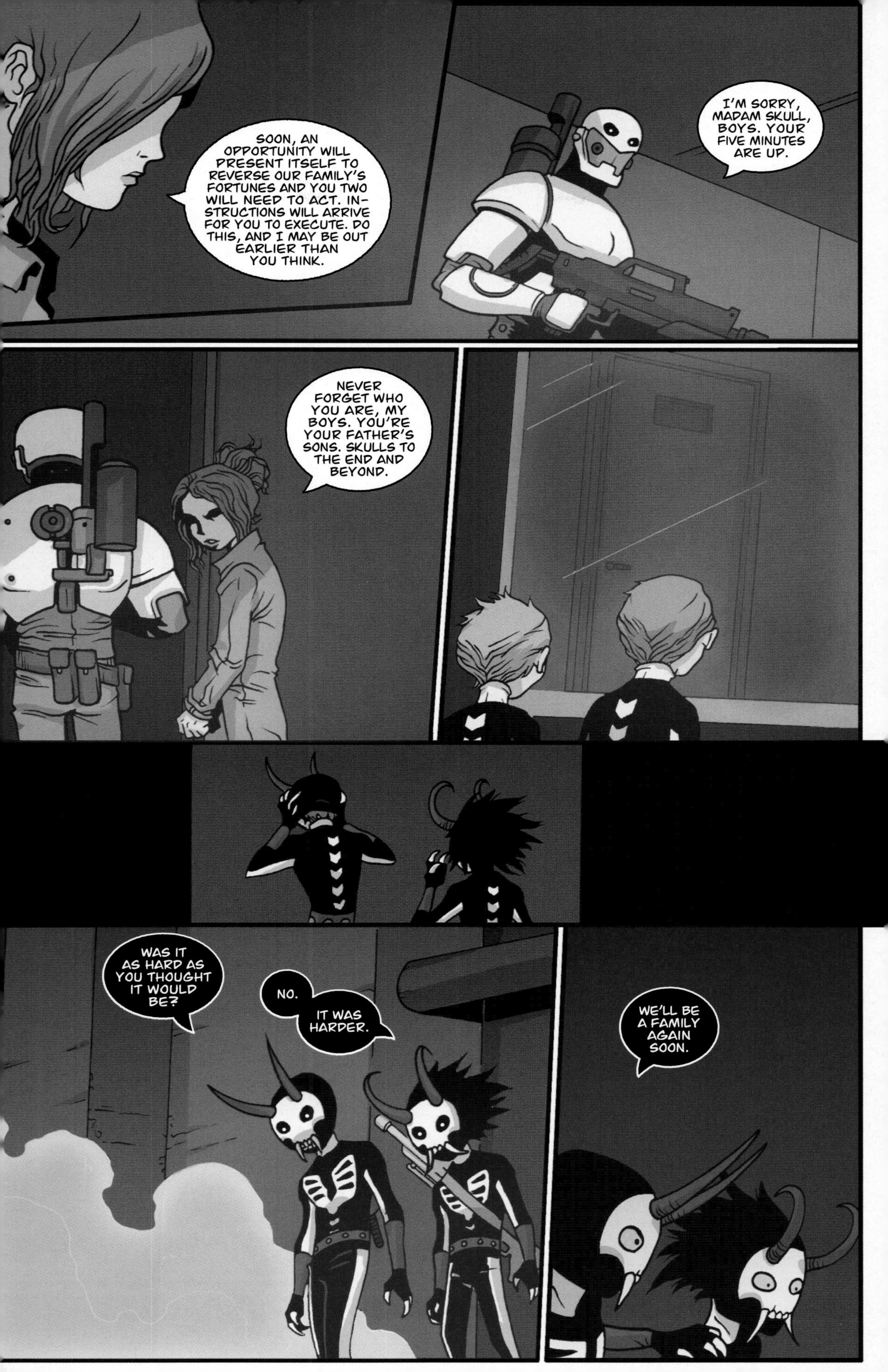
SOON, AN OPPORTUNITY WILL PRESENT ITSELF TO REVERSE OUR FAMILY'S FORTUNES AND YOU TWO WILL NEED TO ACT. INSTRUCTIONS WILL ARRIVE FOR YOU TO EXECUTE. DO THIS, AND I MAY BE OUT EARLIER THAN YOU THINK.
I'M SORRY, MADAM SKULL, BOYS. YOUR FIVE MINUTES ARE UP.
NEVER FORGET WHO YOU ARE, MY BOYS. YOU'RE YOUR FATHER'S SONS. SKULLS TO THE END AND BEYOND.
WAS IT AS HARD AS YOU THOUGHT IT WOULD BE?
NO.
IT WAS HARDER.
WE'LL BE A FAMILY AGAIN SOON.

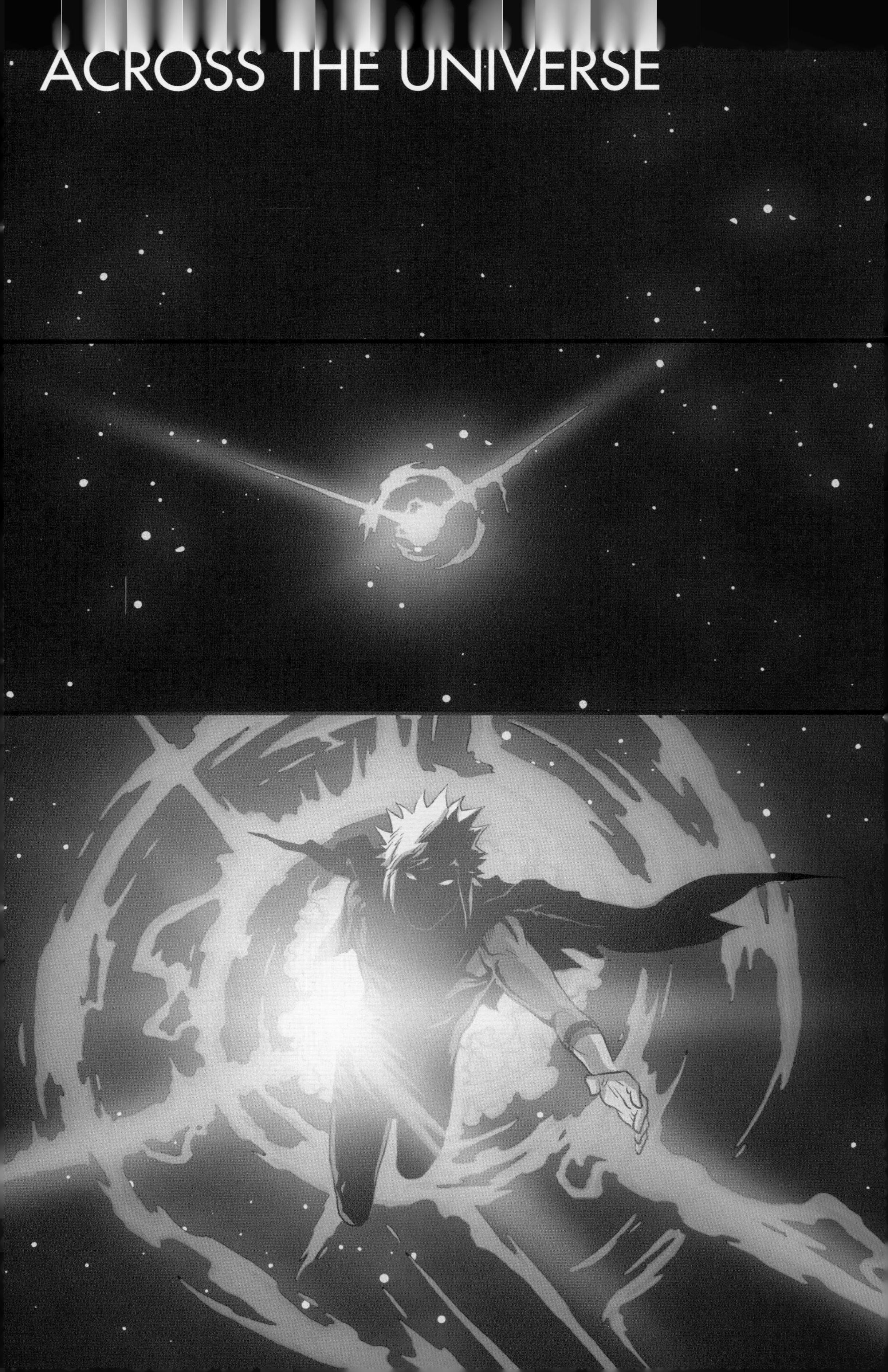
ACROSS THE UNIVERSE

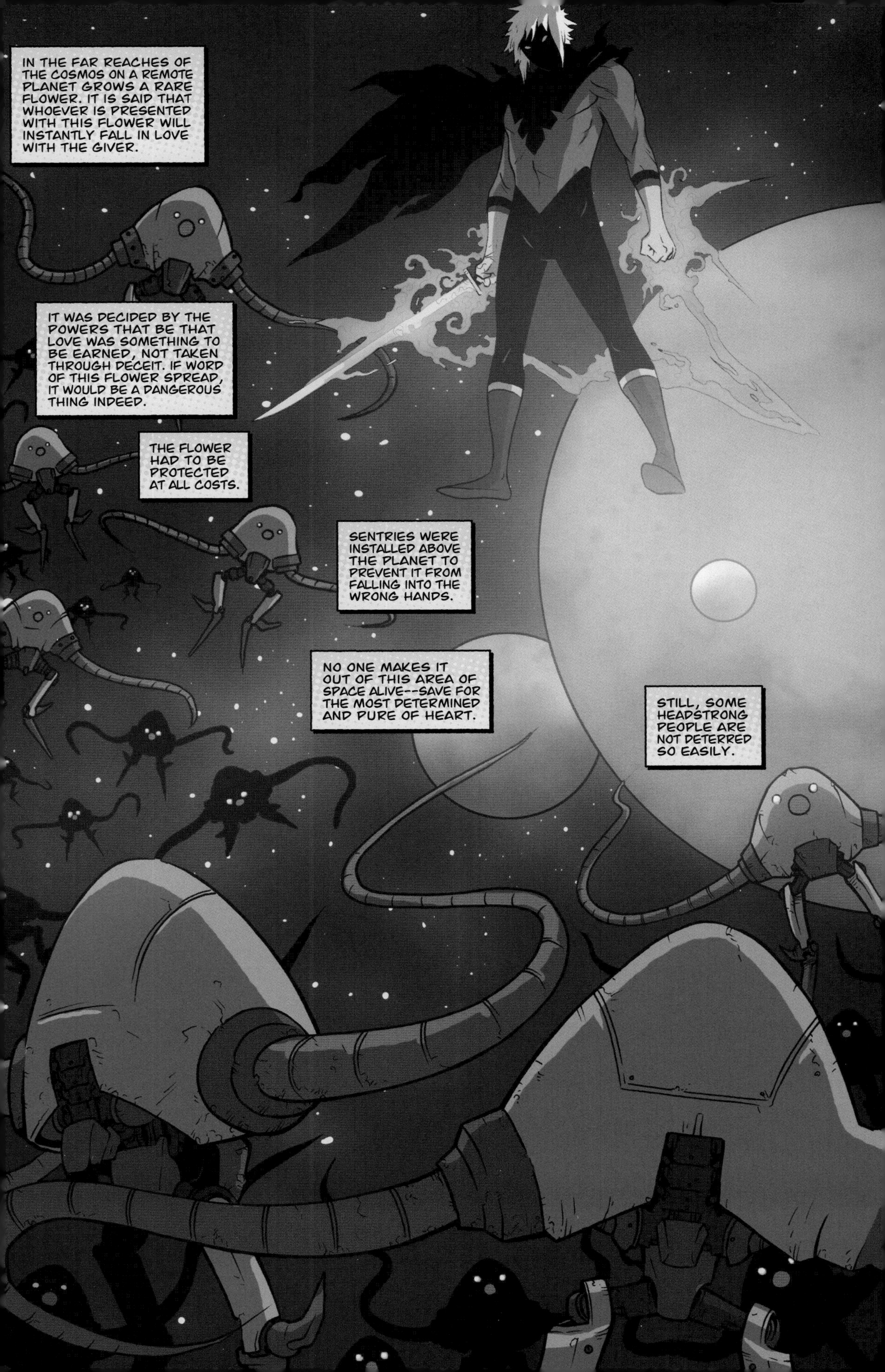
IN THE FAR REACHES OF THE COSMOS ON A REMOTE PLANET GROWS A RARE FLOWER. IT IS SAID THAT WHOEVER IS PRESENTED WITH THIS FLOWER WILL INSTANTLY FALL IN LOVE WITH THE GIVER.
IT WAS DECIDED BY THE POWERS THAT BE THAT LOVE WAS SOMETHING TO BE EARNED, NOT TAKEN THROUGH DECEIT. IF WORD OF THIS FLOWER SPREAD, IT WOULD BE A DANGEROUS THING INDEED.
THE FLOWER HAD TO BE PROTECTED AT ALL COSTS.
SENTRIES WERE INSTALLED ABOVE THE PLANET TO PREVENT IT FROM FALLING INTO THE WRONG HANDS.
NO ONE MAKES IT OUT OF THIS AREA OF SPACE ALIVE--SAVE FOR THE MOST DETERMINED AND PURE OF HEART.
STILL, SOME HEADSTRONG PEOPLE ARE NOT DETERRED SO EASILY.

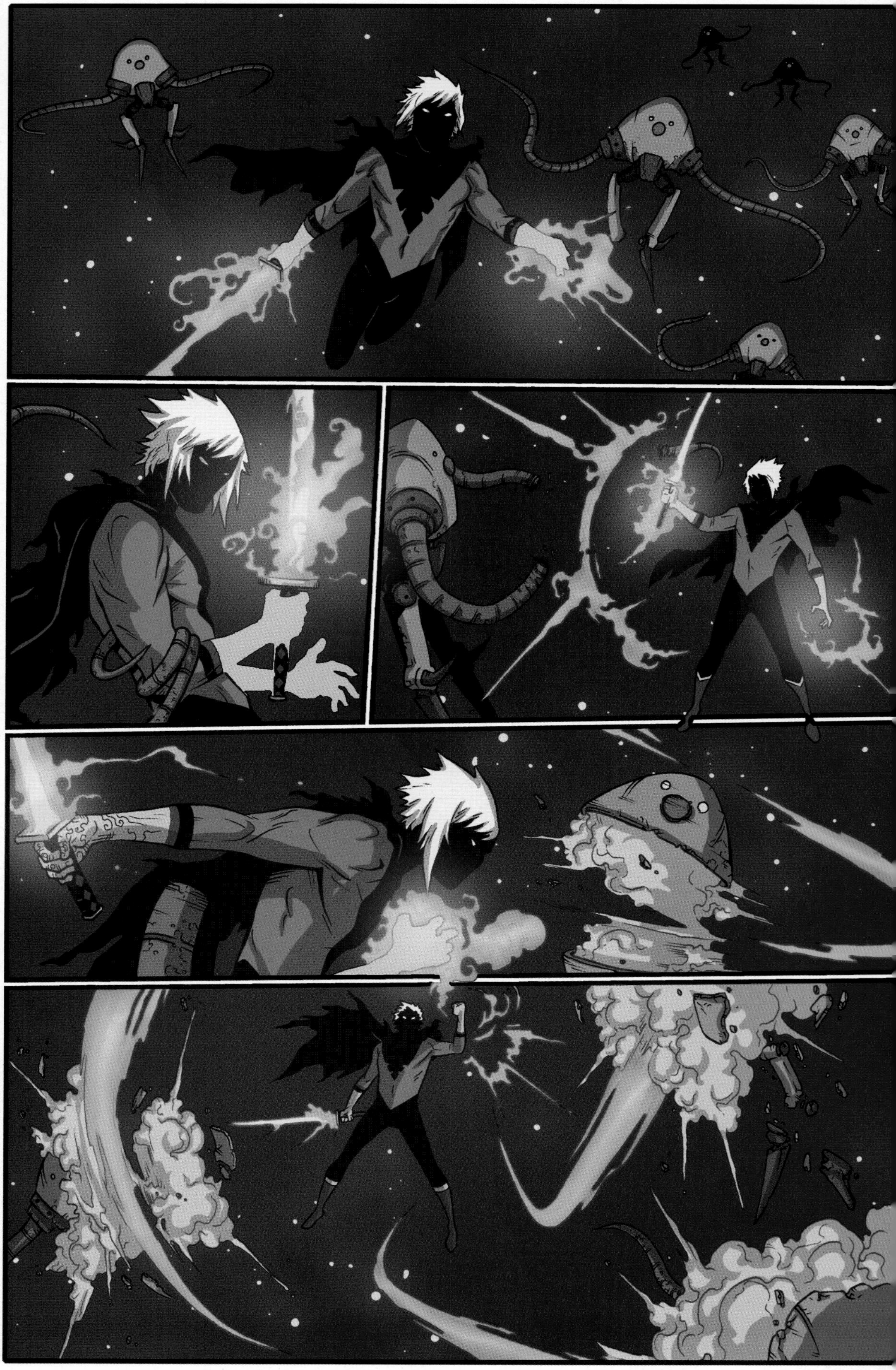

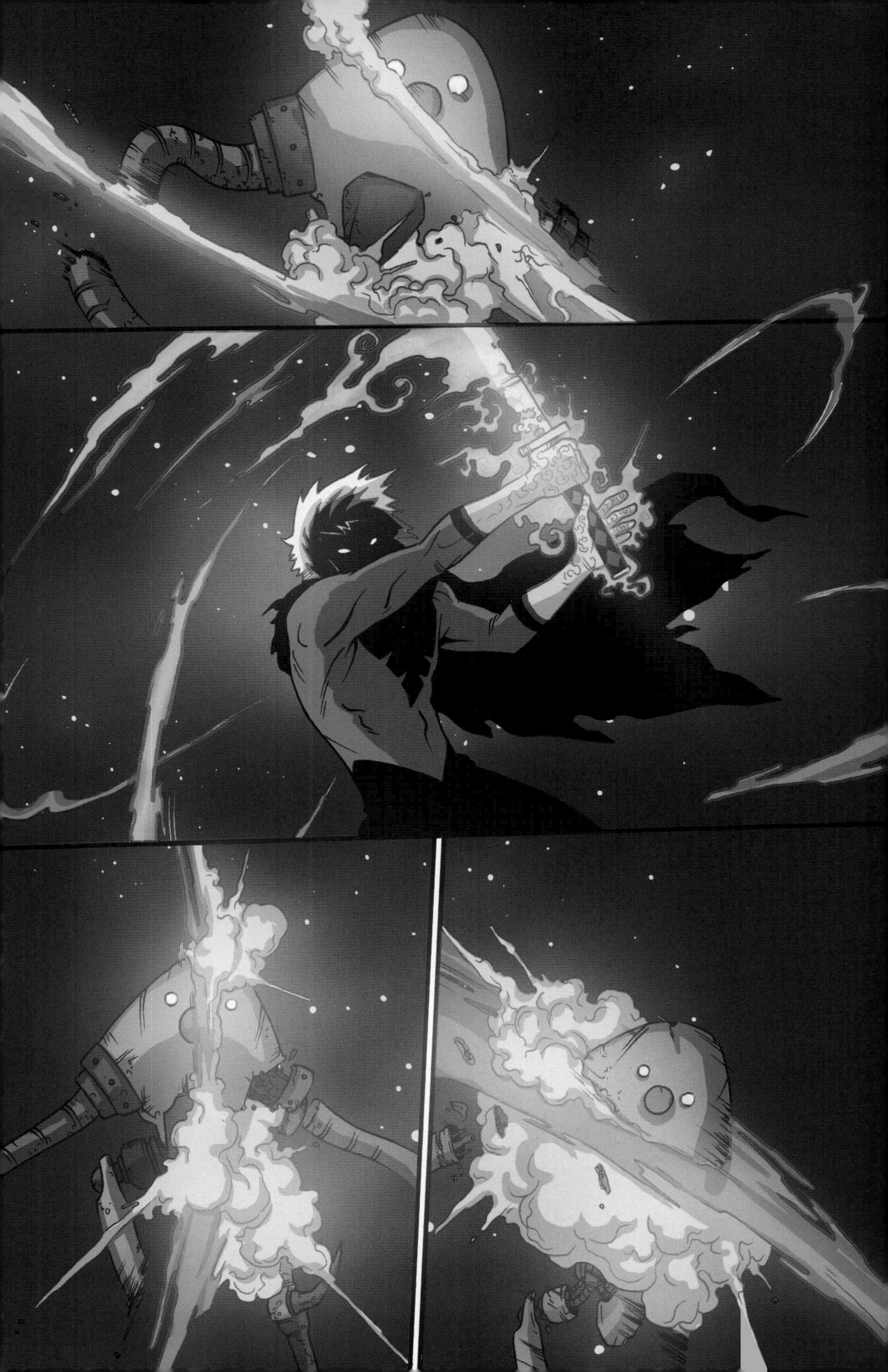

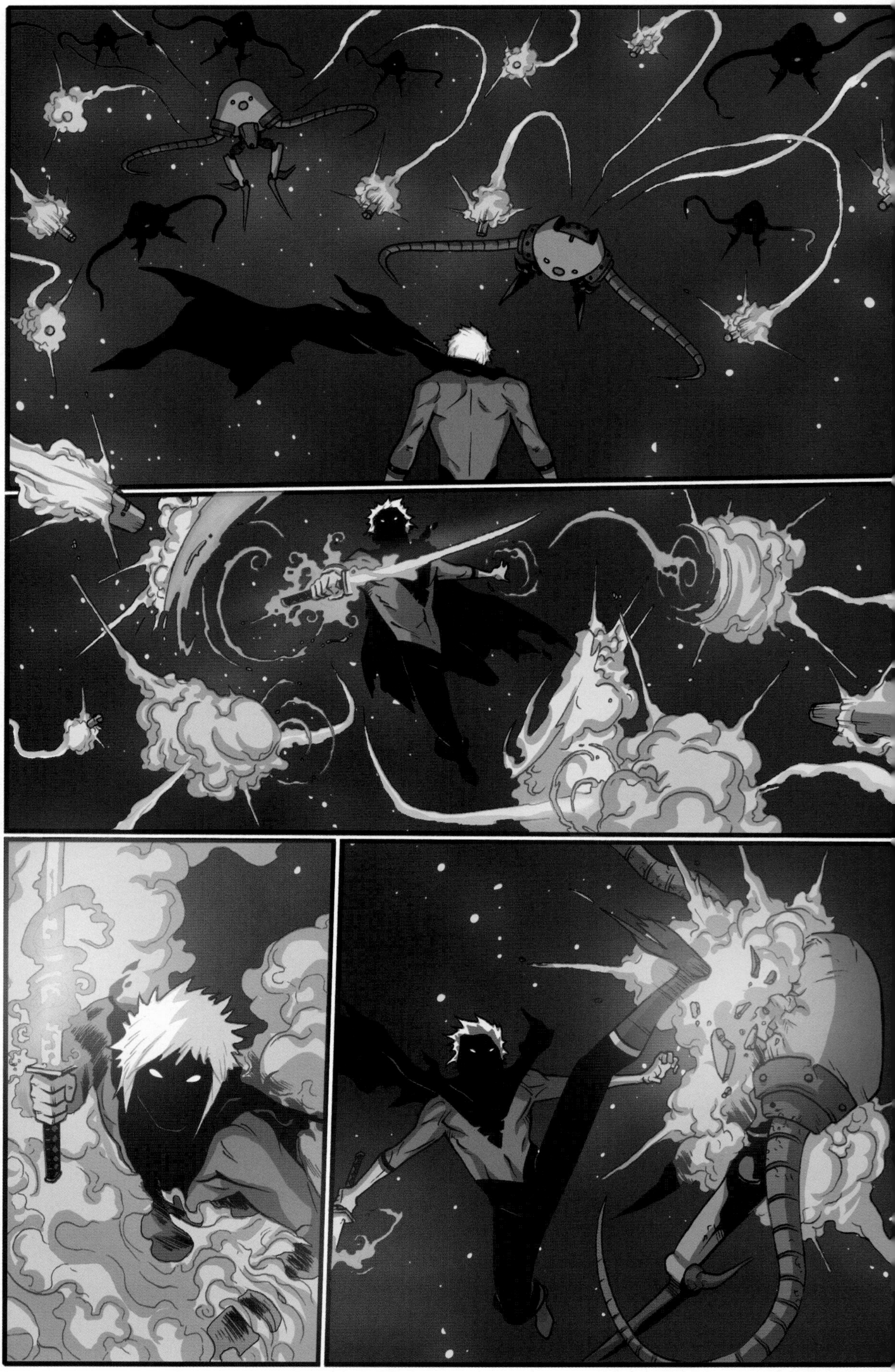

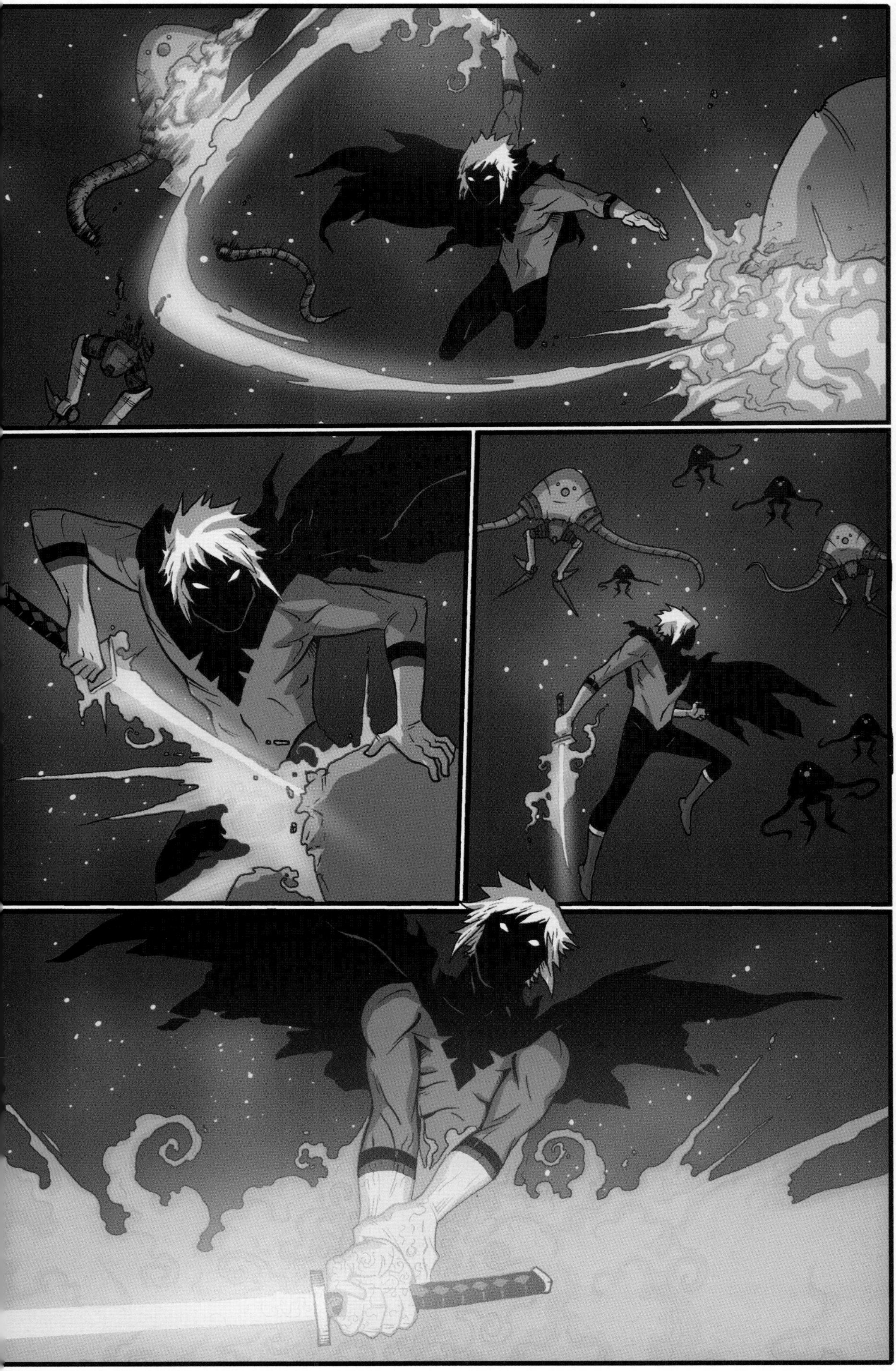

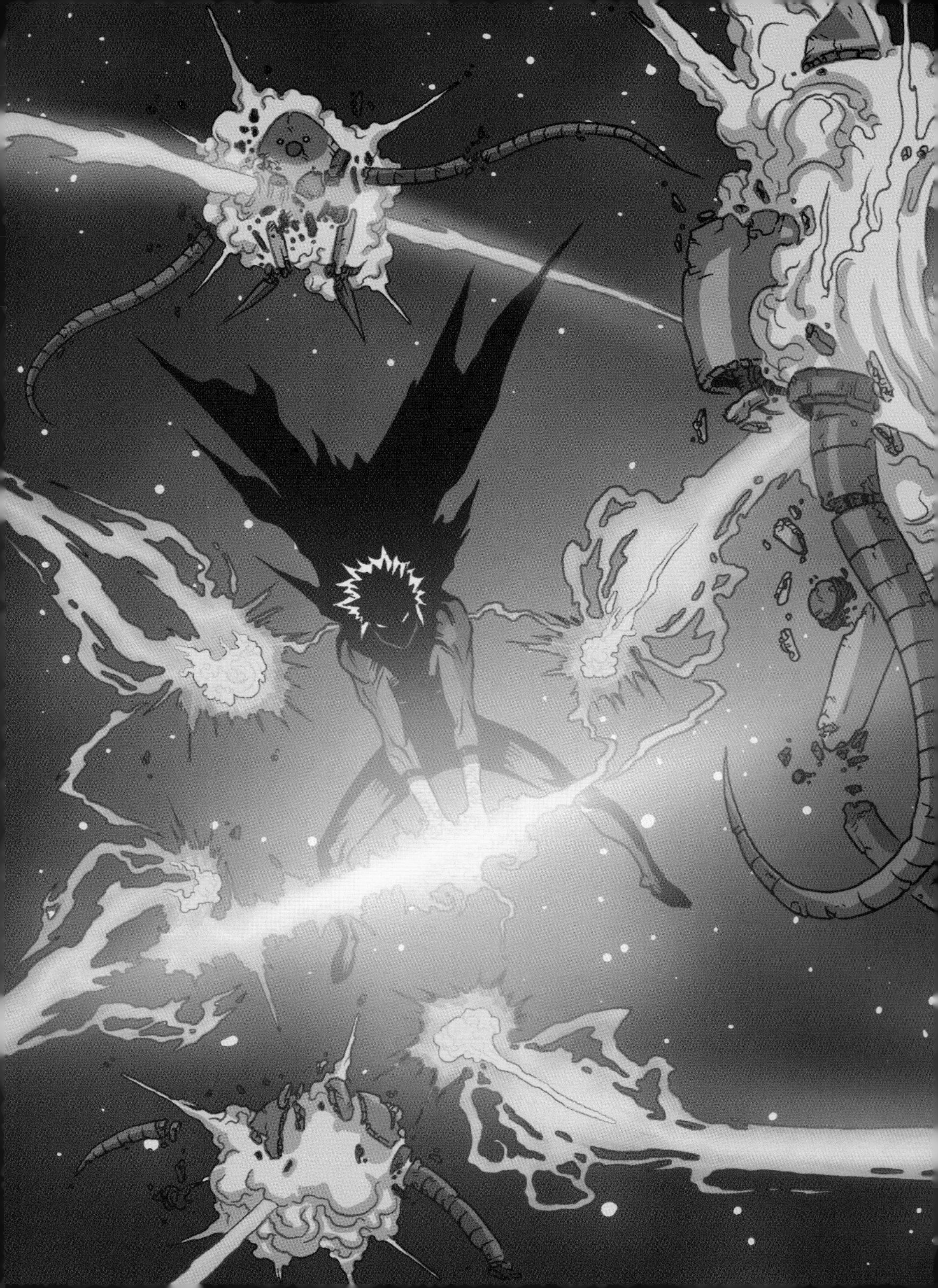

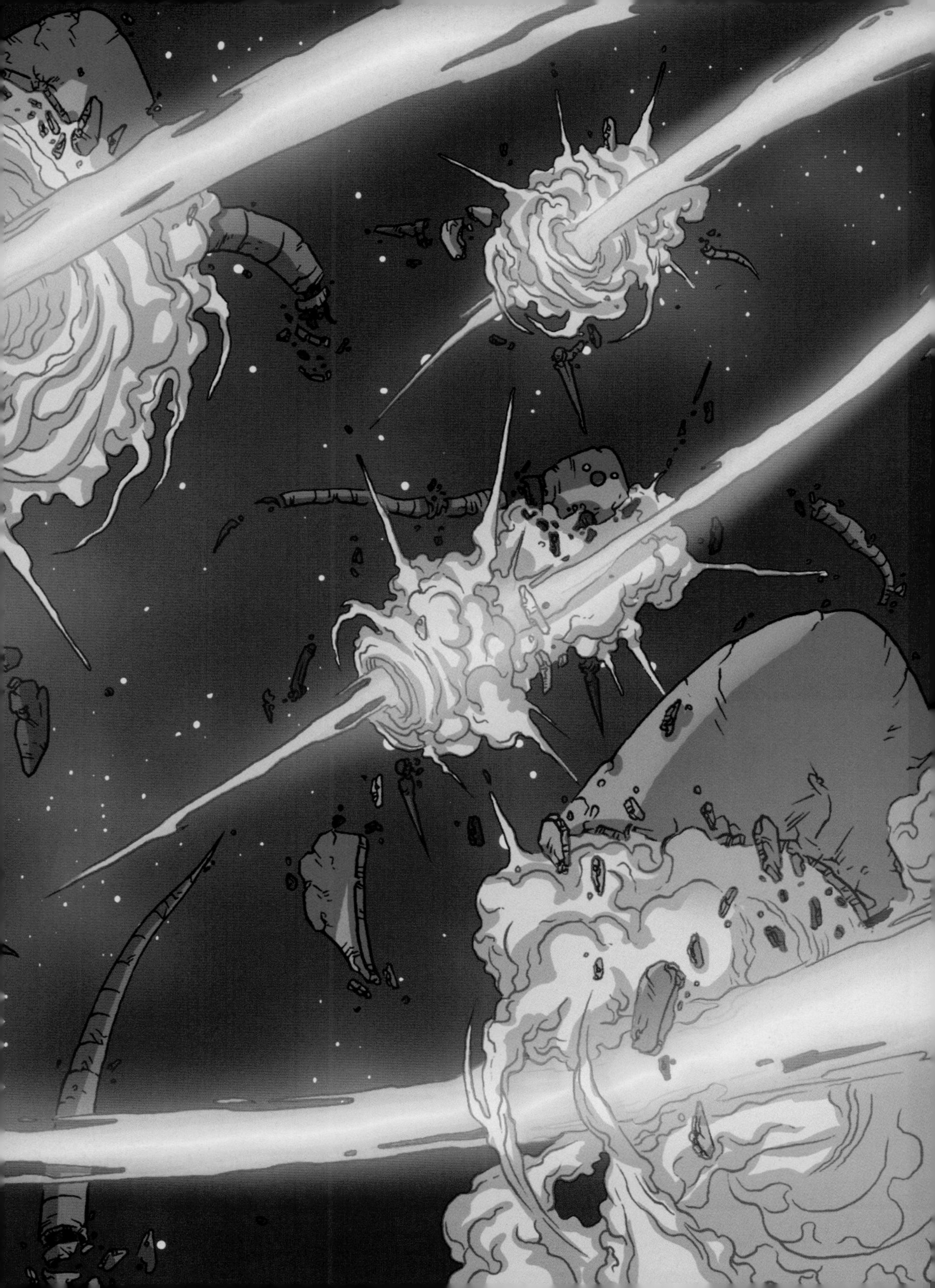

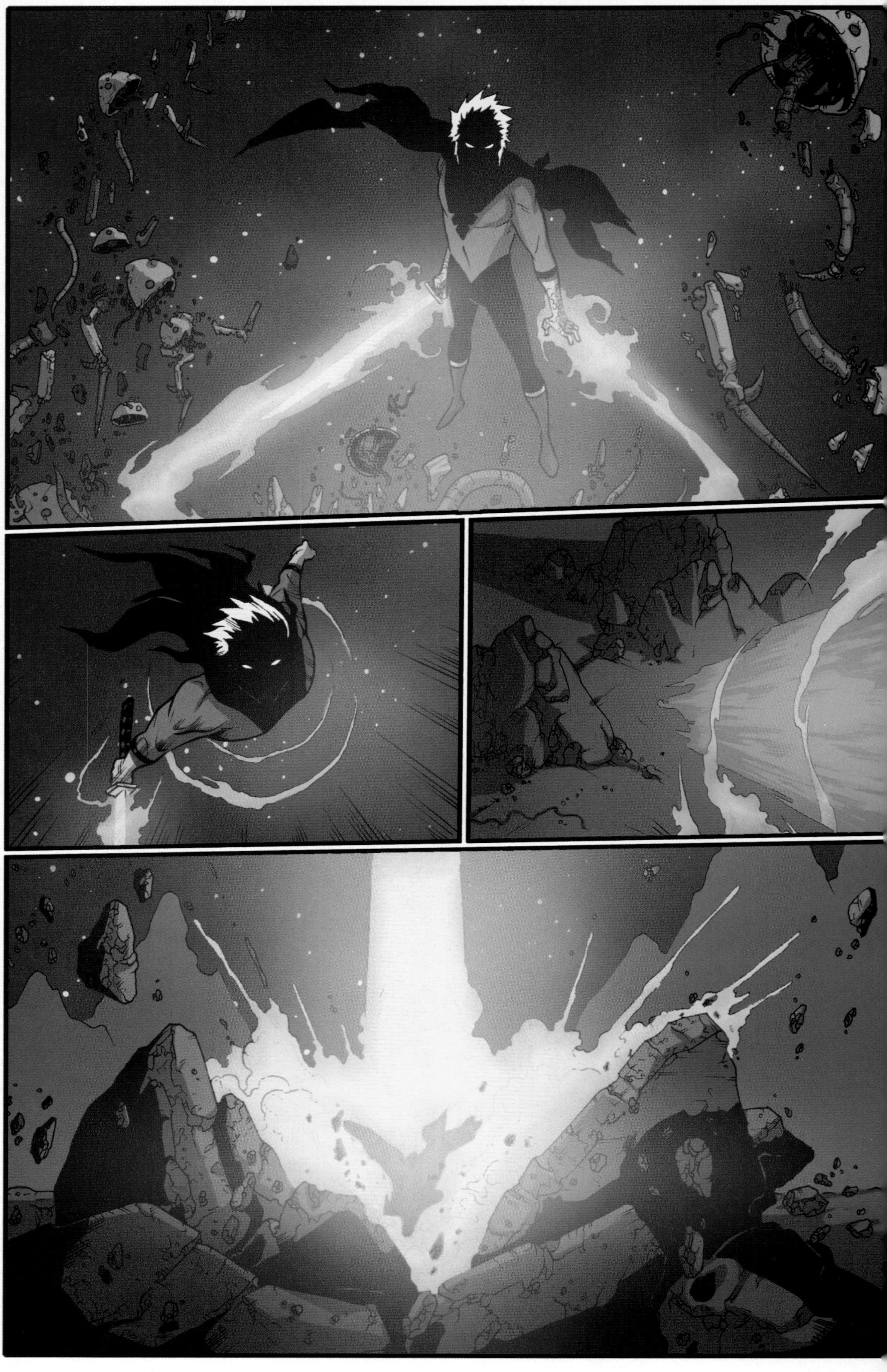

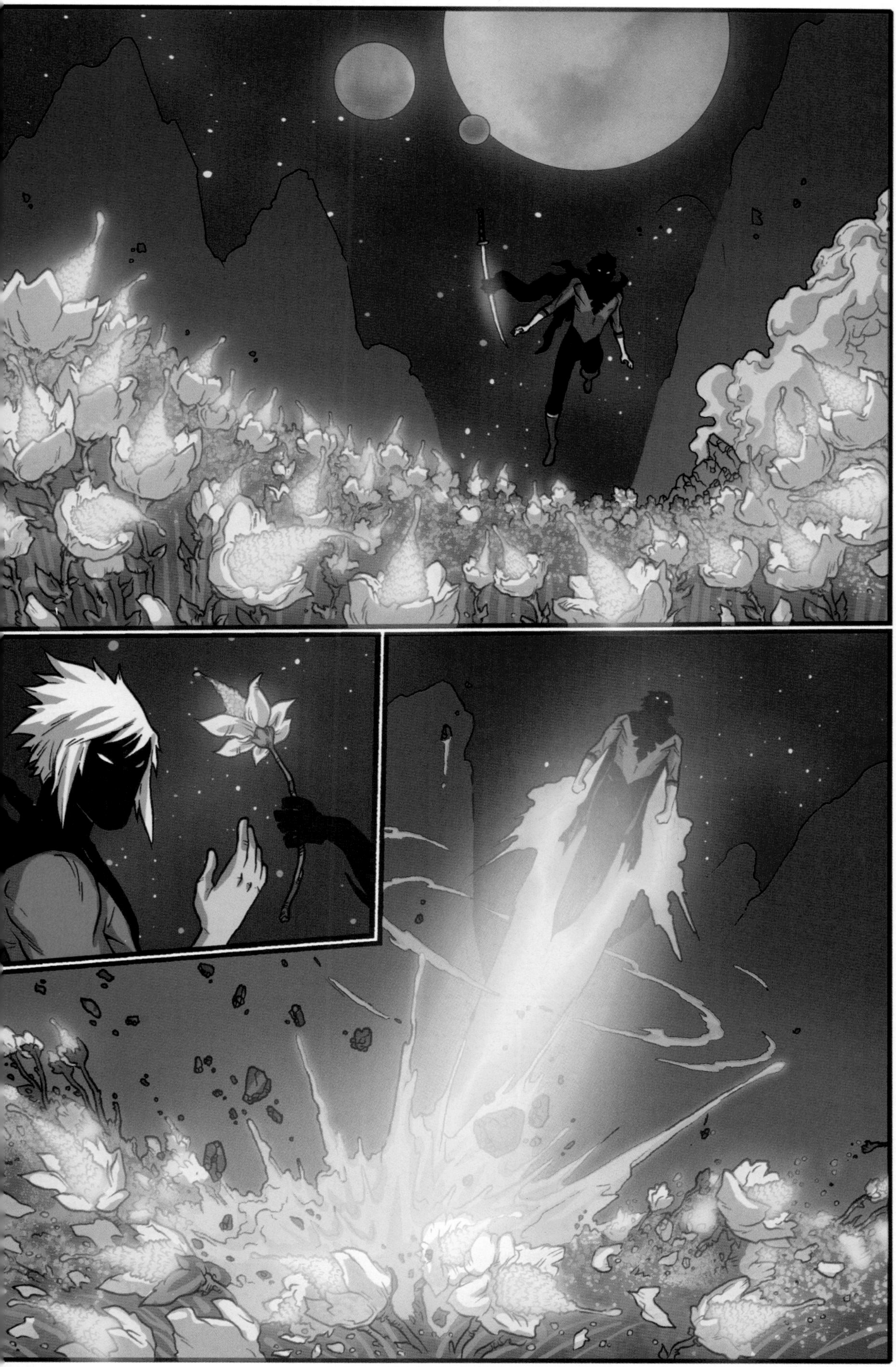

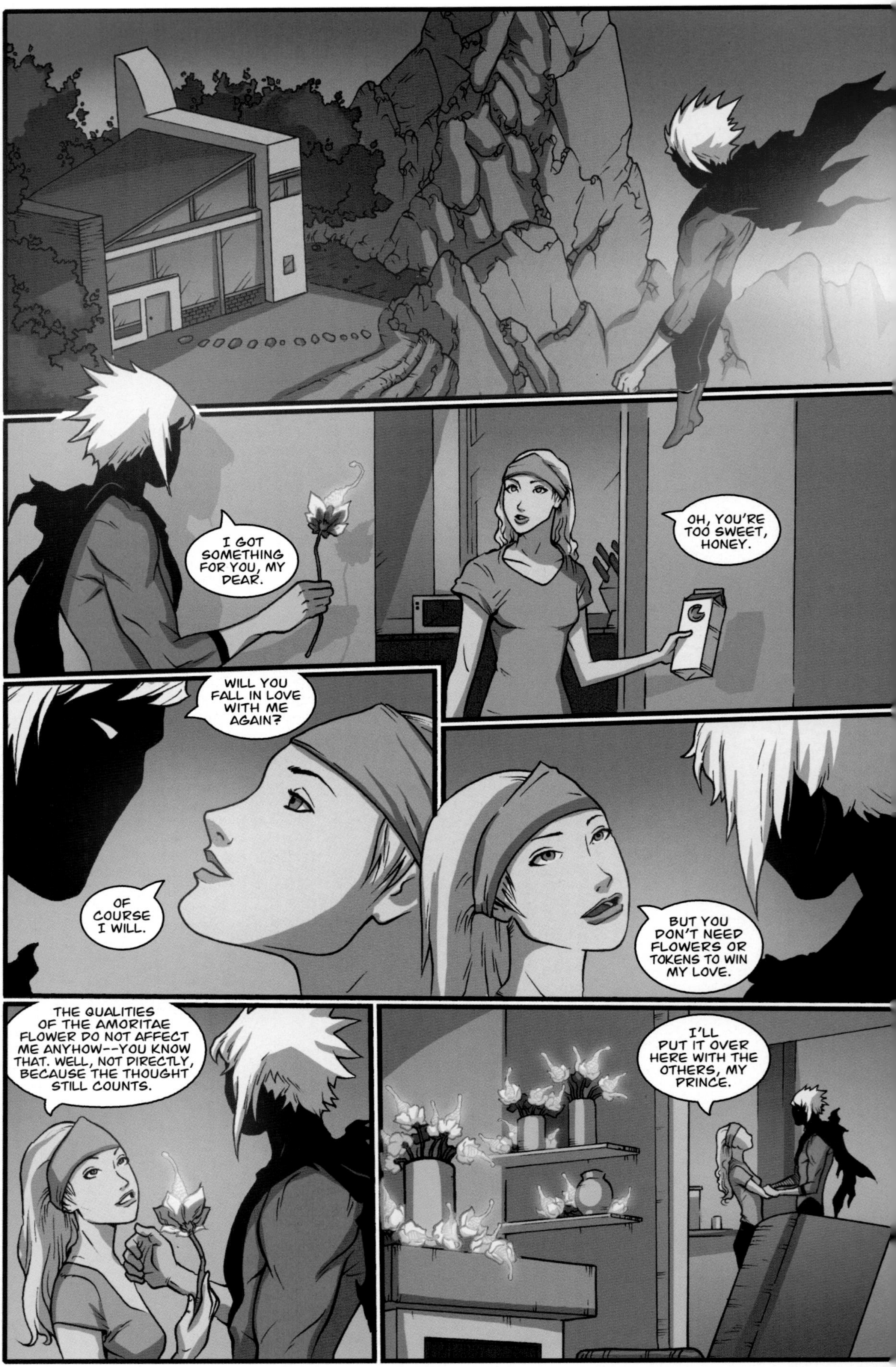

I GOT SOMETHING FOR YOU, MY DEAR.
OH, YOU'RE TOO SWEET, HONEY.
WILL YOU FALL IN LOVE WITH ME AGAIN?
OF COURSE I WILL.
BUT YOU DON'T NEED FLOWERS OR TOKENS TO WIN MY LOVE.
THE QUALITIES OF THE AMORITAE FLOWER DO NOT AFFECT ME ANYHOW--YOU KNOW THAT. WELL, NOT DIRECTLY, BECAUSE THE THOUGHT STILL COUNTS.
I'LL PUT IT OVER HERE WITH THE OTHERS, MY PRINCE.

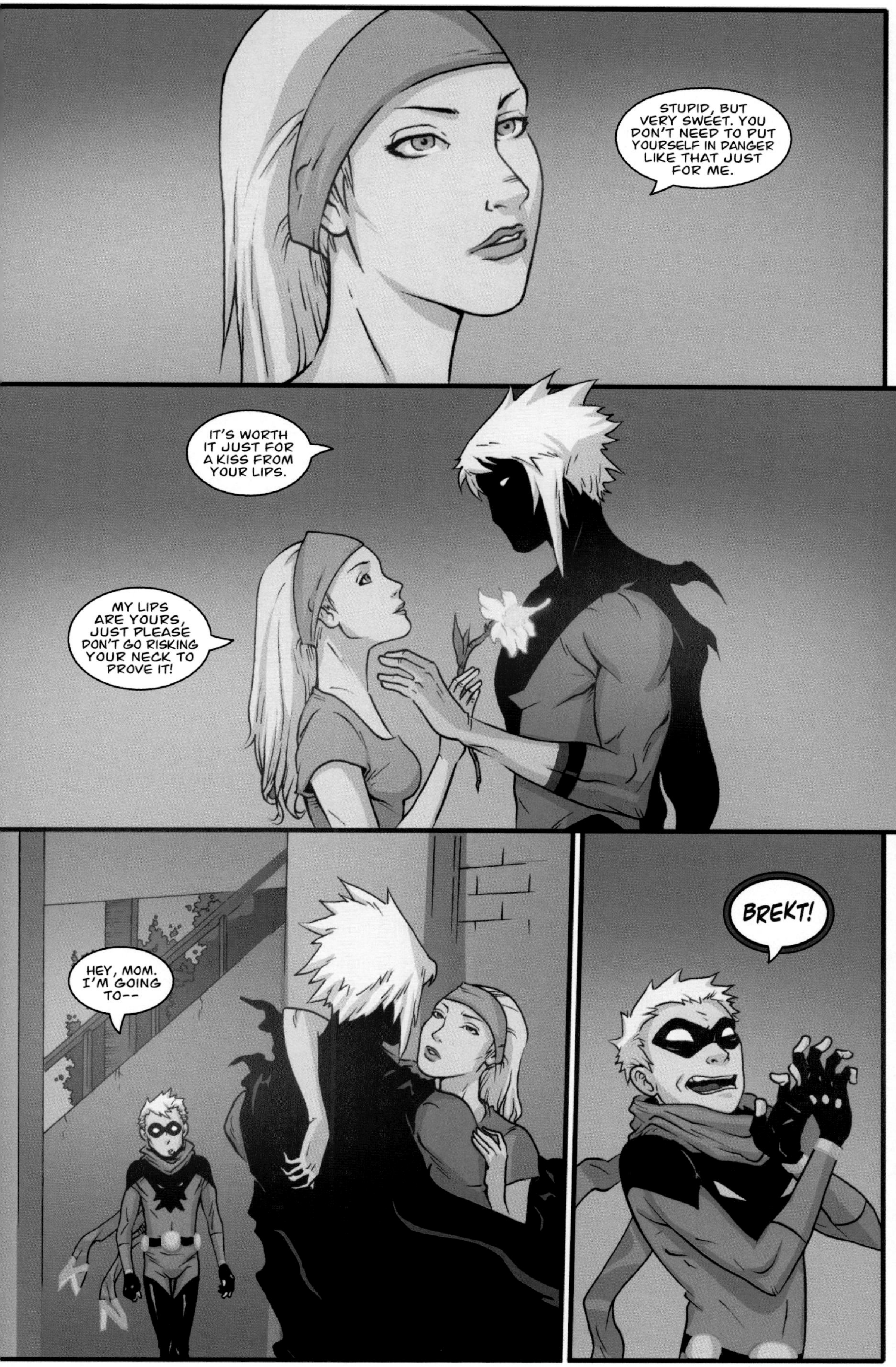
STUPID, BUT VERY SWEET. YOU DON'T NEED TO PUT YOURSELF IN DANGER LIKE THAT JUST FOR ME.
IT'S WORTH IT JUST FOR A KISS FROM YOUR LIPS.
MY LIPS ARE YOURS, JUST PLEASE DON'T GO RISKING YOUR NECK TO PROVE IT!
HEY, MOM. I'M GOING TO--
BREKT!

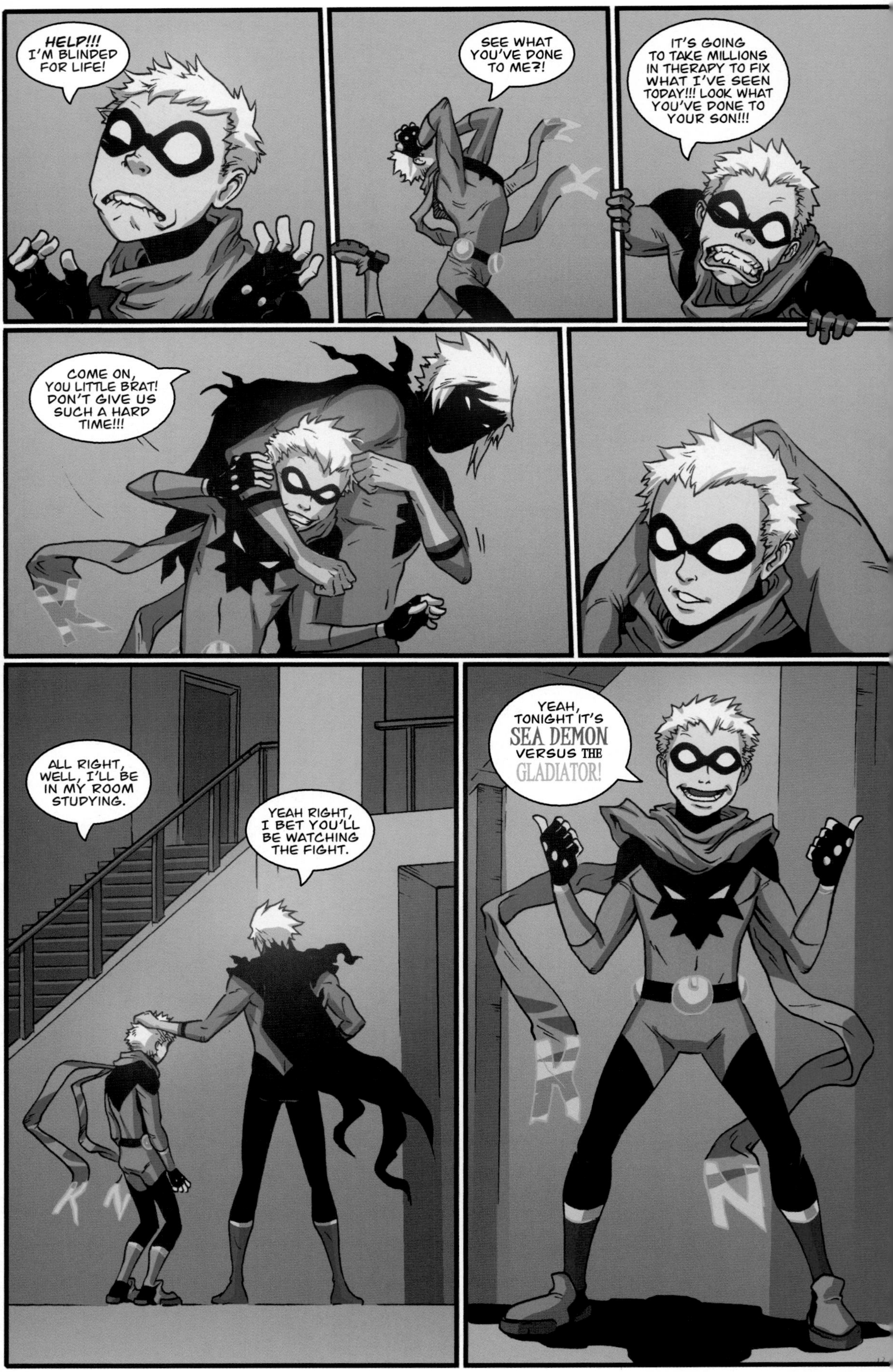
HELP!!! I'M BLINDED FOR LIFE!
SEE WHAT YOU'VE DONE TO ME?!
IT'S GOING TO TAKE MILLIONS IN THERAPY TO FIX WHAT I'VE SEEN TODAY!!! LOOK WHAT YOU'VE DONE TO YOUR SON!!!
COME ON, YOU LITTLE BRAT! DON'T GIVE US SUCH A HARD TIME!!!
ALL RIGHT, WELL, I'LL BE IN MY ROOM STUDYING.
YEAH RIGHT, I BET YOU'LL BE WATCHING THE FIGHT.
YEAH, TONIGHT IT'S SEA DEMON VERSUS THE GLADIATOR!

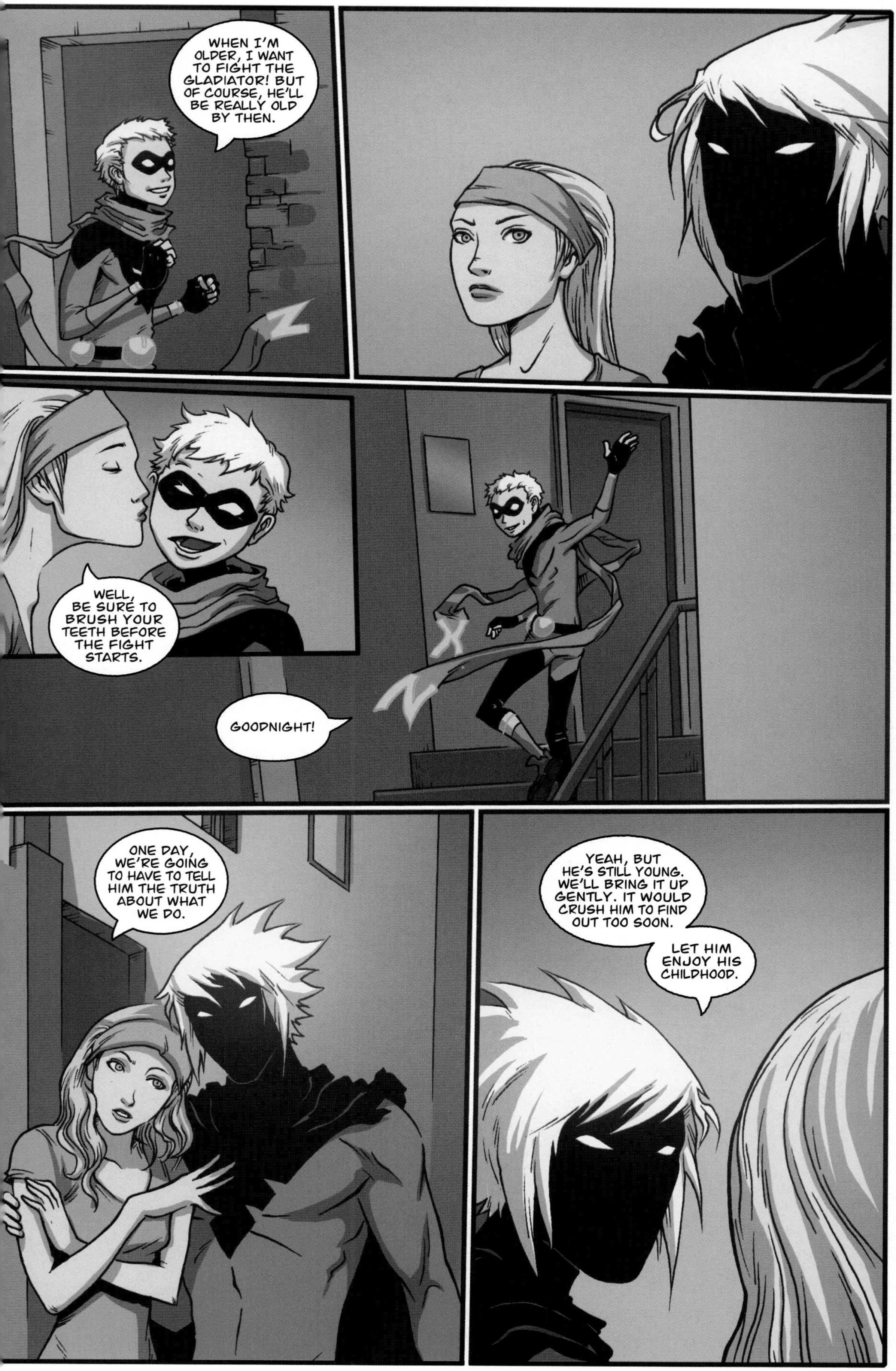
WHEN I'M OLDER, I WANT TO FIGHT THE GLADIATOR! BUT OF COURSE, HE'LL BE REALLY OLD BY THEN.
WELL, BE SURE TO BRUSH YOUR TEETH BEFORE THE FIGHT STARTS.
GOODNIGHT!
ONE DAY, WE'RE GOING TO HAVE TO TELL HIM THE TRUTH ABOUT WHAT WE DO.
YEAH, BUT HE'S STILL YOUNG. WE'LL BRING IT UP GENTLY. IT WOULD CRUSH HIM TO FIND OUT TOO SOON.
LET HIM ENJOY HIS CHILDHOOD.

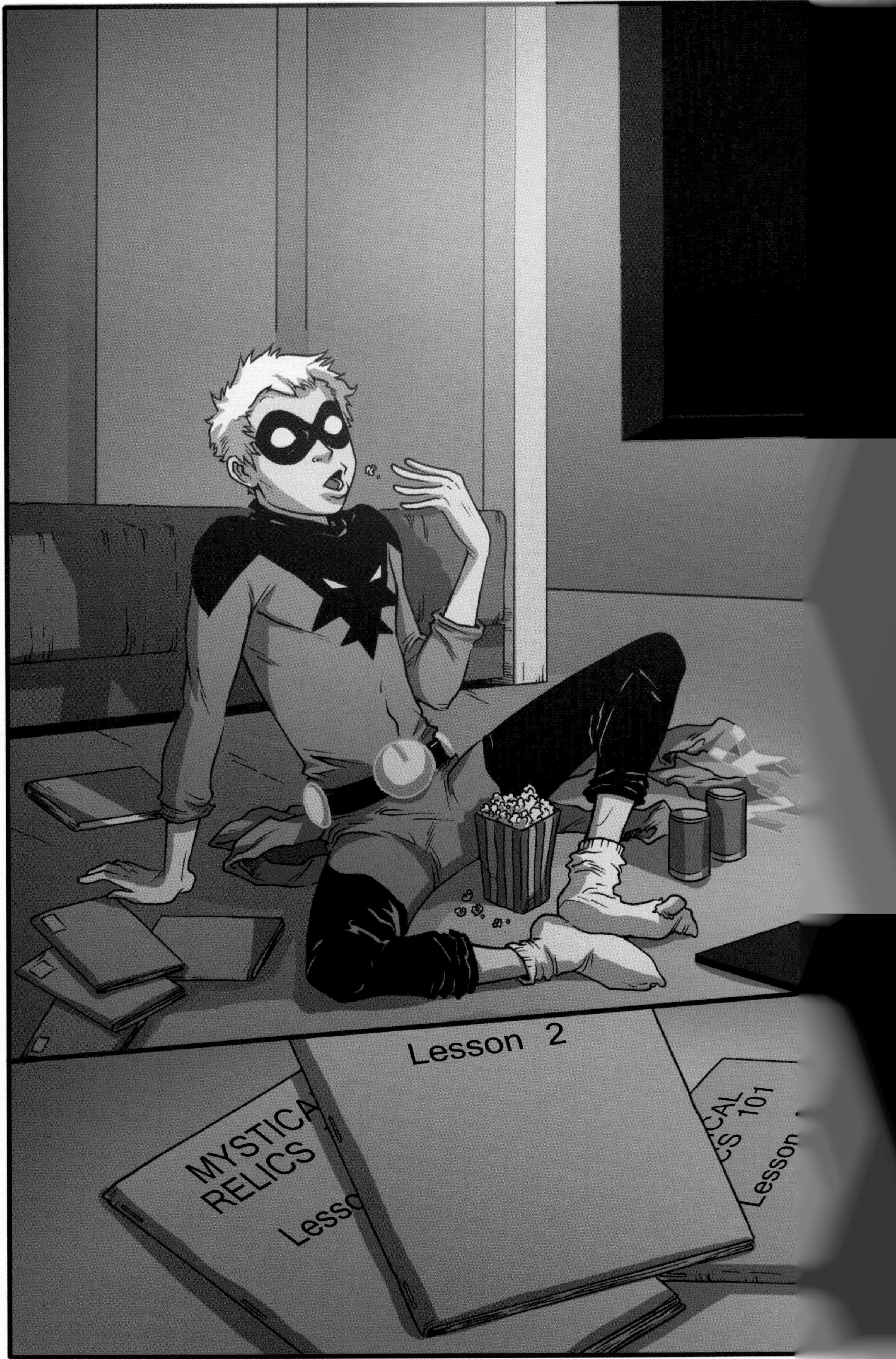
Lesson 2
MYSTICA
RELICS
Lesso
CAL
CS 101
Lesson

CHAPTER 4

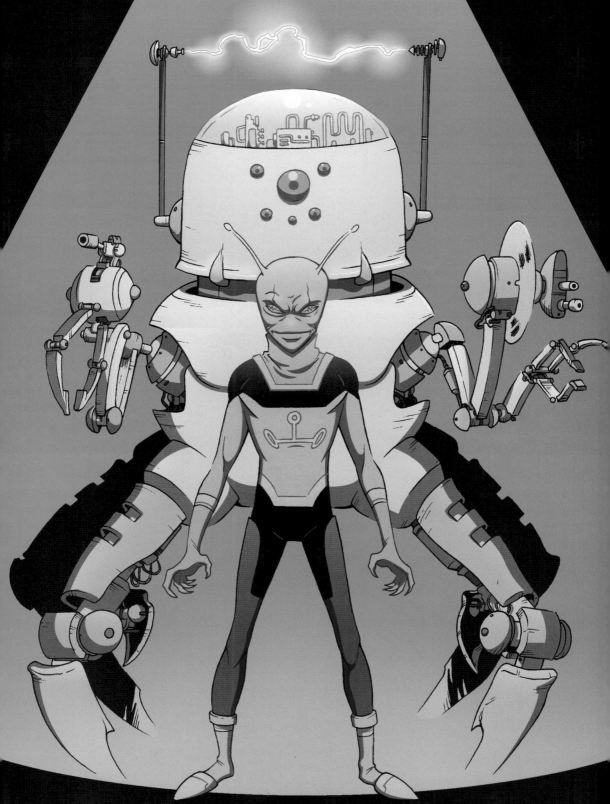

GLADSTONE'S SCHOOL FOR WORLD CONQUERORS

Written by
Mark Andrew Smith

Art & Cover by
Armand Villavert

Colors by
Carlos Carrasco

Letters by
Thomas Mauer

Edits by
Justin Robinson

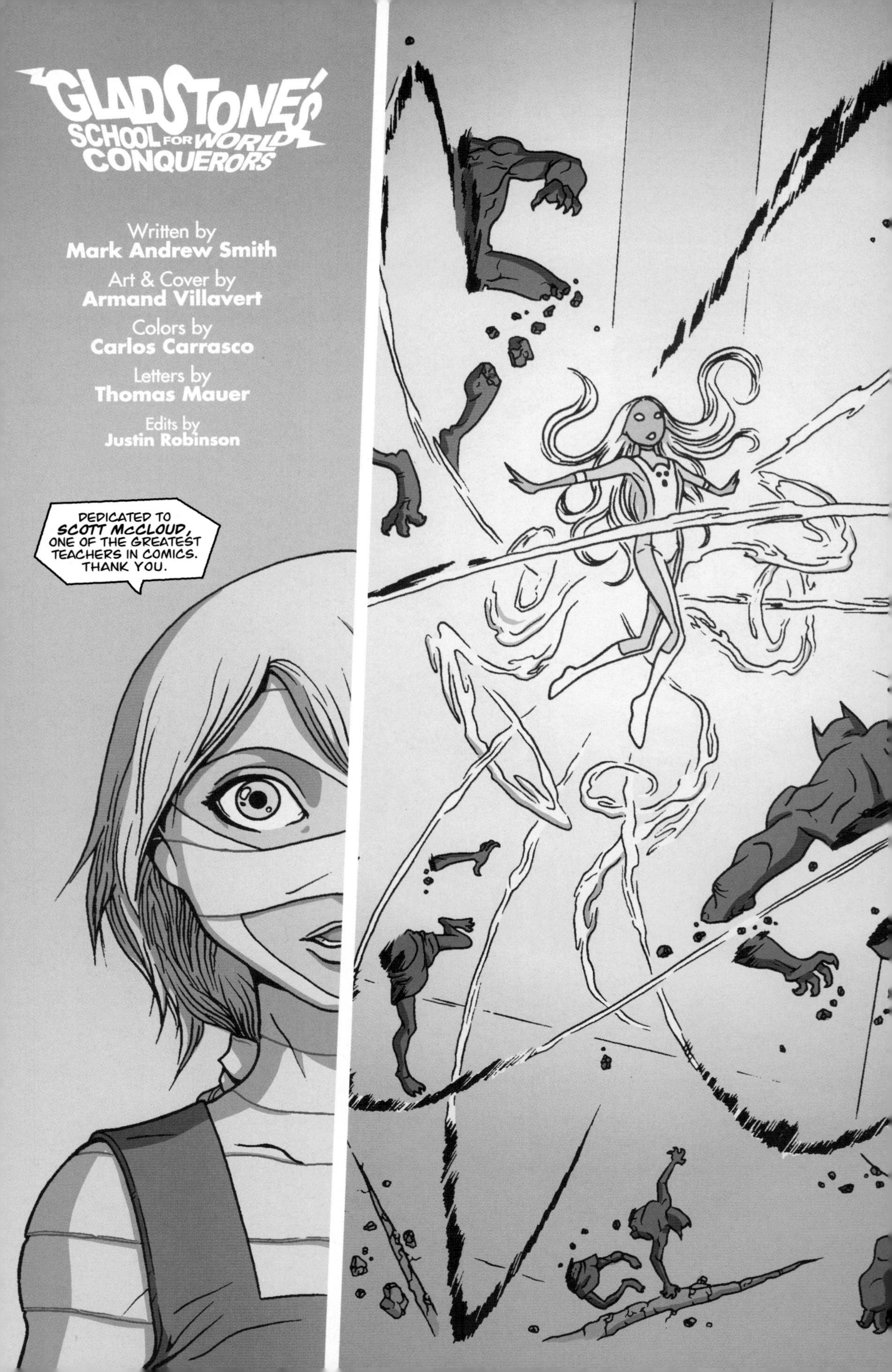
DEDICATED TO SCOTT McCLOUD, ONE OF THE GREATEST TEACHERS IN COMICS. THANK YOU.

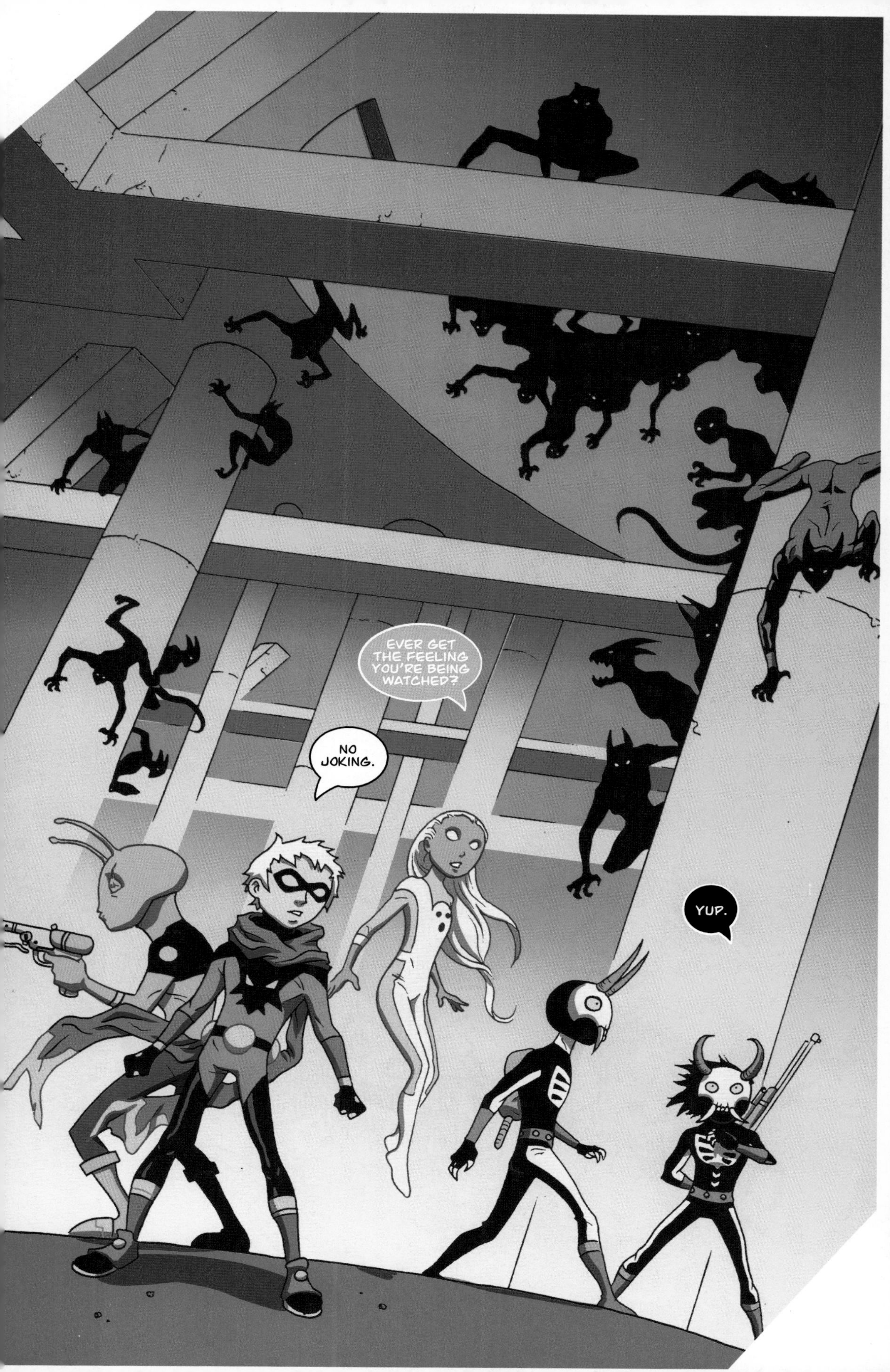
EVER GET THE FEELING YOU'RE BEING WATCHED?
NO JOKING.
YUP.

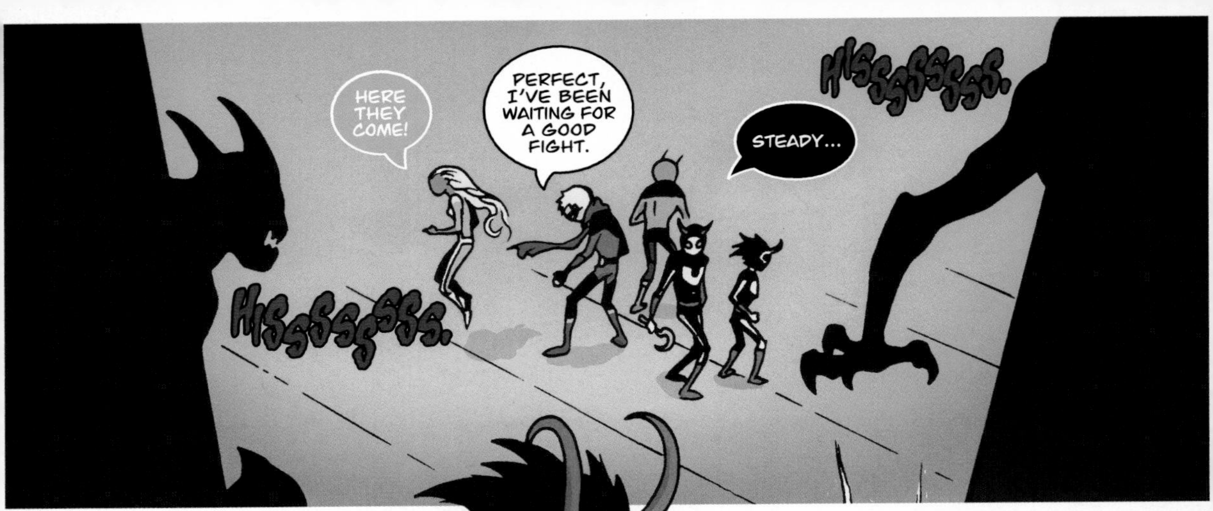
HERE THEY COME!
PERFECT, I'VE BEEN WAITING FOR A GOOD FIGHT.
STEADY...
HISSSSSSSS.
HISSSSSSSS.

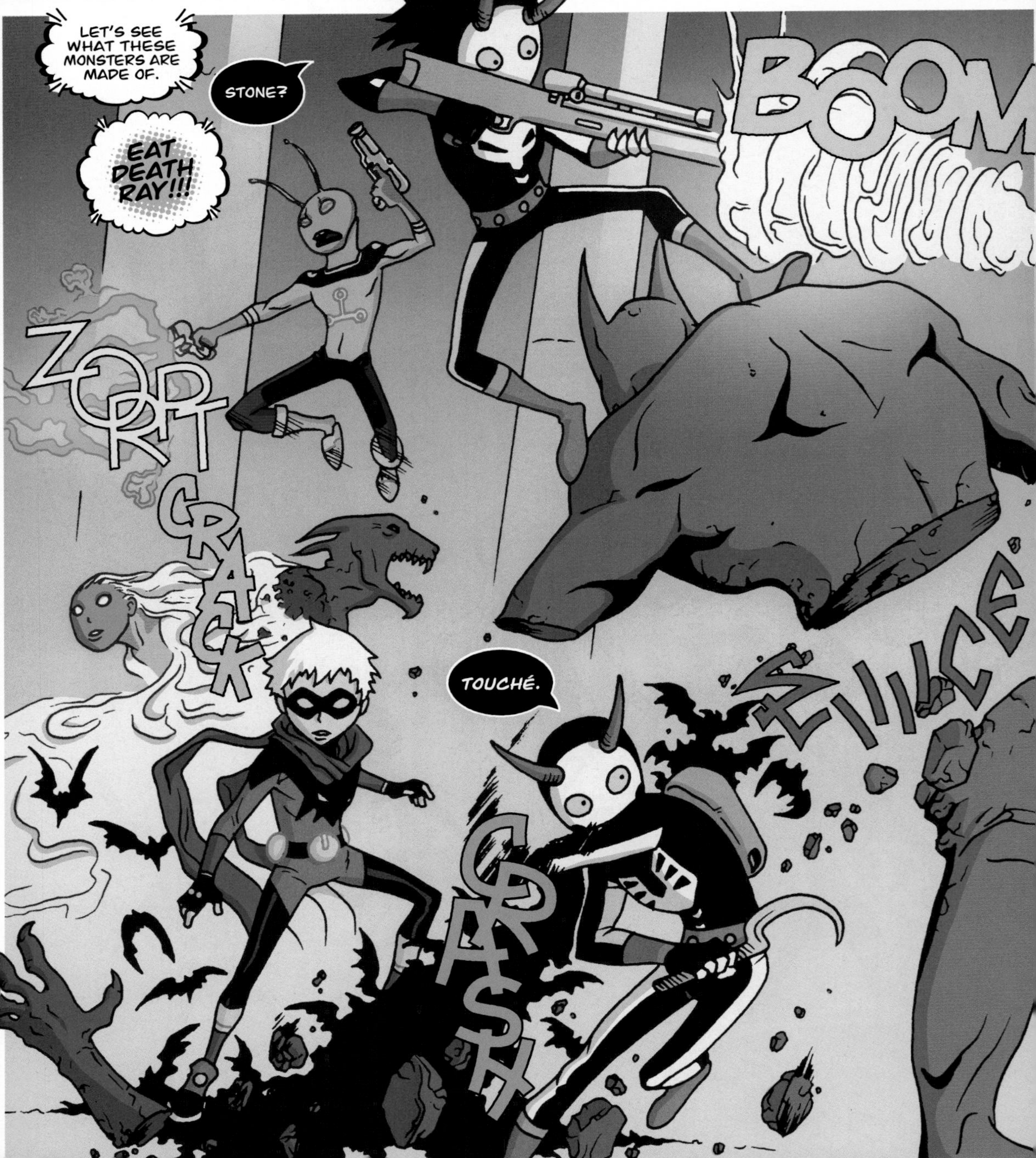
LET'S SEE WHAT THESE MONSTERS ARE MADE OF.
STONE?
EAT DEATH RAY!!!
BOOM
ZORRT
CRACK
TOUCHÉ.
SLIIICE
CRASH

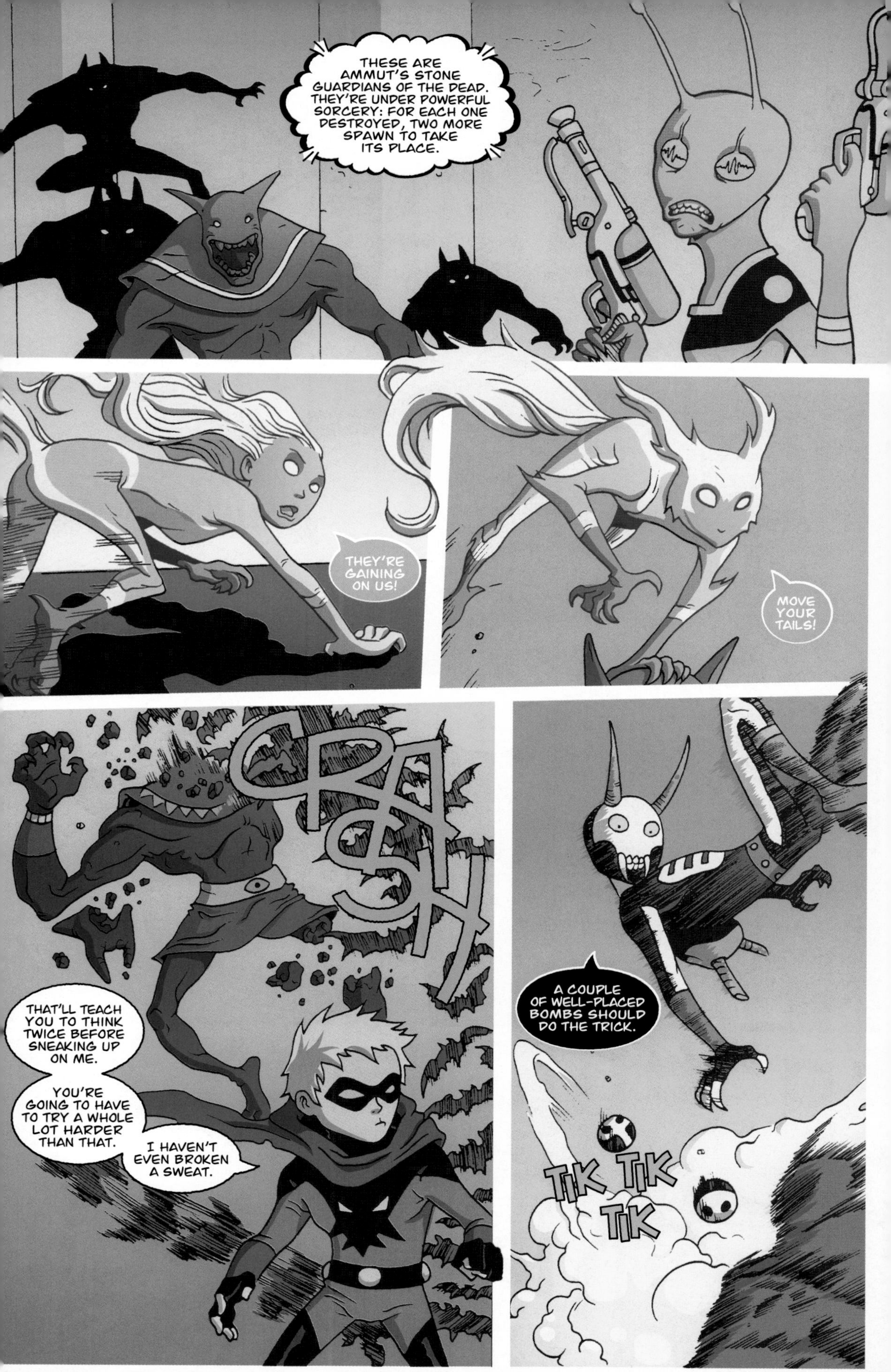
THESE ARE AMMUT'S STONE GUARDIANS OF THE DEAD. THEY'RE UNDER POWERFUL SORCERY: FOR EACH ONE DESTROYED, TWO MORE SPAWN TO TAKE ITS PLACE.
THEY'RE GAINING ON US!
MOVE YOUR TAILS!
CRASH
THAT'LL TEACH YOU TO THINK TWICE BEFORE SNEAKING UP ON ME.
YOU'RE GOING TO HAVE TO TRY A WHOLE LOT HARDER THAN THAT.
I HAVEN'T EVEN BROKEN A SWEAT.
A COUPLE OF WELL-PLACED BOMBS SHOULD DO THE TRICK.
TIK TIK TIK

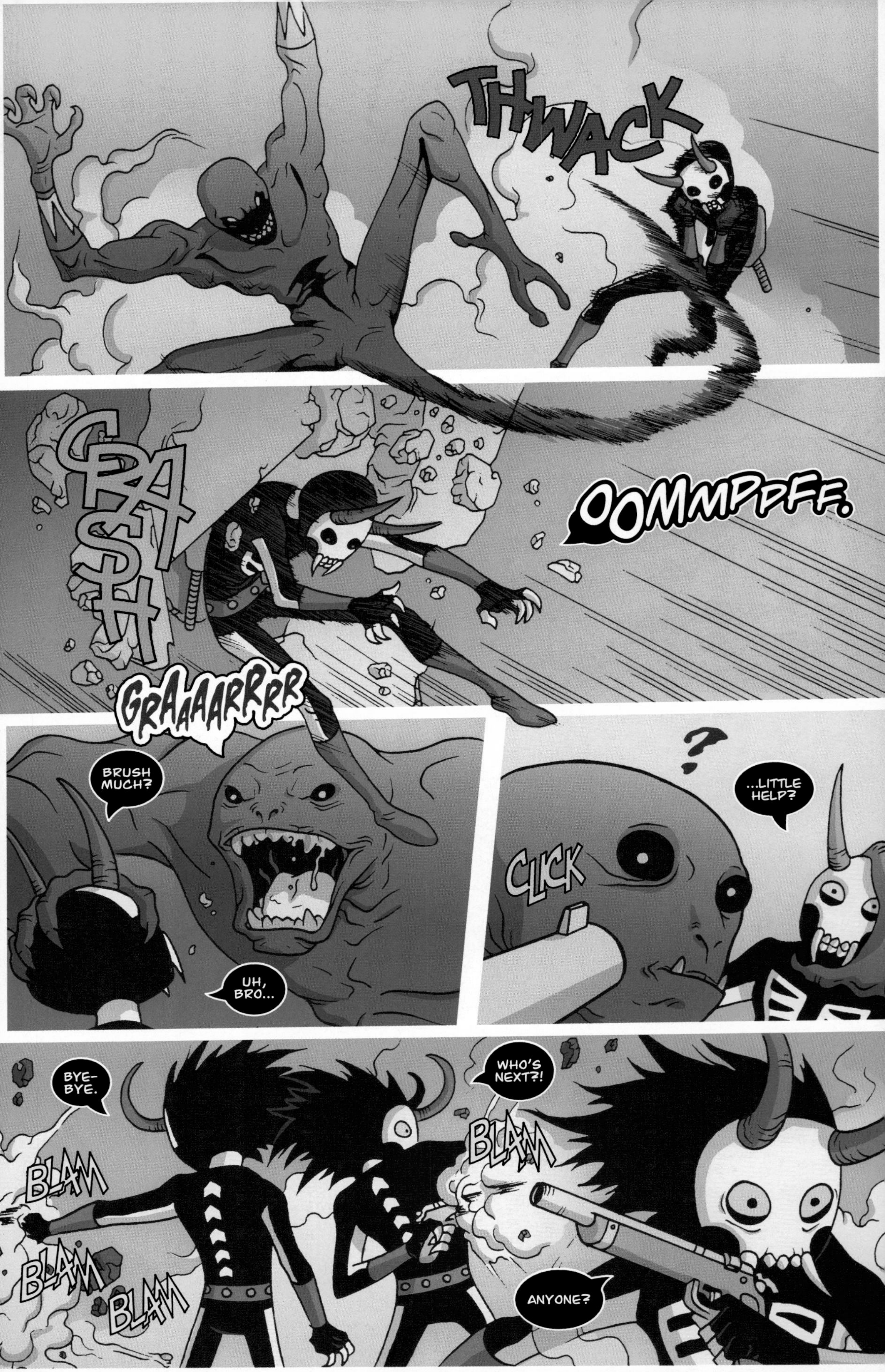
THWACK
CRASH
OOMMPPFF.
GRAAAARRRR
BRUSH MUCH?
UH, BRO...
?
...LITTLE HELP?
CLICK
BYE-BYE.
WHO'S NEXT?!
BLAM
BLAM
BLAM
BLAM
ANYONE?

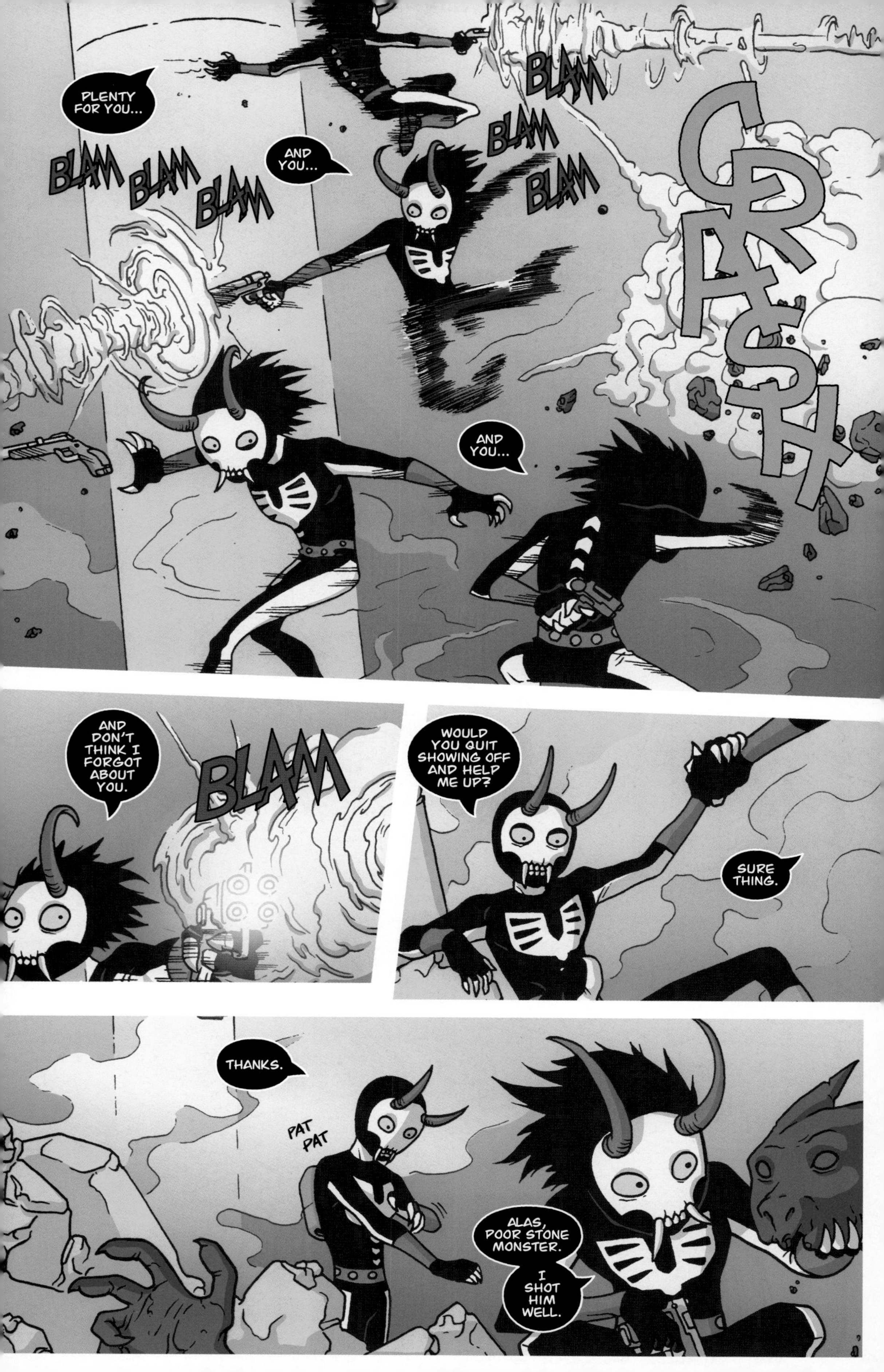
PLENTY FOR YOU...
BLAM
BLAM BLAM BLAM
AND YOU...
BLAM
BLAM
CRASH
AND YOU...
AND DON'T THINK I FORGOT ABOUT YOU.
BLAM
WOULD YOU QUIT SHOWING OFF AND HELP ME UP?
SURE THING.
THANKS.
PAT PAT
ALAS, POOR STONE MONSTER.
I SHOT HIM WELL.

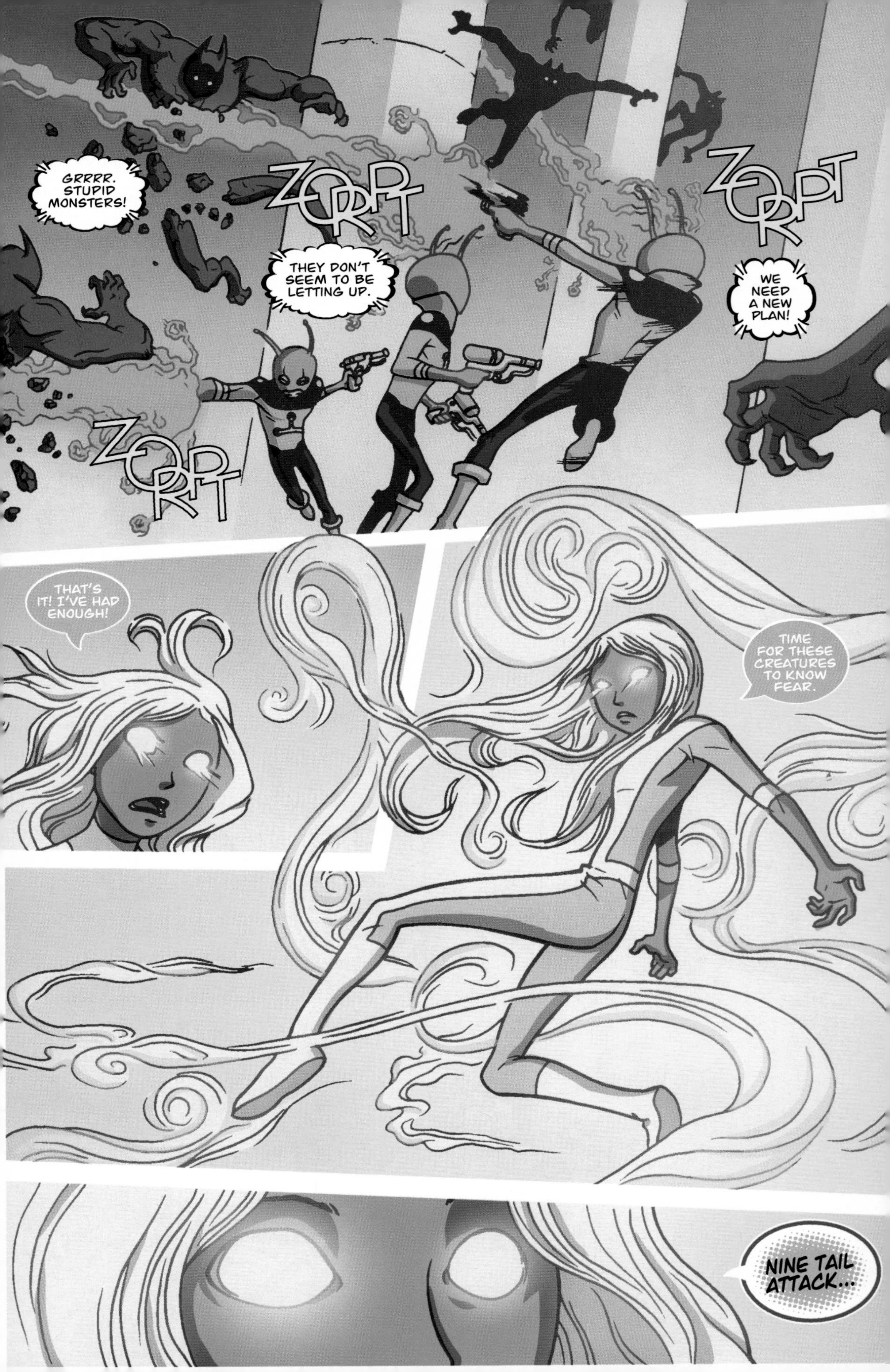
GRRRR. STUPID MONSTERS!
ZORPT
THEY DON'T SEEM TO BE LETTING UP.
ZORPT
WE NEED A NEW PLAN!
ZORPT
THAT'S IT! I'VE HAD ENOUGH!
TIME FOR THESE CREATURES TO KNOW FEAR.
NINE TAIL ATTACK...

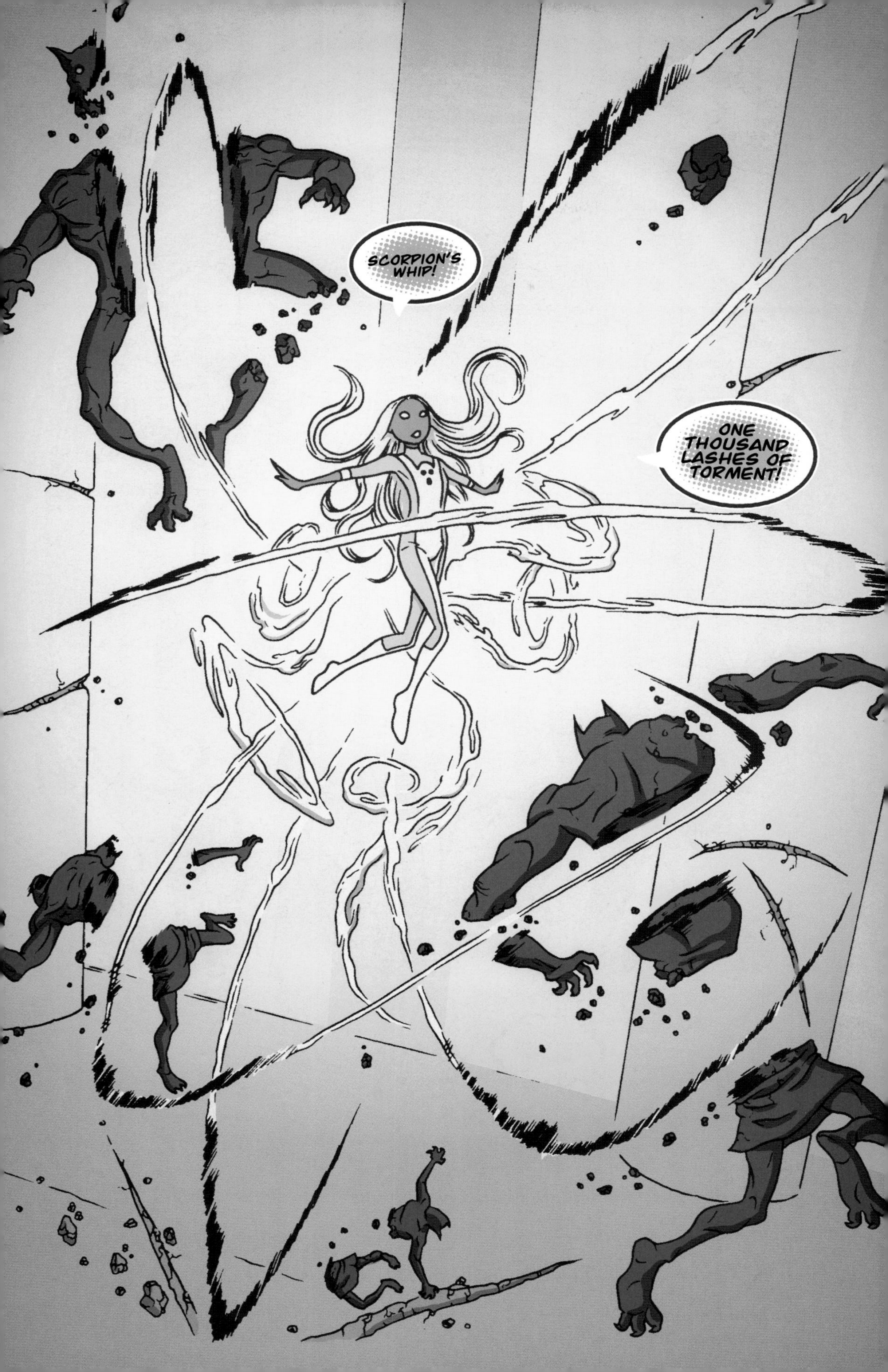
SCORPION'S WHIP!
ONE THOUSAND LASHES OF TORMENT!

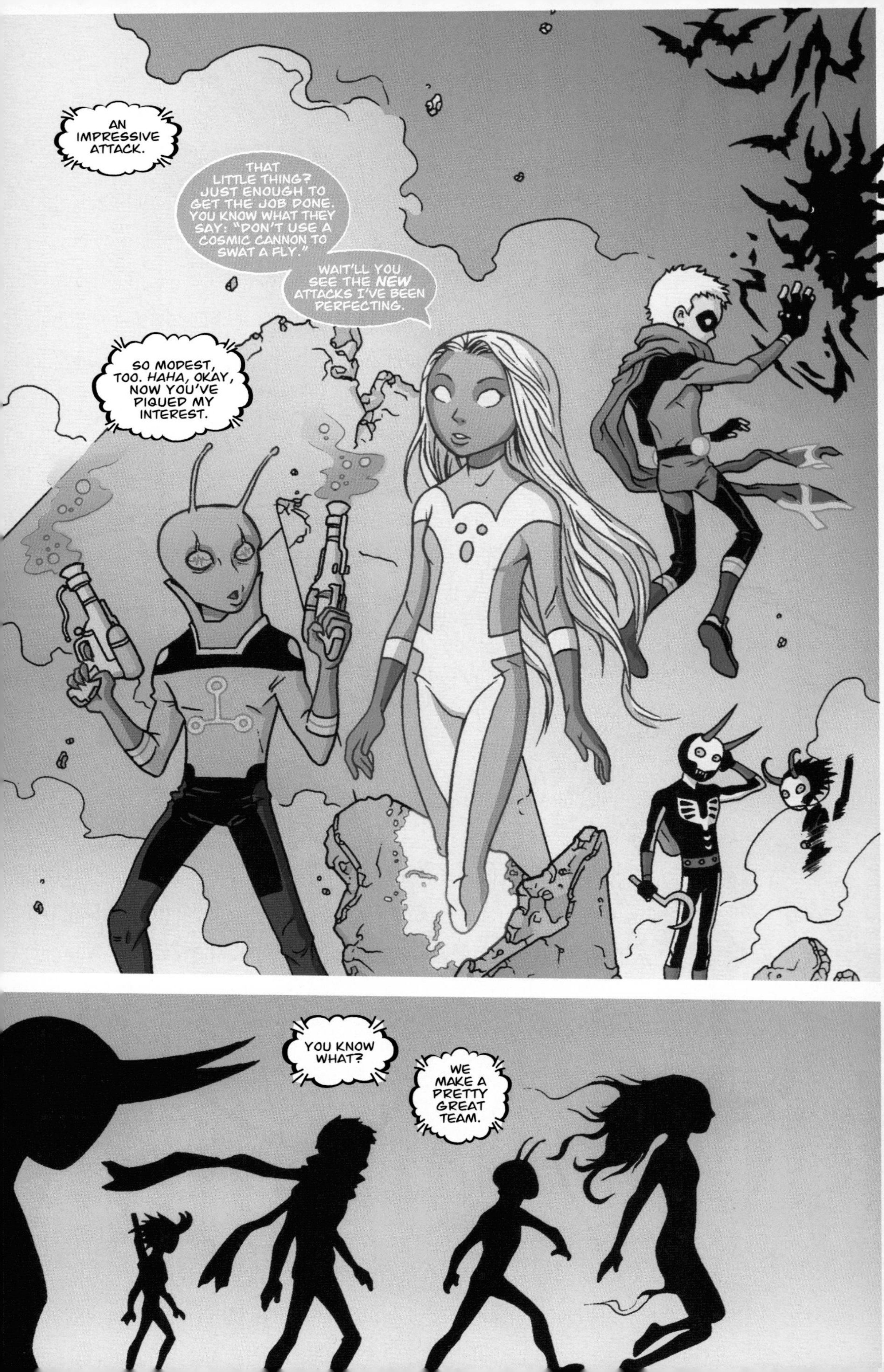
AN IMPRESSIVE ATTACK.
THAT LITTLE THING? JUST ENOUGH TO GET THE JOB DONE. YOU KNOW WHAT THEY SAY: "DON'T USE A COSMIC CANNON TO SWAT A FLY."
WAIT'LL YOU SEE THE NEW ATTACKS I'VE BEEN PERFECTING.
SO MODEST, TOO. HAHA, OKAY, NOW YOU'VE PIQUED MY INTEREST.
YOU KNOW WHAT?
WE MAKE A PRETTY GREAT TEAM.

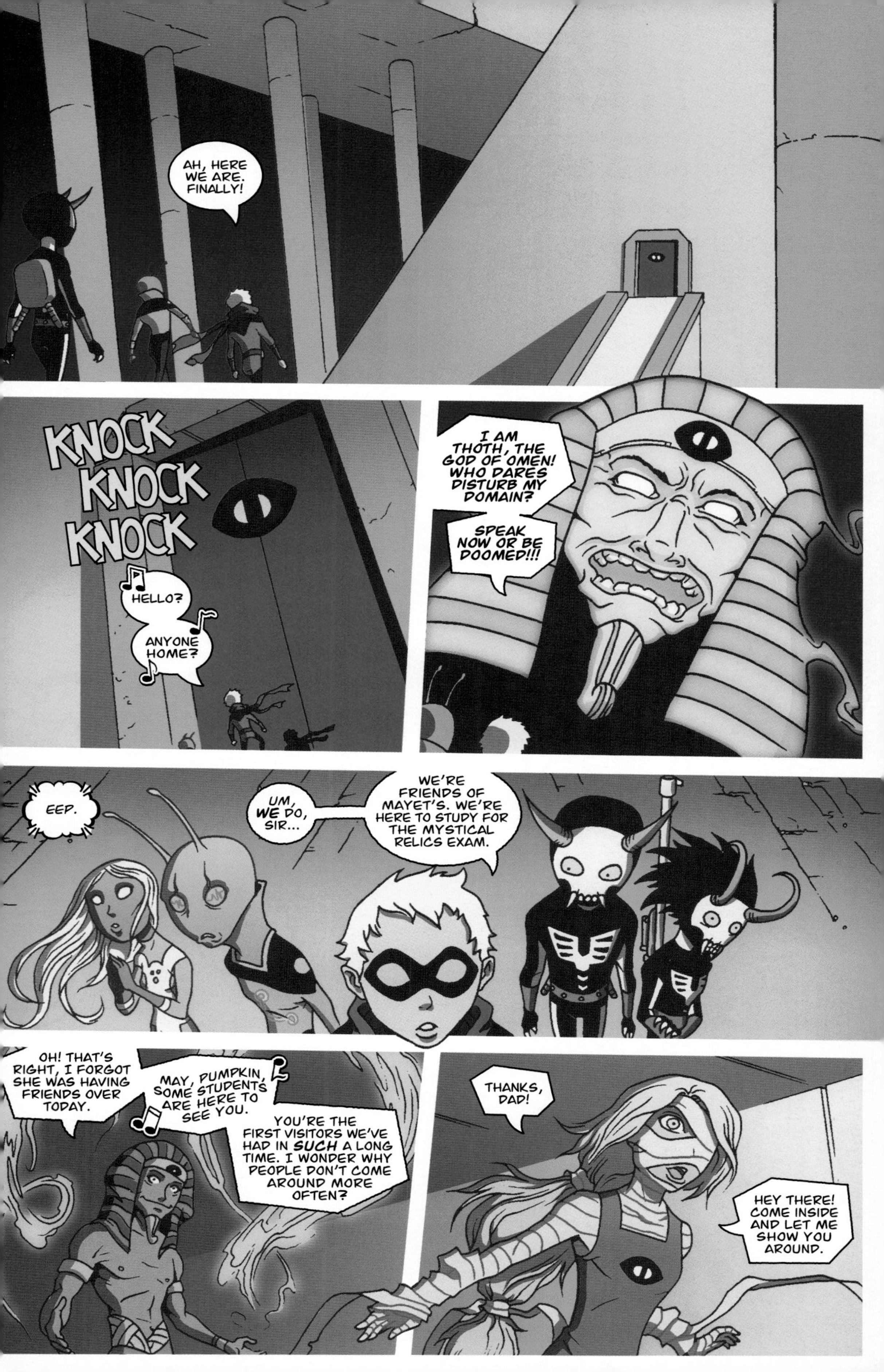
AH, HERE WE ARE. FINALLY!
KNOCK KNOCK KNOCK
HELLO?
ANYONE HOME?
I AM THOTH, THE GOD OF OMEN! WHO DARES DISTURB MY DOMAIN?
SPEAK NOW OR BE DOOMED!!!
EEP.
UM, WE DO, SIR...
WE'RE FRIENDS OF MAYET'S. WE'RE HERE TO STUDY FOR THE MYSTICAL RELICS EXAM.
OH! THAT'S RIGHT, I FORGOT SHE WAS HAVING FRIENDS OVER TODAY.
MAY, PUMPKIN, SOME STUDENTS ARE HERE TO SEE YOU.
YOU'RE THE FIRST VISITORS WE'VE HAD IN SUCH A LONG TIME. I WONDER WHY PEOPLE DON'T COME AROUND MORE OFTEN?
THANKS, DAD!
HEY THERE! COME INSIDE AND LET ME SHOW YOU AROUND.

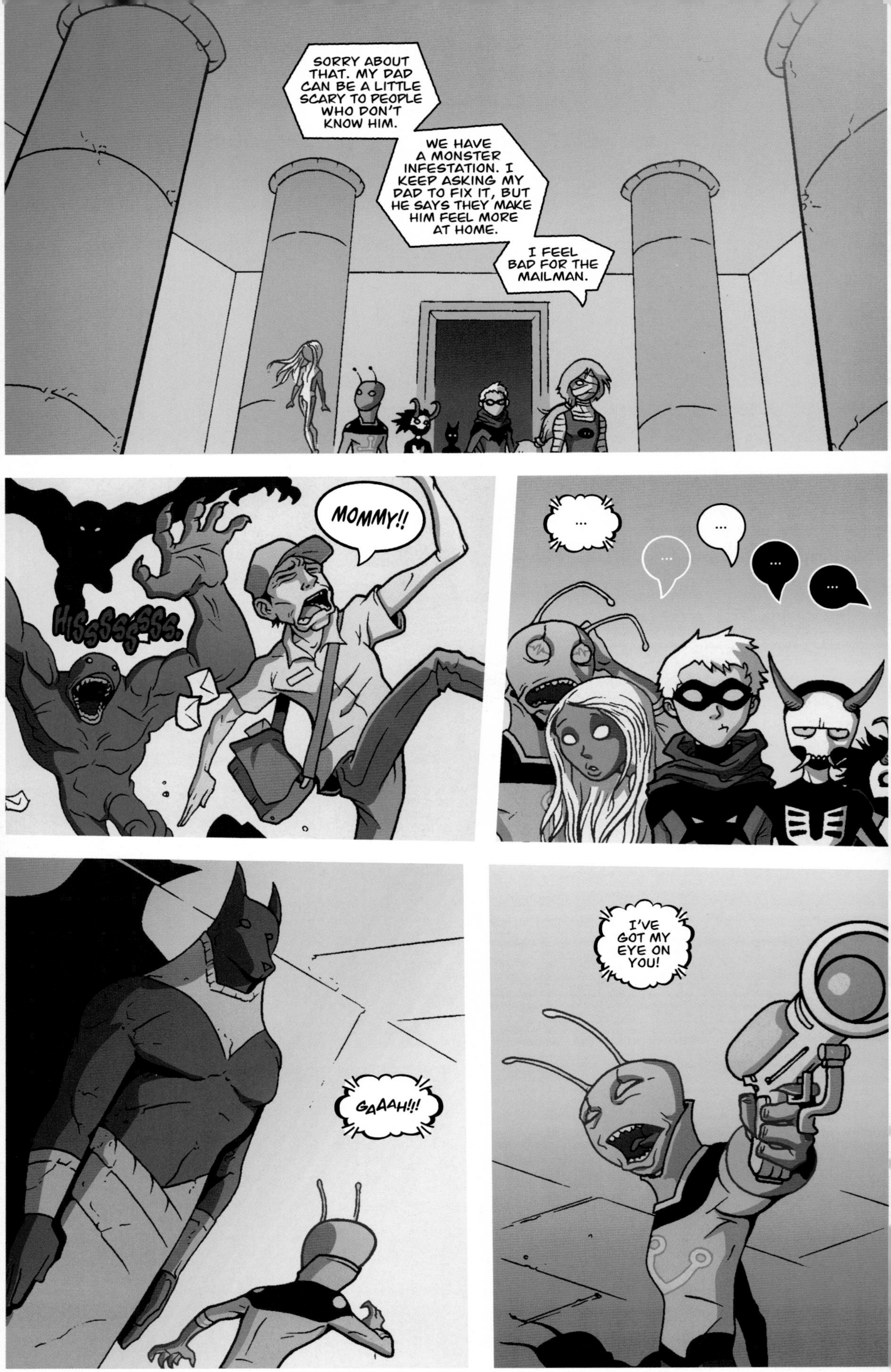
SORRY ABOUT THAT. MY DAD CAN BE A LITTLE SCARY TO PEOPLE WHO DON'T KNOW HIM.
WE HAVE A MONSTER INFESTATION. I KEEP ASKING MY DAD TO FIX IT, BUT HE SAYS THEY MAKE HIM FEEL MORE AT HOME.
I FEEL BAD FOR THE MAILMAN.
HISSSSSSSS.
MOMMY!!
...
...
...
...
...
GAAAH!!!
I'VE GOT MY EYE ON YOU!

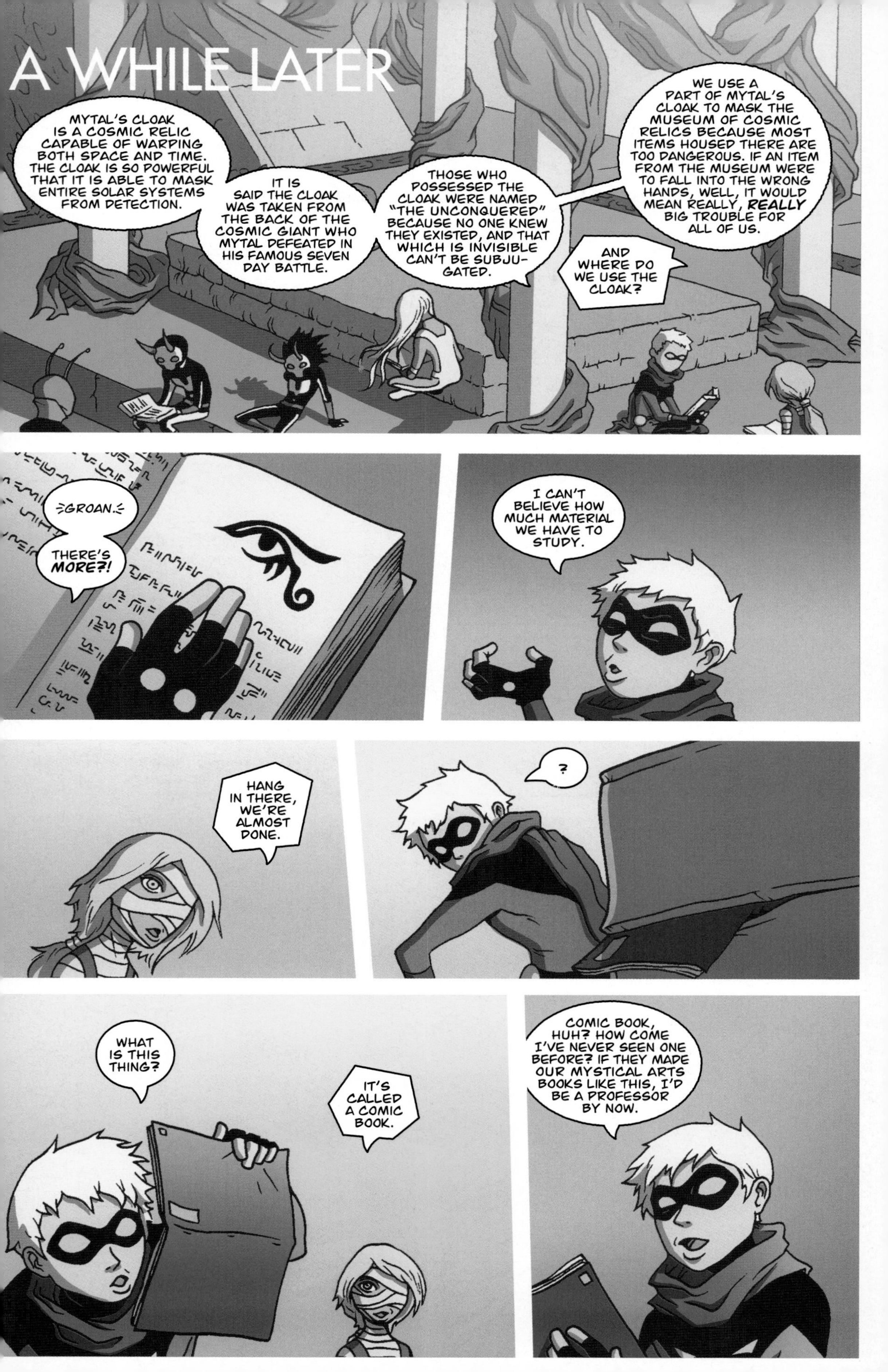
A WHILE LATER
MYTAL'S CLOAK IS A COSMIC RELIC CAPABLE OF WARPING BOTH SPACE AND TIME. THE CLOAK IS SO POWERFUL THAT IT IS ABLE TO MASK ENTIRE SOLAR SYSTEMS FROM DETECTION.
IT IS SAID THE CLOAK WAS TAKEN FROM THE BACK OF THE COSMIC GIANT WHO MYTAL DEFEATED IN HIS FAMOUS SEVEN DAY BATTLE.
THOSE WHO POSSESSED THE CLOAK WERE NAMED "THE UNCONQUERED" BECAUSE NO ONE KNEW THEY EXISTED, AND THAT WHICH IS INVISIBLE CAN'T BE SUBJU-GATED.
WE USE A PART OF MYTAL'S CLOAK TO MASK THE MUSEUM OF COSMIC RELICS BECAUSE MOST ITEMS HOUSED THERE ARE TOO DANGEROUS. IF AN ITEM FROM THE MUSEUM WERE TO FALL INTO THE WRONG HANDS, WELL, IT WOULD MEAN REALLY, REALLY BIG TROUBLE FOR ALL OF US.
AND WHERE DO WE USE THE CLOAK?
GROAN.
THERE'S MORE?!
I CAN'T BELIEVE HOW MUCH MATERIAL WE HAVE TO STUDY.
HANG IN THERE, WE'RE ALMOST DONE.
?
WHAT IS THIS THING?
IT'S CALLED A COMIC BOOK.
COMIC BOOK, HUH? HOW COME I'VE NEVER SEEN ONE BEFORE? IF THEY MADE OUR MYSTICAL ARTS BOOKS LIKE THIS, I'D BE A PROFESSOR BY NOW.

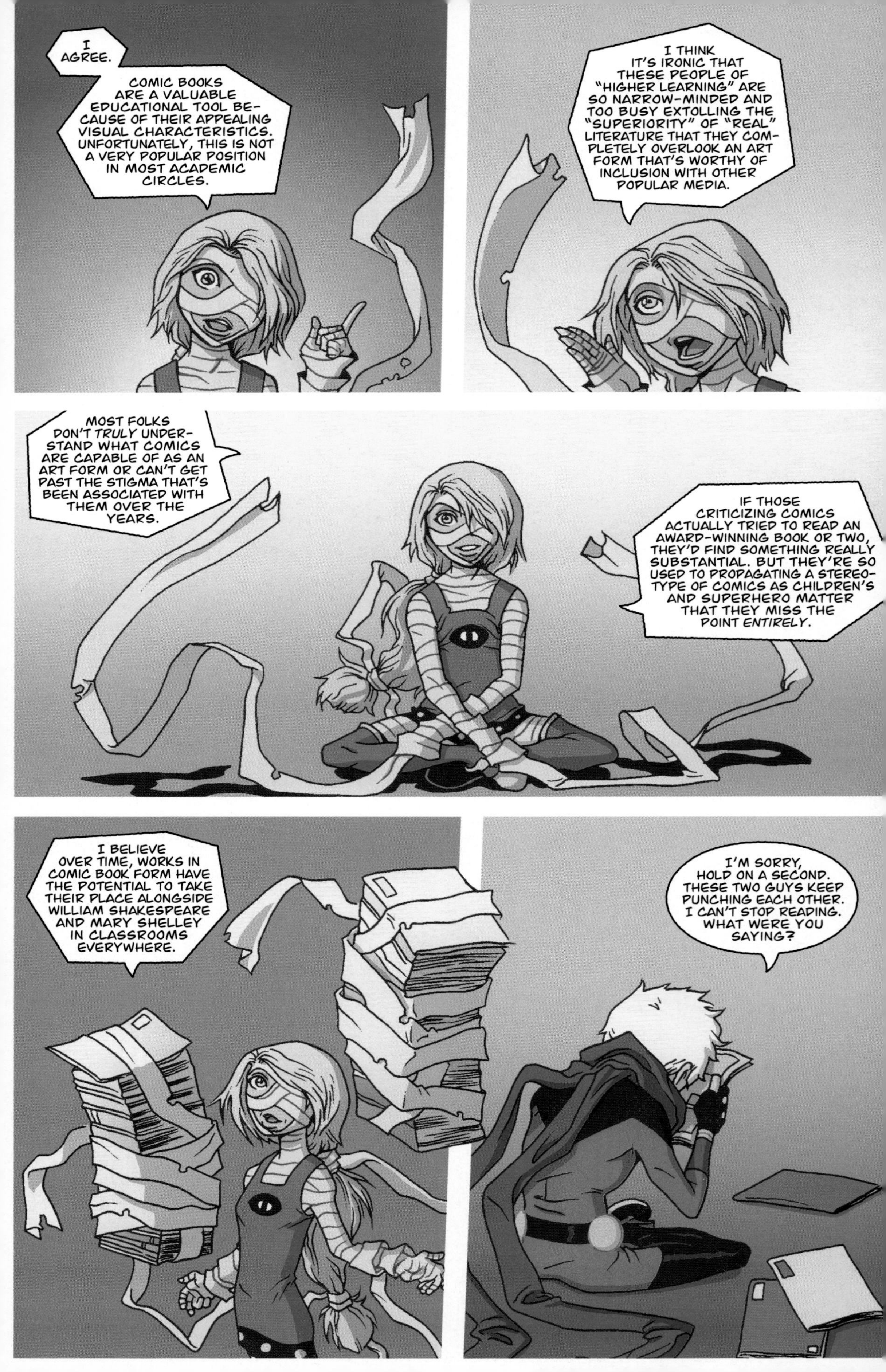
I AGREE.
COMIC BOOKS ARE A VALUABLE EDUCATIONAL TOOL BE-CAUSE OF THEIR APPEALING VISUAL CHARACTERISTICS. UNFORTUNATELY, THIS IS NOT A VERY POPULAR POSITION IN MOST ACADEMIC CIRCLES.
I THINK IT'S IRONIC THAT THESE PEOPLE OF "HIGHER LEARNING" ARE SO NARROW-MINDED AND TOO BUSY EXTOLLING THE "SUPERIORITY" OF "REAL" LITERATURE THAT THEY COM-PLETELY OVERLOOK AN ART FORM THAT'S WORTHY OF INCLUSION WITH OTHER POPULAR MEDIA.
MOST FOLKS DON'T *TRULY* UNDER-STAND WHAT COMICS ARE CAPABLE OF AS AN ART FORM OR CAN'T GET PAST THE STIGMA THAT'S BEEN ASSOCIATED WITH THEM OVER THE YEARS.
IF THOSE CRITICIZING COMICS ACTUALLY TRIED TO READ AN AWARD-WINNING BOOK OR TWO, THEY'D FIND SOMETHING REALLY SUBSTANTIAL. BUT THEY'RE SO USED TO PROPAGATING A STEREO-TYPE OF COMICS AS CHILDREN'S AND SUPERHERO MATTER THAT THEY MISS THE POINT *ENTIRELY*.
I BELIEVE OVER TIME, WORKS IN COMIC BOOK FORM HAVE THE POTENTIAL TO TAKE THEIR PLACE ALONGSIDE WILLIAM SHAKESPEARE AND MARY SHELLEY IN CLASSROOMS EVERYWHERE.
I'M SORRY, HOLD ON A SECOND. THESE TWO GUYS KEEP PUNCHING EACH OTHER. I CAN'T STOP READING. WHAT WERE YOU SAYING?

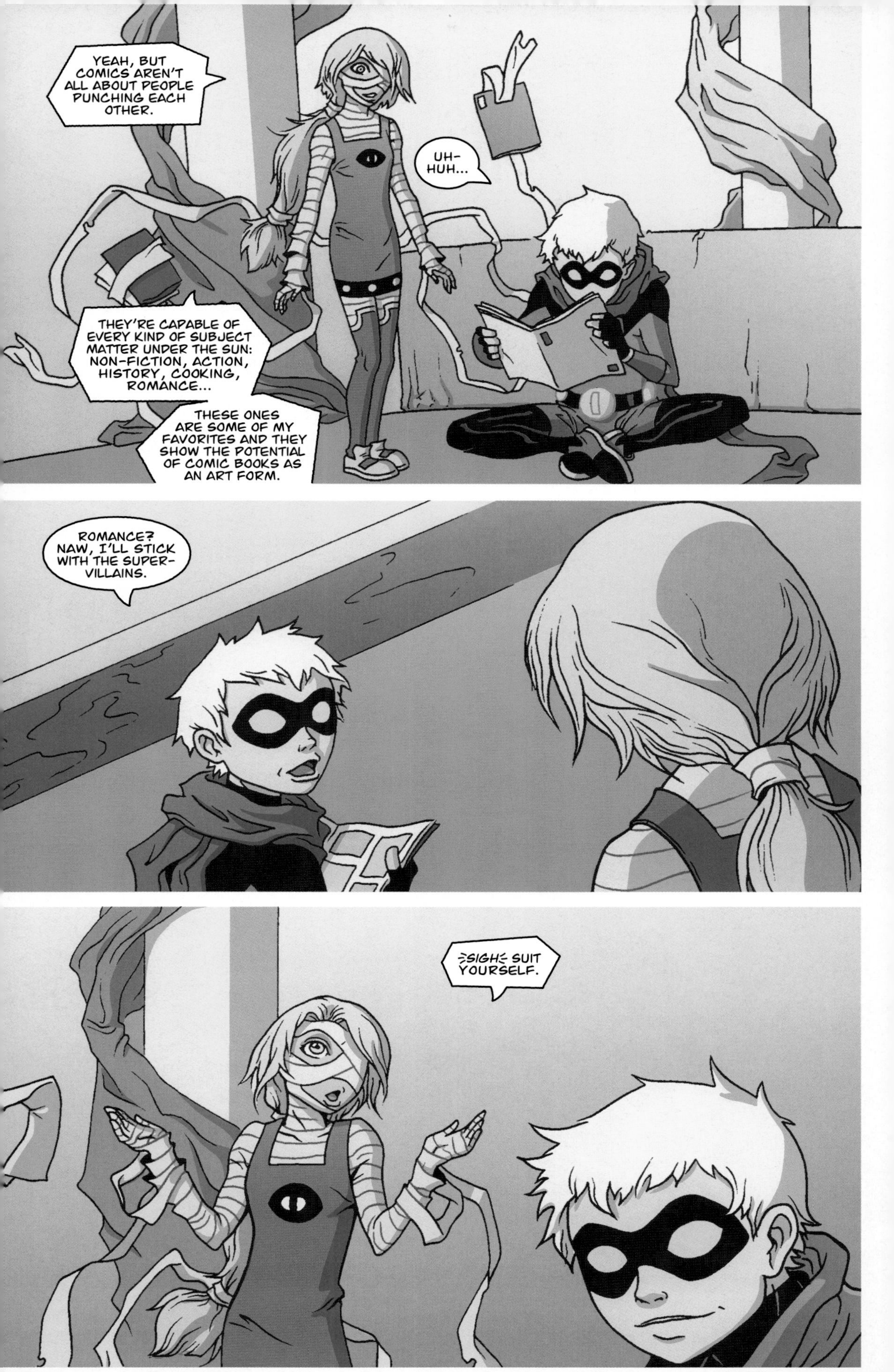
YEAH, BUT COMICS AREN'T ALL ABOUT PEOPLE PUNCHING EACH OTHER.
UH-HUH...
THEY'RE CAPABLE OF EVERY KIND OF SUBJECT MATTER UNDER THE SUN: NON-FICTION, ACTION, HISTORY, COOKING, ROMANCE...
THESE ONES ARE SOME OF MY FAVORITES AND THEY SHOW THE POTENTIAL OF COMIC BOOKS AS AN ART FORM.
ROMANCE? NAW, I'LL STICK WITH THE SUPER-VILLAINS.
SIGH SUIT YOURSELF.

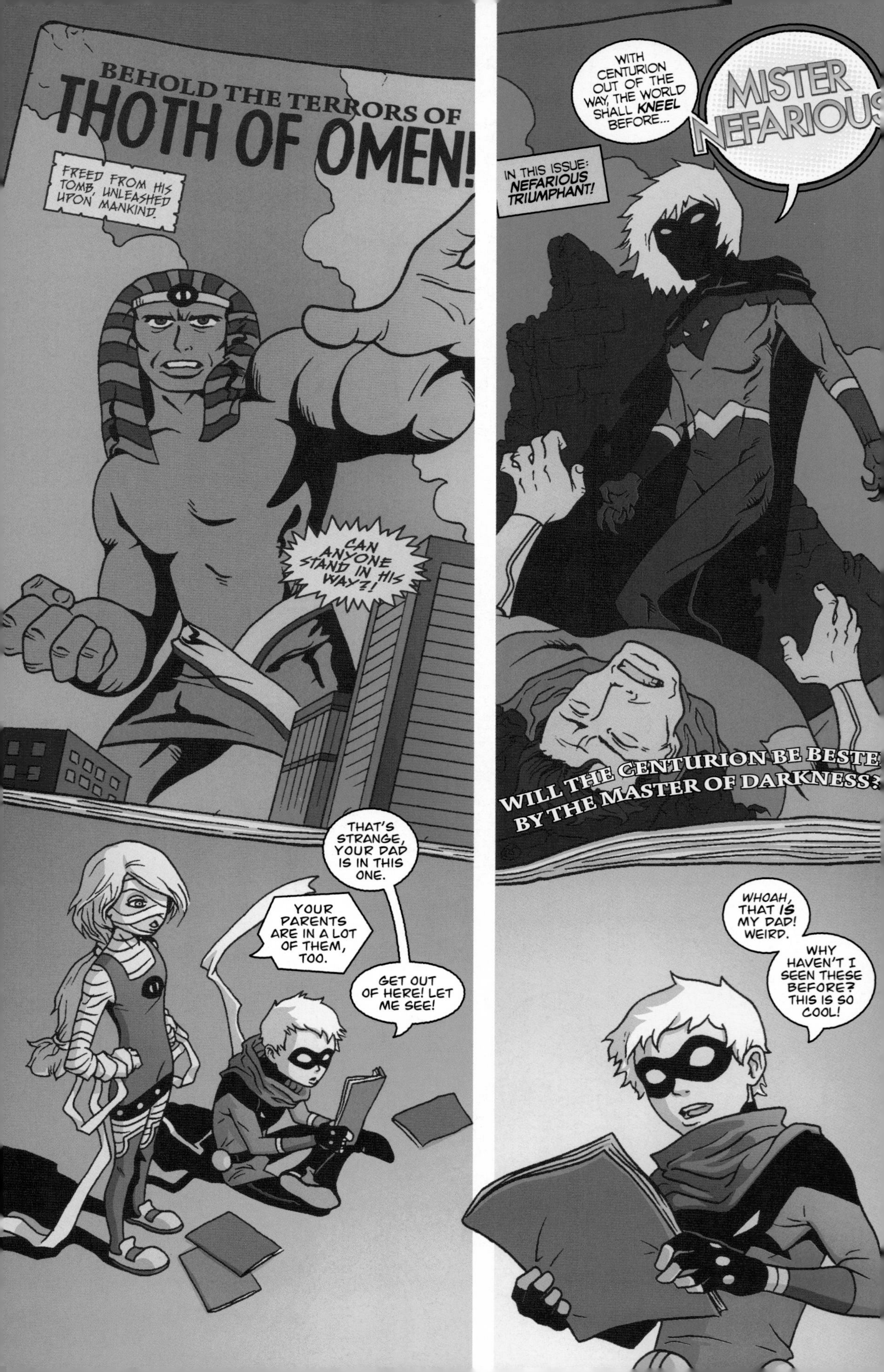
BEHOLD THE TERRORS OF
THOTH OF OMEN!
FREED FROM HIS TOMB, UNLEASHED UPON MANKIND.
CAN ANYONE STAND IN HIS WAY?!
WITH CENTURION OUT OF THE WAY, THE WORLD SHALL KNEEL BEFORE...
MISTER NEFARIOUS
IN THIS ISSUE: NEFARIOUS TRIUMPHANT!
WILL THE CENTURION BE BESTE
BY THE MASTER OF DARKNESS?
THAT'S STRANGE, YOUR DAD IS IN THIS ONE.
YOUR PARENTS ARE IN A LOT OF THEM, TOO.
GET OUT OF HERE! LET ME SEE!
WHOAH, THAT IS MY DAD! WEIRD.
WHY HAVEN'T I SEEN THESE BEFORE? THIS IS SO COOL!

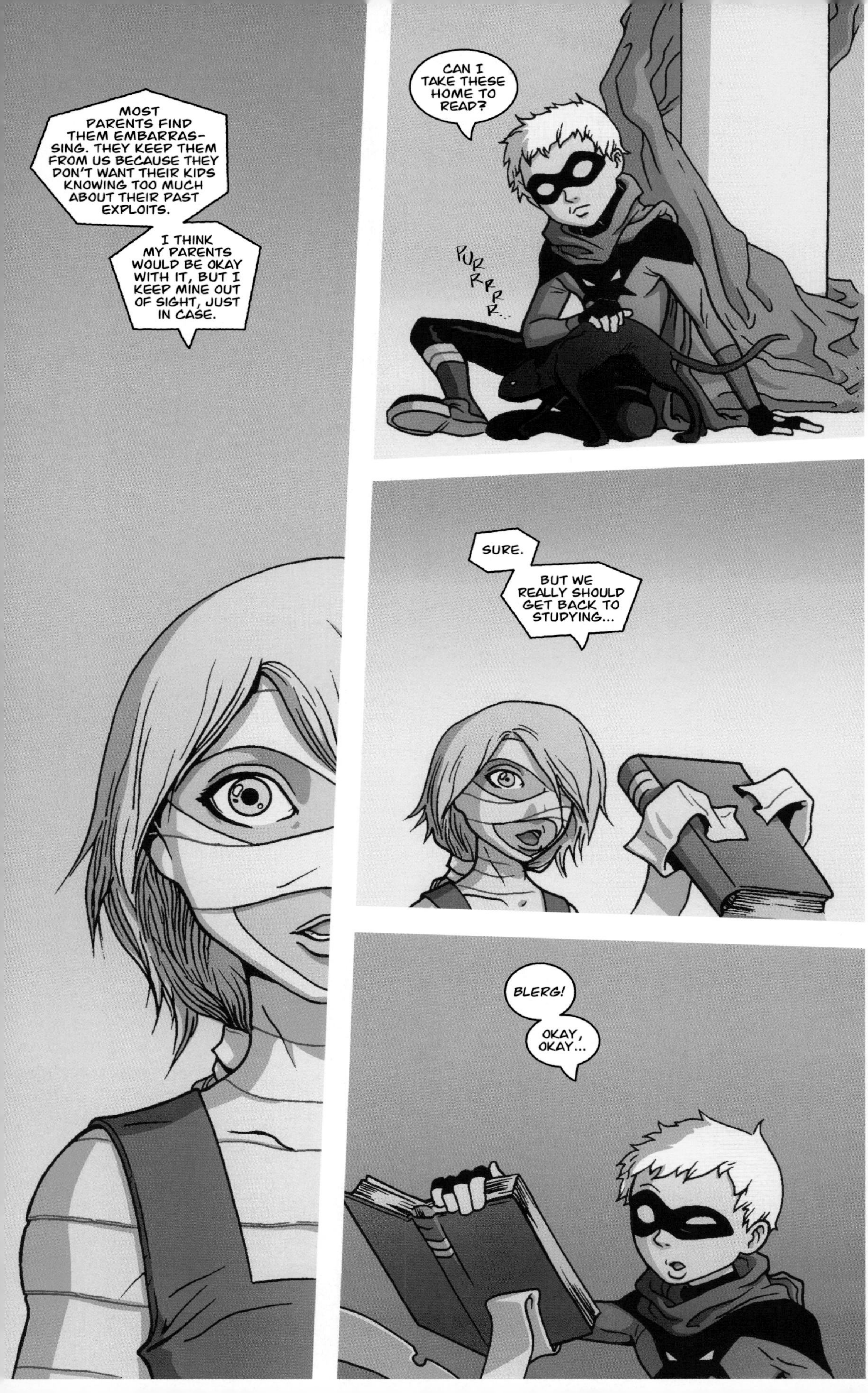
MOST PARENTS FIND THEM EMBARRAS-SING. THEY KEEP THEM FROM US BECAUSE THEY DON'T WANT THEIR KIDS KNOWING TOO MUCH ABOUT THEIR PAST EXPLOITS.
I THINK MY PARENTS WOULD BE OKAY WITH IT, BUT I KEEP MINE OUT OF SIGHT, JUST IN CASE.
CAN I TAKE THESE HOME TO READ?
PURRRRR...
SURE.
BUT WE REALLY SHOULD GET BACK TO STUDYING...
BLERG!
OKAY, OKAY...

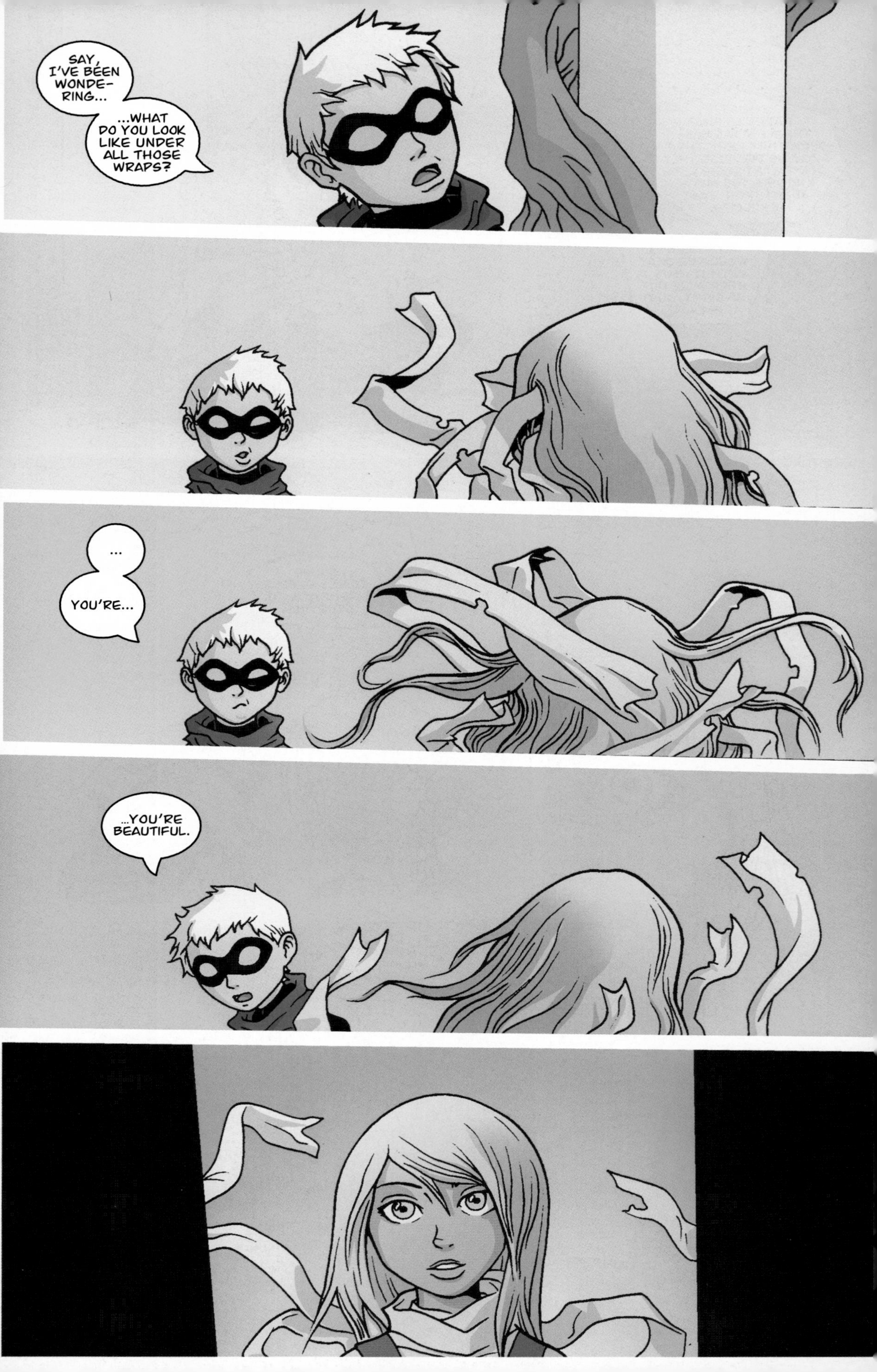
SAY, I'VE BEEN WONDE-RING...
...WHAT DO YOU LOOK LIKE UNDER ALL THOSE WRAPS?
...
YOU'RE...
...YOU'RE BEAUTIFUL.

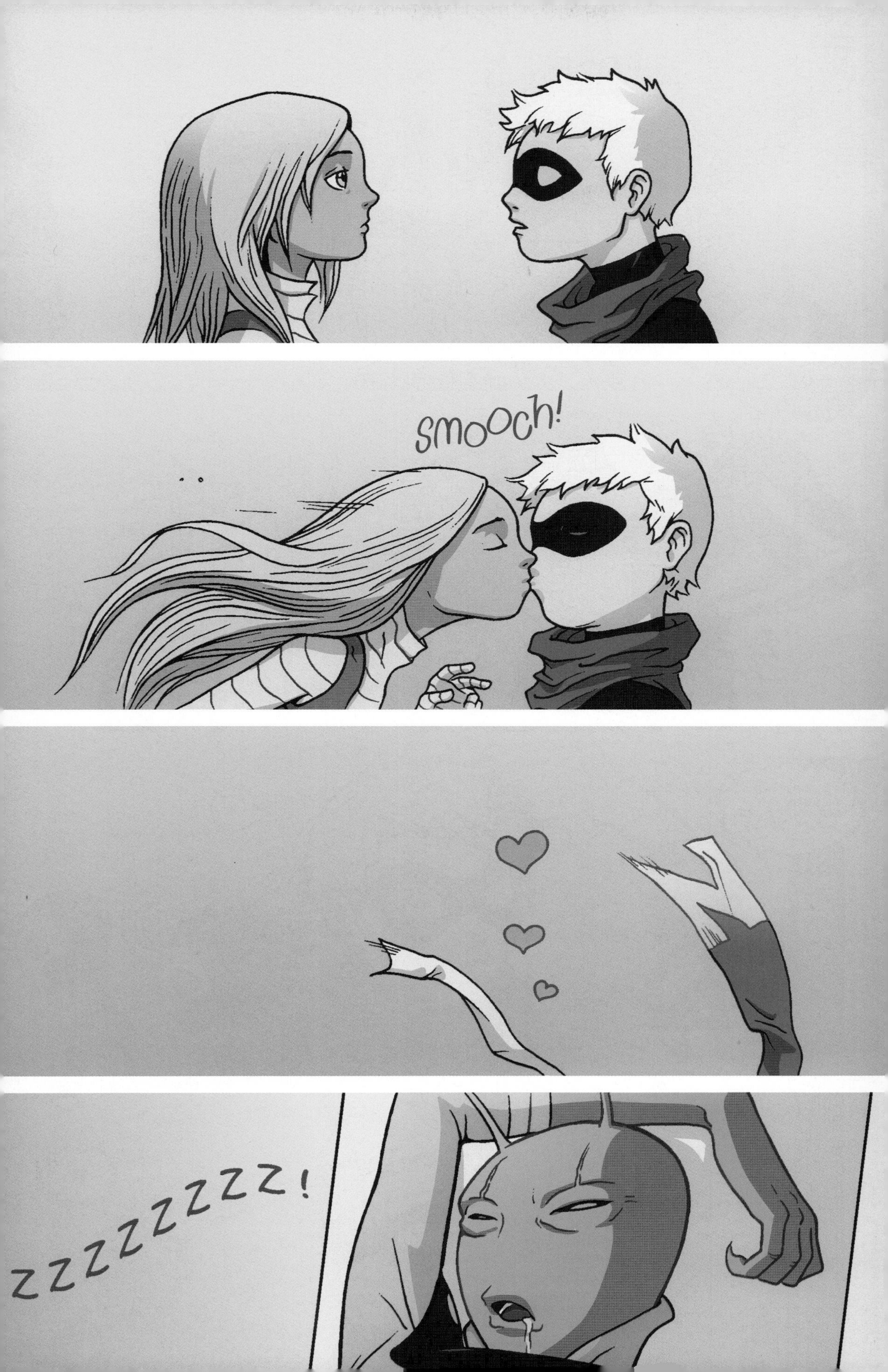
smooch!
ZZZZZZZZZZ!

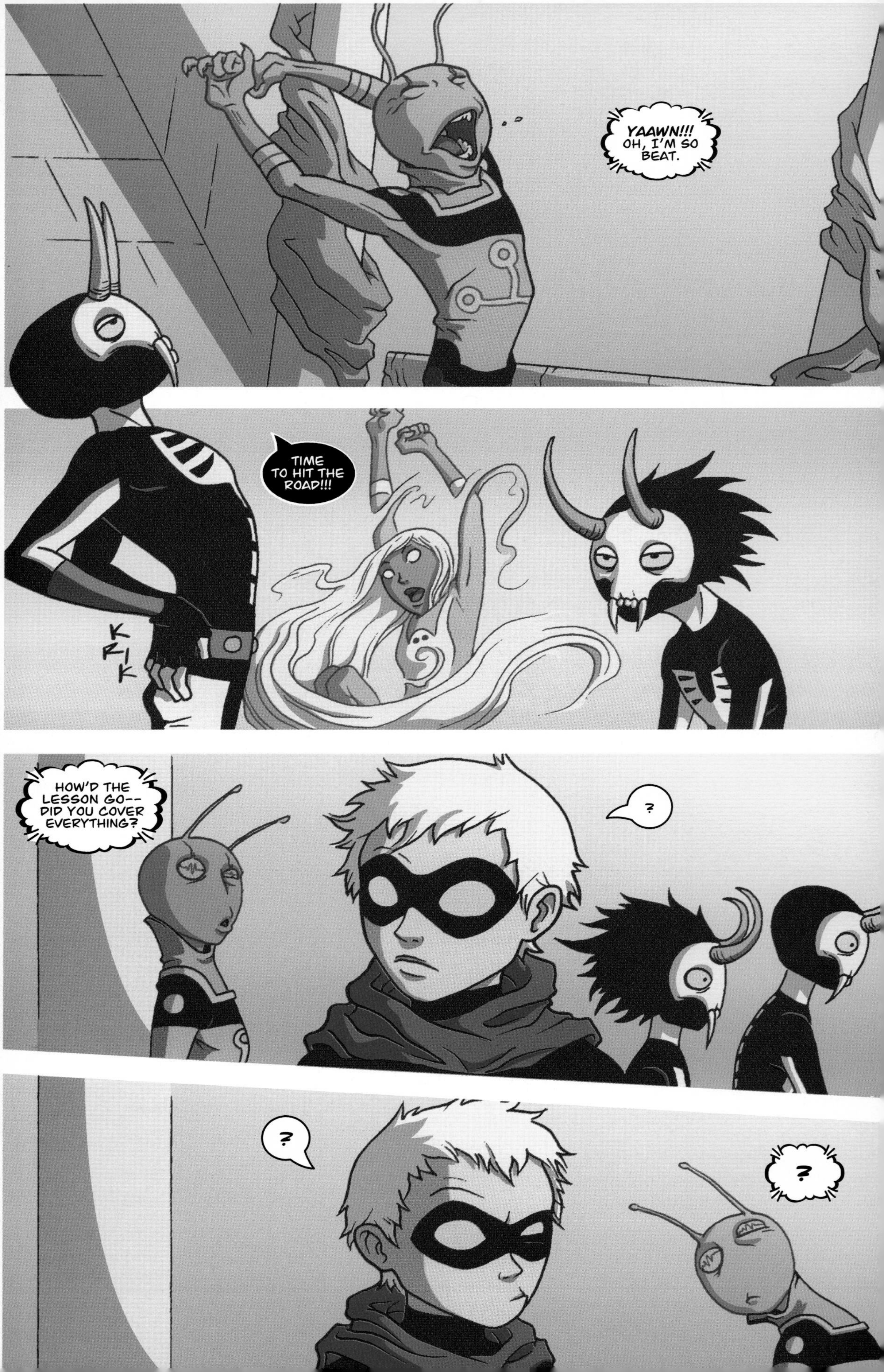
YAAWN!!! OH, I'M SO BEAT.
TIME TO HIT THE ROAD!!!
KRIK
HOW'D THE LESSON GO-- DID YOU COVER EVERYTHING?
?
?
?

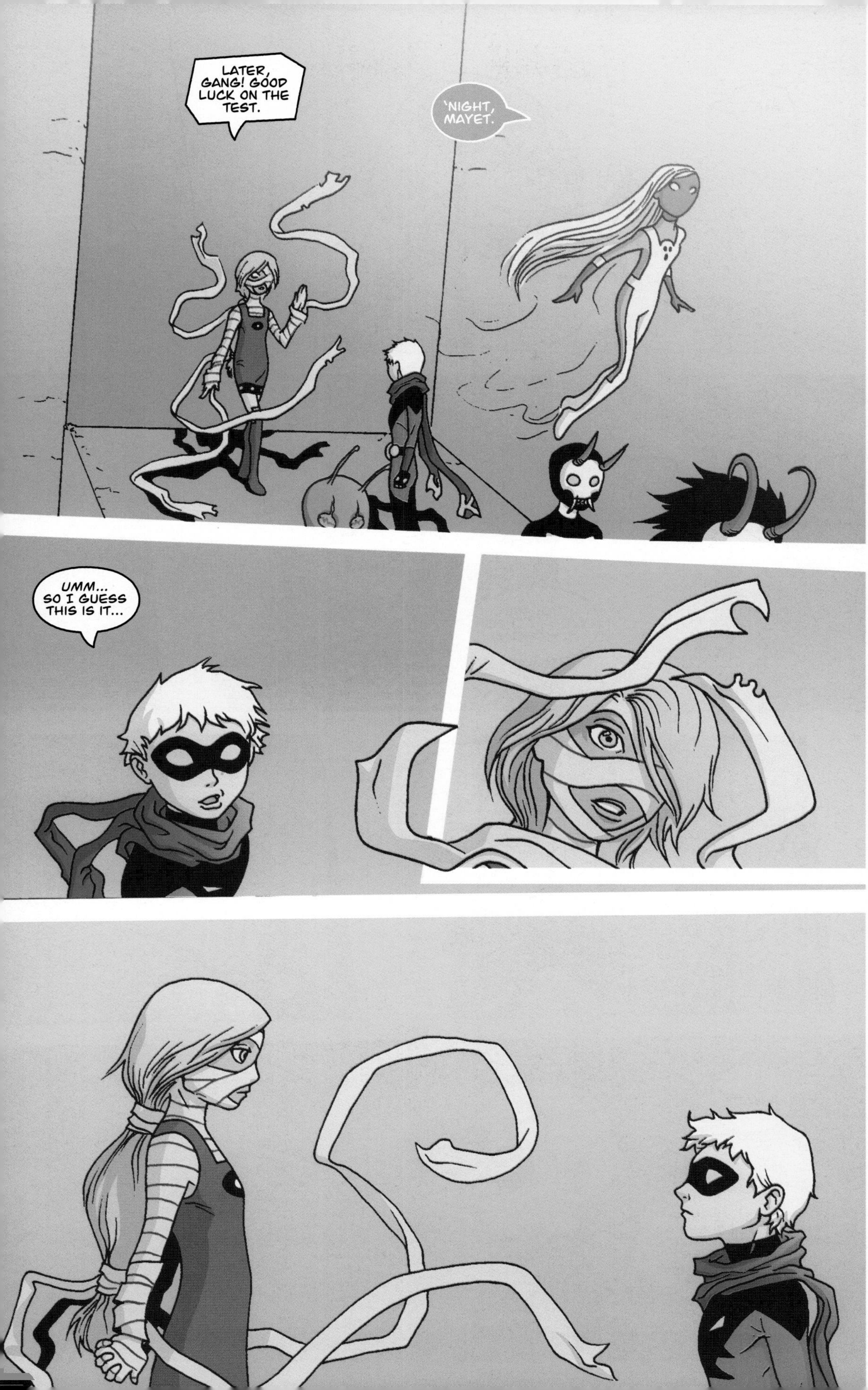
LATER, GANG! GOOD LUCK ON THE TEST.
'NIGHT, MAYET.
UMM... SO I GUESS THIS IS IT...

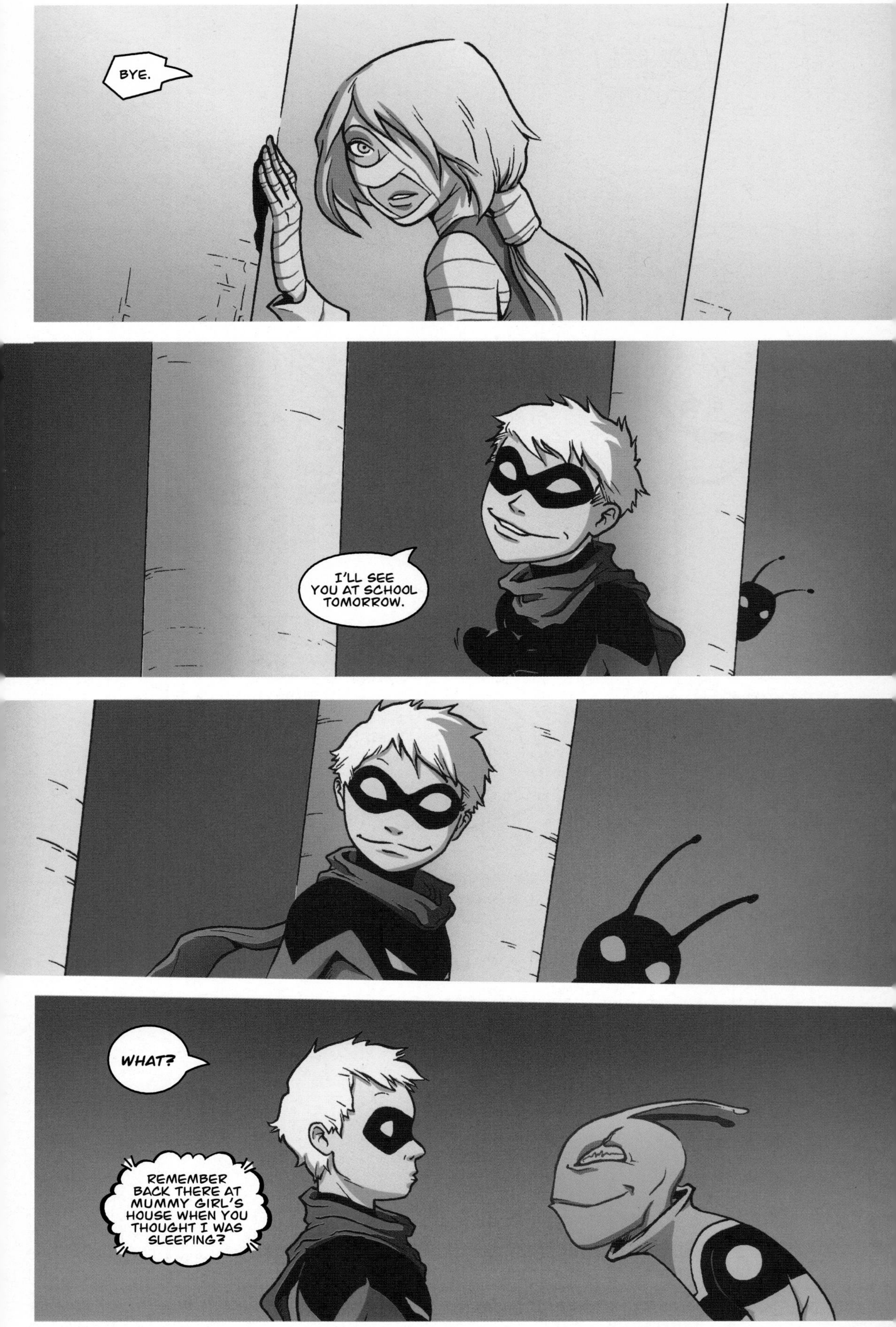
BYE.
I'LL SEE YOU AT SCHOOL TOMORROW.
WHAT?
REMEMBER BACK THERE AT MUMMY GIRL'S HOUSE WHEN YOU THOUGHT I WAS SLEEPING?

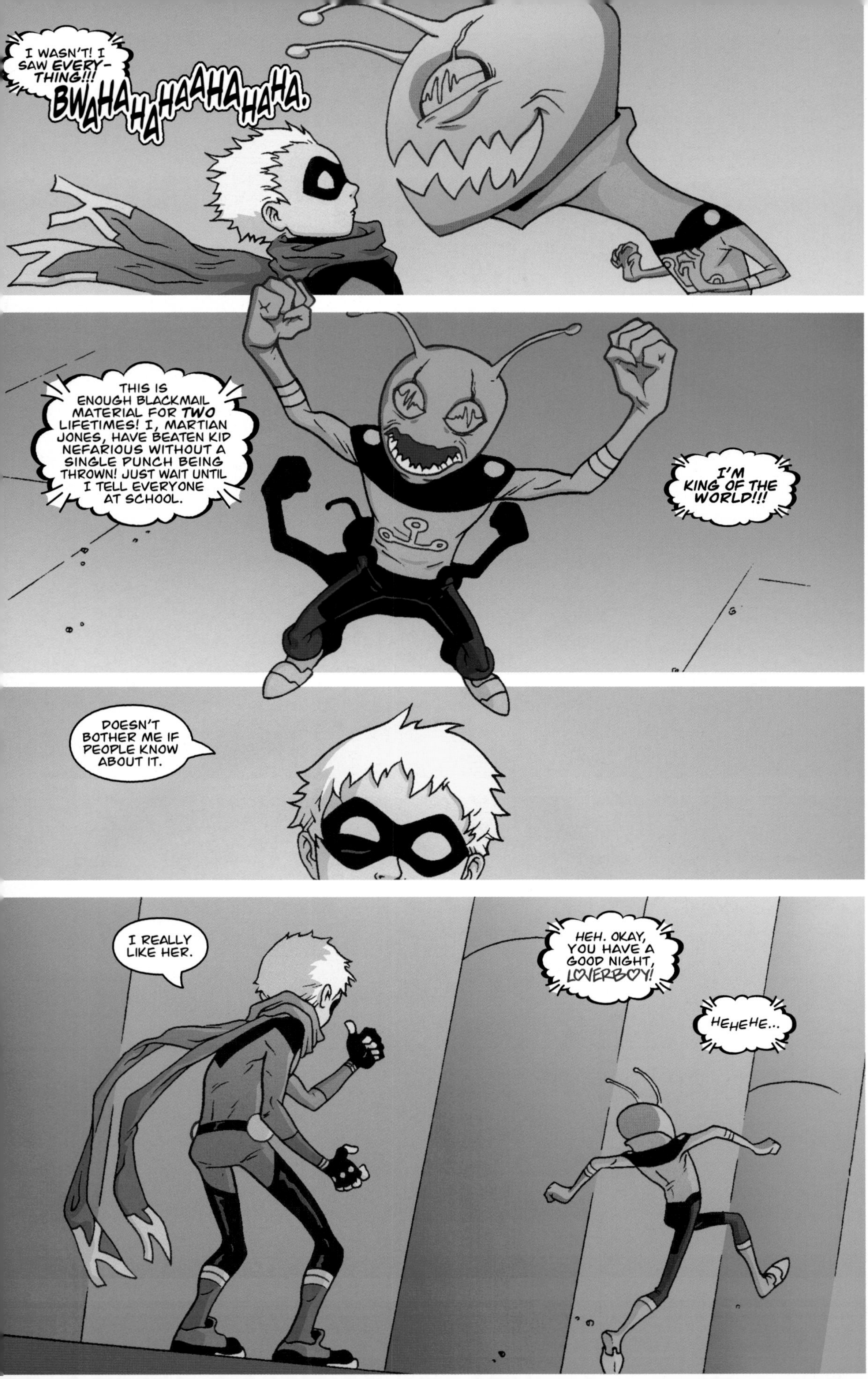
I WASN'T! I SAW EVERY-THING!!!
BWAHAHAHAAHAHAHAHA.
THIS IS ENOUGH BLACKMAIL MATERIAL FOR TWO LIFETIMES! I, MARTIAN JONES, HAVE BEATEN KID NEFARIOUS WITHOUT A SINGLE PUNCH BEING THROWN! JUST WAIT UNTIL I TELL EVERYONE AT SCHOOL.
I'M KING OF THE WORLD!!!
DOESN'T BOTHER ME IF PEOPLE KNOW ABOUT IT.
I REALLY LIKE HER.
HEH. OKAY, YOU HAVE A GOOD NIGHT, LOVERBOY!
HEHEHE...

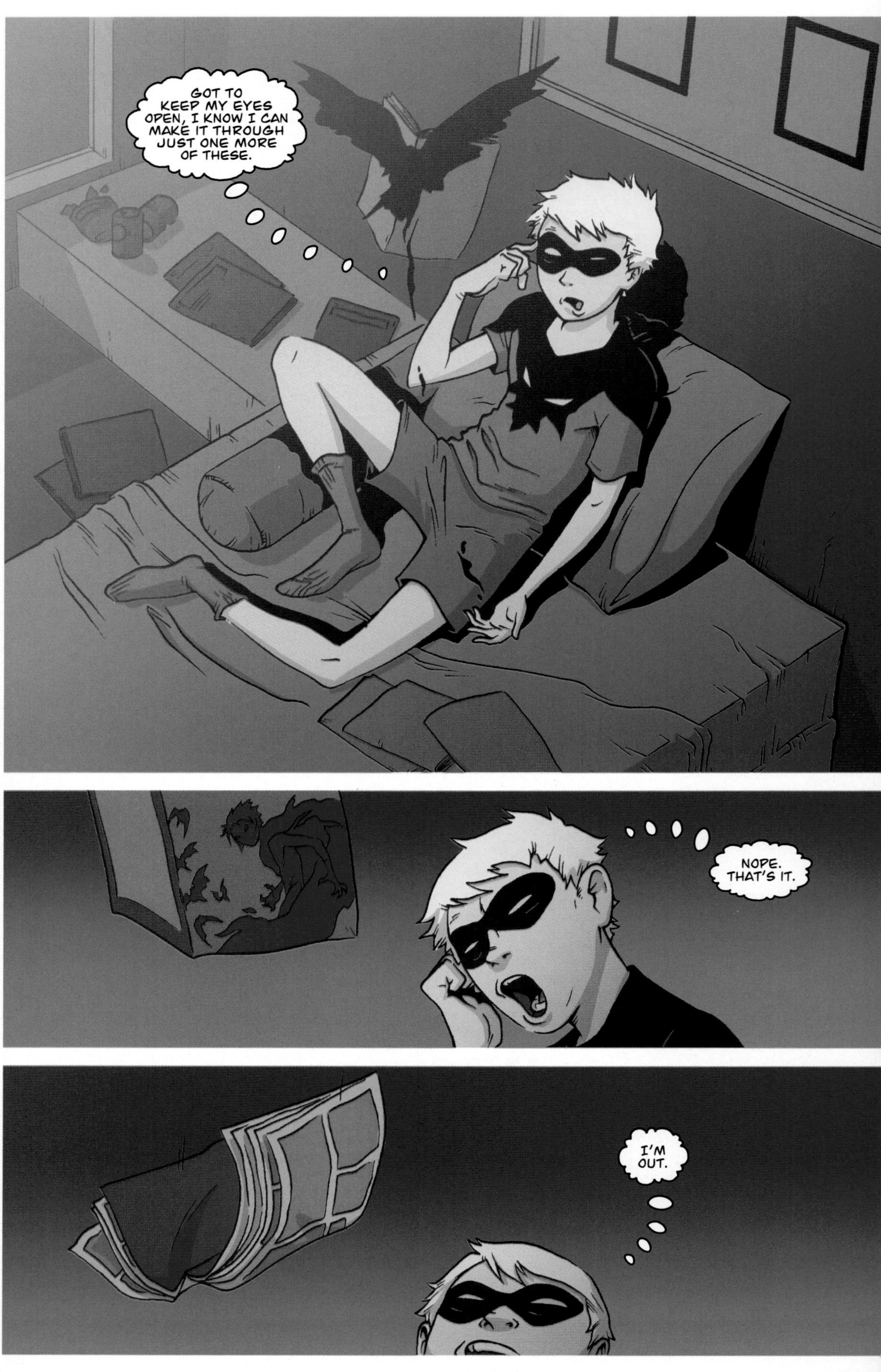
GOT TO KEEP MY EYES OPEN, I KNOW I CAN MAKE IT THROUGH JUST ONE MORE OF THESE.
NOPE. THAT'S IT.
I'M OUT.

CHAPTER 5

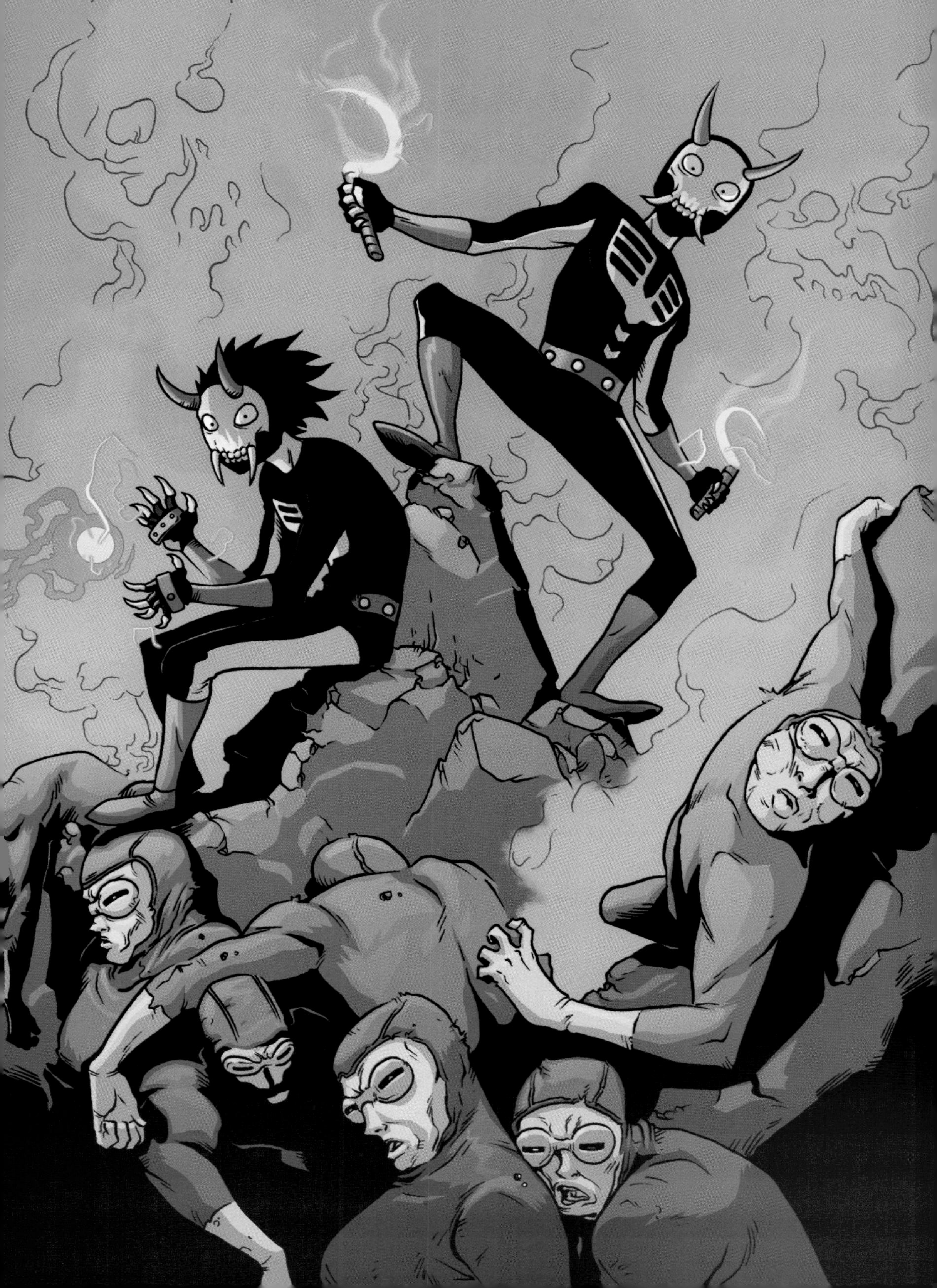

GLADSTONE'S SCHOOL FOR WORLD CONQUERORS

Written by
Mark Andrew Smith

Art & Cover by
Armand Villavert

Colors by
Rodrigo Avilés

Letters by
Thomas Mauer

Edits by
Erick Taggart

INTERGALACTIC BATTLE STRATEGY

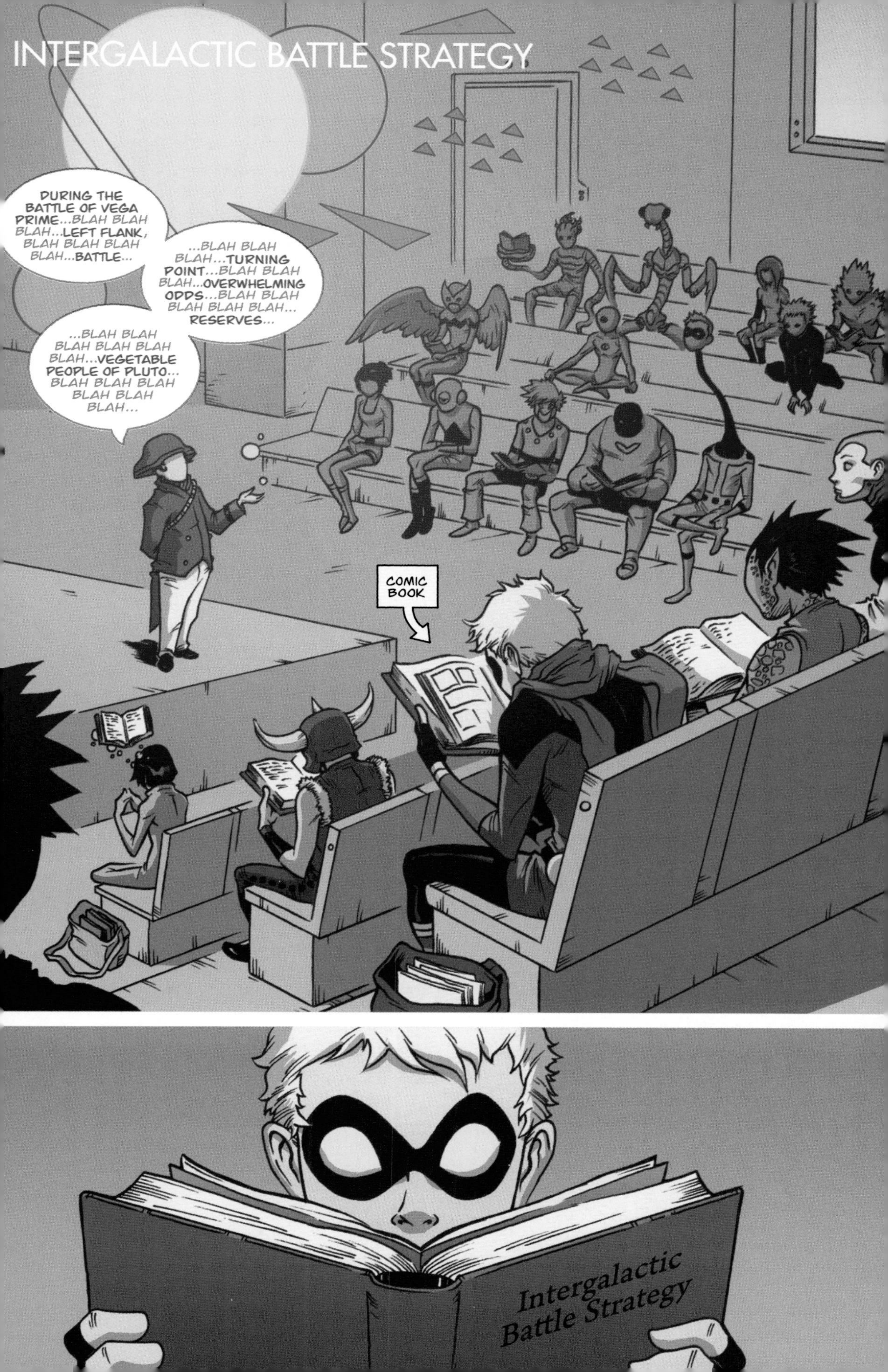
DURING THE BATTLE OF VEGA PRIME...BLAH BLAH BLAH...LEFT FLANK, BLAH BLAH BLAH BLAH...BATTLE...
...BLAH BLAH BLAH...TURNING POINT...BLAH BLAH BLAH...OVERWHELMING ODDS...BLAH BLAH BLAH BLAH BLAH... RESERVES...
...BLAH BLAH BLAH BLAH BLAH BLAH...VEGETABLE PEOPLE OF PLUTO... BLAH BLAH BLAH BLAH BLAH BLAH...
COMIC BOOK
Intergalactic Battle Strategy

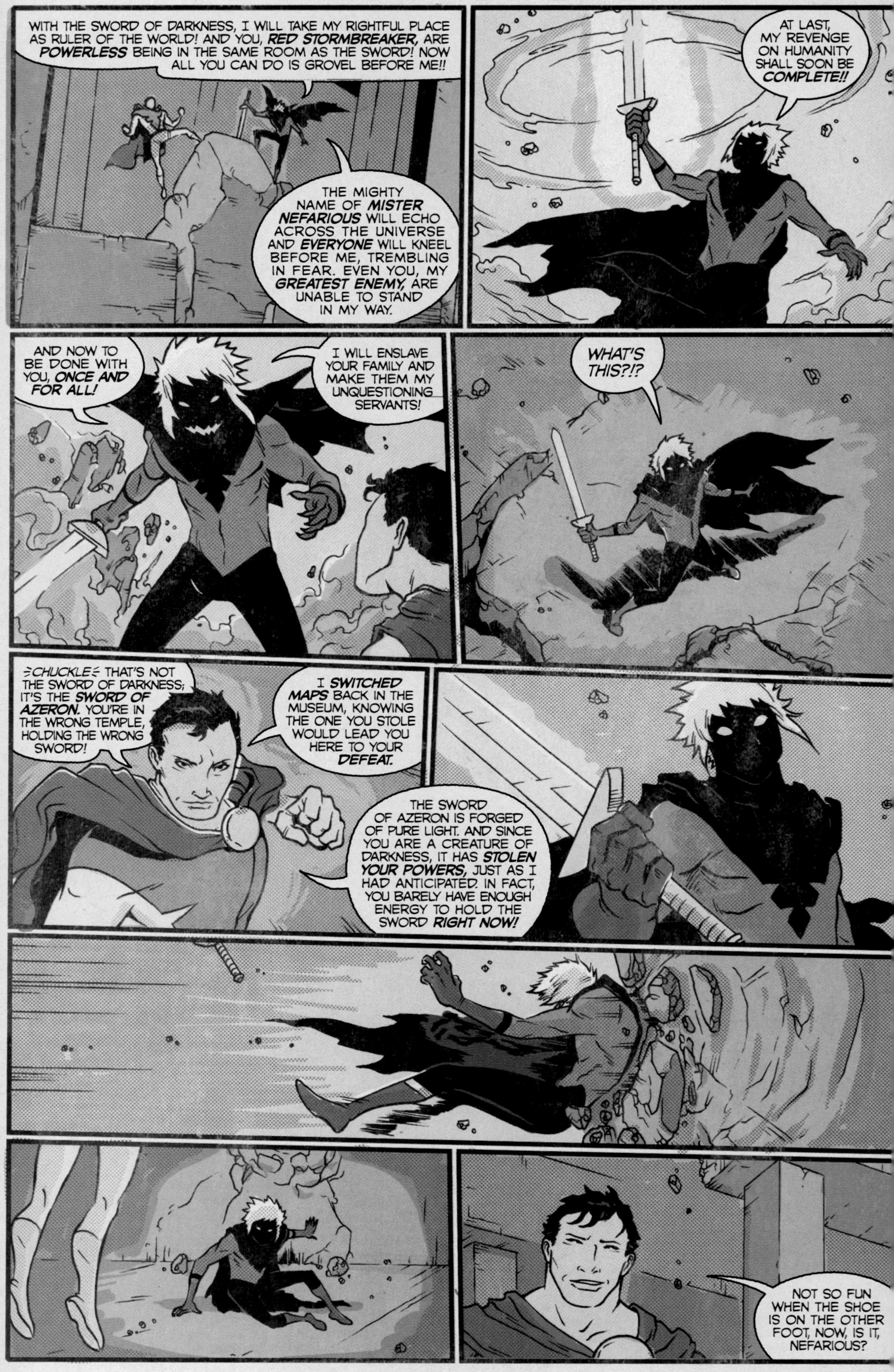
WITH THE SWORD OF DARKNESS, I WILL TAKE MY RIGHTFUL PLACE AS RULER OF THE WORLD! AND YOU, RED STORMBREAKER, ARE POWERLESS BEING IN THE SAME ROOM AS THE SWORD! NOW ALL YOU CAN DO IS GROVEL BEFORE ME!!
THE MIGHTY NAME OF MISTER NEFARIOUS WILL ECHO ACROSS THE UNIVERSE AND EVERYONE WILL KNEEL BEFORE ME, TREMBLING IN FEAR. EVEN YOU, MY GREATEST ENEMY, ARE UNABLE TO STAND IN MY WAY.
AT LAST, MY REVENGE ON HUMANITY SHALL SOON BE COMPLETE!!
AND NOW TO BE DONE WITH YOU, ONCE AND FOR ALL!
I WILL ENSLAVE YOUR FAMILY AND MAKE THEM MY UNQUESTIONING SERVANTS!
WHAT'S THIS?!?
CHUCKLE THAT'S NOT THE SWORD OF DARKNESS; IT'S THE SWORD OF AZERON. YOU'RE IN THE WRONG TEMPLE, HOLDING THE WRONG SWORD!
I SWITCHED MAPS BACK IN THE MUSEUM, KNOWING THE ONE YOU STOLE WOULD LEAD YOU HERE TO YOUR DEFEAT.
THE SWORD OF AZERON IS FORGED OF PURE LIGHT. AND SINCE YOU ARE A CREATURE OF DARKNESS, IT HAS STOLEN YOUR POWERS, JUST AS I HAD ANTICIPATED. IN FACT, YOU BARELY HAVE ENOUGH ENERGY TO HOLD THE SWORD RIGHT NOW!
NOT SO FUN WHEN THE SHOE IS ON THE OTHER FOOT, NOW, IS IT, NEFARIOUS?

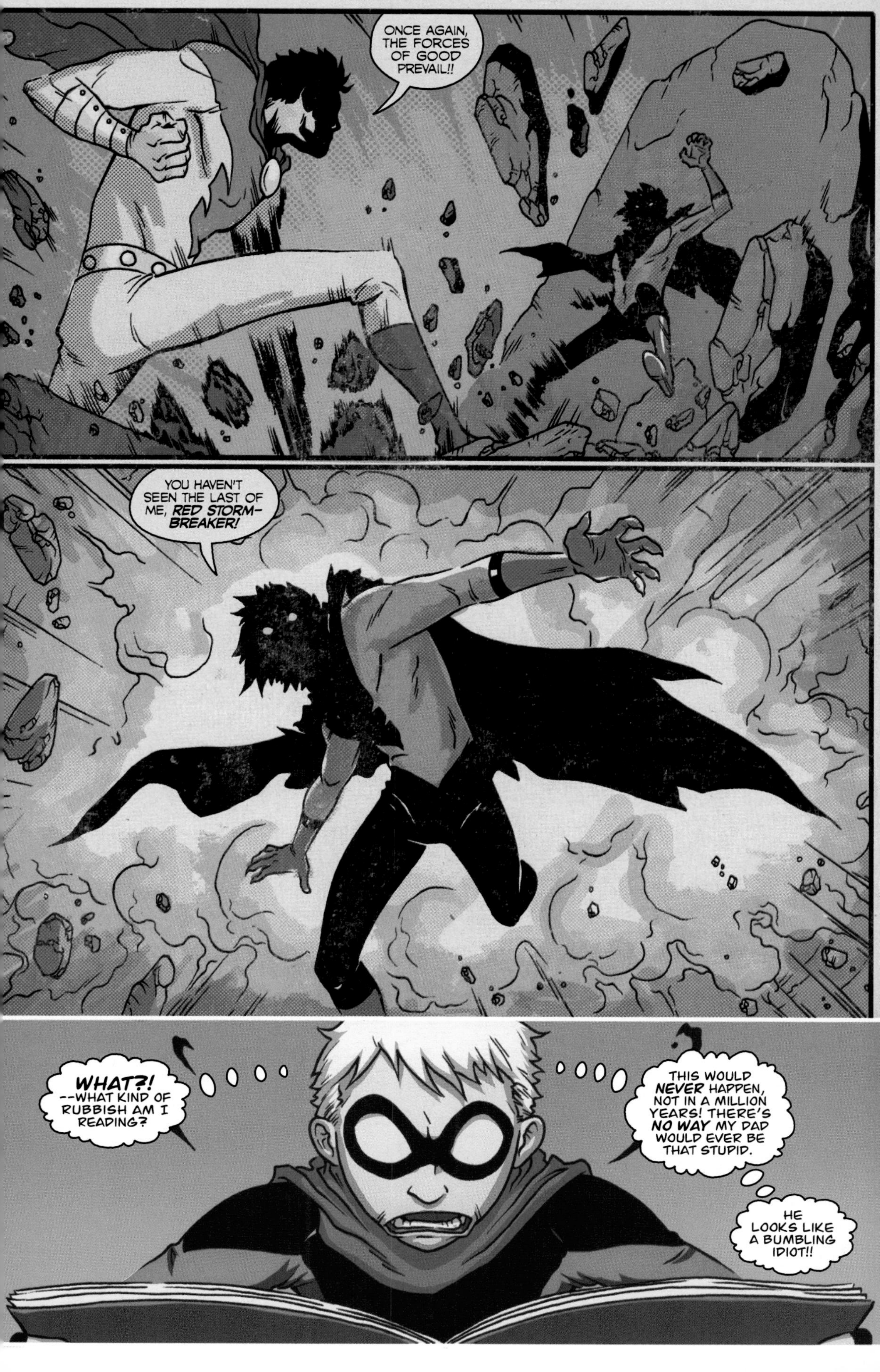

ONCE AGAIN, THE FORCES OF GOOD PREVAIL!!
YOU HAVEN'T SEEN THE LAST OF ME, *RED STORM-BREAKER!*
WHAT?! --WHAT KIND OF RUBBISH AM I READING?
THIS WOULD *NEVER* HAPPEN, NOT IN A MILLION YEARS! THERE'S *NO WAY* MY DAD WOULD EVER BE THAT STUPID.
HE LOOKS LIKE A BUMBLING IDIOT!!

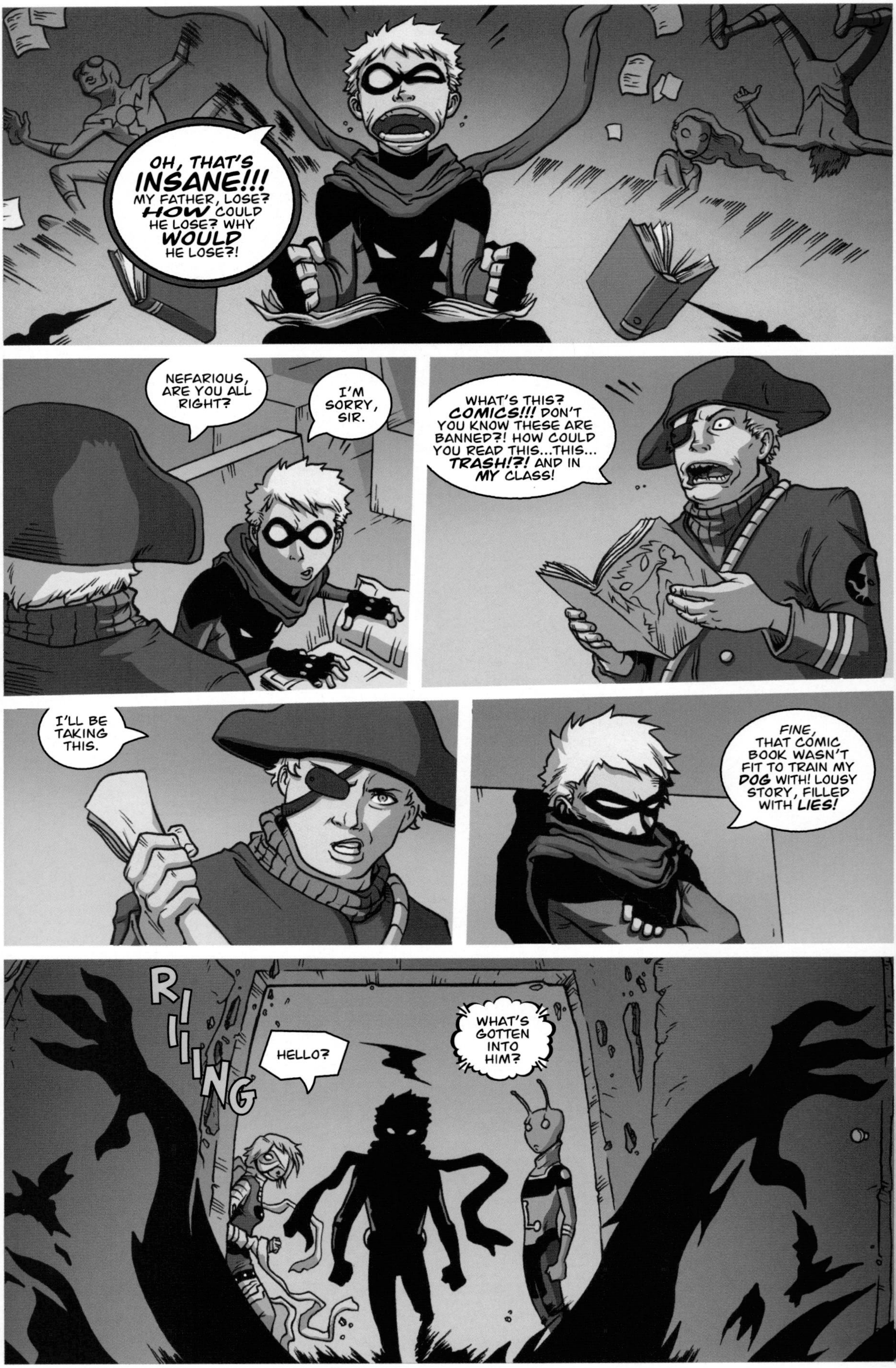
OH, THAT'S INSANE!!! MY FATHER, LOSE? HOW COULD HE LOSE? WHY WOULD HE LOSE?!
NEFARIOUS, ARE YOU ALL RIGHT?
I'M SORRY, SIR.
WHAT'S THIS? COMICS!!! DON'T YOU KNOW THESE ARE BANNED?! HOW COULD YOU READ THIS...THIS... TRASH!?! AND IN MY CLASS!
I'LL BE TAKING THIS.
FINE, THAT COMIC BOOK WASN'T FIT TO TRAIN MY DOG WITH! LOUSY STORY, FILLED WITH LIES!
RIIIING
HELLO?
WHAT'S GOTTEN INTO HIM?

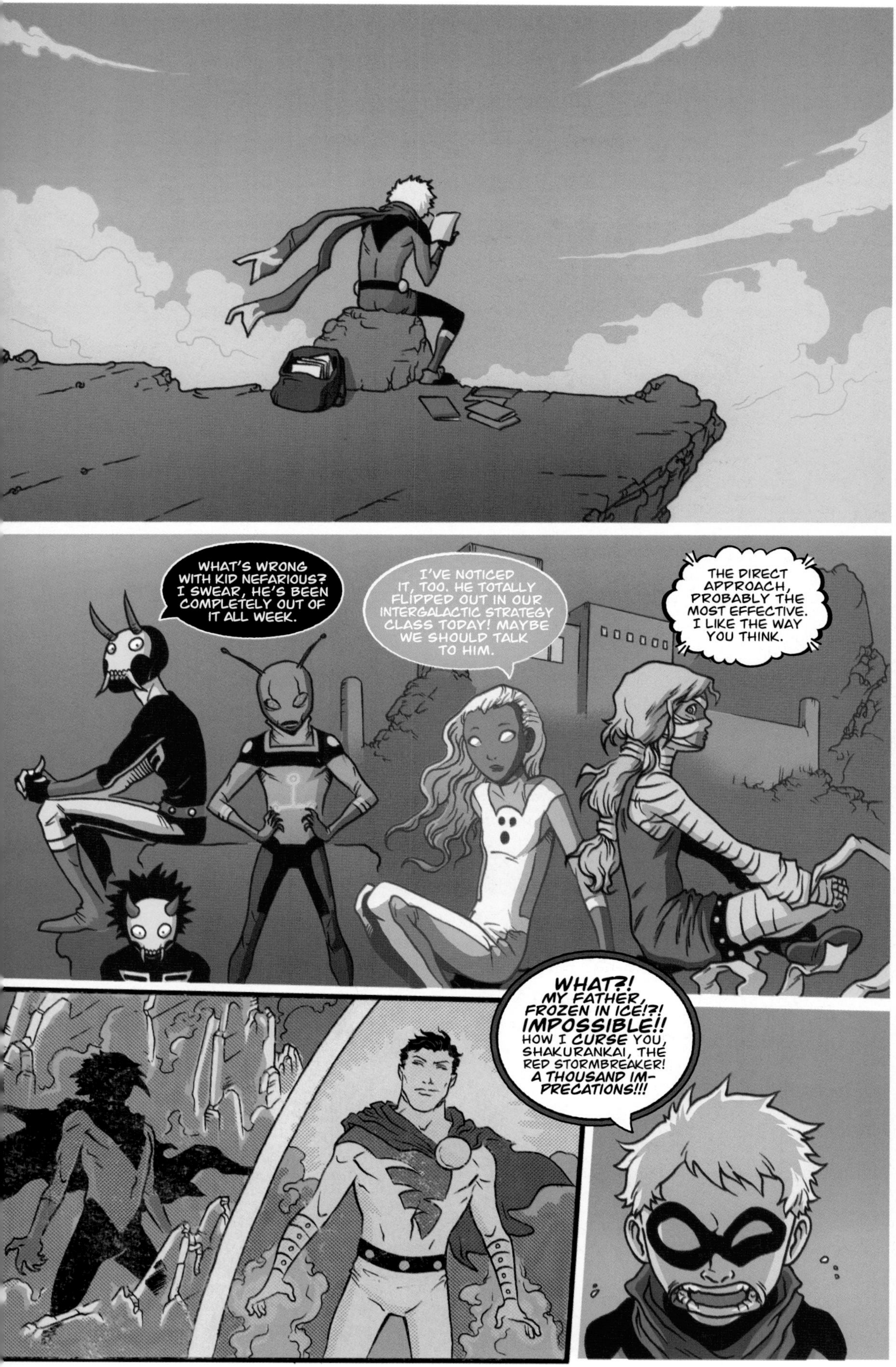
WHAT'S WRONG WITH KID NEFARIOUS? I SWEAR, HE'S BEEN COMPLETELY OUT OF IT ALL WEEK.
I'VE NOTICED IT, TOO. HE TOTALLY FLIPPED OUT IN OUR INTERGALACTIC STRATEGY CLASS TODAY! MAYBE WE SHOULD TALK TO HIM.
THE DIRECT APPROACH, PROBABLY THE MOST EFFECTIVE. I LIKE THE WAY YOU THINK.
WHAT?! MY FATHER, FROZEN IN ICE!?! IMPOSSIBLE!! HOW I CURSE YOU, SHAKURANKAI, THE RED STORMBREAKER! A THOUSAND IMPRECATIONS!!!

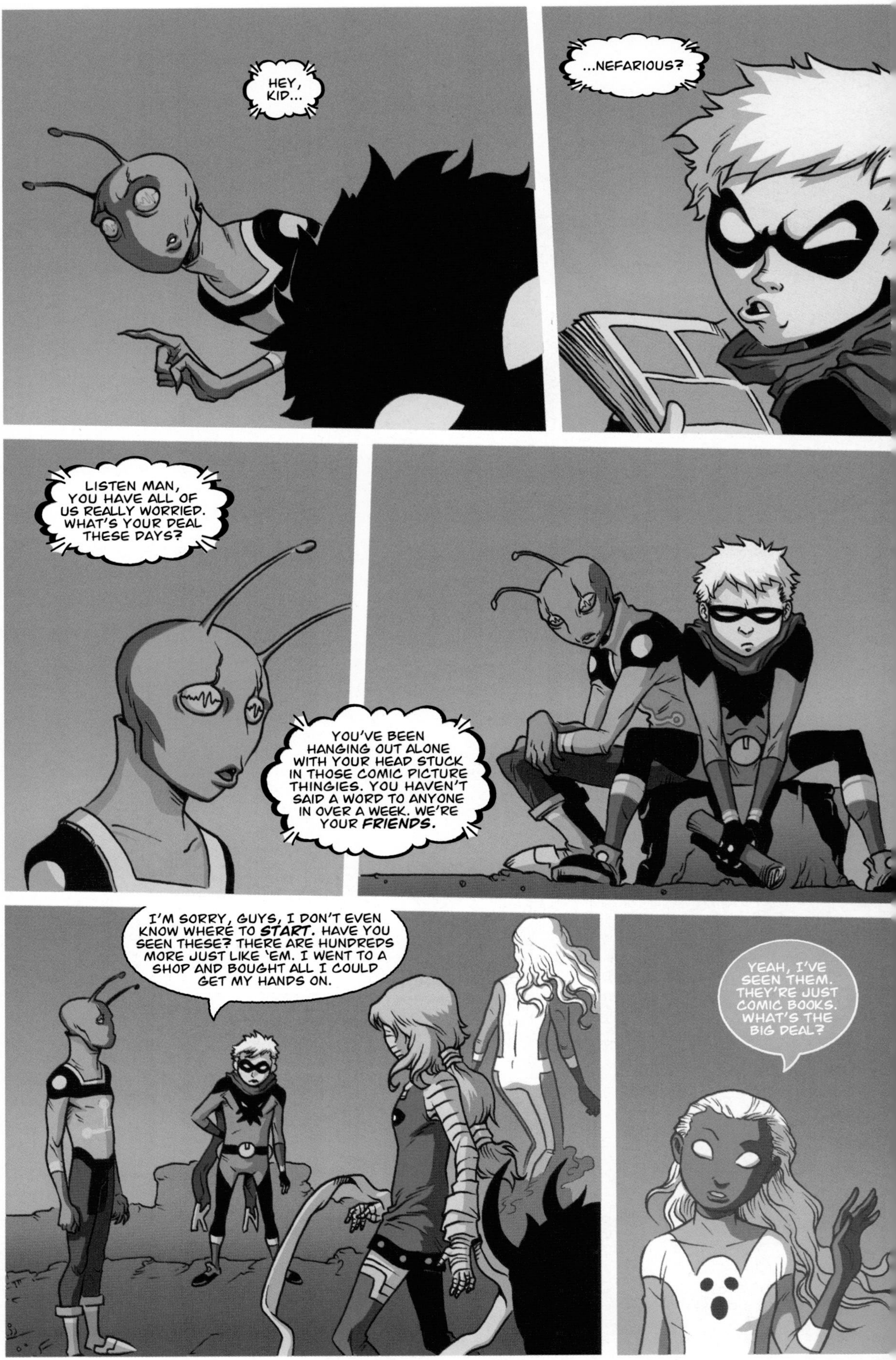
HEY, KID...
...NEFARIOUS?
LISTEN MAN, YOU HAVE ALL OF US REALLY WORRIED. WHAT'S YOUR DEAL THESE DAYS?
YOU'VE BEEN HANGING OUT ALONE WITH YOUR HEAD STUCK IN THOSE COMIC PICTURE THINGIES. YOU HAVEN'T SAID A WORD TO ANYONE IN OVER A WEEK. WE'RE YOUR FRIENDS.
I'M SORRY, GUYS, I DON'T EVEN KNOW WHERE TO START. HAVE YOU SEEN THESE? THERE ARE HUNDREDS MORE JUST LIKE 'EM. I WENT TO A SHOP AND BOUGHT ALL I COULD GET MY HANDS ON.
YEAH, I'VE SEEN THEM. THEY'RE JUST COMIC BOOKS. WHAT'S THE BIG DEAL?

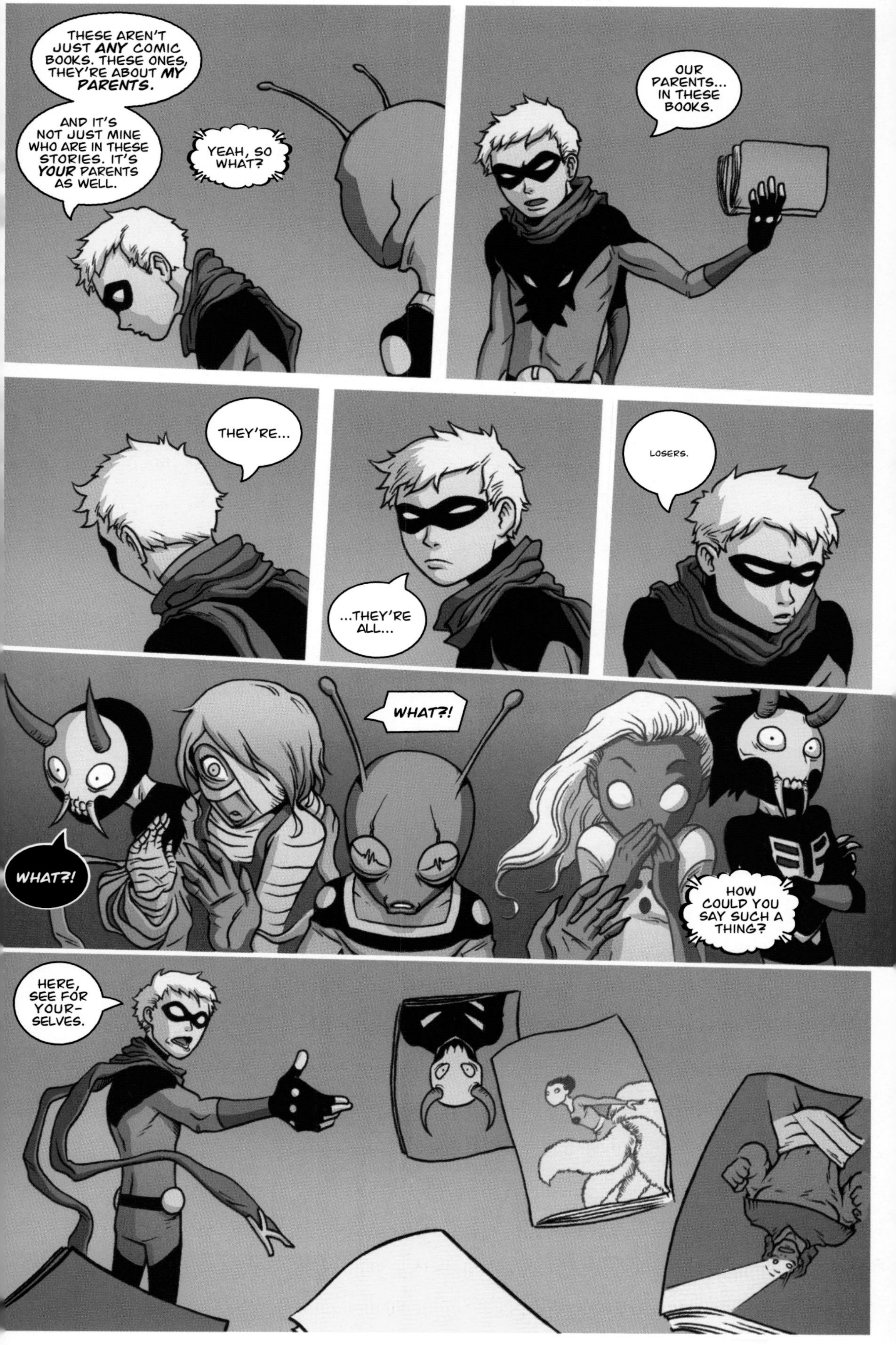

THESE AREN'T JUST ANY COMIC BOOKS. THESE ONES, THEY'RE ABOUT MY PARENTS.
AND IT'S NOT JUST MINE WHO ARE IN THESE STORIES. IT'S YOUR PARENTS AS WELL.
YEAH, SO WHAT?
OUR PARENTS... IN THESE BOOKS.
THEY'RE...
...THEY'RE ALL...
LOSERS.
WHAT?!
WHAT?!
HOW COULD YOU SAY SUCH A THING?
HERE, SEE FOR YOUR-SELVES.

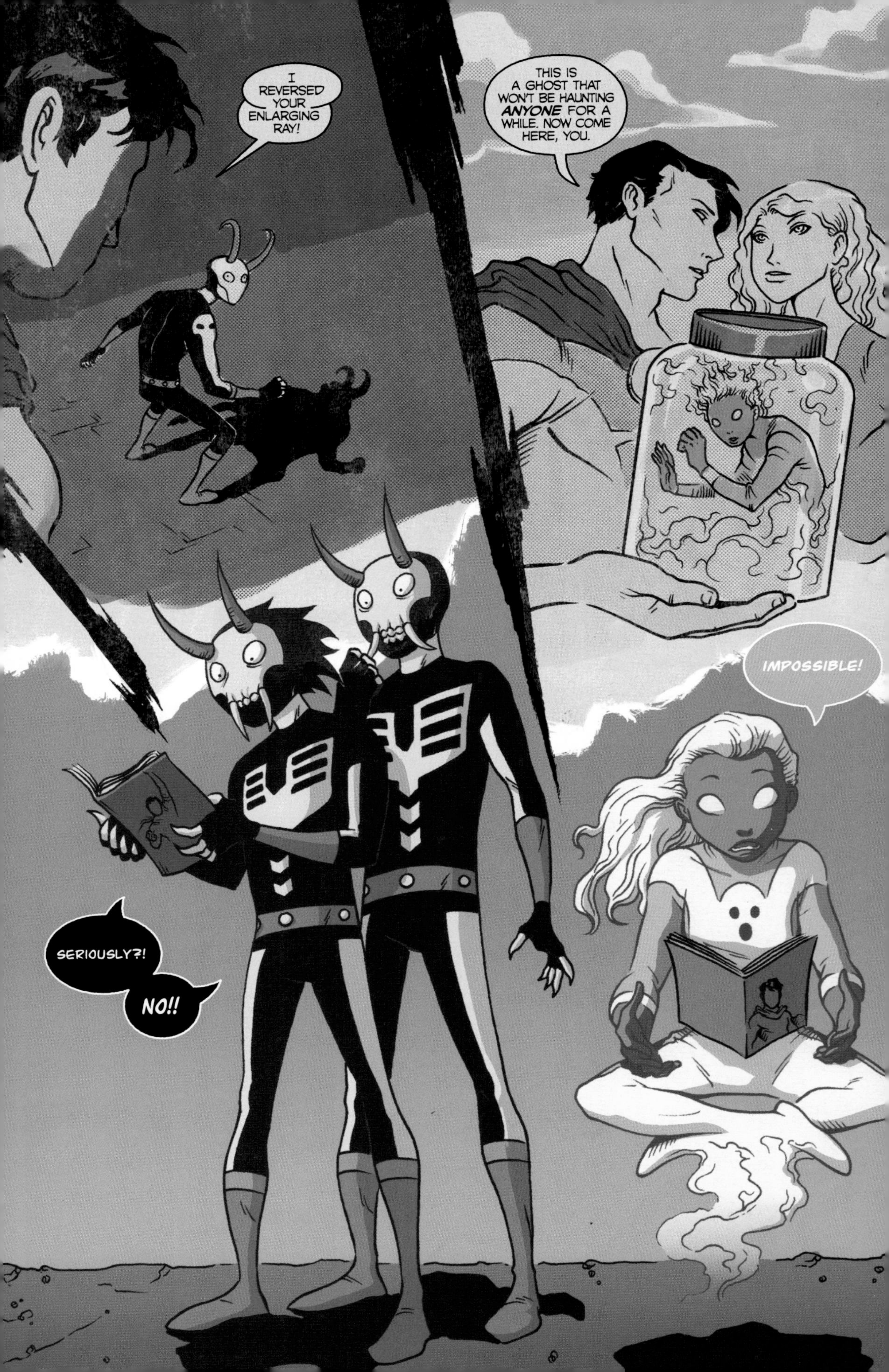
I REVERSED YOUR ENLARGING RAY!
THIS IS A GHOST THAT WON'T BE HAUNTING ANYONE FOR A WHILE. NOW COME HERE, YOU.
IMPOSSIBLE!
SERIOUSLY?!
NO!!

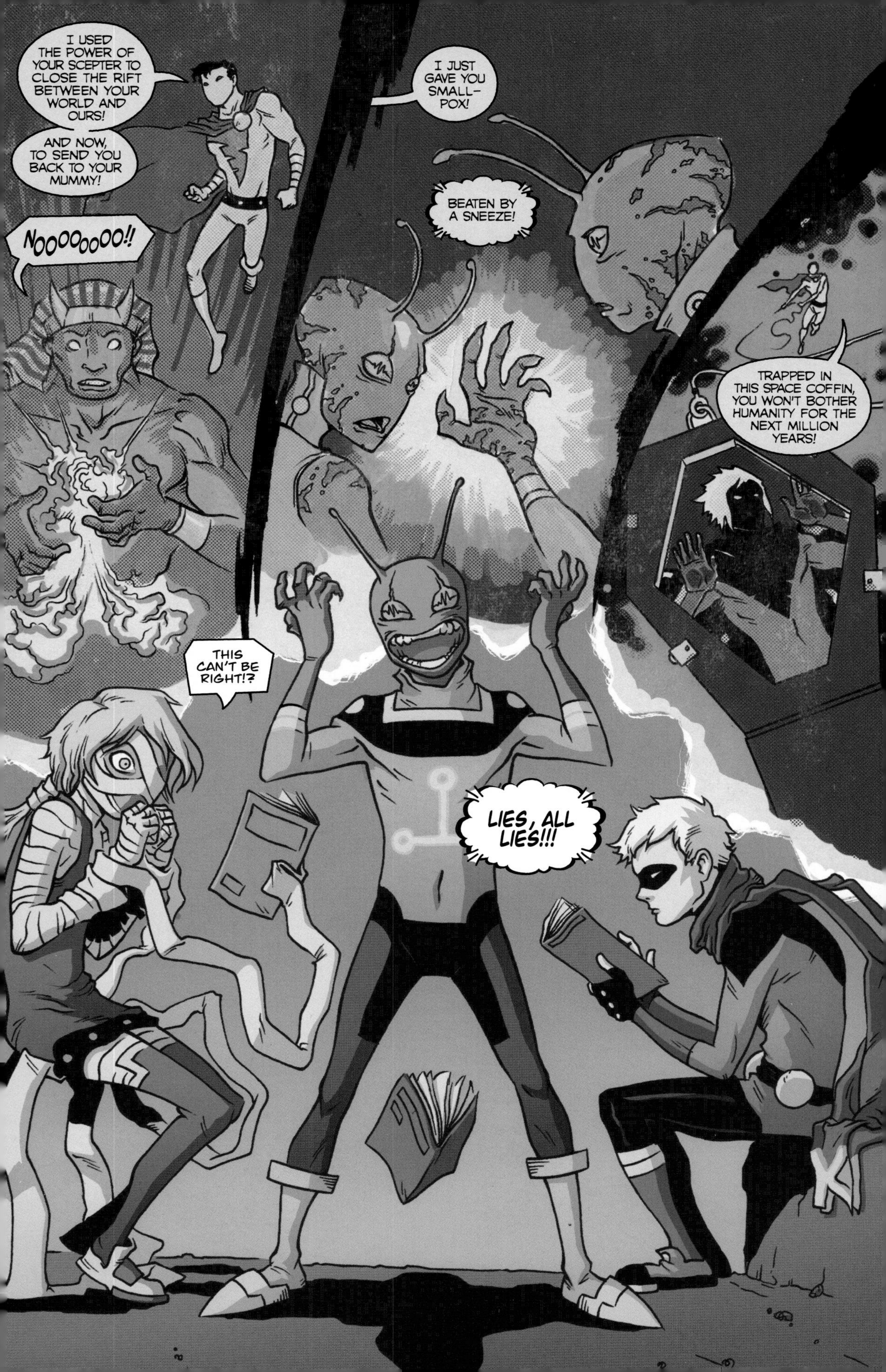
I USED THE POWER OF YOUR SCEPTER TO CLOSE THE RIFT BETWEEN YOUR WORLD AND OURS!
AND NOW, TO SEND YOU BACK TO YOUR MUMMY!
NOOOOOOOO!!
I JUST GAVE YOU SMALL-POX!
BEATEN BY A SNEEZE!
TRAPPED IN THIS SPACE COFFIN, YOU WON'T BOTHER HUMANITY FOR THE NEXT MILLION YEARS!
THIS CAN'T BE RIGHT!?
LIES, ALL LIES!!!

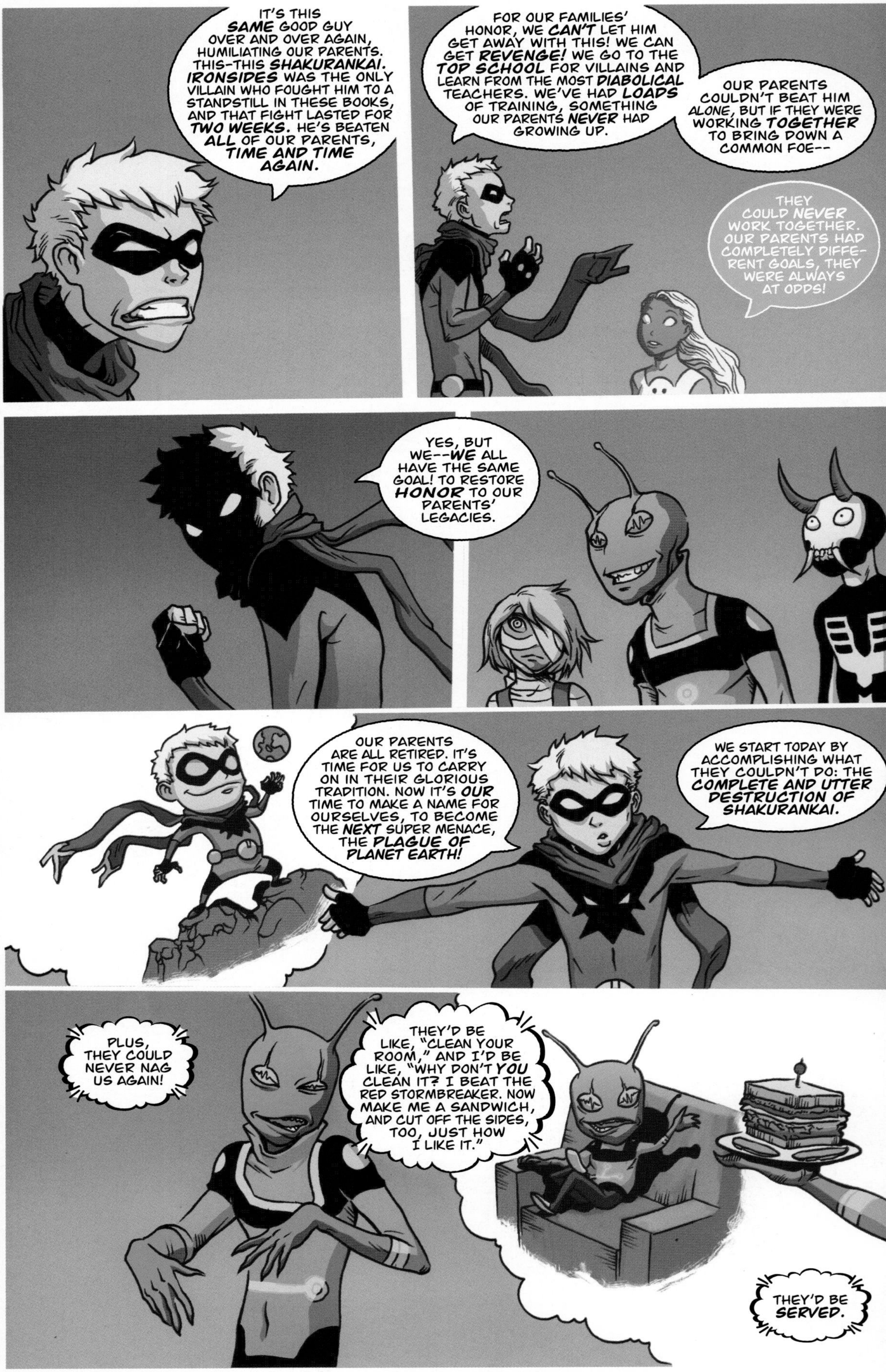
IT'S THIS SAME GOOD GUY OVER AND OVER AGAIN, HUMILIATING OUR PARENTS. THIS-THIS SHAKURANKAI. IRONSIDES WAS THE ONLY VILLAIN WHO FOUGHT HIM TO A STANDSTILL IN THESE BOOKS, AND THAT FIGHT LASTED FOR TWO WEEKS. HE'S BEATEN ALL OF OUR PARENTS, TIME AND TIME AGAIN.
FOR OUR FAMILIES' HONOR, WE CAN'T LET HIM GET AWAY WITH THIS! WE CAN GET REVENGE! WE GO TO THE TOP SCHOOL FOR VILLAINS AND LEARN FROM THE MOST DIABOLICAL TEACHERS. WE'VE HAD LOADS OF TRAINING, SOMETHING OUR PARENTS NEVER HAD GROWING UP.
OUR PARENTS COULDN'T BEAT HIM ALONE, BUT IF THEY WERE WORKING TOGETHER TO BRING DOWN A COMMON FOE--
THEY COULD NEVER WORK TOGETHER. OUR PARENTS HAD COMPLETELY DIFFERENT GOALS, THEY WERE ALWAYS AT ODDS!
YES, BUT WE--WE ALL HAVE THE SAME GOAL! TO RESTORE HONOR TO OUR PARENTS' LEGACIES.
OUR PARENTS ARE ALL RETIRED. IT'S TIME FOR US TO CARRY ON IN THEIR GLORIOUS TRADITION. NOW IT'S OUR TIME TO MAKE A NAME FOR OURSELVES, TO BECOME THE NEXT SUPER MENACE, THE PLAGUE OF PLANET EARTH!
WE START TODAY BY ACCOMPLISHING WHAT THEY COULDN'T DO: THE COMPLETE AND UTTER DESTRUCTION OF SHAKURANKAI.
PLUS, THEY COULD NEVER NAG US AGAIN!
THEY'D BE LIKE, "CLEAN YOUR ROOM," AND I'D BE LIKE, "WHY DON'T YOU CLEAN IT? I BEAT THE RED STORMBREAKER. NOW MAKE ME A SANDWICH, AND CUT OFF THE SIDES, TOO, JUST HOW I LIKE IT."
THEY'D BE SERVED.

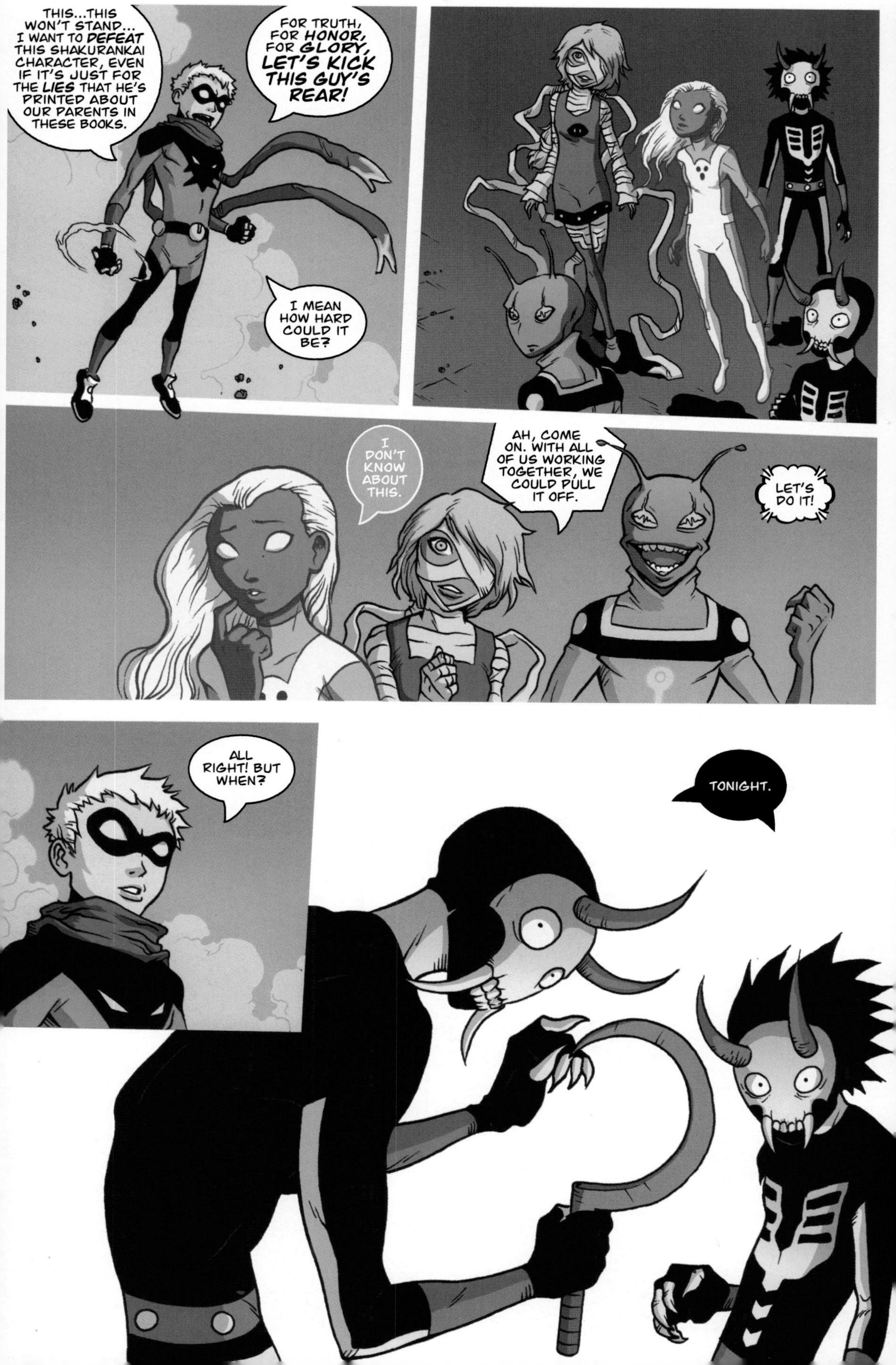
THIS...THIS WON'T STAND... I WANT TO DEFEAT THIS SHAKURANKAI CHARACTER, EVEN IF IT'S JUST FOR THE LIES THAT HE'S PRINTED ABOUT OUR PARENTS IN THESE BOOKS.
FOR TRUTH, FOR HONOR, FOR GLORY, LET'S KICK THIS GUY'S REAR!
I MEAN HOW HARD COULD IT BE?
I DON'T KNOW ABOUT THIS.
AH, COME ON. WITH ALL OF US WORKING TOGETHER, WE COULD PULL IT OFF.
LET'S DO IT!
ALL RIGHT! BUT WHEN?
TONIGHT.

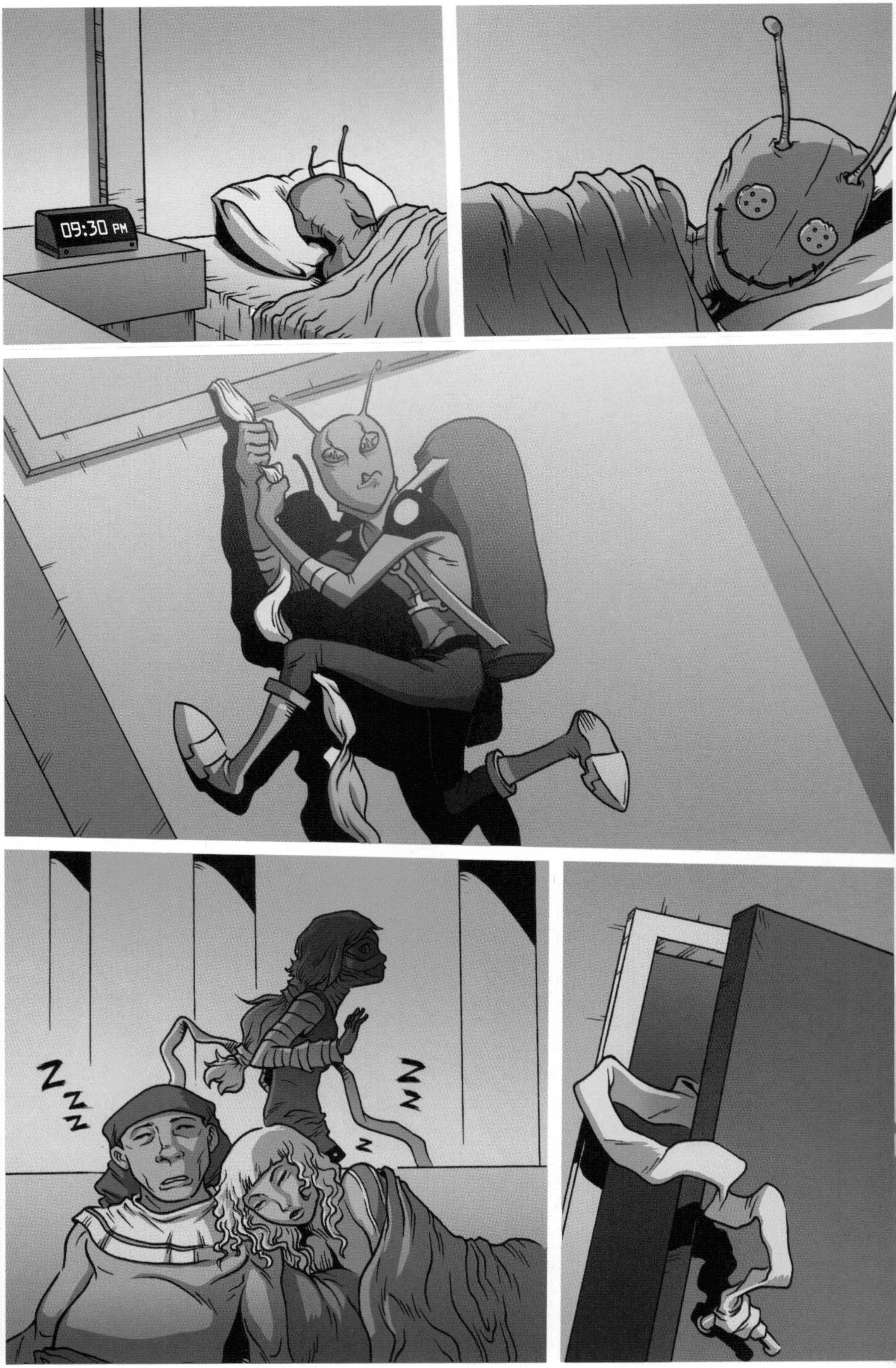
09:30 PM
ZZZ
ZZ
Z

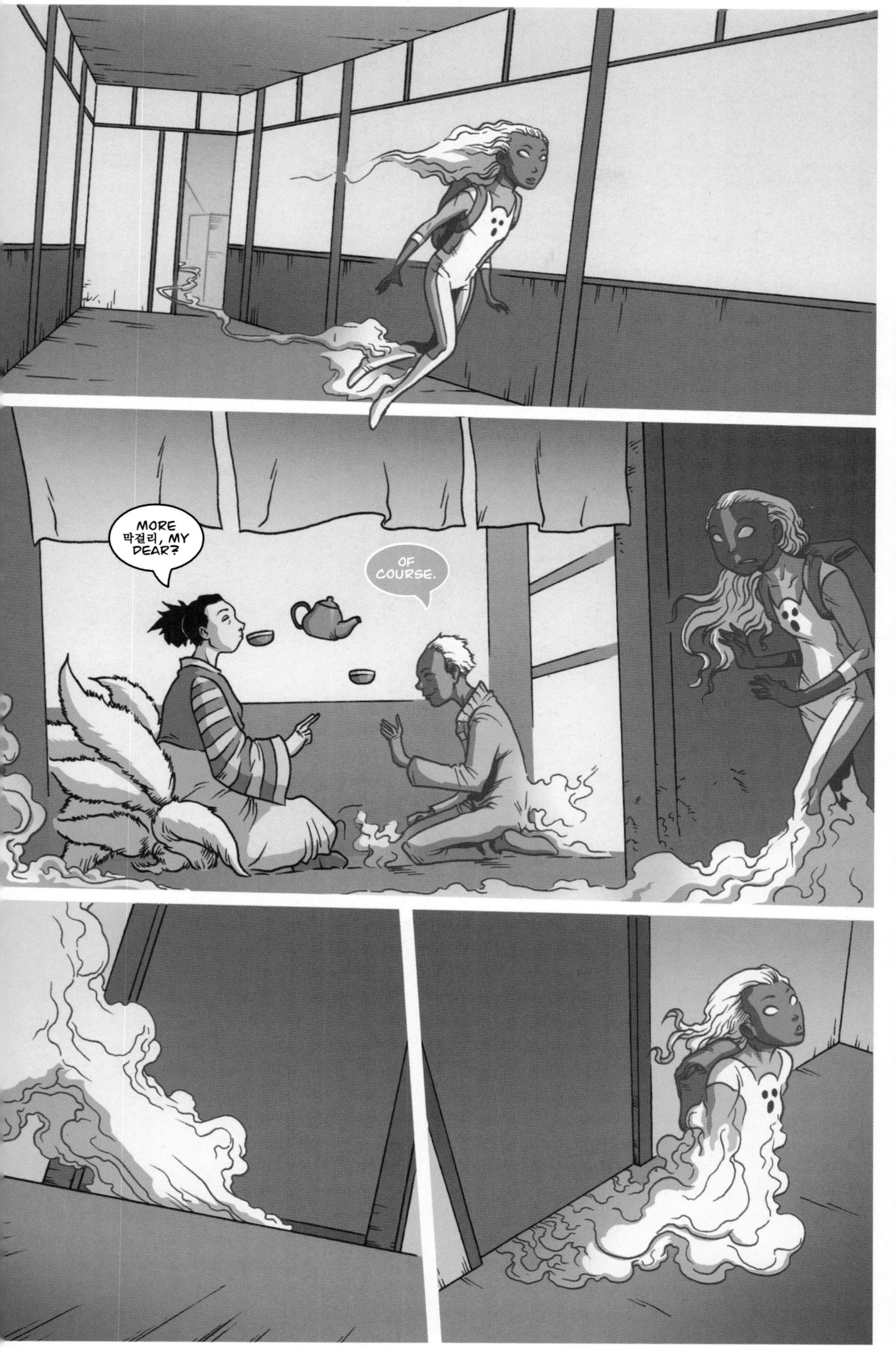
MORE 막걸리, MY DEAR?
OF COURSE.

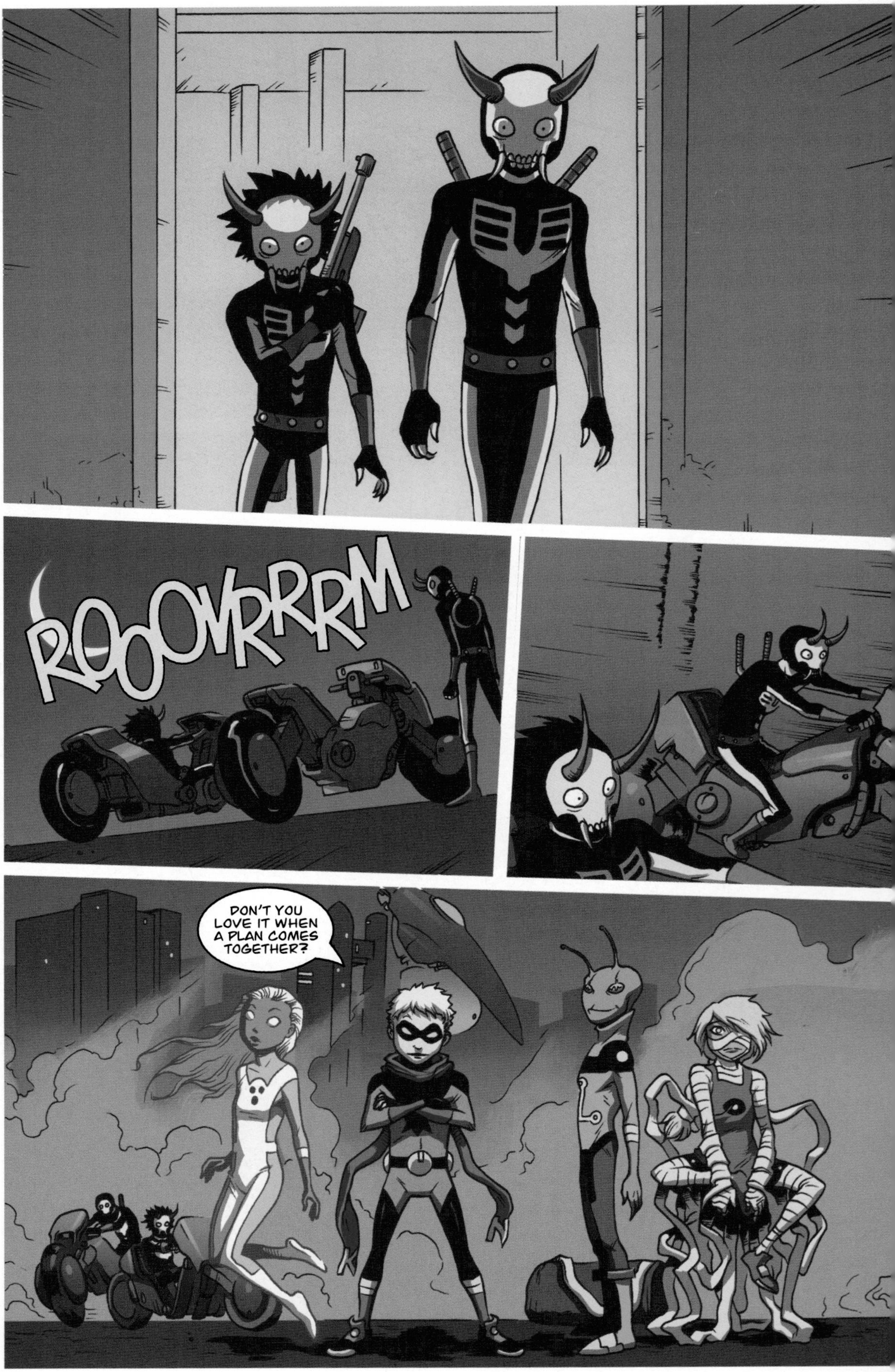
ROOOVRRRM
DON'T YOU LOVE IT WHEN A PLAN COMES TOGETHER?

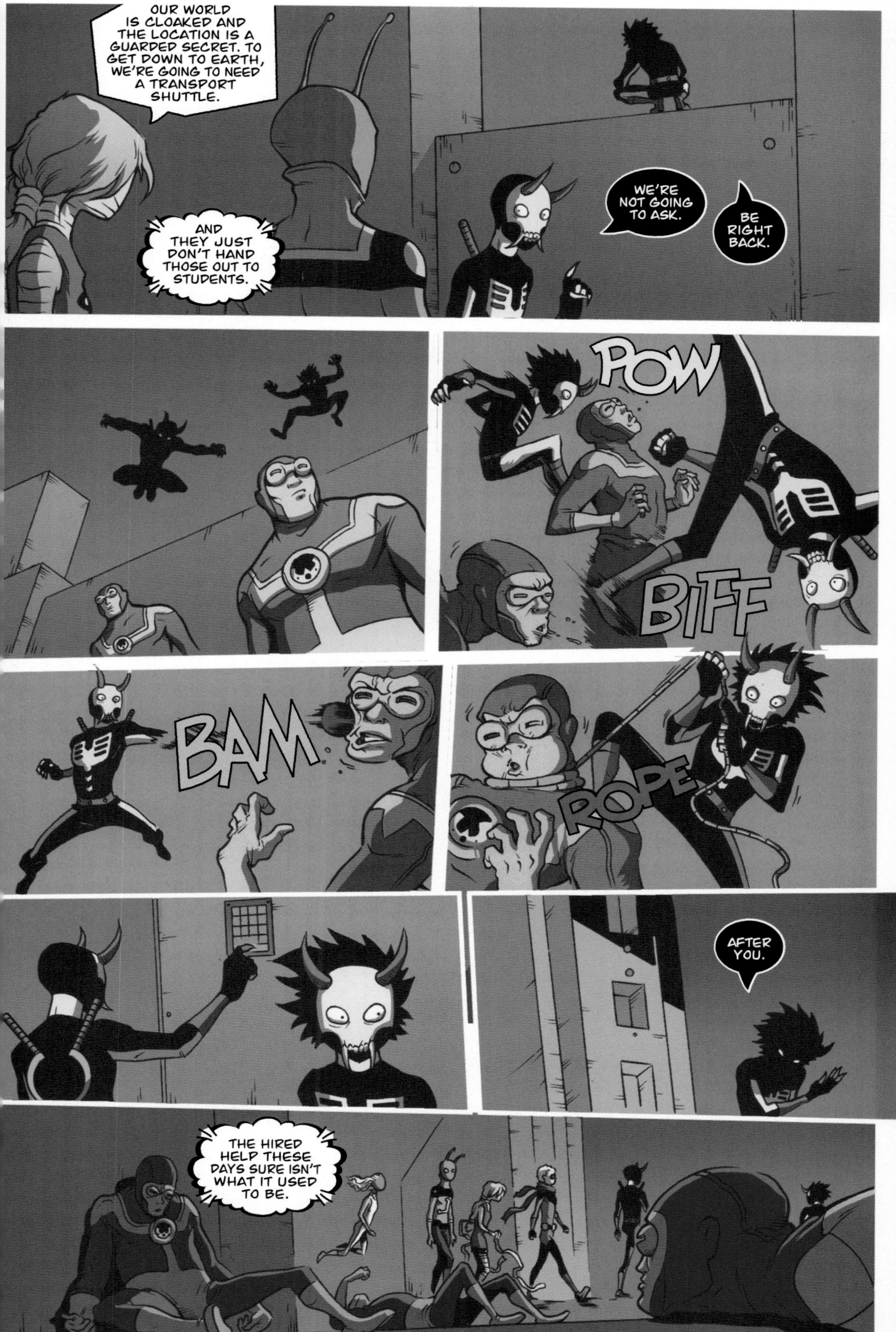

OUR WORLD IS CLOAKED AND THE LOCATION IS A GUARDED SECRET. TO GET DOWN TO EARTH, WE'RE GOING TO NEED A TRANSPORT SHUTTLE.
AND THEY JUST DON'T HAND THOSE OUT TO STUDENTS.
WE'RE NOT GOING TO ASK.
BE RIGHT BACK.
POW
BIFF
BAM
ROPE
AFTER YOU.
THE HIRED HELP THESE DAYS SURE ISN'T WHAT IT USED TO BE.

LADIES AND GENTLEMEN, THIS IS YOUR CAPTAIN SPEAKING. PLEASE FASTEN YOUR SEATBELTS AND ROLL UP YOUR WINDOWS BECAUSE WE'RE ABOUT TO GO **REEAAALLY**, REALLY, FAST!

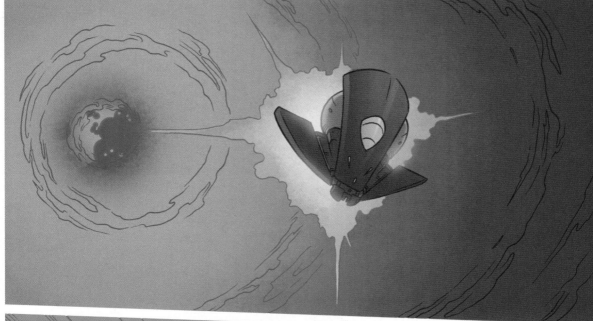

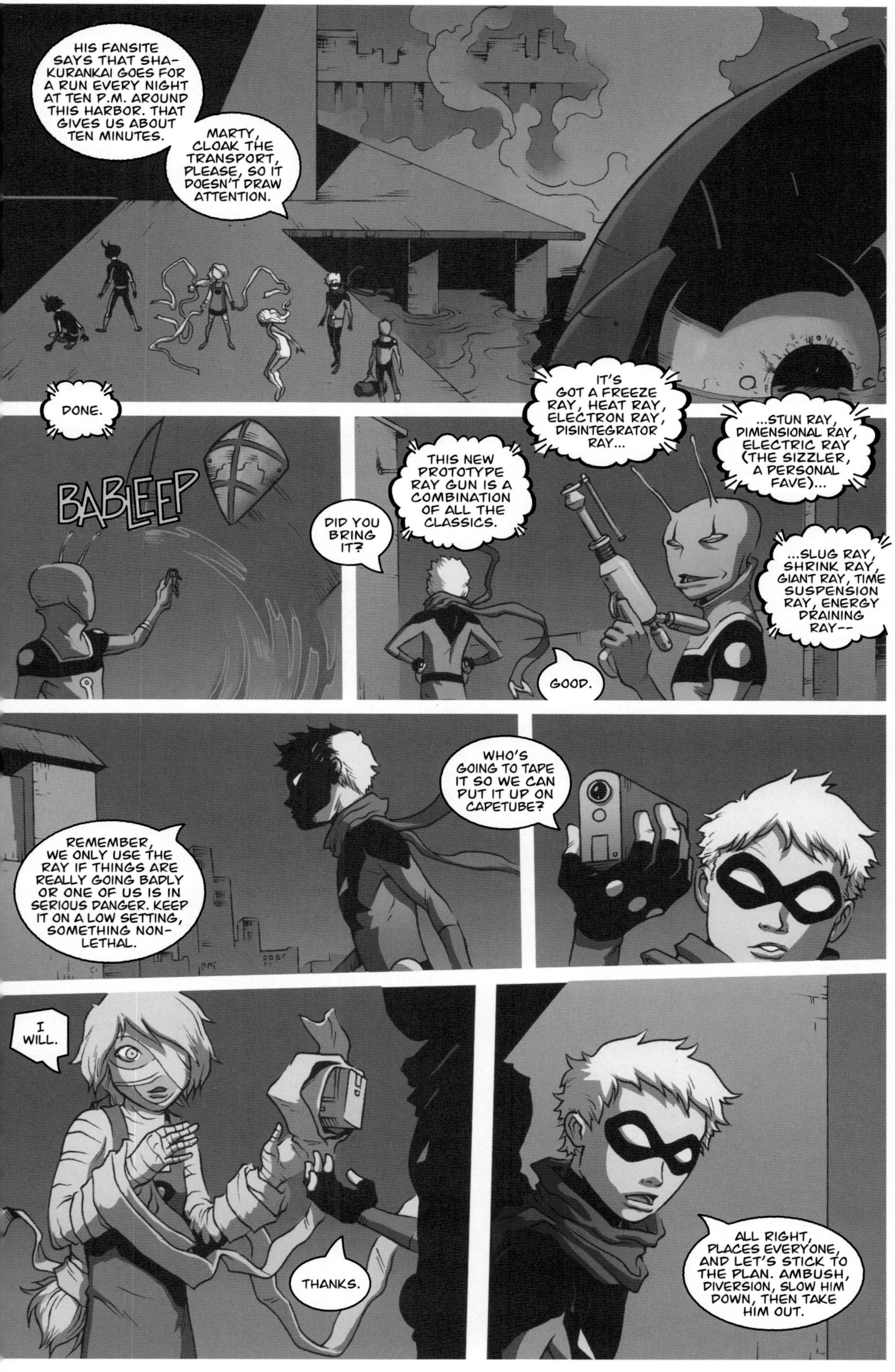
HIS FANSITE SAYS THAT SHA-KURANKAI GOES FOR A RUN EVERY NIGHT AT TEN P.M. AROUND THIS HARBOR. THAT GIVES US ABOUT TEN MINUTES.
MARTY, CLOAK THE TRANSPORT, PLEASE, SO IT DOESN'T DRAW ATTENTION.
DONE.
BABLEEP
DID YOU BRING IT?
THIS NEW PROTOTYPE RAY GUN IS A COMBINATION OF ALL THE CLASSICS.
IT'S GOT A FREEZE RAY, HEAT RAY, ELECTRON RAY, DISINTEGRATOR RAY...
...STUN RAY, DIMENSIONAL RAY, ELECTRIC RAY (THE SIZZLER, A PERSONAL FAVE)...
...SLUG RAY, SHRINK RAY, GIANT RAY, TIME SUSPENSION RAY, ENERGY DRAINING RAY--
GOOD.
REMEMBER, WE ONLY USE THE RAY IF THINGS ARE REALLY GOING BADLY OR ONE OF US IS IN SERIOUS DANGER. KEEP IT ON A LOW SETTING, SOMETHING NON-LETHAL.
WHO'S GOING TO TAPE IT SO WE CAN PUT IT UP ON CAPETUBE?
I WILL.
THANKS.
ALL RIGHT, PLACES EVERYONE, AND LET'S STICK TO THE PLAN. AMBUSH, DIVERSION, SLOW HIM DOWN, THEN TAKE HIM OUT.

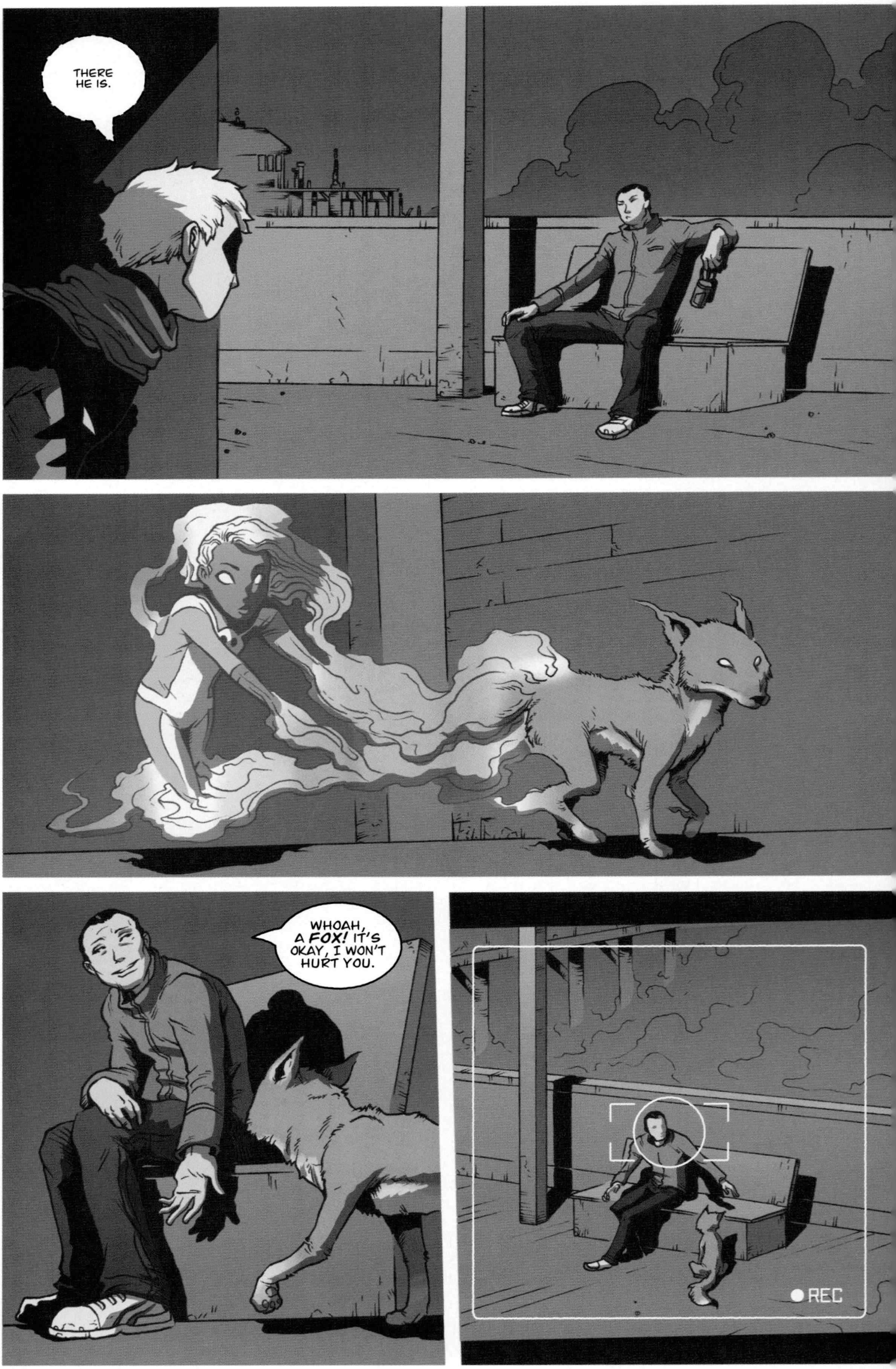
THERE HE IS.
WHOAH, A FOX! IT'S OKAY, I WON'T HURT YOU.
REC

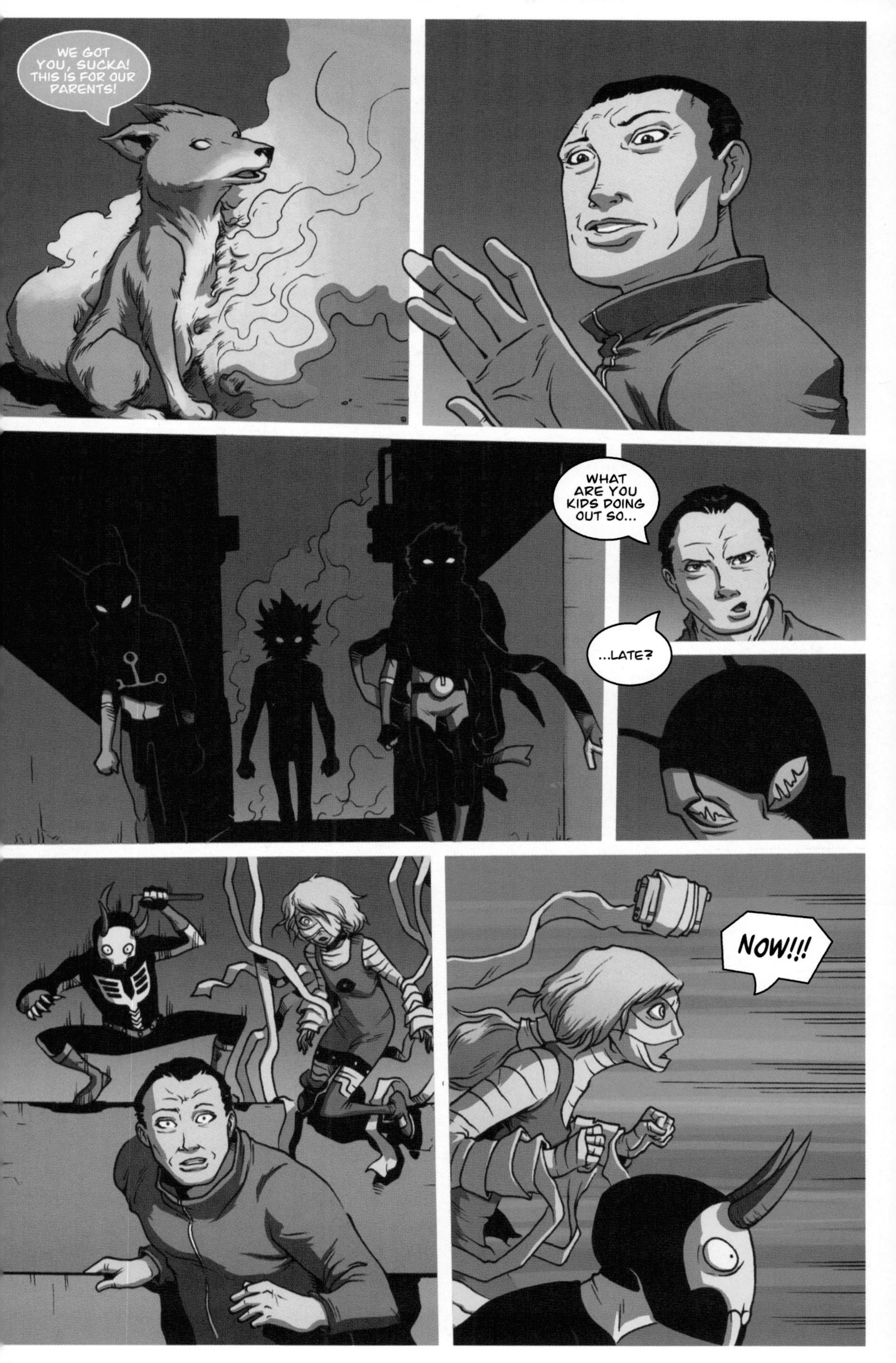
WE GOT YOU, SUCKA! THIS IS FOR OUR PARENTS!
WHAT ARE YOU KIDS DOING OUT SO...
...LATE?
NOW!!!

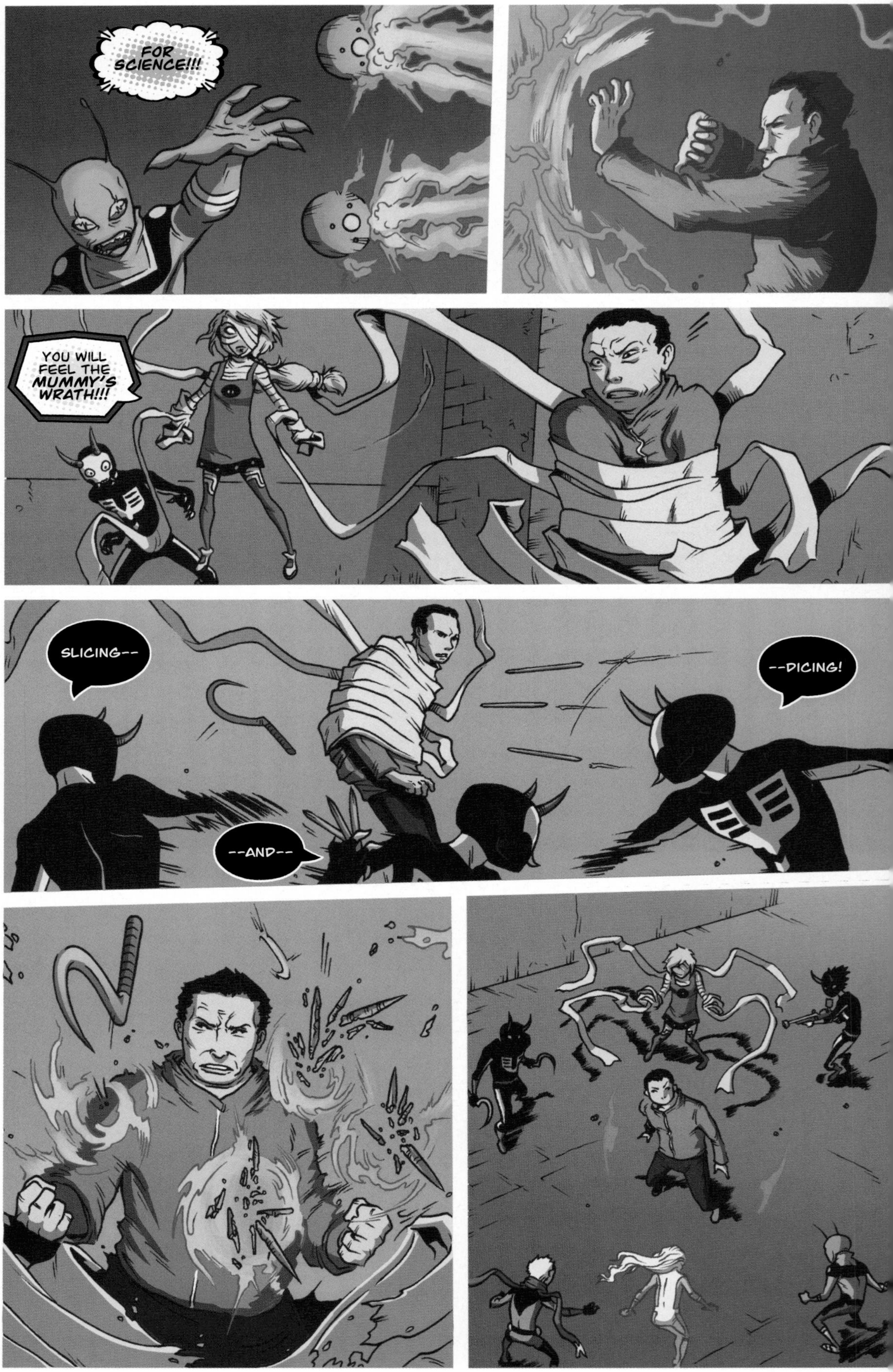
FOR SCIENCE!!!
YOU WILL FEEL THE MUMMY'S WRATH!!!
SLICING--
--DICING!
--AND--

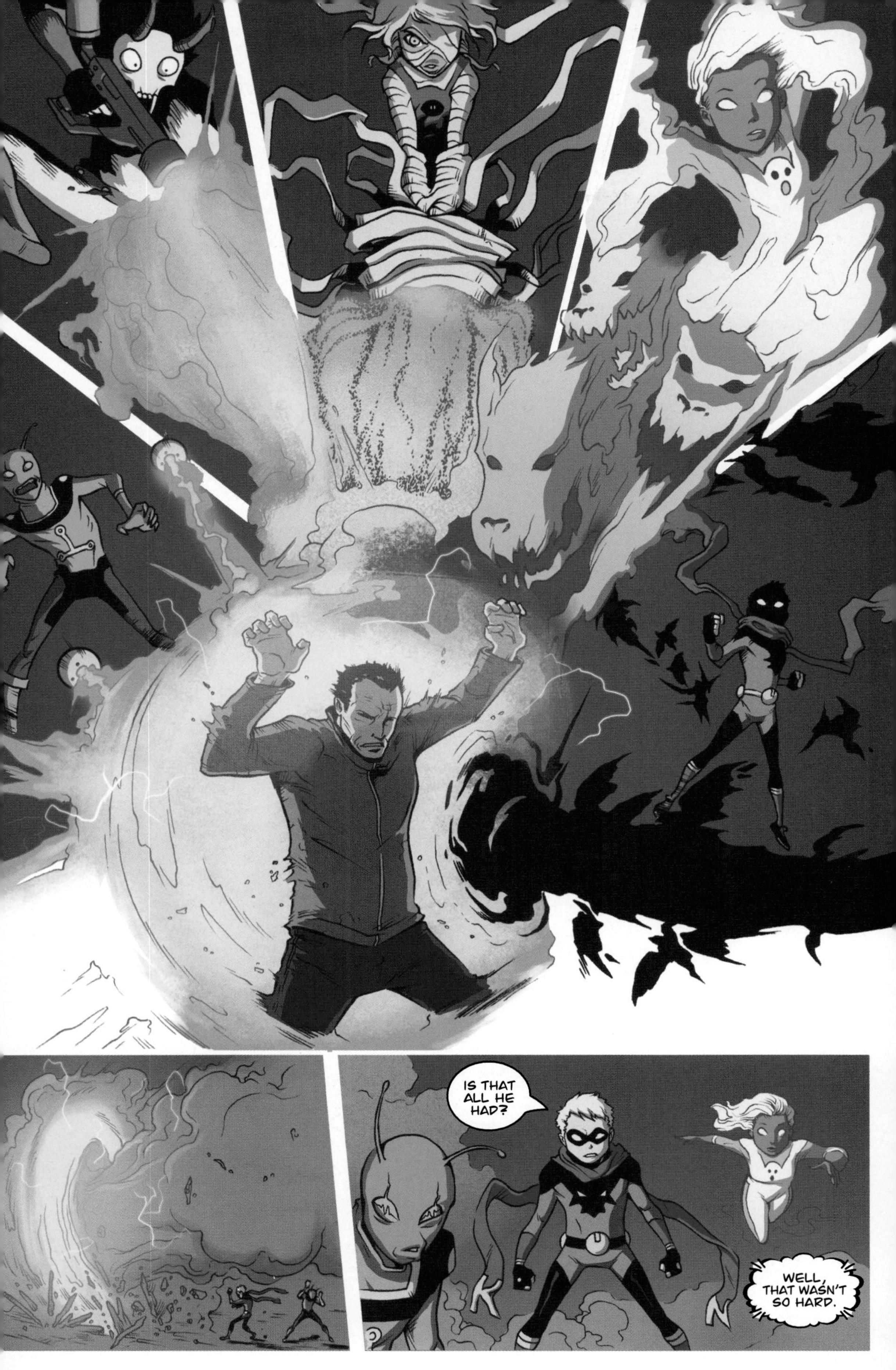
IS THAT ALL HE HAD?
WELL, THAT WASN'T SO HARD.

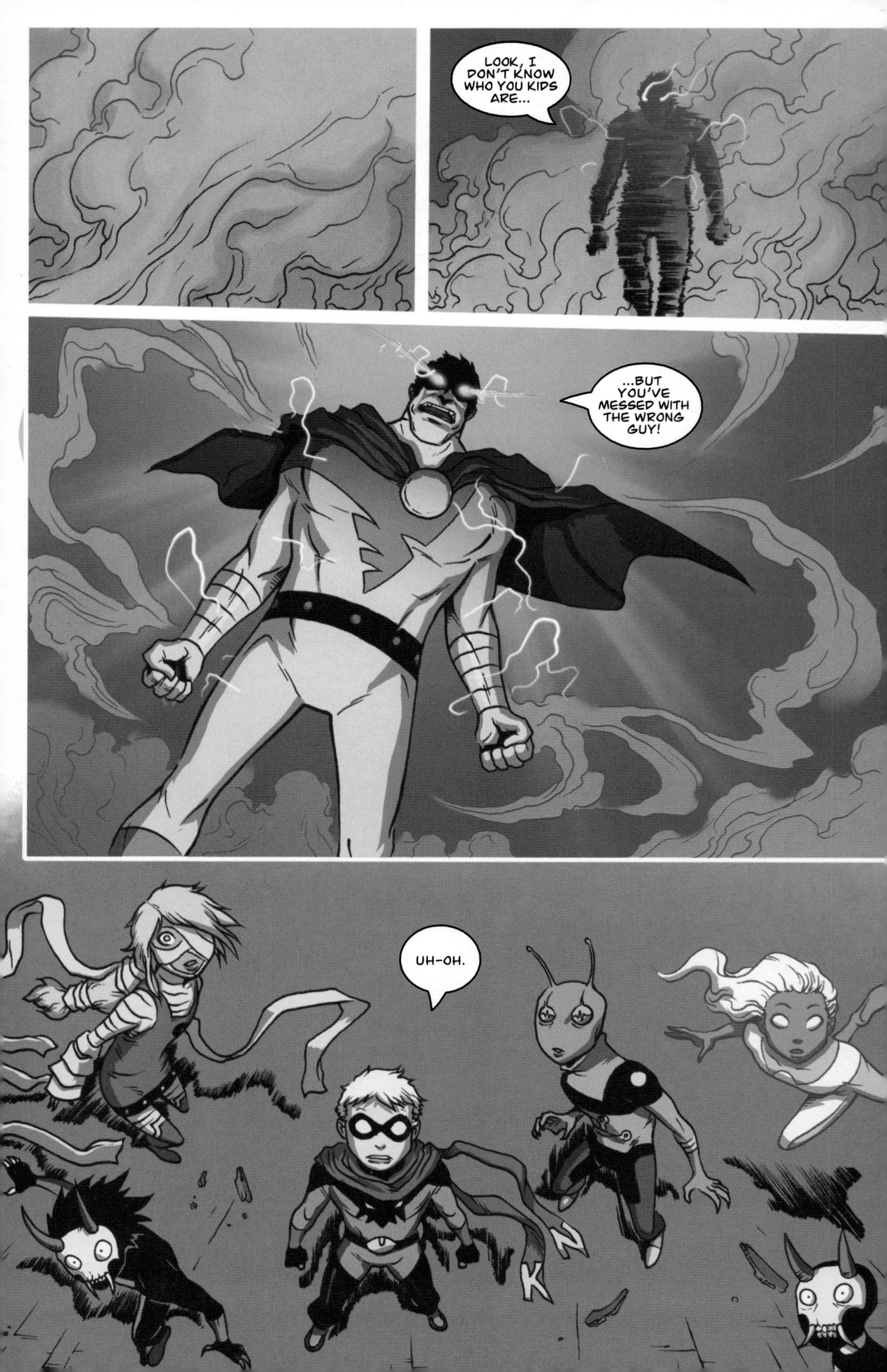

LOOK, I DON'T KNOW WHO YOU KIDS ARE...
...BUT YOU'VE MESSED WITH THE WRONG GUY!
UH-OH.

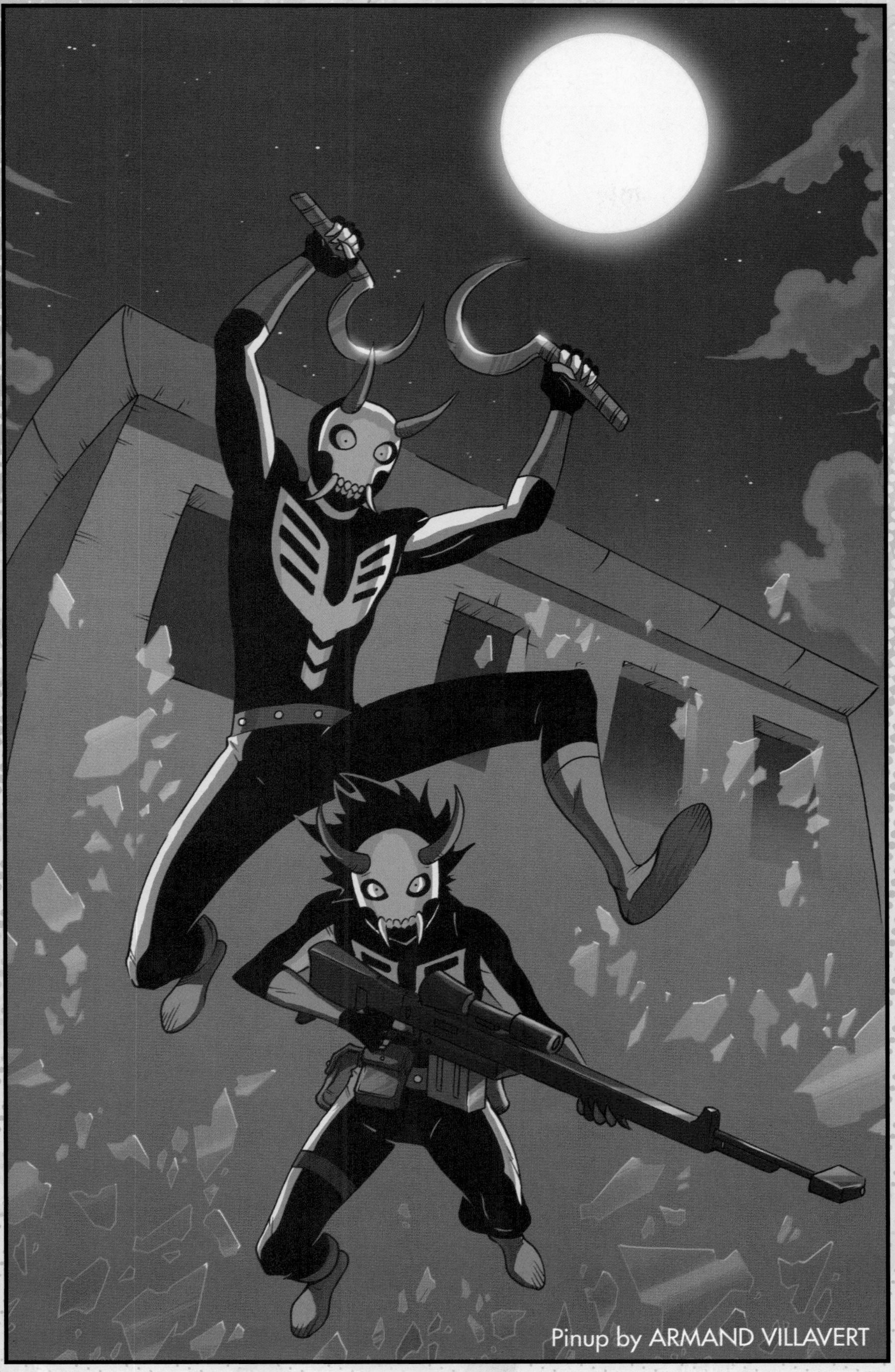
Pinup by ARMAND VILLAVERT

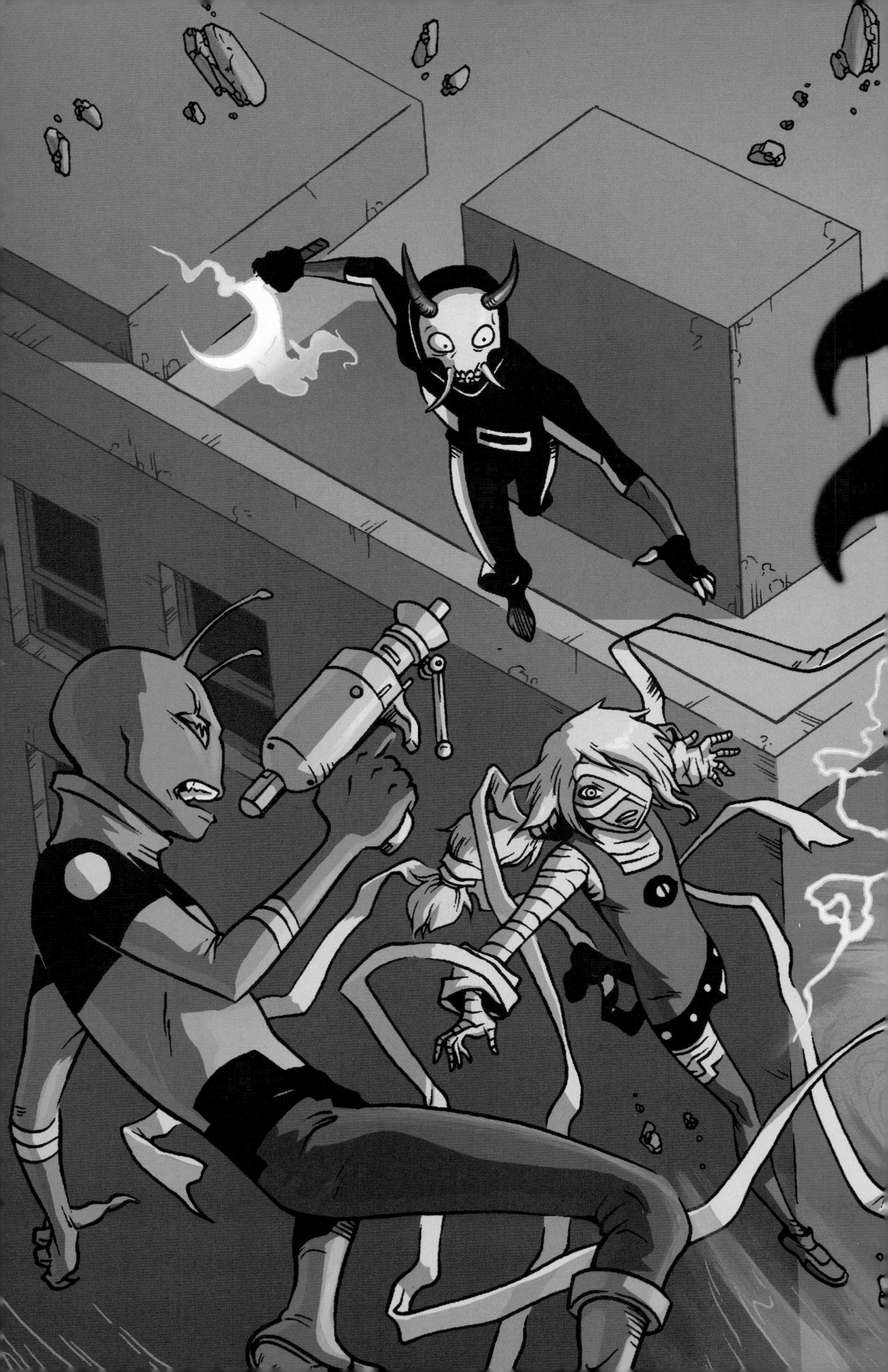

CHAPTER 6

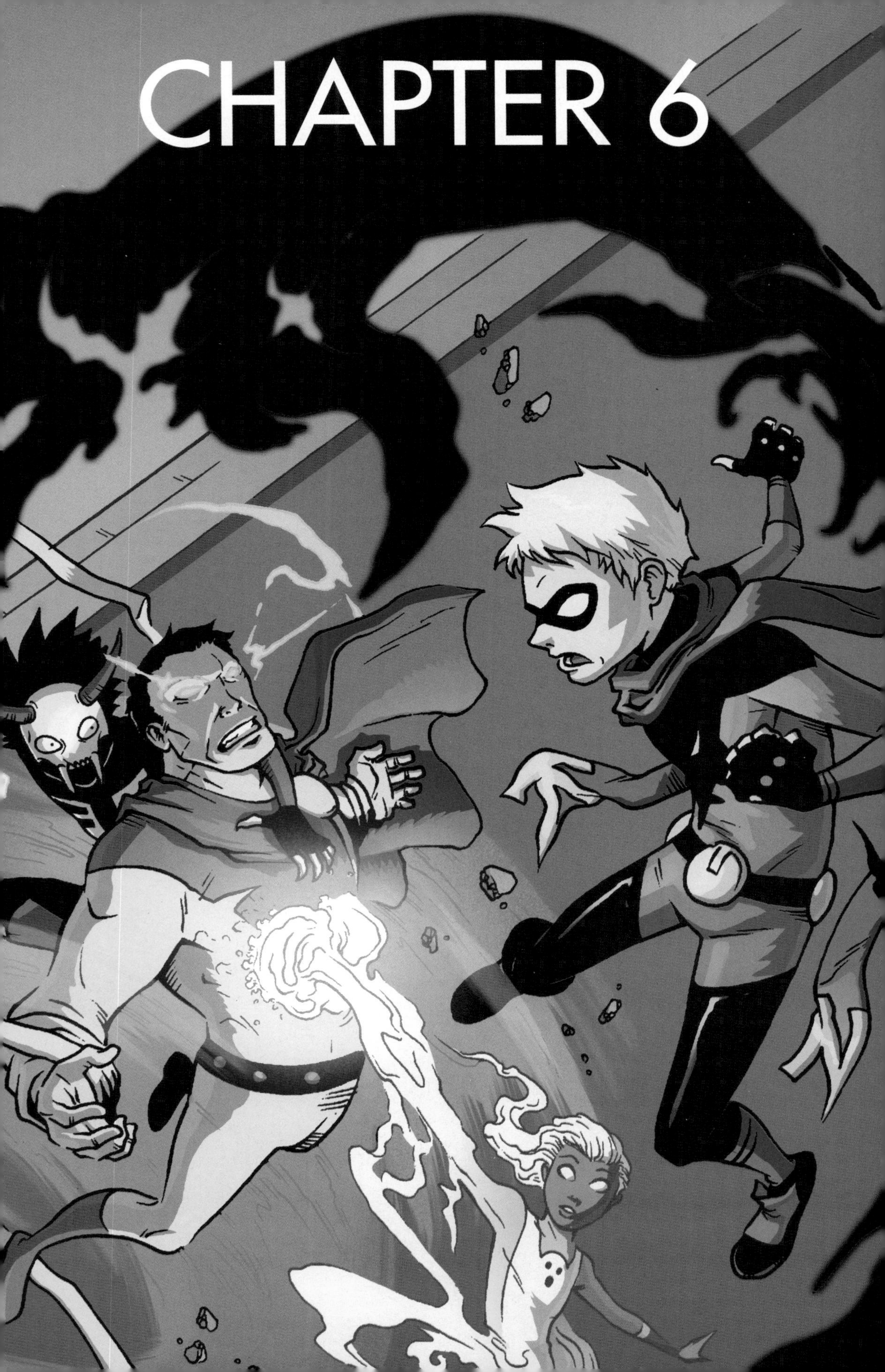

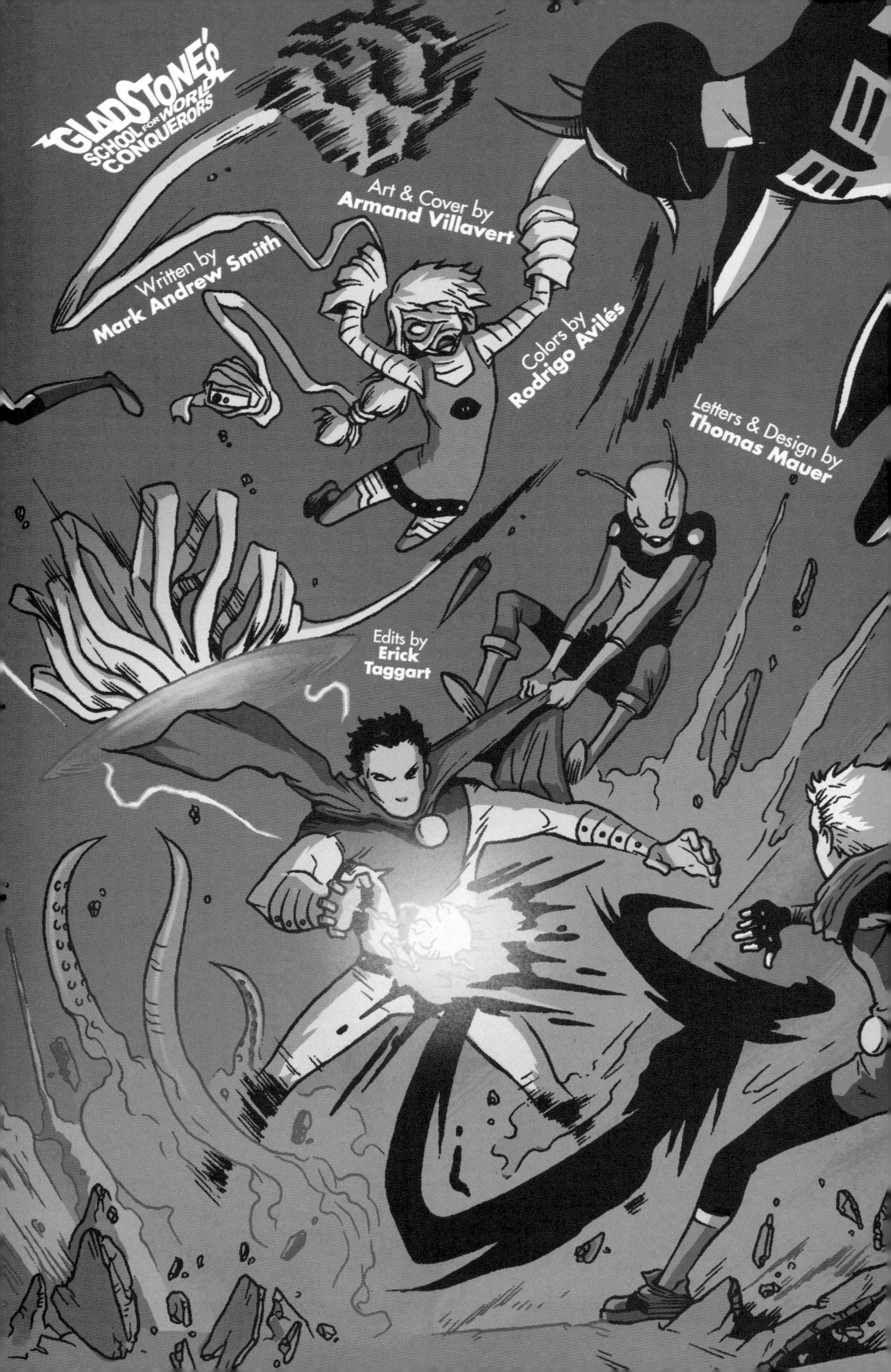

GLADSTONE'S SCHOOL FOR WORLD CONQUERORS
Art & Cover by Armand Villavert
Written by Mark Andrew Smith
Colors by Rodrigo Avilés
Letters & Design by Thomas Mauer
Edits by Erick Taggart

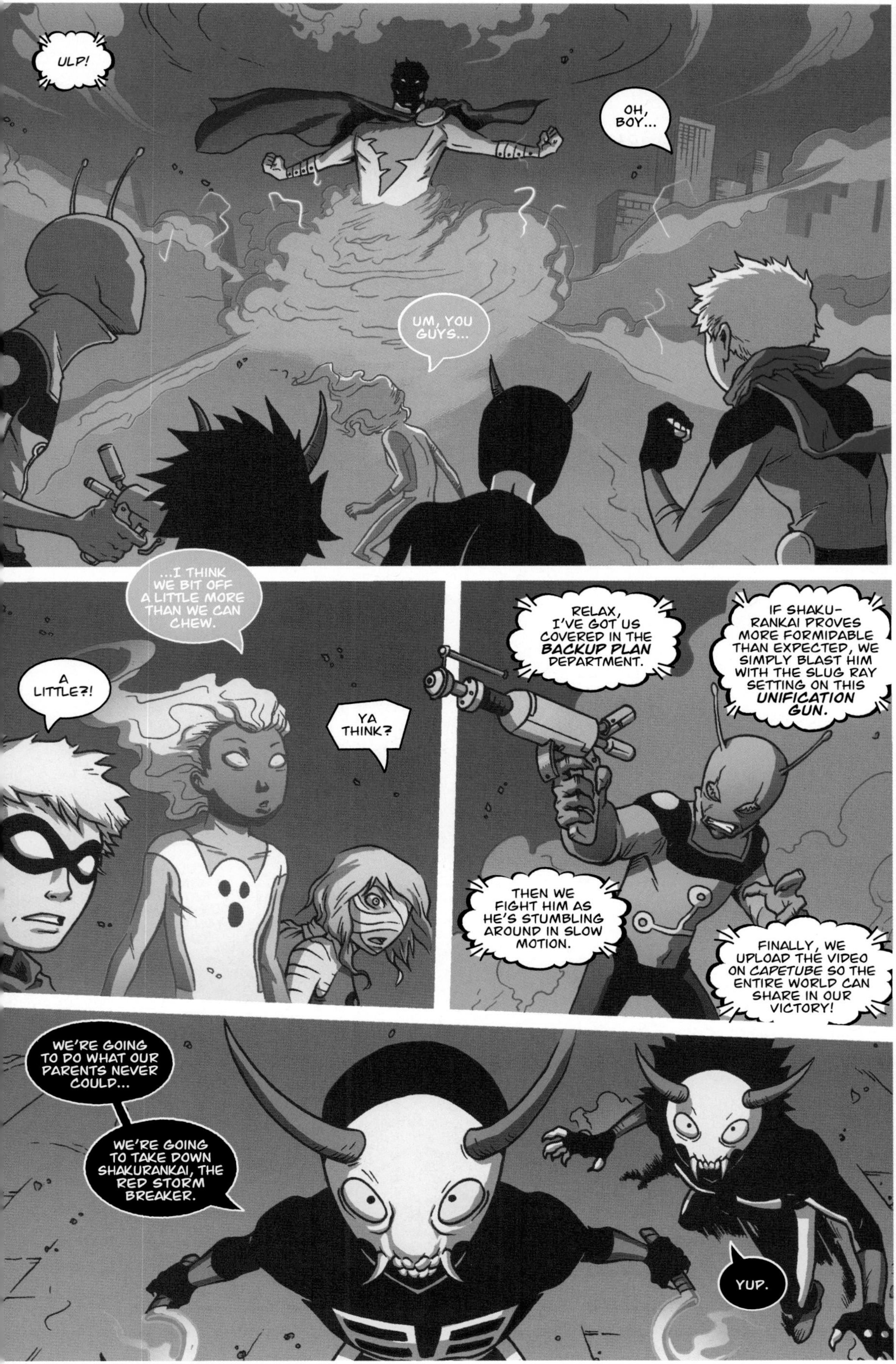
ULP!
OH, BOY...
UM, YOU GUYS...
...I THINK WE BIT OFF A LITTLE MORE THAN WE CAN CHEW.
A LITTLE?!
YA THINK?
RELAX, I'VE GOT US COVERED IN THE BACKUP PLAN DEPARTMENT.
IF SHAKU-RANKAI PROVES MORE FORMIDABLE THAN EXPECTED, WE SIMPLY BLAST HIM WITH THE SLUG RAY SETTING ON THIS UNIFICATION GUN.
THEN WE FIGHT HIM AS HE'S STUMBLING AROUND IN SLOW MOTION.
FINALLY, WE UPLOAD THE VIDEO ON CAPETUBE SO THE ENTIRE WORLD CAN SHARE IN OUR VICTORY!
WE'RE GOING TO DO WHAT OUR PARENTS NEVER COULD...
WE'RE GOING TO TAKE DOWN SHAKURANKAI, THE RED STORM BREAKER.
YUP.

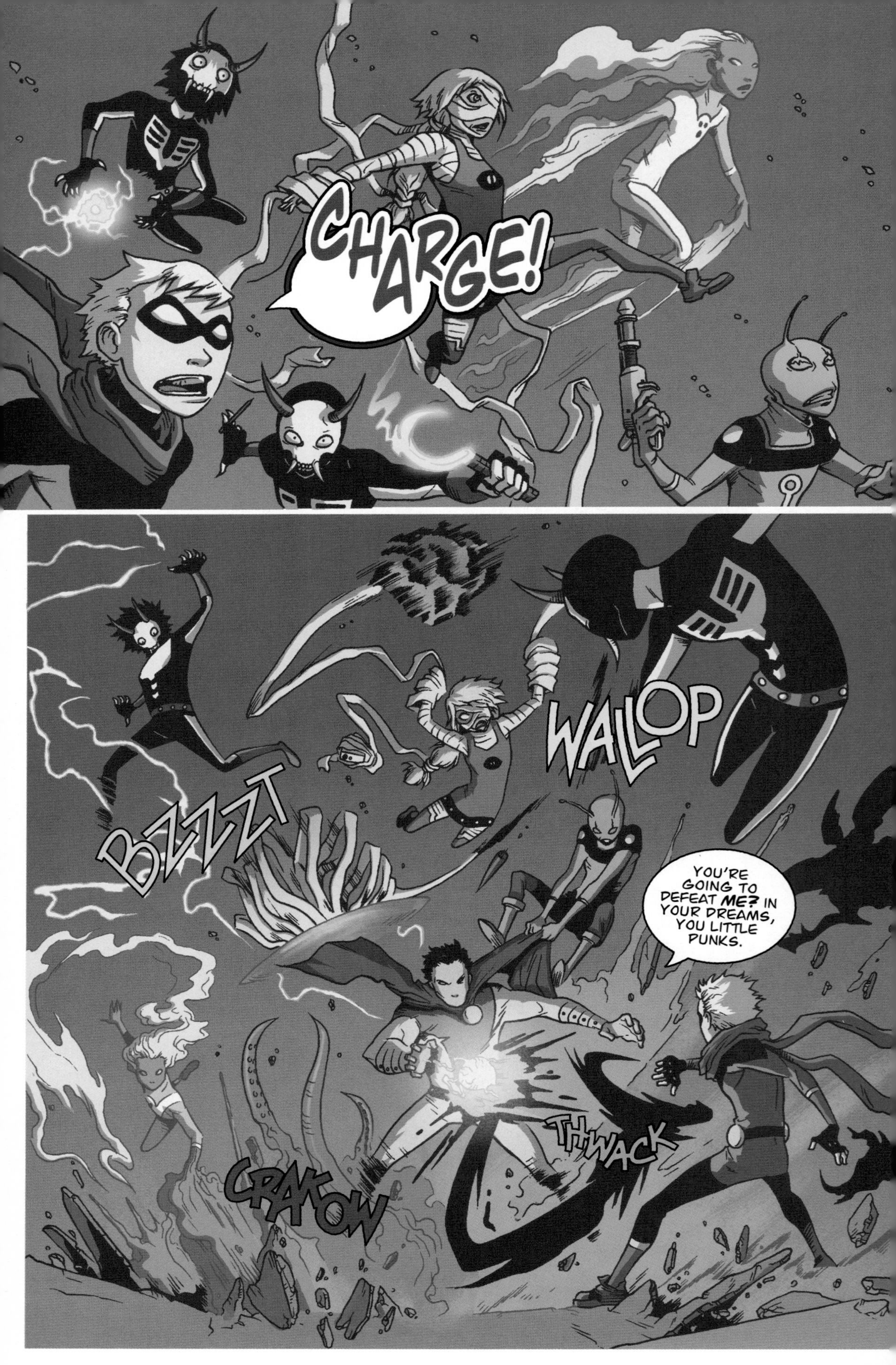
CHARGE!
BZZZZT
WALLOP
YOU'RE GOING TO DEFEAT ME? IN YOUR DREAMS, YOU LITTLE PUNKS.
THWACK
CRAKOW

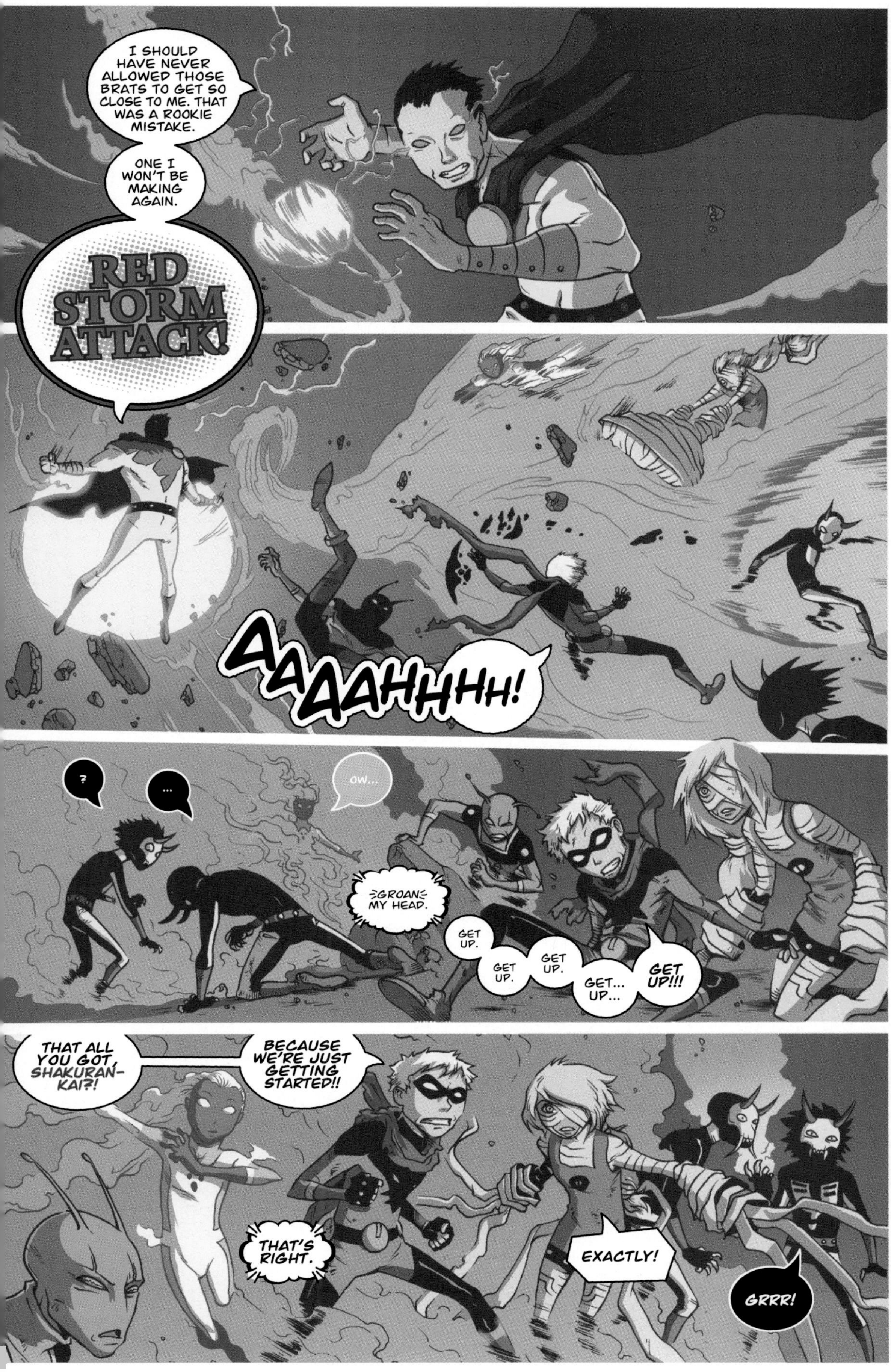
I SHOULD HAVE NEVER ALLOWED THOSE BRATS TO GET SO CLOSE TO ME. THAT WAS A ROOKIE MISTAKE.
ONE I WON'T BE MAKING AGAIN.
RED STORM ATTACK!
AAAAHHHH!
?
...
OW...
GROAN MY HEAD.
GET UP.
GET UP.
GET UP.
GET... UP...
GET UP!!!
THAT ALL YOU GOT, SHAKURAN-KAI?!
BECAUSE WE'RE JUST GETTING STARTED!!
THAT'S RIGHT.
EXACTLY!
GRRR!

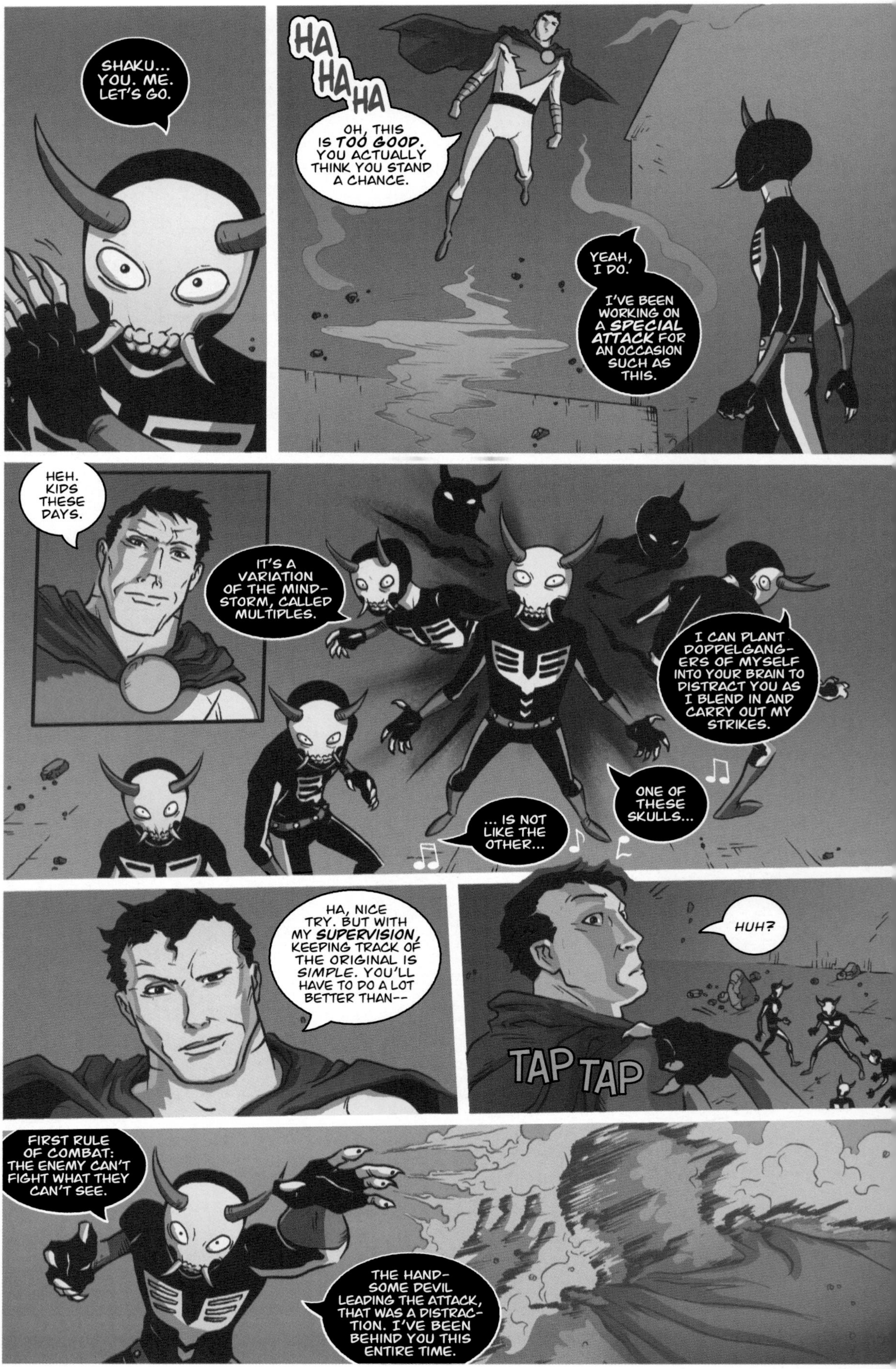
SHAKU... YOU. ME. LET'S GO.
HA HA HA
OH, THIS IS TOO GOOD. YOU ACTUALLY THINK YOU STAND A CHANCE.
YEAH, I DO.
I'VE BEEN WORKING ON A SPECIAL ATTACK FOR AN OCCASION SUCH AS THIS.
HEH. KIDS THESE DAYS.
IT'S A VARIATION OF THE MIND-STORM, CALLED MULTIPLES.
I CAN PLANT DOPPELGANGERS OF MYSELF INTO YOUR BRAIN TO DISTRACT YOU AS I BLEND IN AND CARRY OUT MY STRIKES.
ONE OF THESE SKULLS...
... IS NOT LIKE THE OTHER...
HA, NICE TRY. BUT WITH MY SUPERVISION, KEEPING TRACK OF THE ORIGINAL IS SIMPLE. YOU'LL HAVE TO DO A LOT BETTER THAN--
HUH?
TAP TAP
FIRST RULE OF COMBAT: THE ENEMY CAN'T FIGHT WHAT THEY CAN'T SEE.
THE HANDSOME DEVIL LEADING THE ATTACK, THAT WAS A DISTRACTION. I'VE BEEN BEHIND YOU THIS ENTIRE TIME.

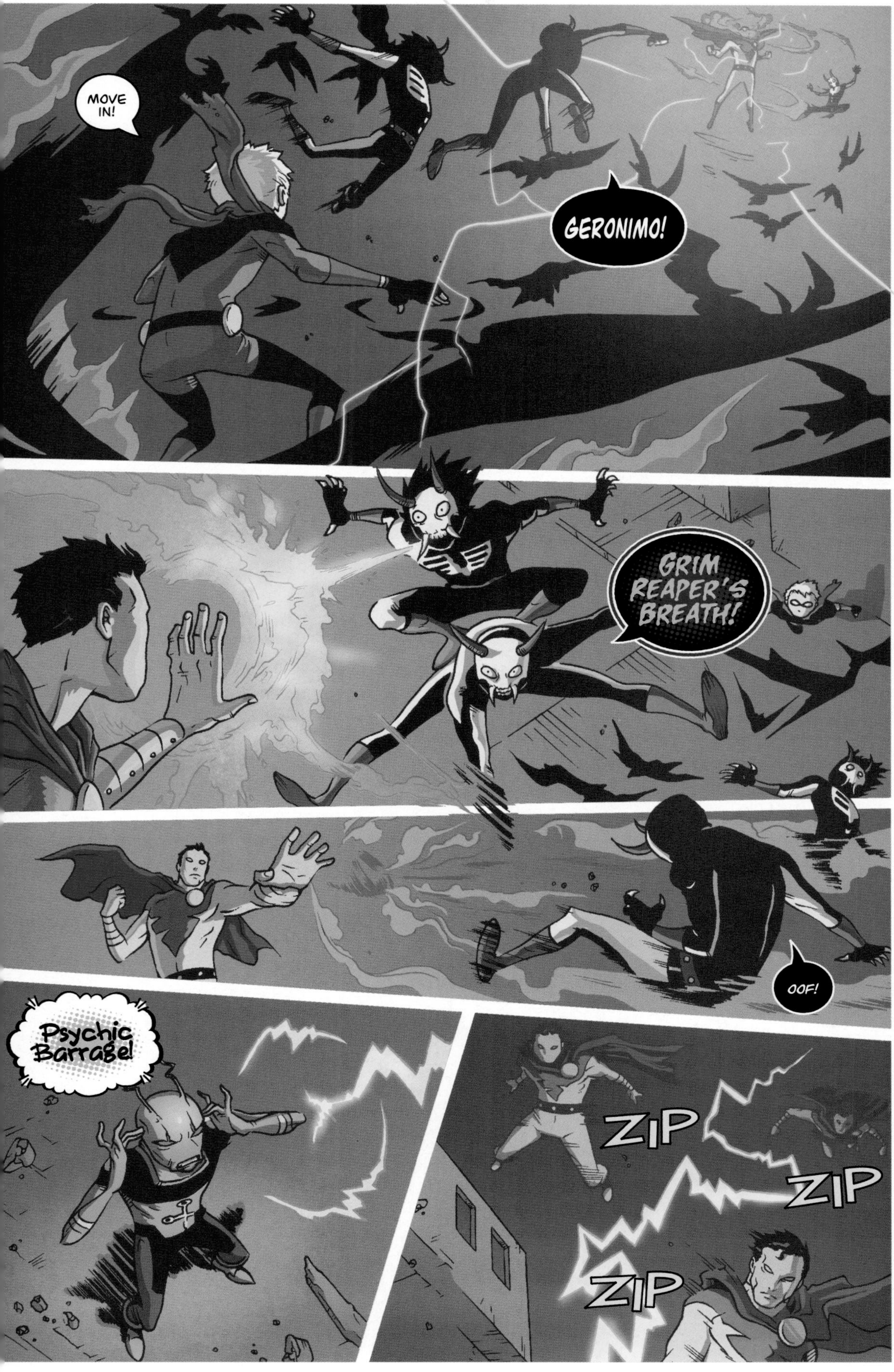
MOVE IN!
GERONIMO!
GRIM REAPER'S BREATH!
OOF!
Psychic Barrage!
ZIP
ZIP
ZIP

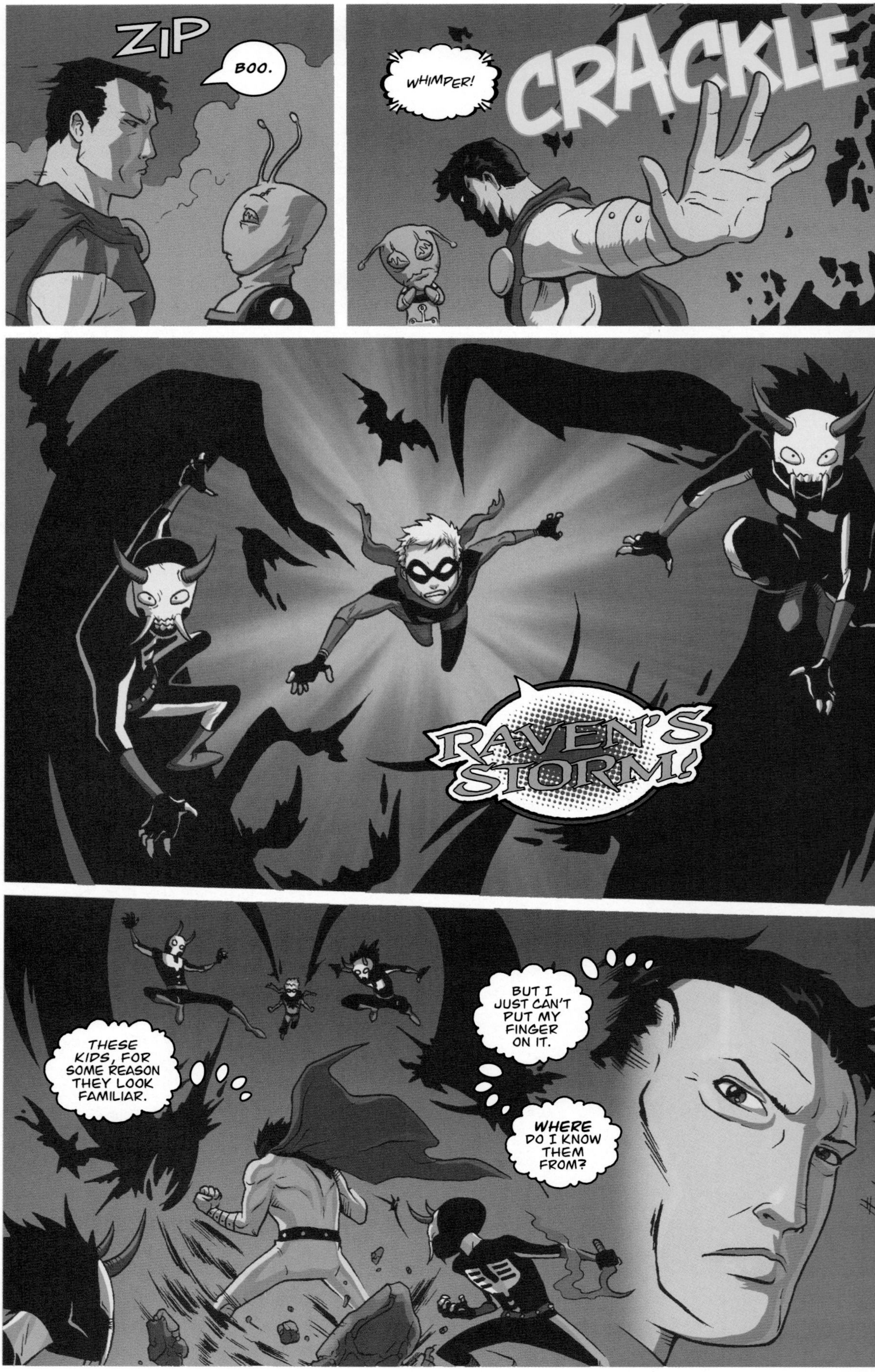
ZIP
BOO.
WHIMPER!
CRACKLE
RAVEN'S STORM!
THESE KIDS, FOR SOME REASON THEY LOOK FAMILIAR.
BUT I JUST CAN'T PUT MY FINGER ON IT.
WHERE DO I KNOW THEM FROM?

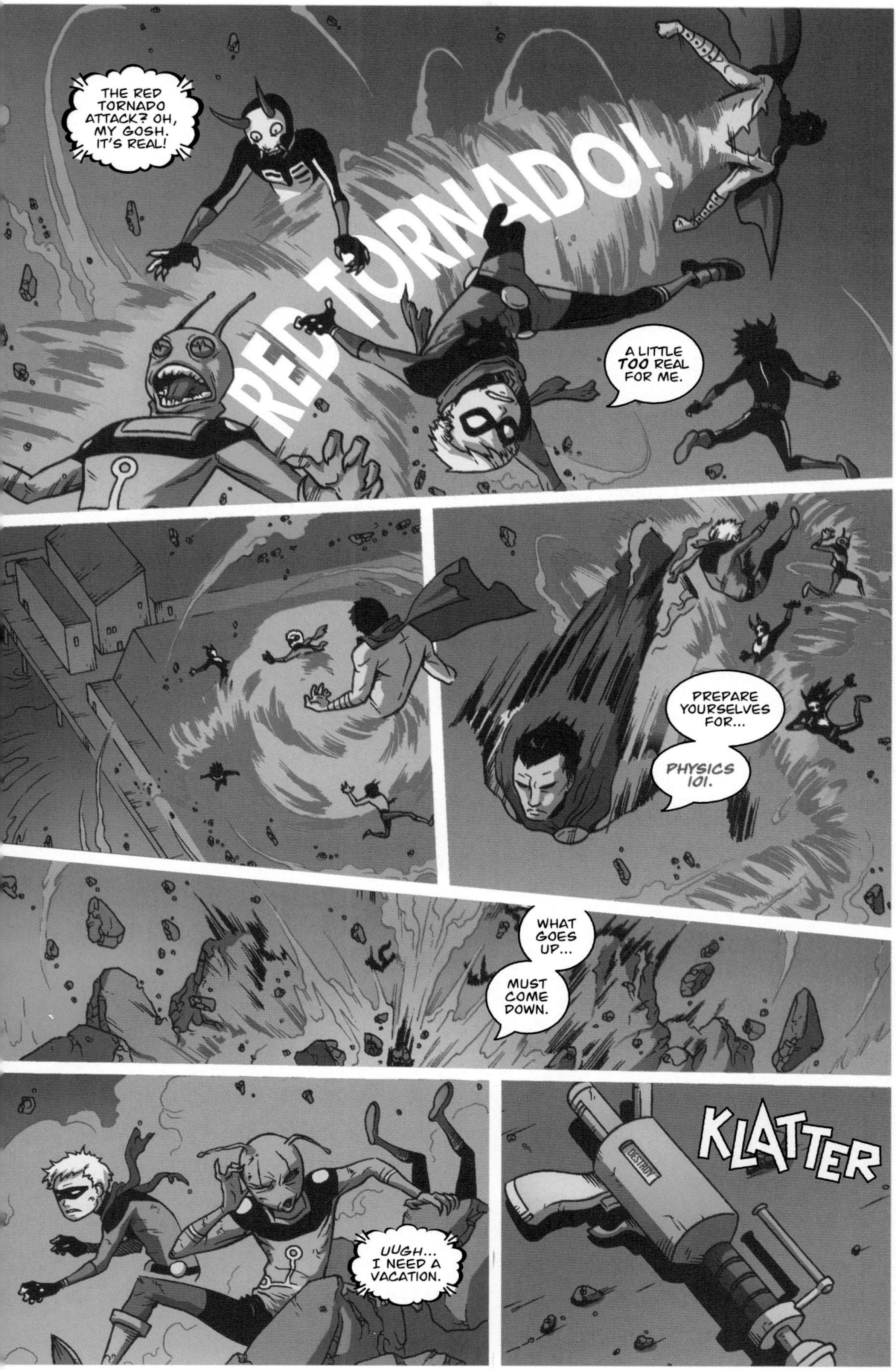
THE RED TORNADO ATTACK? OH, MY GOSH. IT'S REAL!
RED TORNADO!
A LITTLE TOO REAL FOR ME.
PREPARE YOURSELVES FOR...
PHYSICS 101.
WHAT GOES UP...
MUST COME DOWN.
UUGH... I NEED A VACATION.
KLATTER
DESTROY

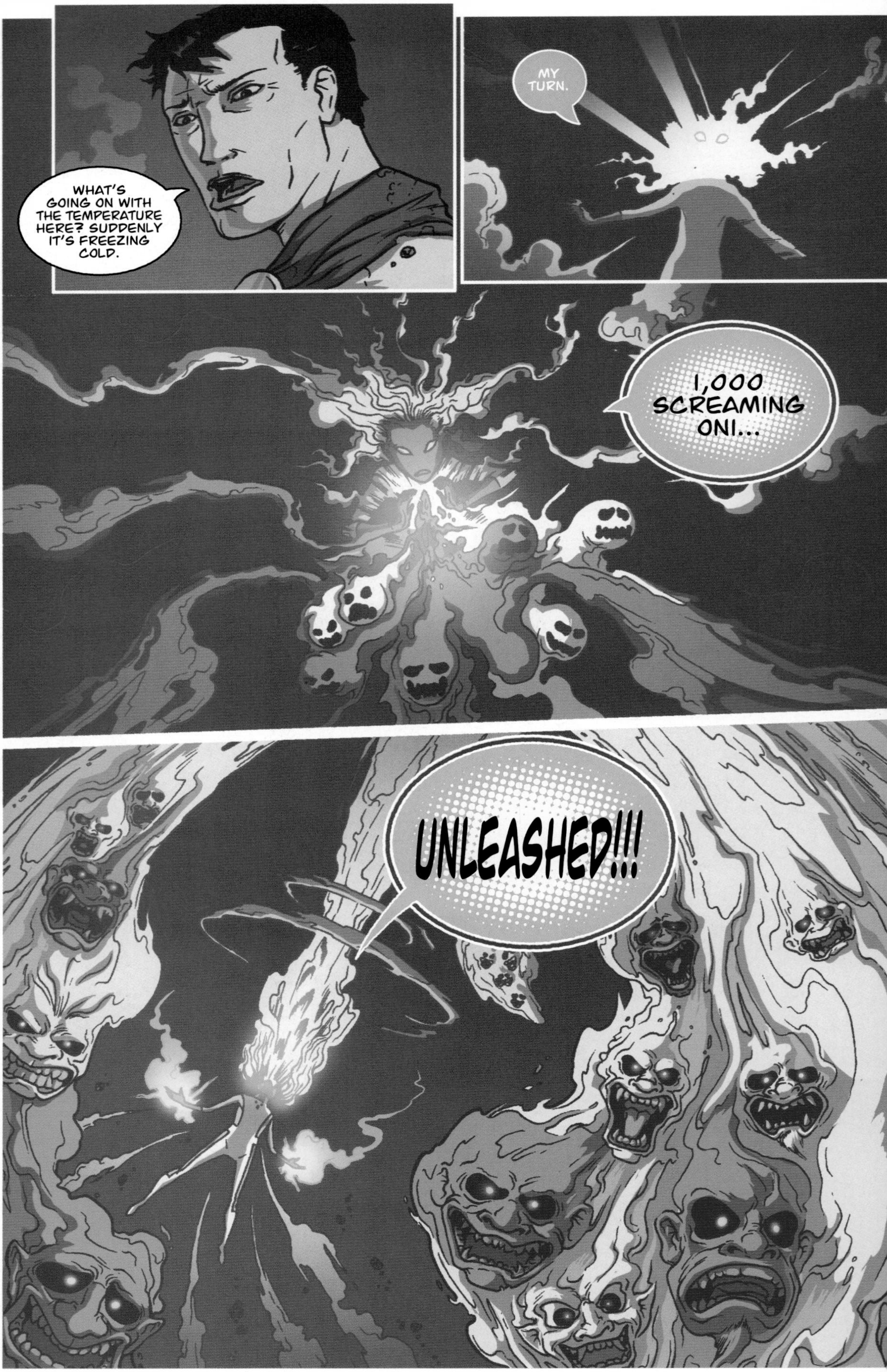
WHAT'S GOING ON WITH THE TEMPERATURE HERE? SUDDENLY IT'S FREEZING COLD.
MY TURN.
1,000 SCREAMING ONI...
UNLEASHED!!!

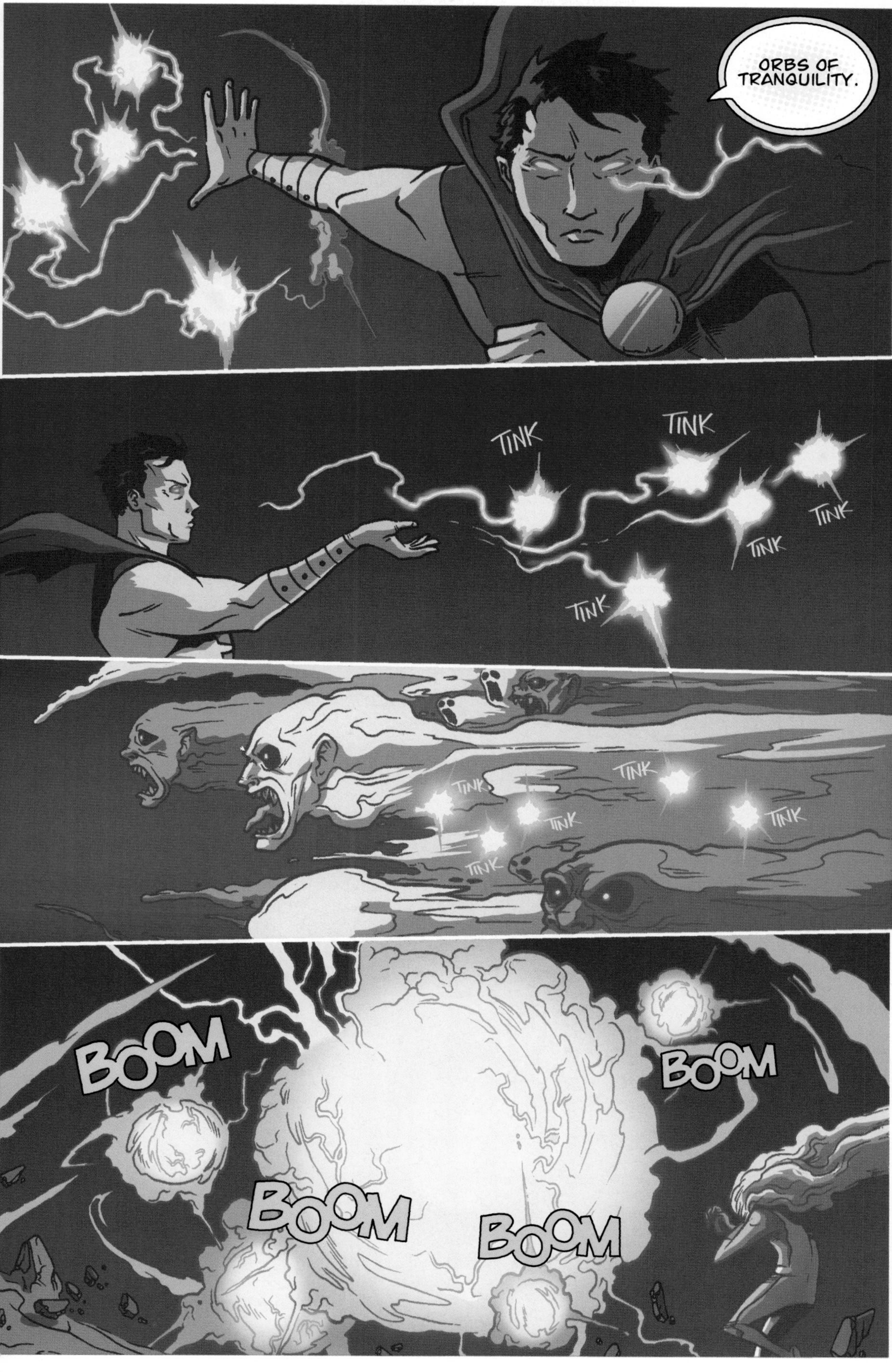
ORBS OF TRANQUILITY.
TINK
TINK
TINK
TINK
TINK
TINK
TINK
TINK
TINK
TINK
TINK
BOOM
BOOM
BOOM
BOOM

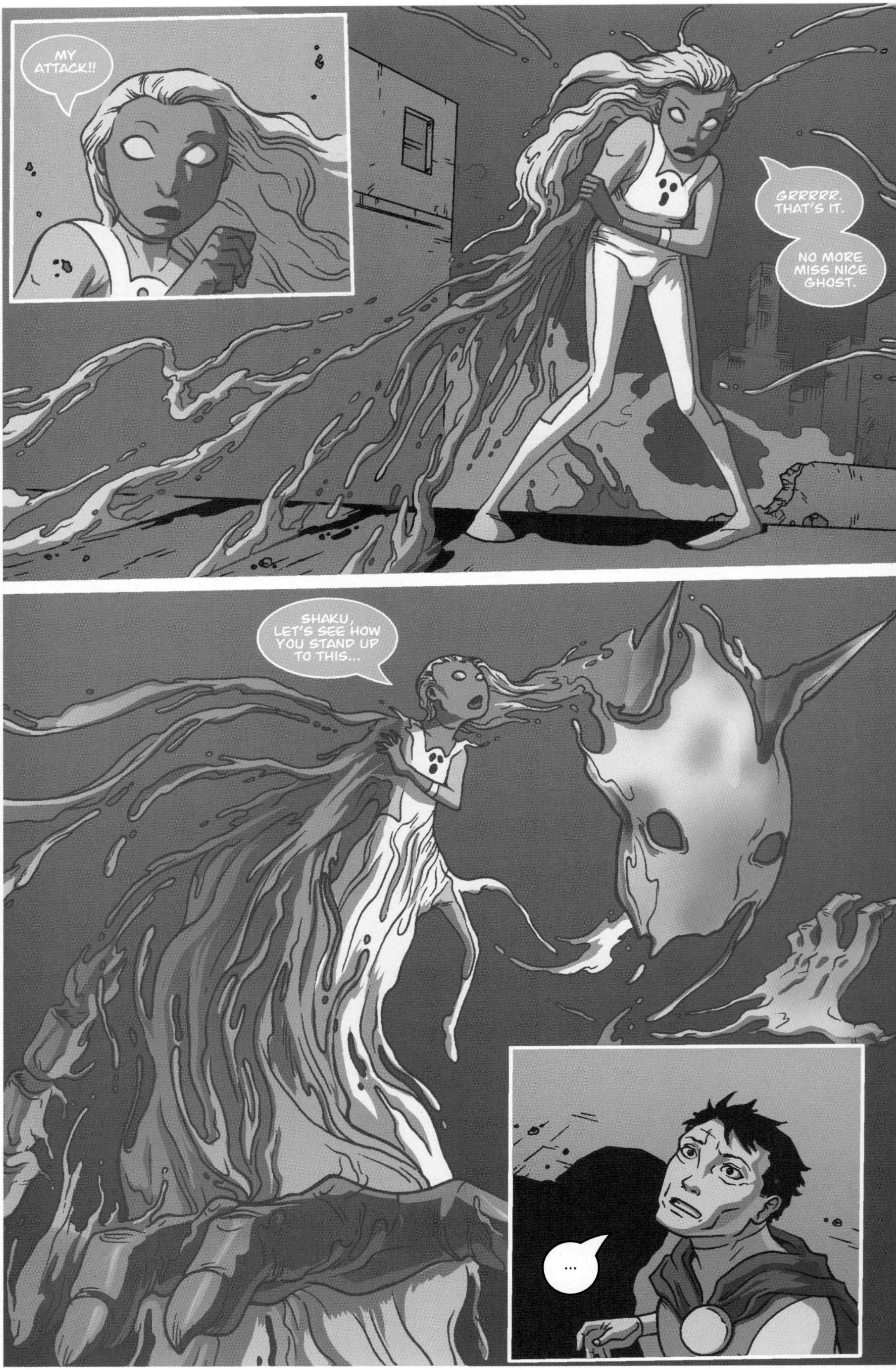
MY ATTACK!!
GRRRRR. THAT'S IT.
NO MORE MISS NICE GHOST.
SHAKU, LET'S SEE HOW YOU STAND UP TO THIS...
...

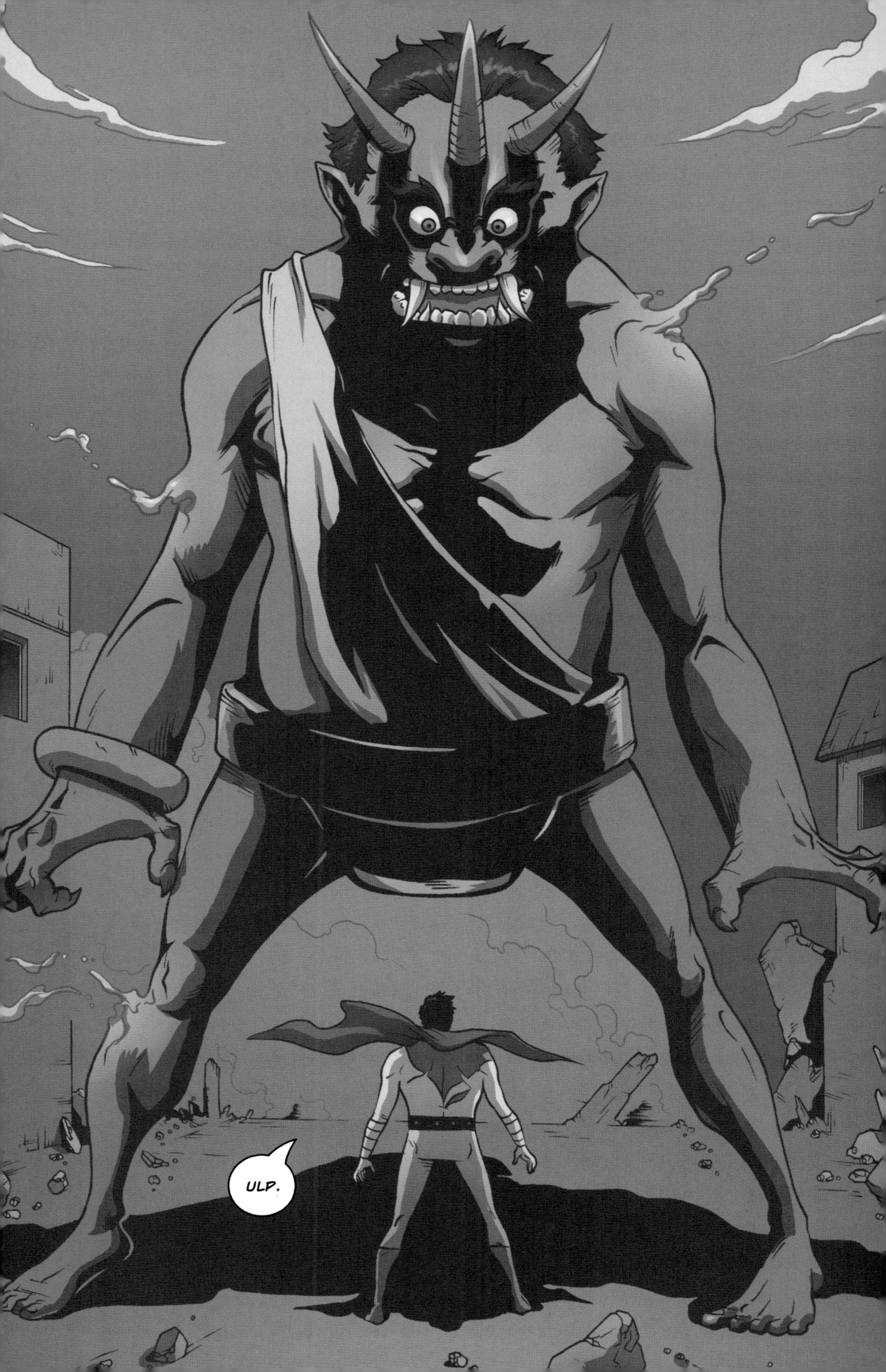
ULP.

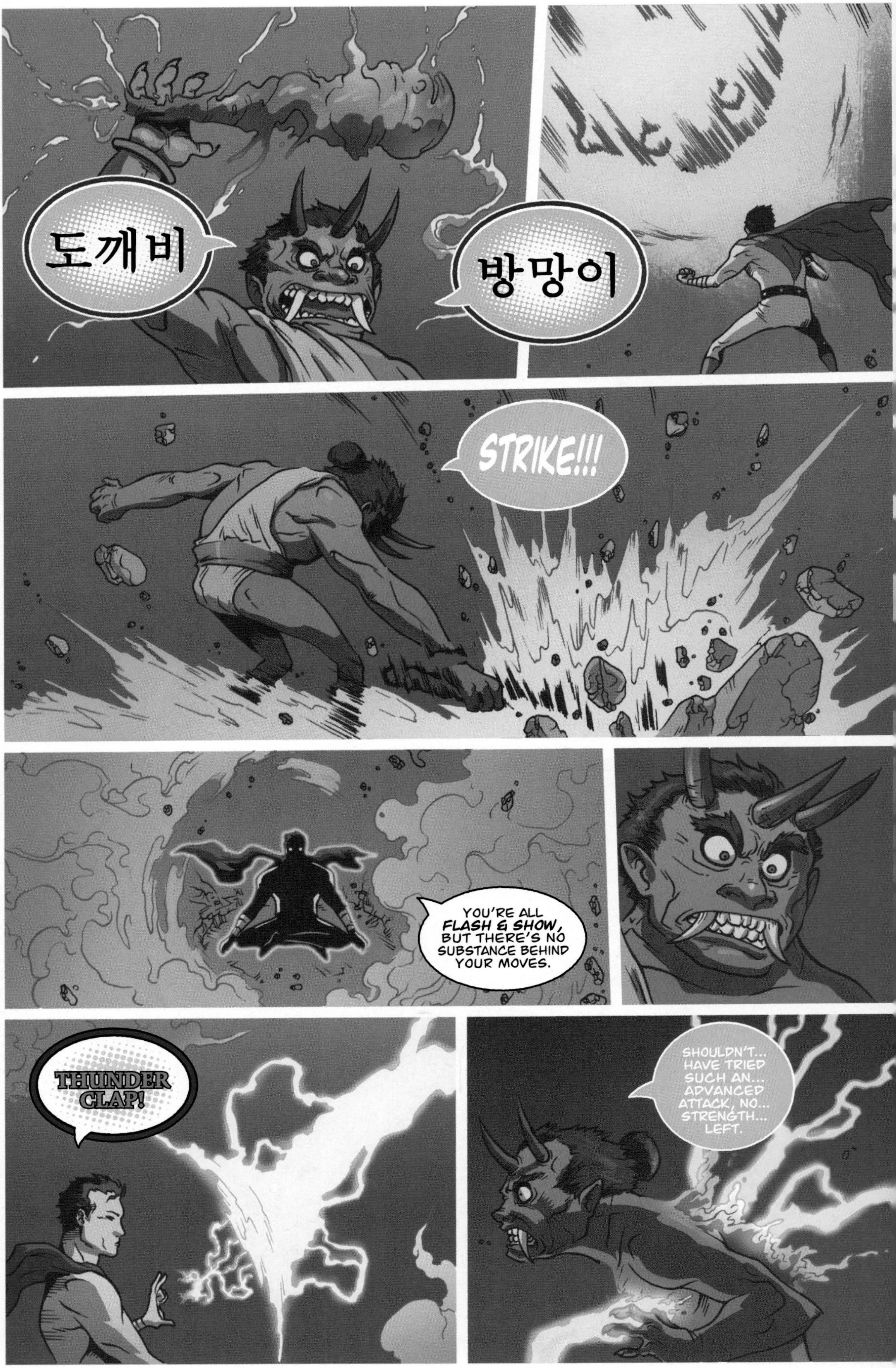
도깨비
방망이
STRIKE!!!
YOU'RE ALL FLASH & SHOW, BUT THERE'S NO SUBSTANCE BEHIND YOUR MOVES.
THUNDER CLAP!
SHOULDN'T... HAVE TRIED SUCH AN... ADVANCED ATTACK, NO... STRENGTH... LEFT.

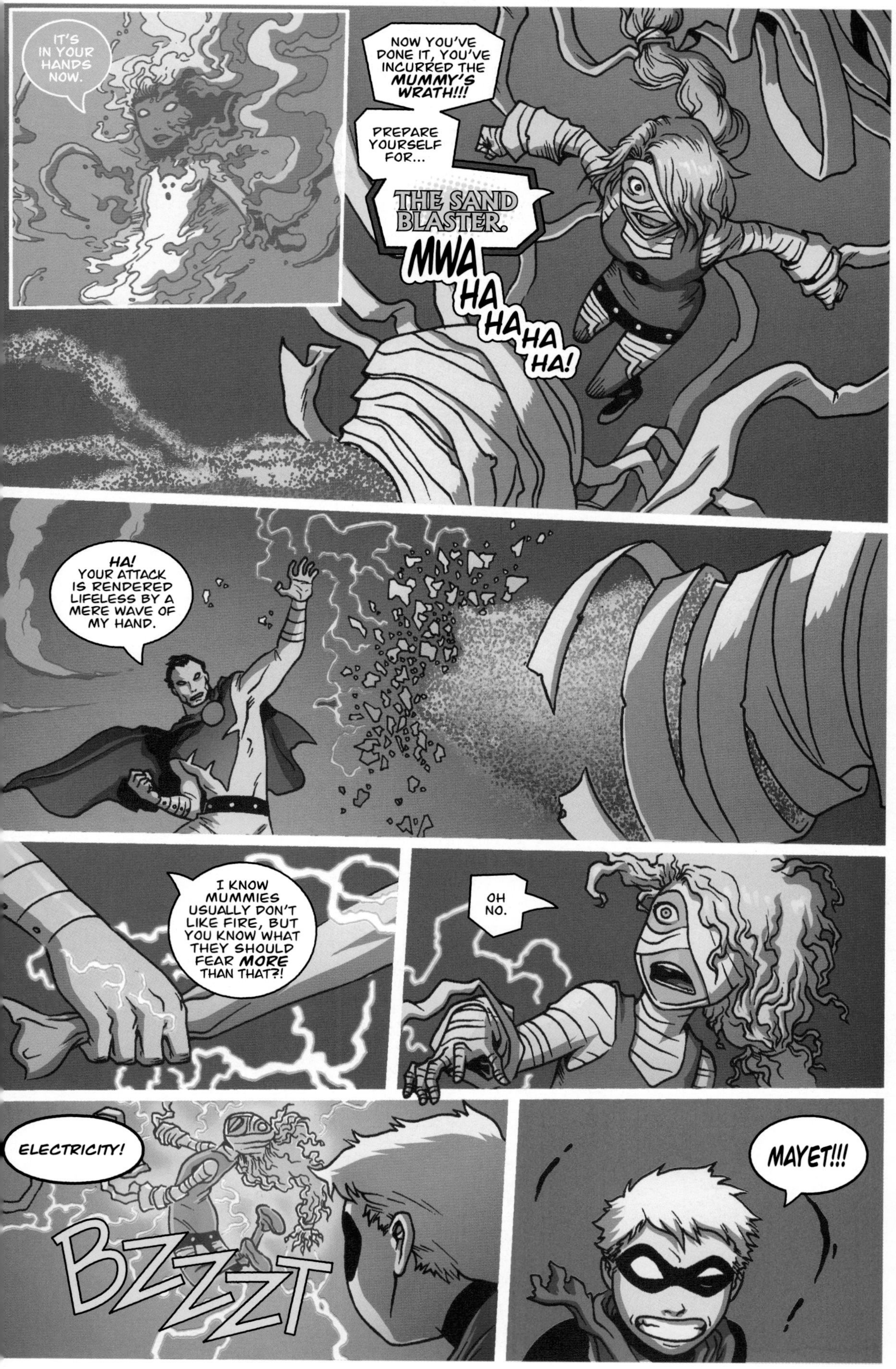
IT'S IN YOUR HANDS NOW.
NOW YOU'VE DONE IT, YOU'VE INCURRED THE MUMMY'S WRATH!!!
PREPARE YOURSELF FOR...
THE SAND BLASTER.
MWA HA HA HA HA!
HA! YOUR ATTACK IS RENDERED LIFELESS BY A MERE WAVE OF MY HAND.
I KNOW MUMMIES USUALLY DON'T LIKE FIRE, BUT YOU KNOW WHAT THEY SHOULD FEAR MORE THAN THAT?!
OH NO.
ELECTRICITY!
BZZZT
MAYET!!!

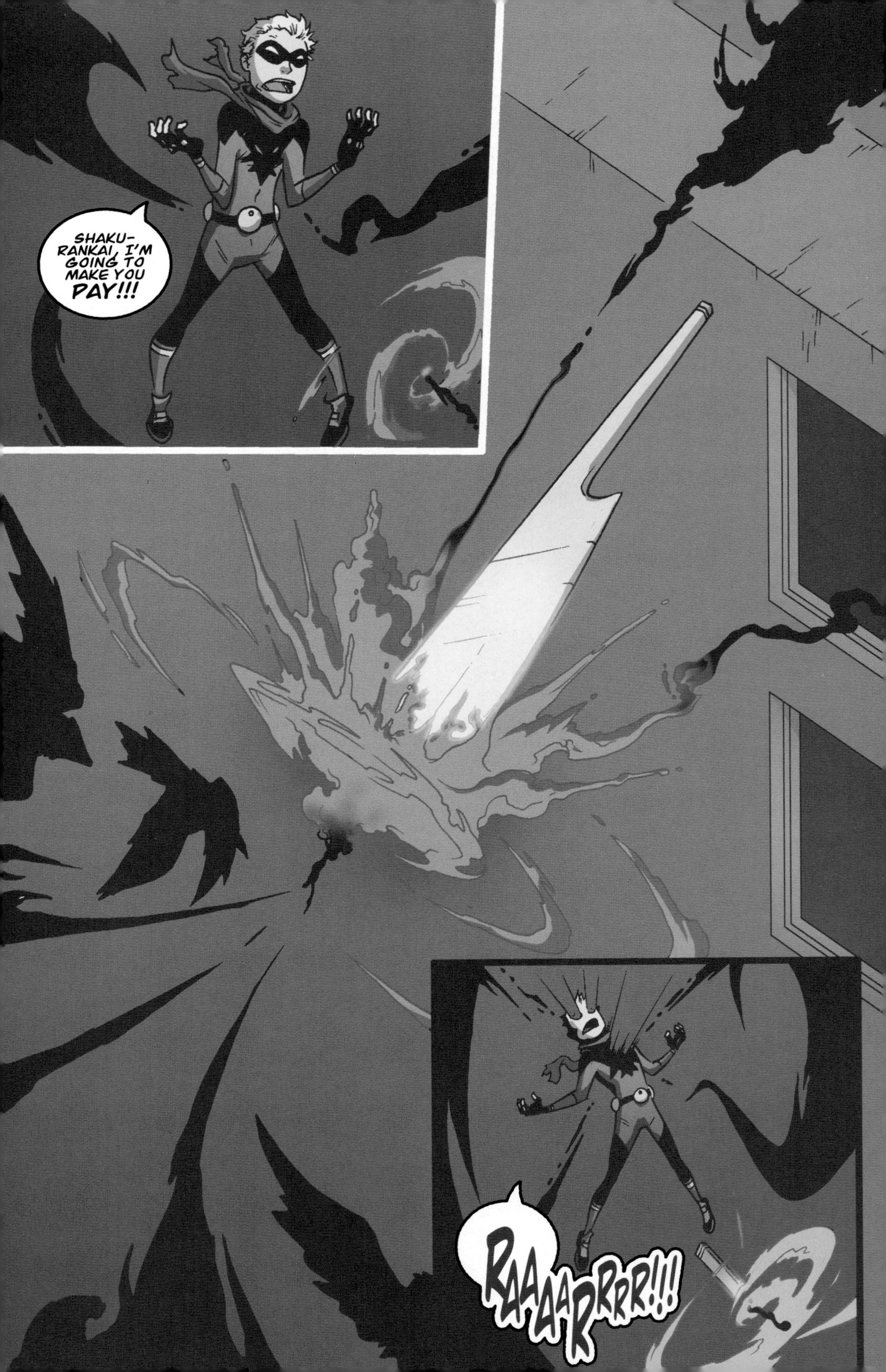
SHAKU-RANKAI, I'M GOING TO MAKE YOU PAY!!!
RAAAAARRRR!!!

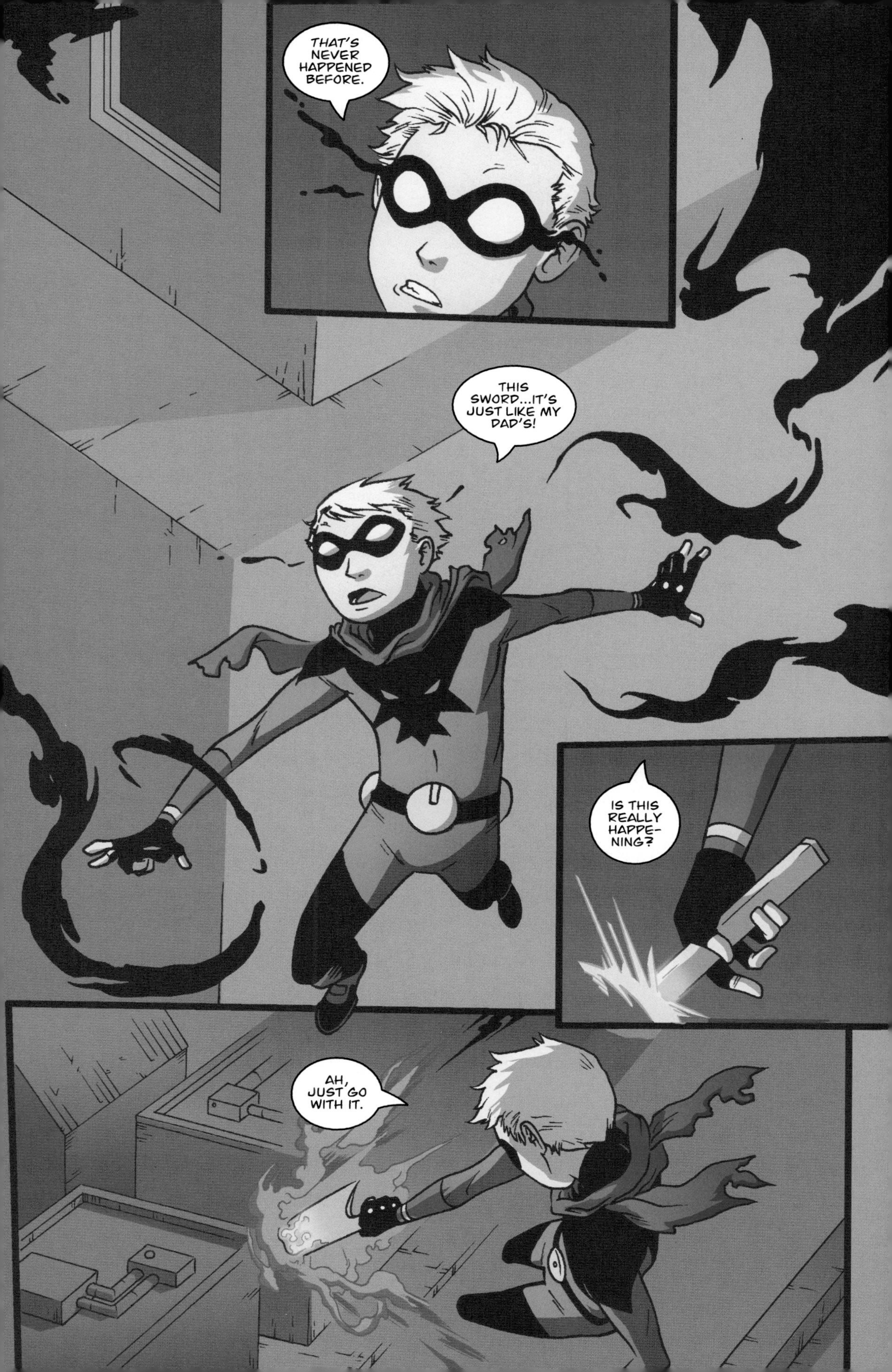
THAT'S NEVER HAPPENED BEFORE.
THIS SWORD...IT'S JUST LIKE MY DAD'S!
IS THIS REALLY HAPPE-NING?
AH, JUST GO WITH IT.

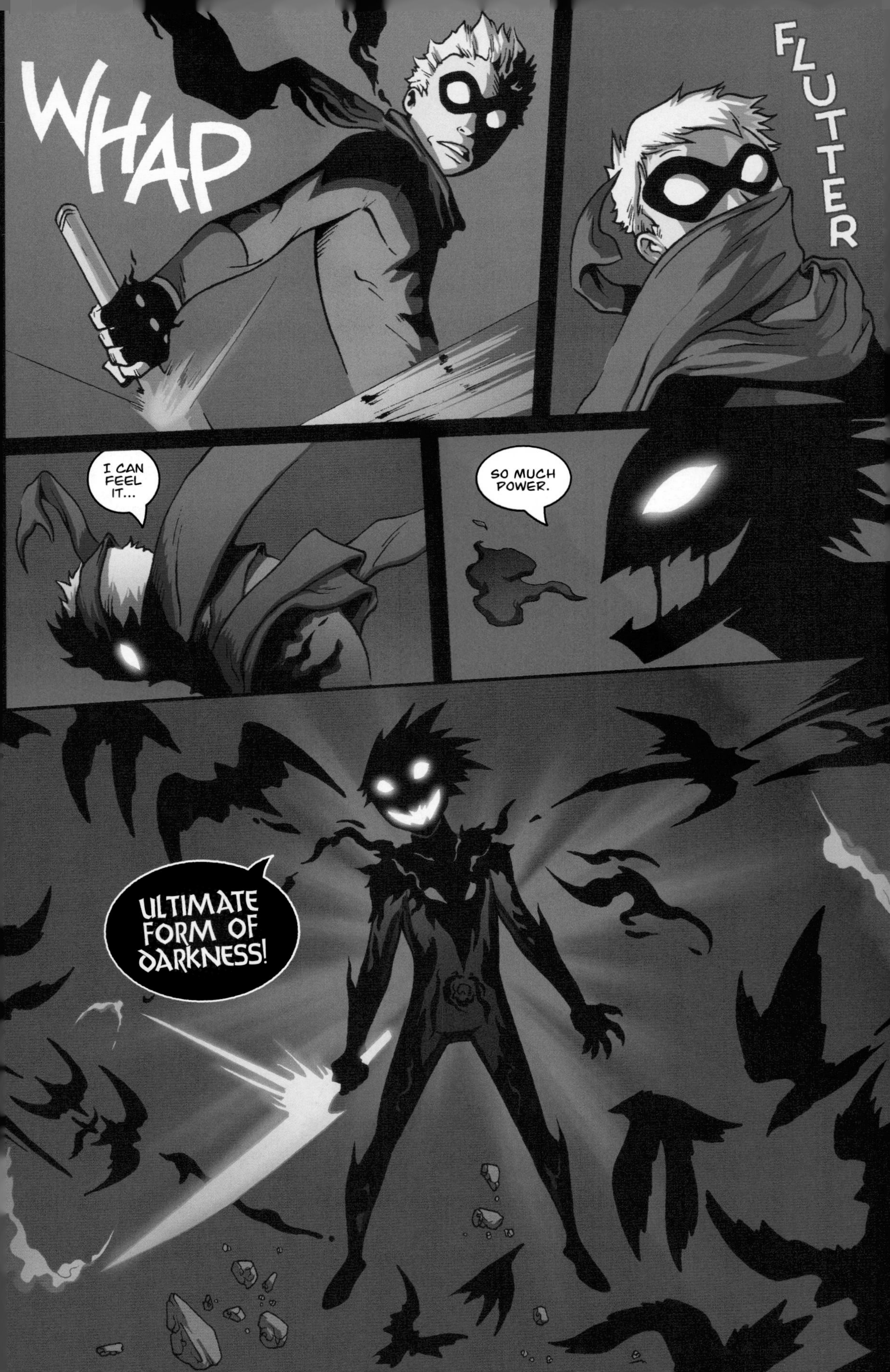
WHAP
FLUTTER
I CAN FEEL IT...
SO MUCH POWER.
ULTIMATE FORM OF DARKNESS!

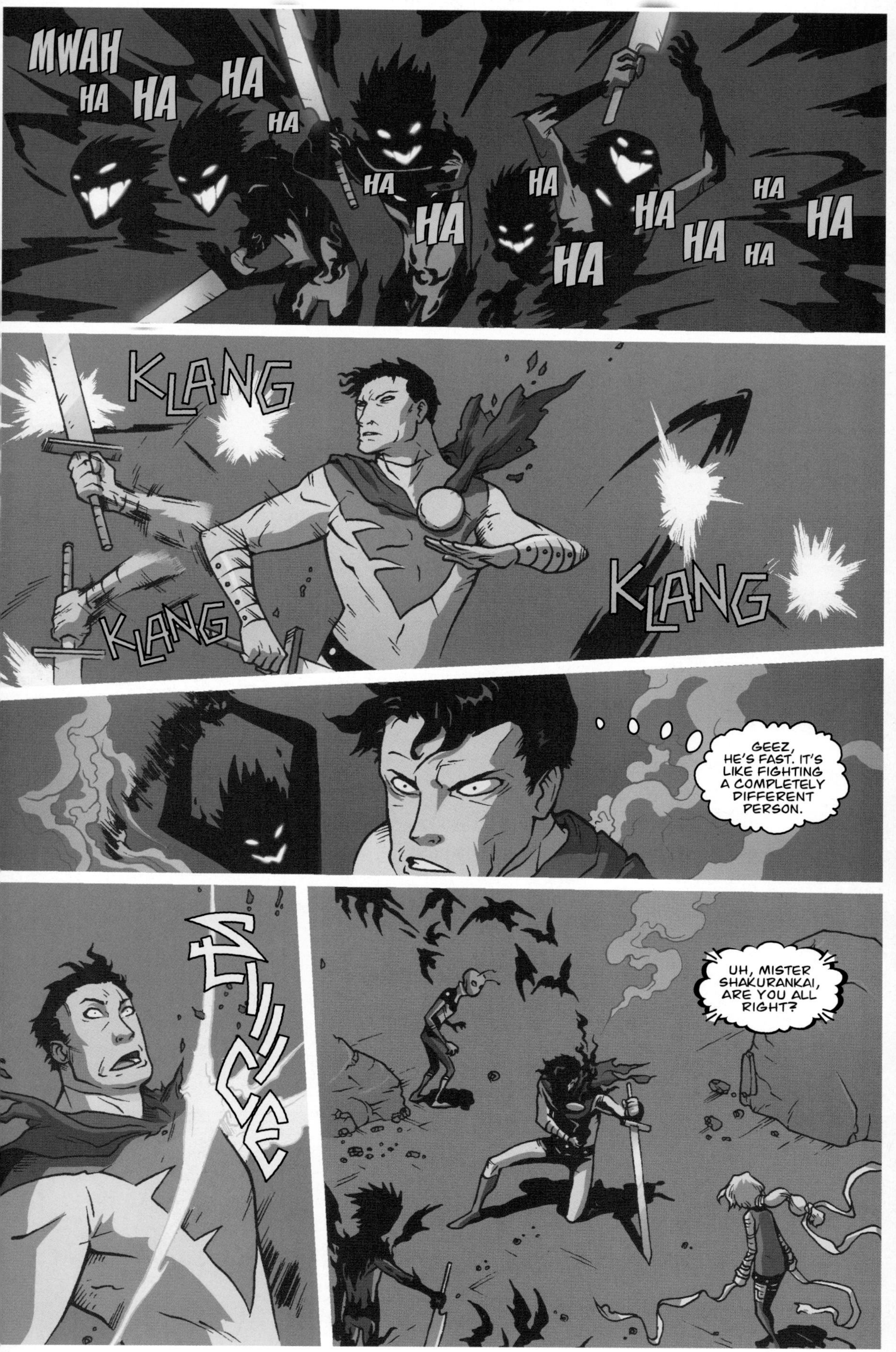
MWAH
HA HA HA HA HA HA HA HA HA HA HA HA HA
KLANG
KLANG
KLANG
GEEZ, HE'S FAST. IT'S LIKE FIGHTING A COMPLETELY DIFFERENT PERSON.
SLIIIICE
UH, MISTER SHAKURANKAI, ARE YOU ALL RIGHT?

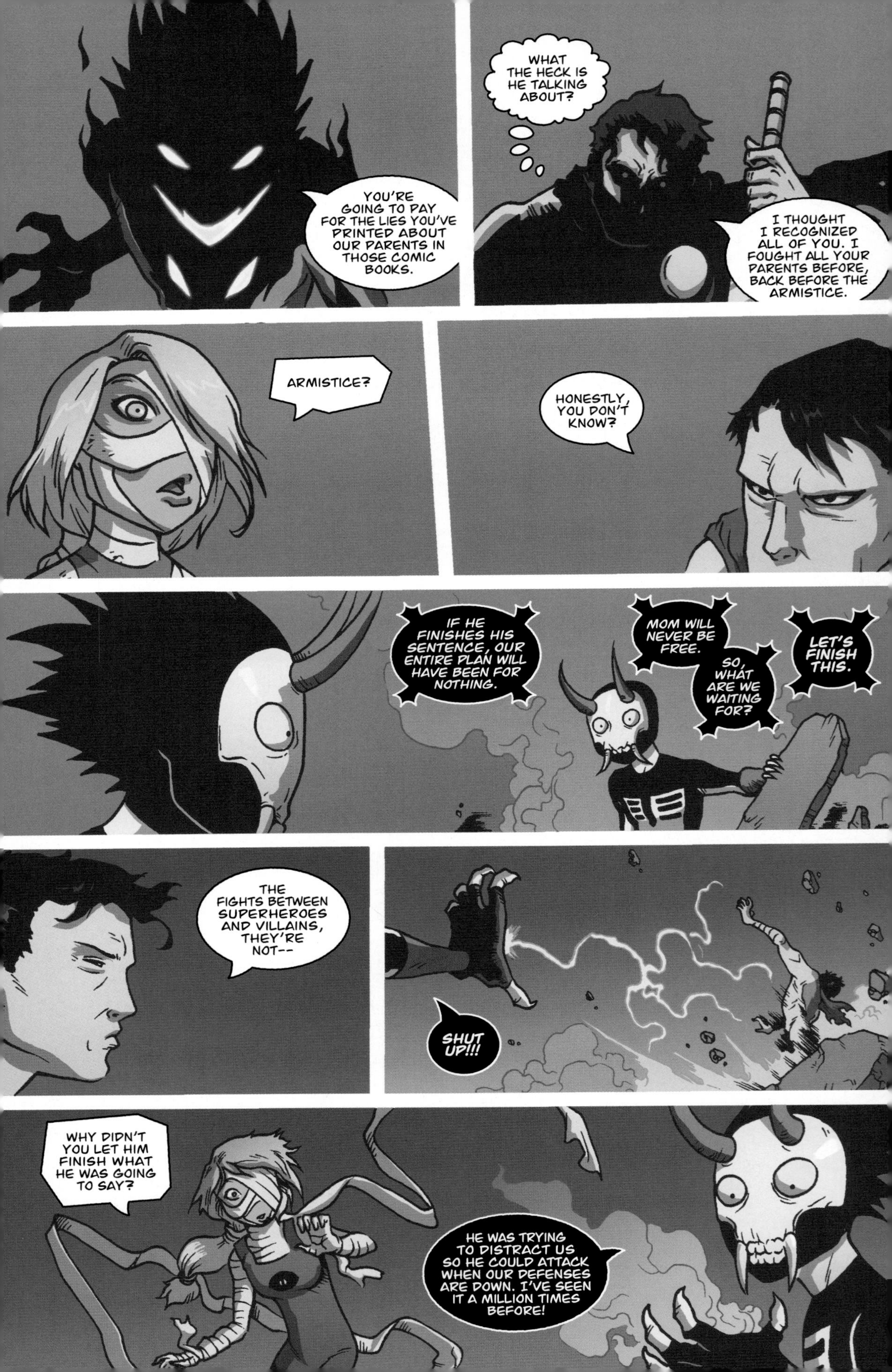
YOU'RE GOING TO PAY FOR THE LIES YOU'VE PRINTED ABOUT OUR PARENTS IN THOSE COMIC BOOKS.
WHAT THE HECK IS HE TALKING ABOUT?
I THOUGHT I RECOGNIZED ALL OF YOU. I FOUGHT ALL YOUR PARENTS BEFORE, BACK BEFORE THE ARMISTICE.
ARMISTICE?
HONESTLY, YOU DON'T KNOW?
IF HE FINISHES HIS SENTENCE, OUR ENTIRE PLAN WILL HAVE BEEN FOR NOTHING.
MOM WILL NEVER BE FREE.
SO, WHAT ARE WE WAITING FOR?
LET'S FINISH THIS.
THE FIGHTS BETWEEN SUPERHEROES AND VILLAINS, THEY'RE NOT--
SHUT UP!!!
WHY DIDN'T YOU LET HIM FINISH WHAT HE WAS GOING TO SAY?
HE WAS TRYING TO DISTRACT US SO HE COULD ATTACK WHEN OUR DEFENSES ARE DOWN. I'VE SEEN IT A MILLION TIMES BEFORE!

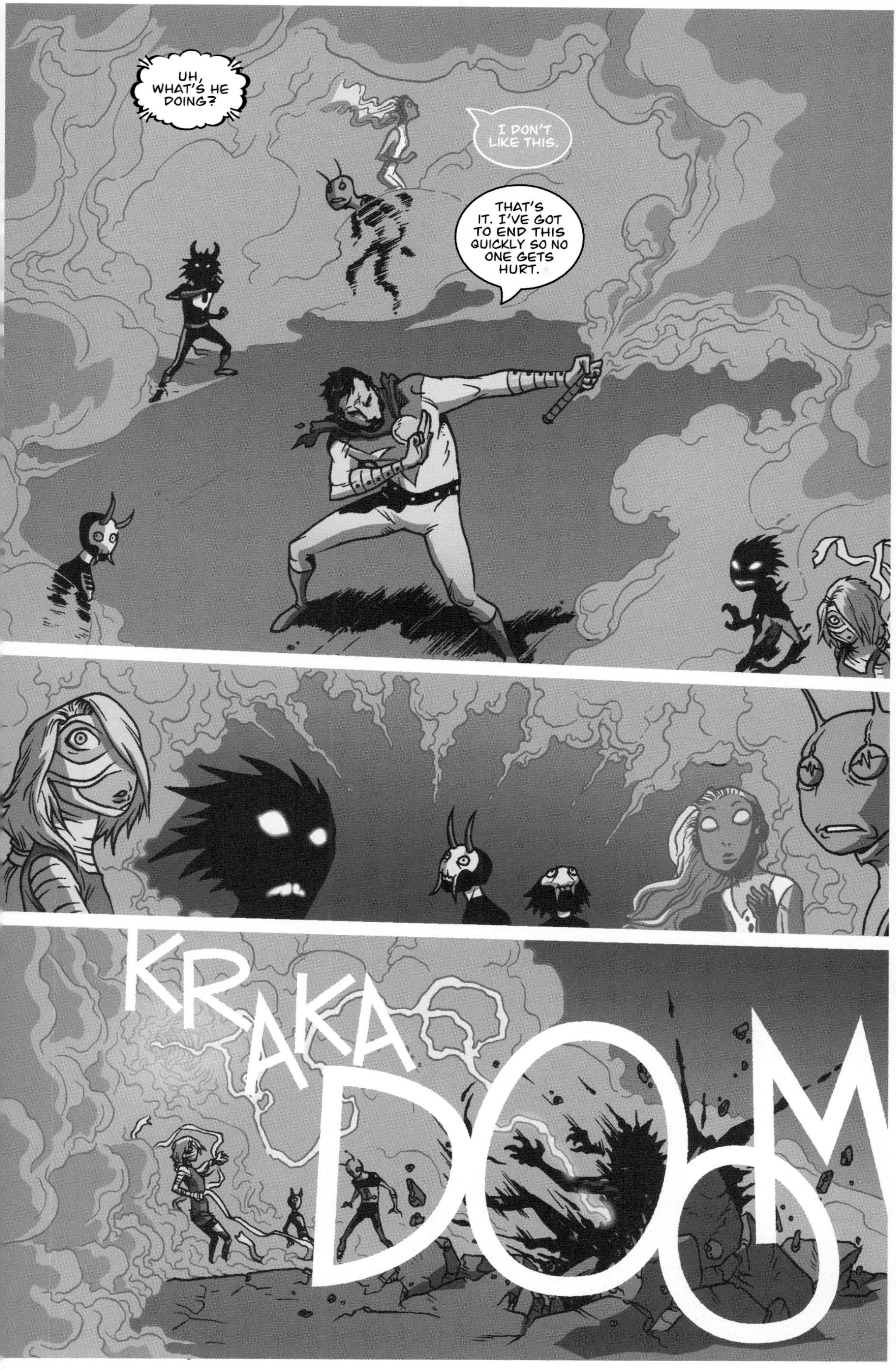
UH, WHAT'S HE DOING?
I DON'T LIKE THIS.
THAT'S IT. I'VE GOT TO END THIS QUICKLY SO NO ONE GETS HURT.
KRAKADOOM

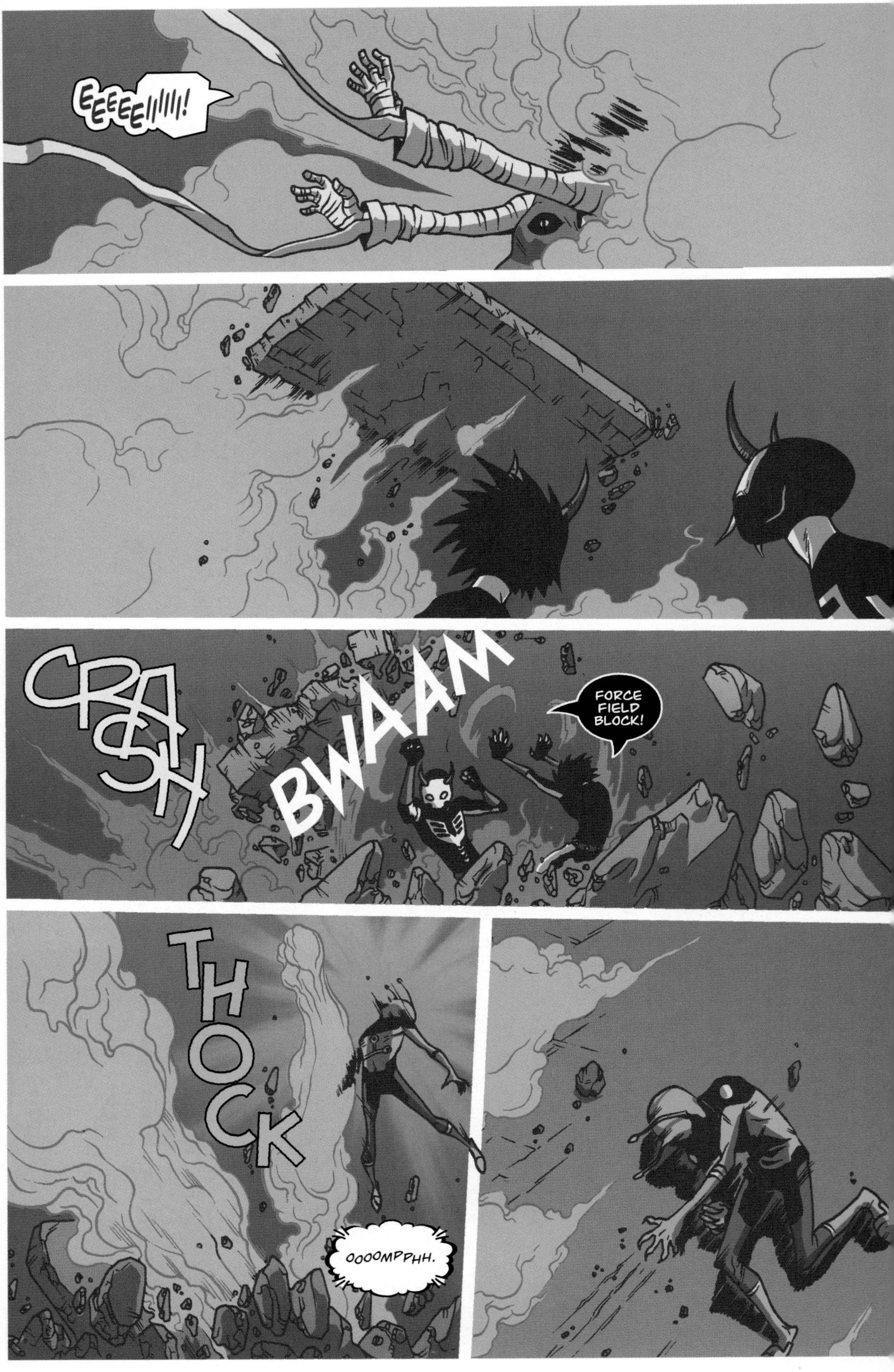
EEEEE!!!!!!!!
CRASH
BWAAM
FORCE FIELD BLOCK!
THOCK
OOOOMPPHH.

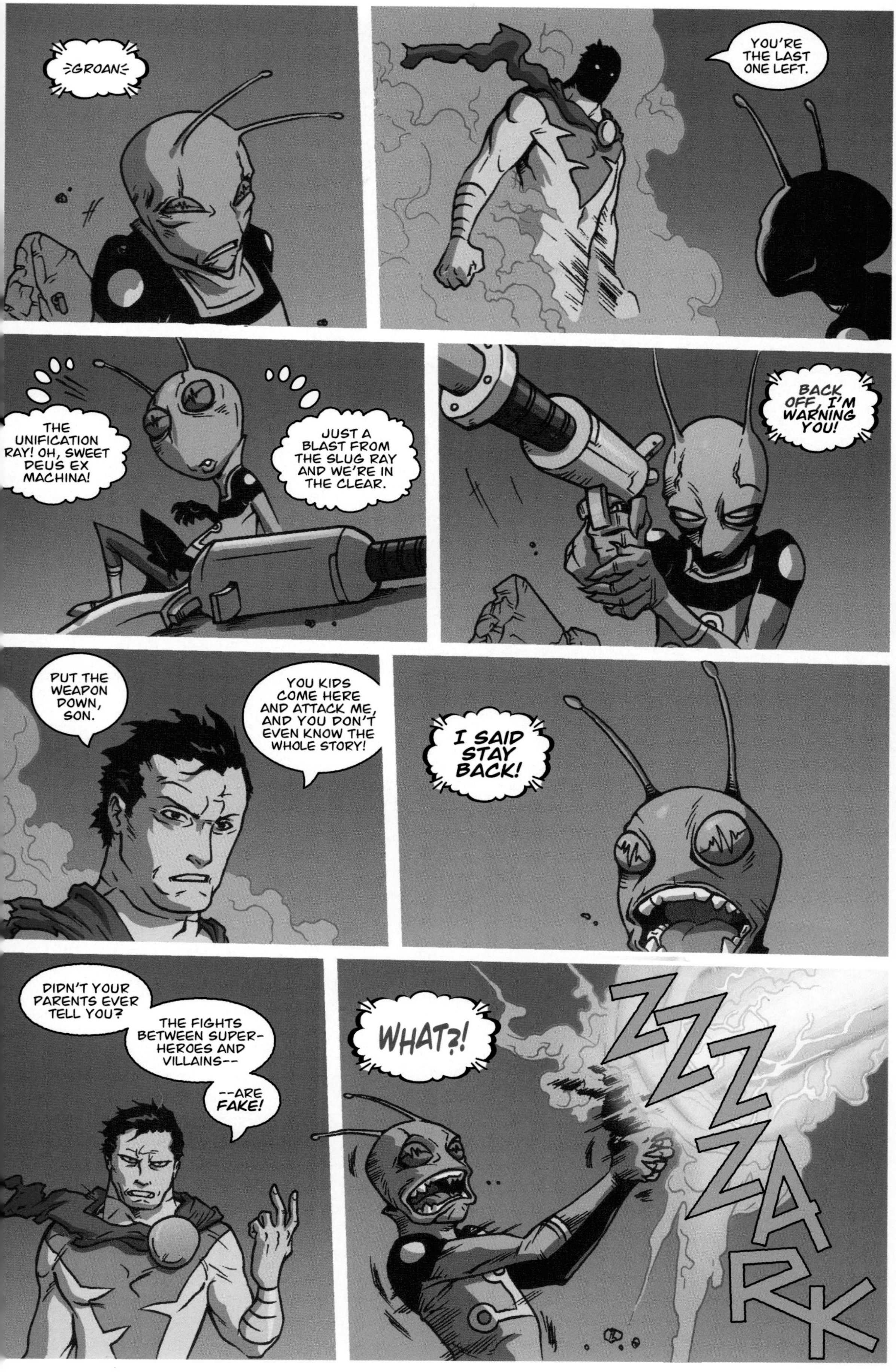
GROAN
YOU'RE THE LAST ONE LEFT.
THE UNIFICATION RAY! OH, SWEET DEUS EX MACHINA!
JUST A BLAST FROM THE SLUG RAY AND WE'RE IN THE CLEAR.
BACK OFF, I'M WARNING YOU!
PUT THE WEAPON DOWN, SON.
YOU KIDS COME HERE AND ATTACK ME, AND YOU DON'T EVEN KNOW THE WHOLE STORY!
I SAID STAY BACK!
DIDN'T YOUR PARENTS EVER TELL YOU?
THE FIGHTS BETWEEN SUPER-HEROES AND VILLAINS--
--ARE FAKE!
WHAT?!
ZZZZARK

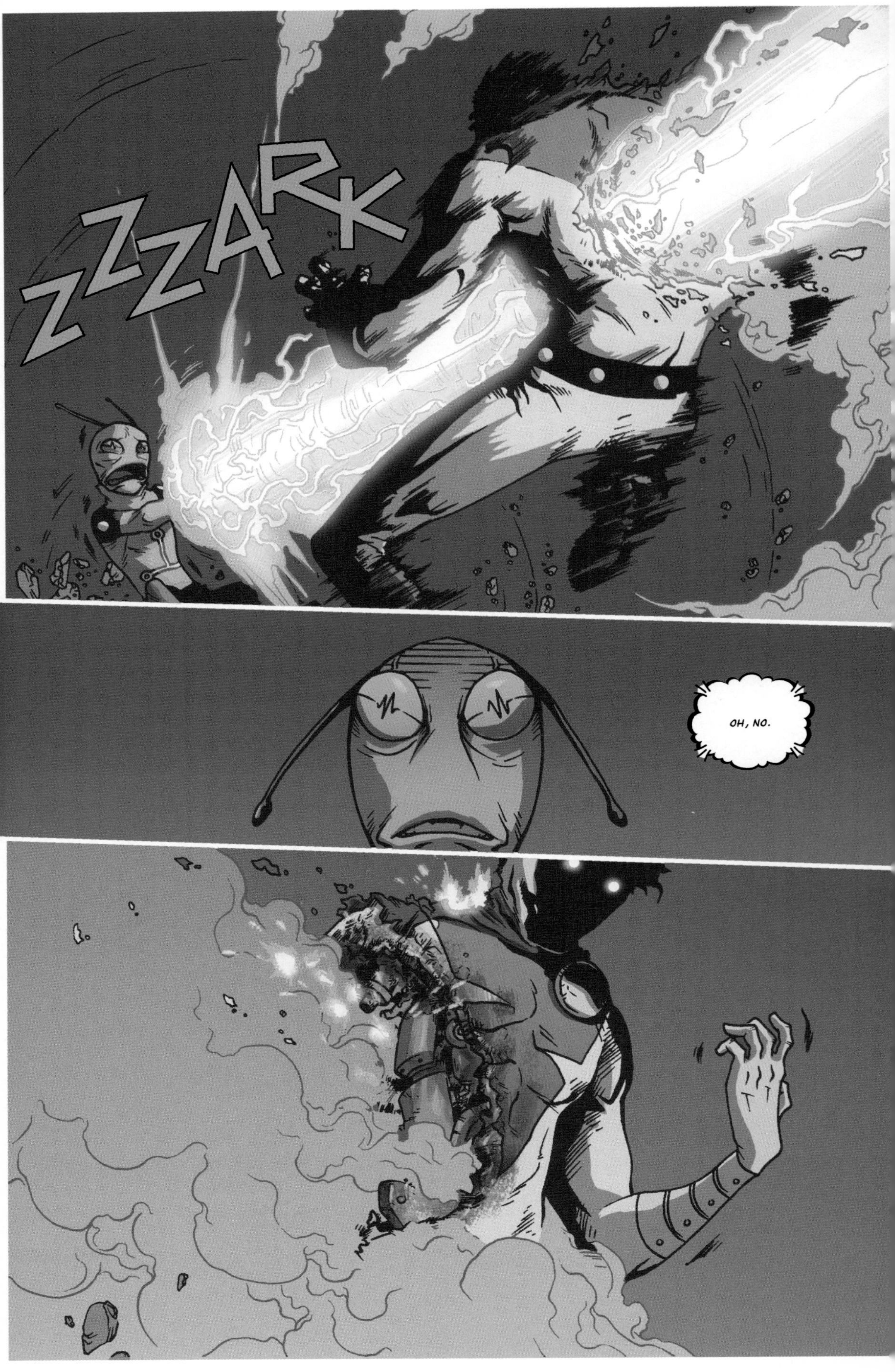
ZZZARK
OH, NO.

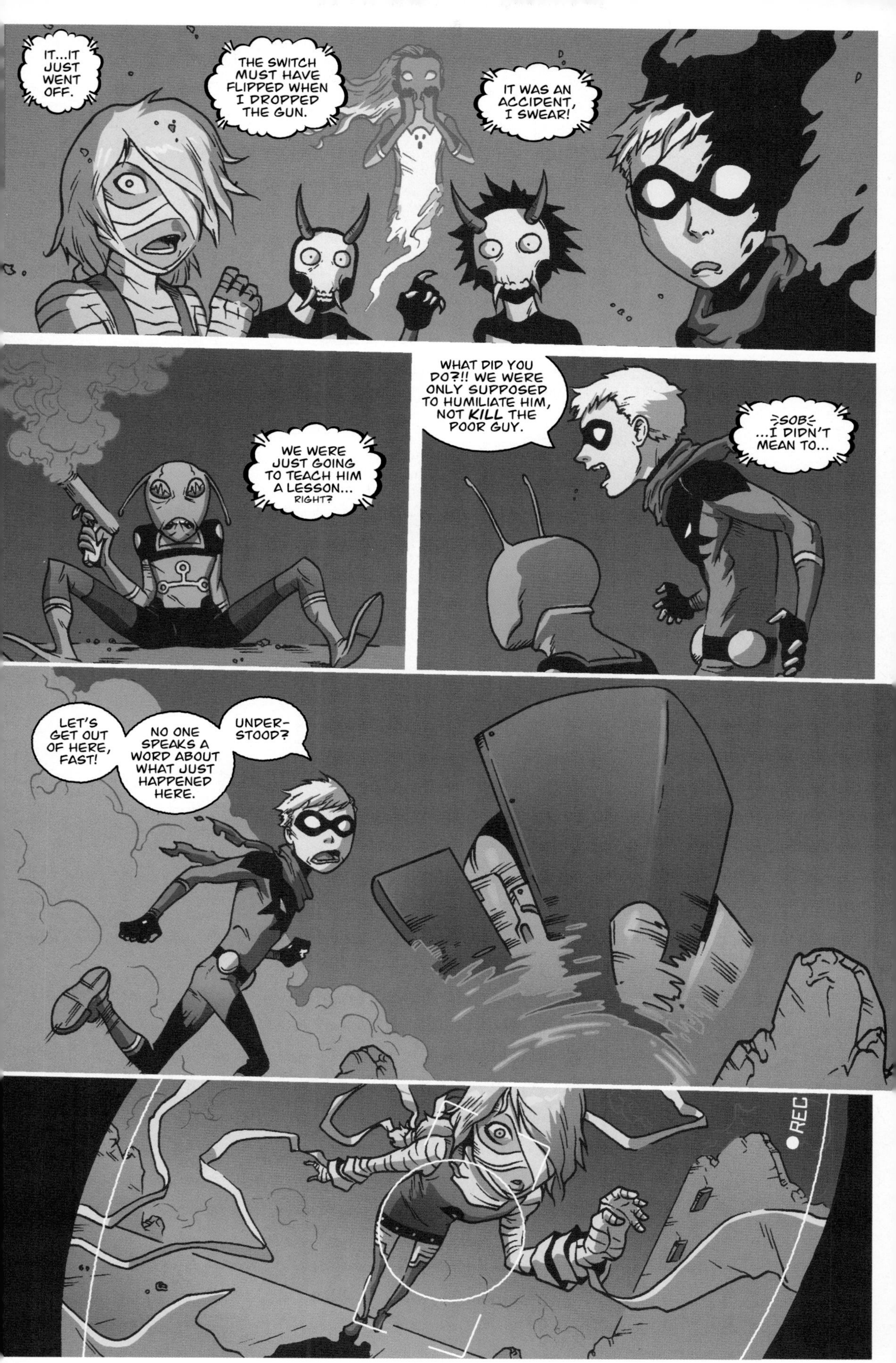

IT...IT JUST WENT OFF.
THE SWITCH MUST HAVE FLIPPED WHEN I DROPPED THE GUN.
IT WAS AN ACCIDENT, I SWEAR!
WE WERE JUST GOING TO TEACH HIM A LESSON... RIGHT?
WHAT DID YOU DO?!! WE WERE ONLY SUPPOSED TO HUMILIATE HIM, NOT KILL THE POOR GUY.
SOB ...I DIDN'T MEAN TO...
LET'S GET OUT OF HERE, FAST!
NO ONE SPEAKS A WORD ABOUT WHAT JUST HAPPENED HERE.
UNDER-STOOD?
REC

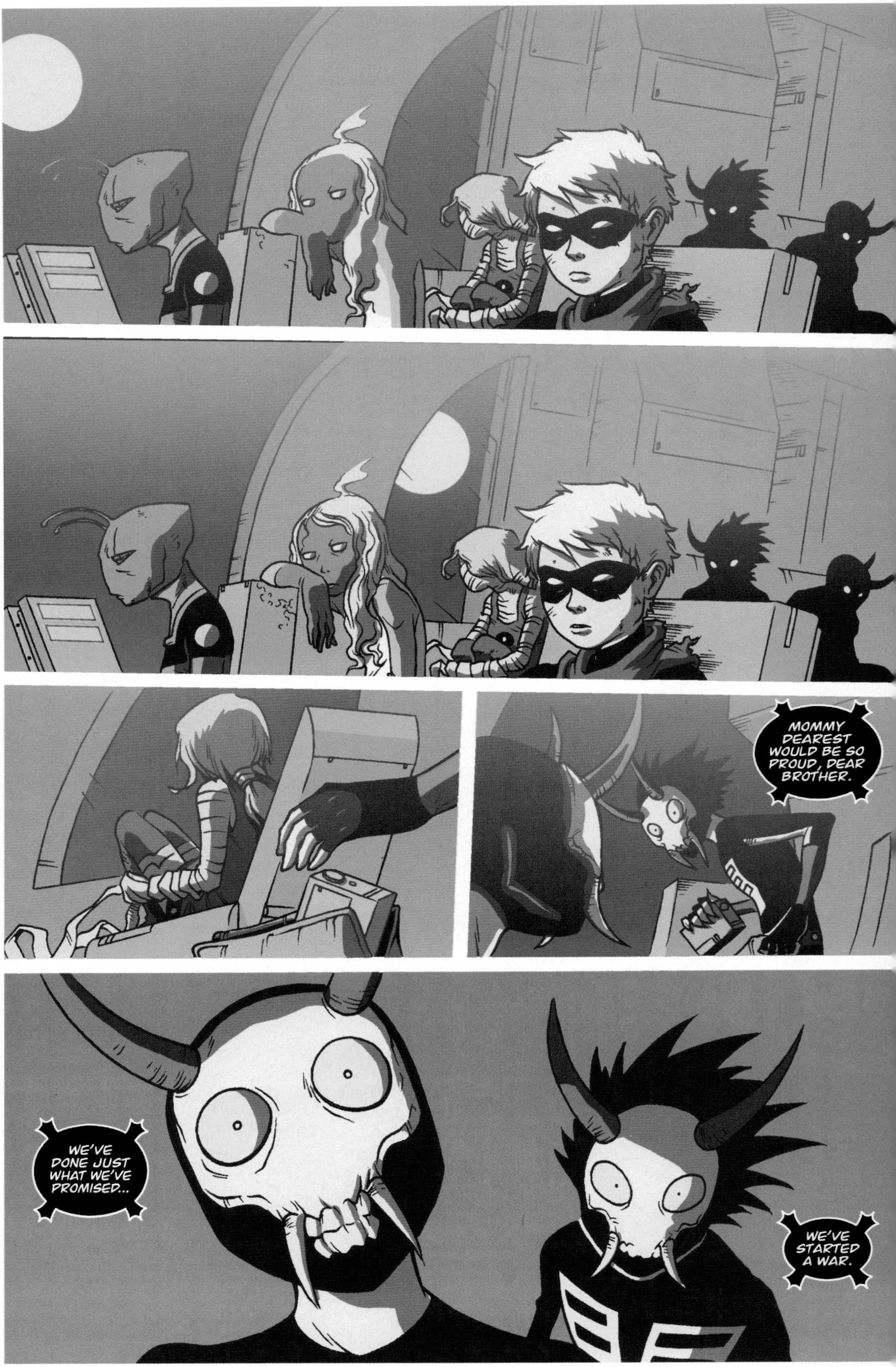
MOMMY DEAREST WOULD BE SO PROUD, DEAR BROTHER.
WE'VE DONE JUST WHAT WE'VE PROMISED...
WE'VE STARTED A WAR.

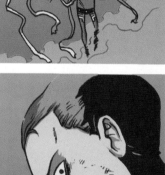

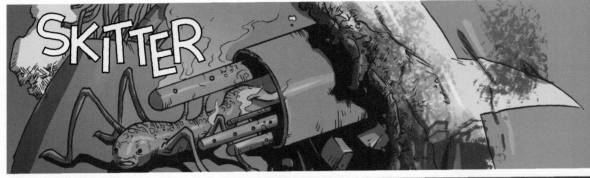

SKITTER

SKITTER

SPLOOSH

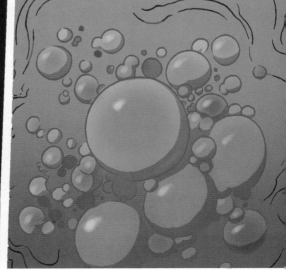

HALFWAY ACROSS THE GALAXY ...

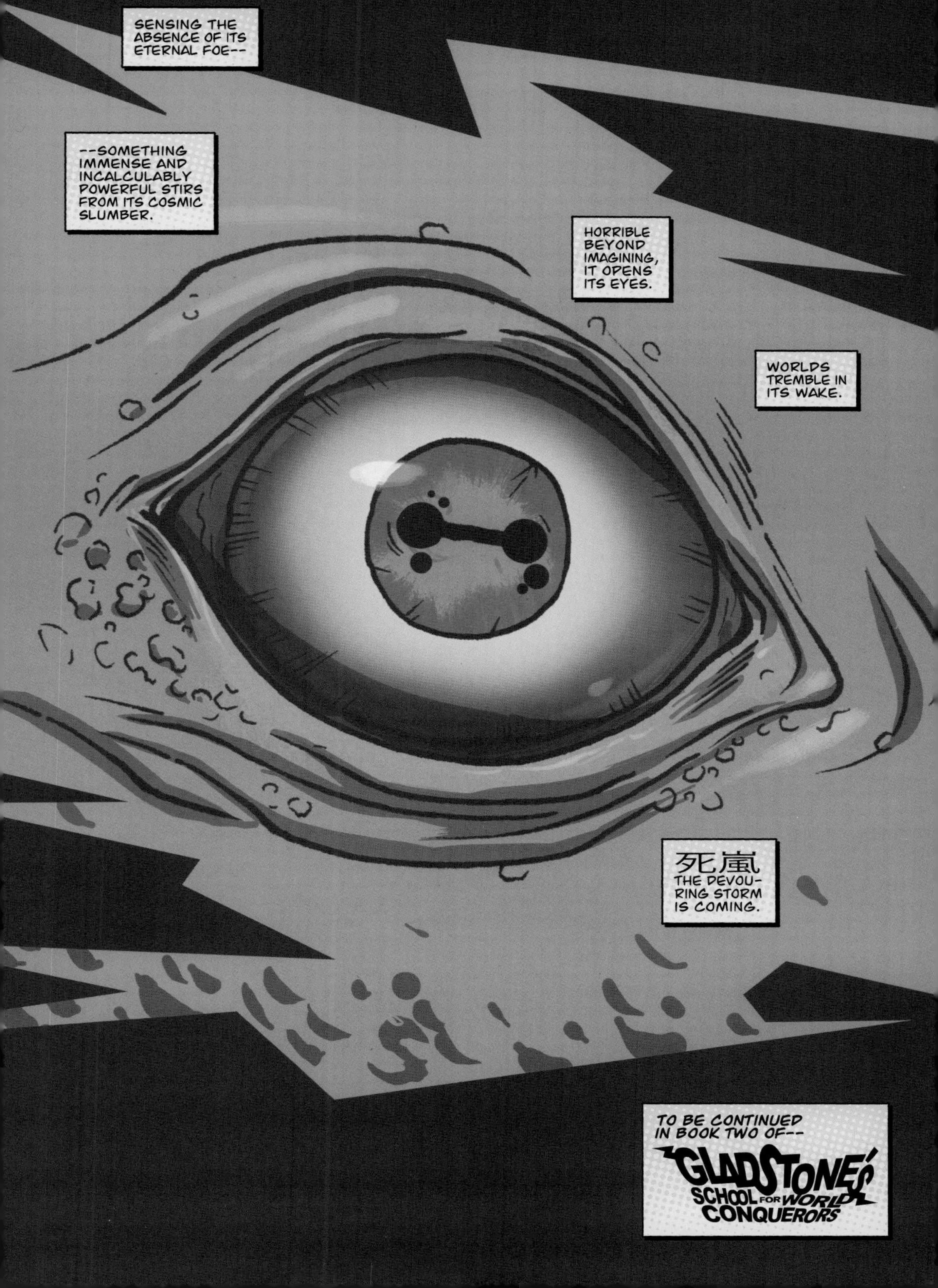
SENSING THE ABSENCE OF ITS ETERNAL FOE--
--SOMETHING IMMENSE AND INCALCULABLY POWERFUL STIRS FROM ITS COSMIC SLUMBER.
HORRIBLE BEYOND IMAGINING, IT OPENS ITS EYES.
WORLDS TREMBLE IN ITS WAKE.
死嵐 THE DEVOURING STORM IS COMING.
TO BE CONTINUED IN BOOK TWO OF--
GLADSTONE'S SCHOOL FOR WORLD CONQUERORS

Pinup by ARMAND VILLAVERT

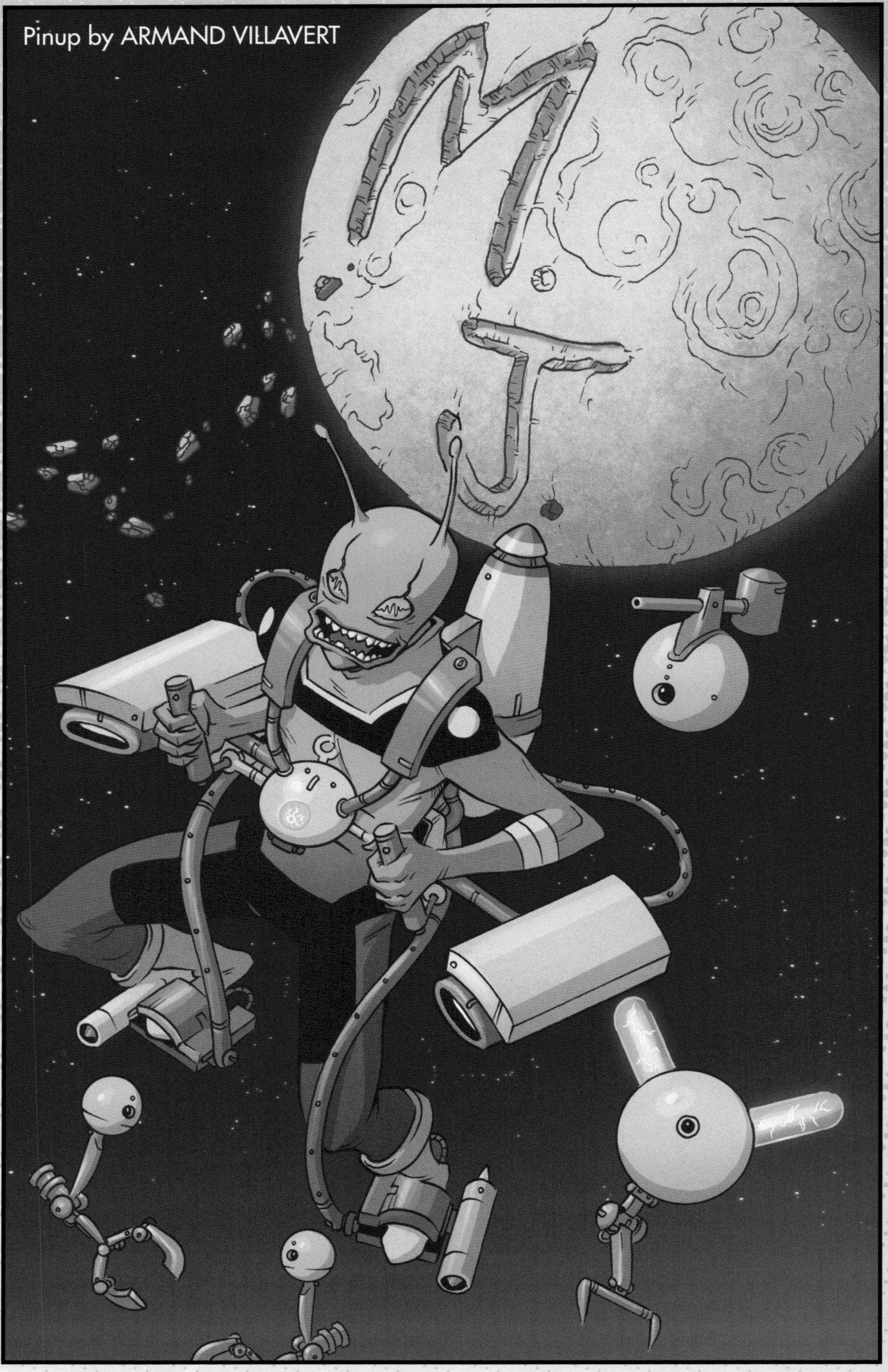

YOU DON'T GET TO CONQUER THE WORLD WITHOUT THE HELP OF A FEW FRIENDS

A CALL TO ACTION!

Thank you for reading *GLADSTONE'S SCHOOL FOR WORLD CONQUERORS.* If you've liked the series and would like to read future volumes, please support the comic by spreading the word and helping us connect with more readers.

Some easy ways to do this are on Facebook, Twitter, Google+ — as well as old-fashioned word of mouth or loaning a copy of this book to a friend. And if they like it, hopefully they'll post about it online and pick up the next volumes or single issues — thus the cycle of support continues!

Only by connecting with a larger readership will we be able to ensure future volumes of *GLADSTONE'S* and get the chance to tell our epic story — and boy is it ever an epic one!

We would love to be able to play in the *GLADSTONE'S* universe that we've set up here for the next thirty years, and are very excited about what's coming up next in the *GLADSTONE'S* saga...

It's been a pleasure creating this series for you.

Follow us on Twitter and our Facebook group for updates and news about the series:

@MarkAndrewSmith
@ArmandArtist

— *Mark Andrew Smith*
Phuket, 2011

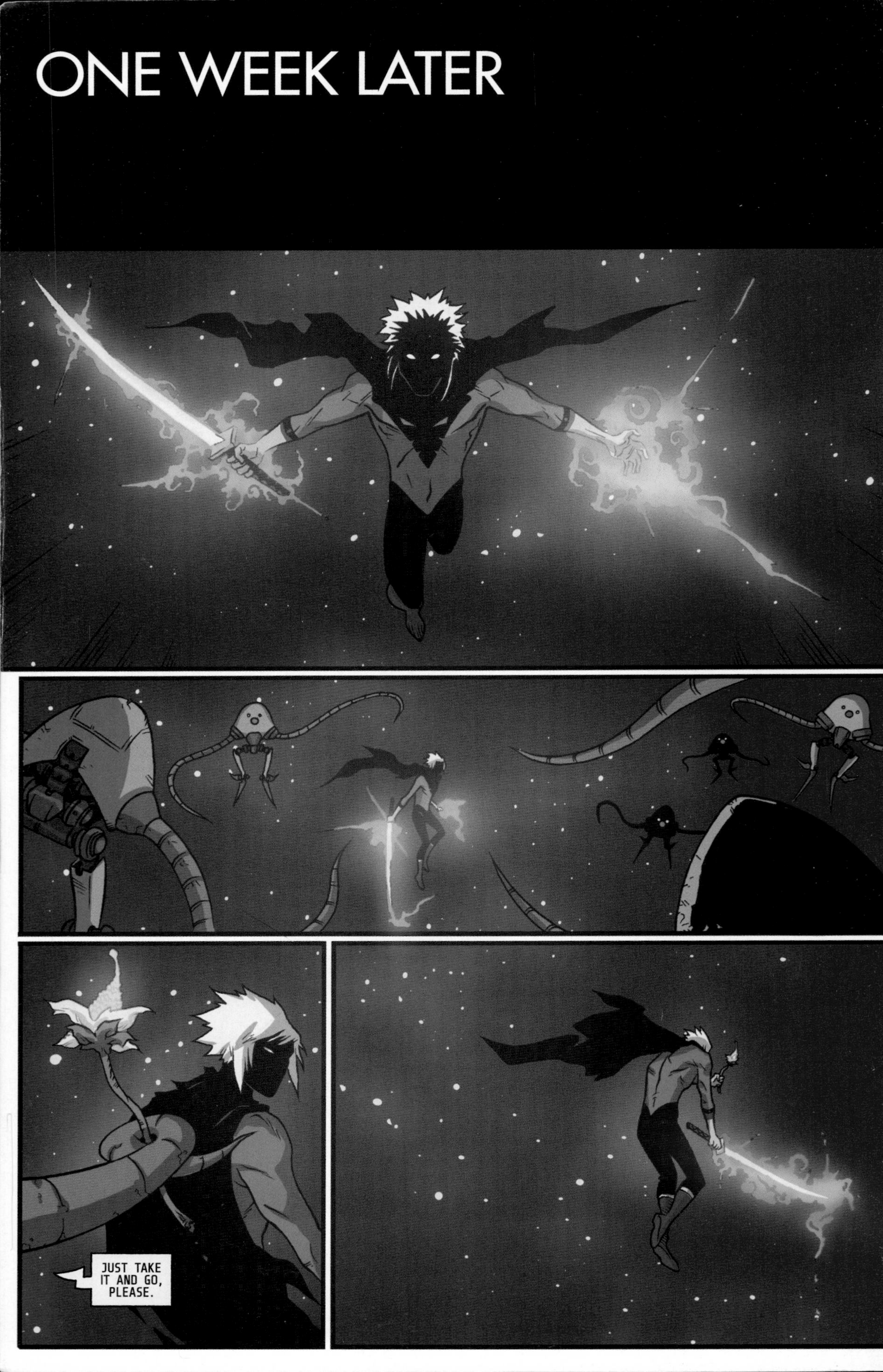
ONE WEEK LATER
JUST TAKE IT AND GO, PLEASE.